Theories of Knowledge and Reality

An Introduction to the Problems and Arguments of Philosophy
Second Edition

J.A. Cover
Purdue University

Rudy L. Garns
Northern Kentucky University

McGraw-Hill, Inc.
College Custom Series

New York   St. Louis   San Francisco   Auckland   Bogotá
Caracas   Lisbon   London   Madrid   Mexico City   Milan
Montreal   New Delhi   San Juan   Singapore
Sydney   Tokyo   Toronto

McGraw-Hill's **College Custom Series** consists of products that are produced from camera-ready copy. Peer review, class testing, and accuracy are primarily the responsibility of the author(s).

THEORIES OF KNOWLEDGE AND REALITY
An Introduction to the Problems and Arguments of Philosophy

4 5 6 7 8 9 10 11 12 13 14 BKMBKM 9 9 8 7 6

ISBN 07-013269-0

Editor: Margaret A. Hollander

Preface to the Second Edition

THEORIES of Knowledge and Reality introduces students to the central problems, arguments and methods of philosophy. One reason for offering a new text is that critical thinking skills, largely overlooked in other introductory texts, can and should be given serious attention along with the traditional fare of lower division philosophy courses. Traditional philosophical topics offer a particularly suitable medium in which to teach those skills, and students grasp the topics more handily if they are provided with the tools necessary for critically treating them. Indeed, students with critical thinking skills come away with much more than can be realistically expected of them otherwise, and stand better-prepared for other courses. Even if most freshmen and sophomores will forget the details of this or that theory in (say) the philosophy of mind, they will retain habits of good thinking if properly instructed. This text will help to instill such habits while making difficult topics more accessible.

Our text offers material and insight that an anthology alone cannot provide. While an instructor can teach critical skills on his own, alongside discussion of readings from an anthology, a text in which those skills are explicitly treated puts this material immediately in the hands of the instructor and the student, available for illustration and for review. Furthermore, most anthologized articles are not by themselves particularly accessible to freshmen and sophomores. We find that beginning students progress more efficiently when first presented with material aimed at their level. If primary sources are to be effectively employed, the student needs discussions that motivate assigned readings, provide thematic considerations, and illustrate critical evaluation of the primary sources. Historical and contemporary writings will fall more cleanly into place when they follow extended introductory material. This text is meant to incorporate just enough historical flavor to be used alone (without divorcing traditional problems from their most famous treatments by philosophers), or it may be used in tandem with anthologies.

Theories of Knowledge and Reality was developed over the past nine years in conjunction with a large-enrollment introductory course at Syracuse University. That course is primarily an introduction to metaphysics and epistemology, and the text is designed to present this material on a level accessible to the average freshman and sophomore college student. An interesting and helpful discussion of that course and the role this text plays in that course can be found in Michael Patten's "Teaching Graduate Students to Teach," *Teaching Philosophy* 15 (1992). Various portions of the text, in manuscript form, have been used for several years at Syracuse, Hobart and William Smith Colleges, Purdue University and Northern Kentucky University. We have also circulated the book at various stages amongst teaching colleagues at Ohio State University, University of Arkansas, Northern Illinois University, and University of California Riverside.

Several distinctive features of the text have proven successful and offer substantial advantages over existing texts.

1. In our chapter on tools of philosophical analysis we discuss *arguments*—their purpose, structure, and how they are to be evaluated. The use of argument is then reinforced throughout the book in contexts of discussing philosophical problems. For example, introductory texts will typically offer discussions of teleological arguments for God's existence and of the Problem of Other Minds: neither of these topics in their classical renditions can be treated adequately without previous work on standards by which we assess inductive argument forms. Our chapter on rationality and the existence of God takes seriously the forms that traditional arguments for and against the existence of God have taken; understanding and assessing such arguments requires a working knowledge of deductive and inductive forms and the relevant methods of evaluation. We introduce the student to important fallacies and the art of counterexample, and provide an opportunity to obtain a good grasp of the concepts of validity, soundness, and convincingness.

2. In addition to presenting and using basic logical tools, we provide a section on relevant topics in the philosophy of language, which include standard discussions of vagueness and ambiguity, meaning and definition. These latter topics, conjoined with the logical material presented earlier, allow us to treat explicitly what we call *conceptual analysis*. While many texts present the notions of necessary and sufficient conditions, few offer them as the core of a method of

analysis, useful in assessing philosophical arguments. More importantly, we distinguish sentences from propositions in a way that allows us to move naturally from our treatment of necessity and sufficiency (as linguistic notions) to the problem of modality.

3. Our treatment of modality is perhaps one of the most distinctive features of the text. Modal concepts—ones having to do with possibility and necessity—have fairly recently been incorporated into a standard branch of formal logic. The most pervasive and useful model in such treatments is the notion of a *possible world*, which has not made its way into introductory texts, but can be extremely useful there. We treat possible worlds, naturally and intuitively, as a tool for thinking about modal concepts. The possible-worlds model offers an indispensable tool for understanding both traditional and contemporary discussions of so-called modal arguments for God's existence, and it allows for a more insightful discussion of so-called "contingency" versions of the Cosmological Argument. Many texts, offering little more than the notions of analyticity and self-contradiction as criteria for necessity and impossibility, ignore the important fact that individual propositions may not themselves be *obviously* necessary or impossible—hat questions of modality must often be decided in contexts involving a broad range of propositions.

4. While these tools of philosophical analysis are presented in a single chapter early in the book, all of the chapters are written so as to be unified and self-contained, providing for an unusual amount of *versatility*: An instructor can skip the preliminary material, and pause at various points when discussing the philosophical problems to treat the relevant analytic topics. The text is also organized into a series of short labeled subsections to keep the reader's attention, facilitate focus on the topic at hand, and aid in cross-referencing. Each chapter can stand on its own. Instructors can select topics in any order and with omissions.

5. In addition to introducing and developing tools of philosophical reasoning, a separate overarching feature of the book animates much of our presentation of standard philosophical topics. Showing someone how to do philosophy requires not only these "local" tools of critical thought, but also an understanding of the more global, big-picture dynamics of philosophical theorizing. We construct our latter chapters with an eye toward illustrating different strategies in what might be called *philosophical methodology*. In the chapter on God, we show how to defend positions by reconstructing arguments in light of objections. For example, several versions of the Causal Argument

are presented, each an improvement over the last, and our discussion of the Contingency Argument displays an attempt to both salvage important themes essential to cosmological arguments and overcome what are presented as fatal objections to the Causal Argument. A chapter on the Mind-Body Problem illustrates the dialectical nature of philosophical interchange, allowing theories (Dualism and Materialism, in this case) to play off each other. The chapter on perception and the external world incorporates a historical approach to philosophy, which allows us at the same time to show how a theory may be developed as the natural outgrowth of previous less successful theories. We present Representative Realism as a response to Direct Realism and Idealism as following naturally from Representative Realism. Our final chapter on Free Will and Determinism illustrates, in the context of a dilemma, the important decisions philosophers must sometimes make when well-entrenched beliefs are threatened by carefully constructed argument.

6. The second edition of *Theories of Knowledge and Reality* includes a new chapter in which we introduce the student to the nature, methods and purpose of philosophy. Some advice for working with the text is offered. A more detailed table of contents is also included, giving the reader more help in locating specific sections and subsections. We've added study questions at the end of most sections and a short list of related readings at the end of each chapter. In light of the many helpful comments we've received over the years, we've been able to rework many sections of the text, making the discussions more accurate and more accessible to the student.

Advice from our readers on all facets of this work is welcomed. We encourage those with comments to write us:

Jan A. Cover   Rudy L. Garns
Department of Philosophy   Philosophy Program
Purdue University   Northern Kentucky University
West Lafayette, IN 47907   Highland Heights, KY 41076

Acknowledgements

The earliest stage of writing for this project was supported by a textbook development grant from the College of Arts and Sciences at Syracuse University, which we gratefully acknowledge. Special thanks is due to Alexander Rosenberg, for initiating the project; to Tom Senor, who helped helped us extensively with an an early draft and has supported us throughout; to C. L. Hardin, who advised and encouraged us from the beginning; and to our teaching colleagues at Syracuse University (past and present), who made significant recommendations on how the book might be improved: Ralph Baergen, Paul Bloomfield, Terry Christlieb, Gregory Ganssle, Phil Goggins, Raja Halwani, Glenn Hartz, Dan Howard-Snyder, Frances Howard-Snyder, Michael Lynch, Neil Manson, Alastair Norcross, Michael Patten, Karen Taylor, Robert Van Gulick, Mark Webb, and David Woodruff. We are grateful to Constance Ditzel and Margaret Hollander at McGraw-Hill for their helpful advice and patience.

May 1993   J.A.C.
                                                              R.L.G.

TABLE OF CONTENTS

CHAPTER 1 | Doing Philosophy

Section 1: WHAT IS PHILOSOPHY?

Defining Philosophy

ANY STUDENT of philosophy might expect that the question "What is philosophy?" would be answered early in an introductory philosophy textbook. After all, such a text is meant to introduce the student to philosophy, and one could reasonably expect to find out, at least in some general way, what it is that one is being introduced to at the start. How else could one appreciate the problems studied as being philosophical problems unless one has already some sense of what is philosophical? On the other hand, it could plausibly be argued that such a question is best left for the end of the text book, to be examined in the light of all that has come before. Only after one has investigated some of the problems of philosophy and ways in which philosophers approach those problems can one really appreciate and understand what philosophy is and how it is done.

Both approaches have merit. It will be enough for our purposes, early in this text, to offer a general description of philosophy, its area of concern and its method of investigation, and leave a more sophisticated grasp of its nature for later. If one follows carefully and thoughtfully the discussions of the problems presented throughout, a better understanding of philosophy, and what it is to be philosophical, is sure to follow.

If we expect a precise answer, the question "What is philosophy?" is one of the most difficult questions a philosopher faces. The difficulty arises, in part, with the expected precision. As with many ordinary concepts, even once we can correctly identify many or most cases as belonging to the concept, the criteria for belonging are complicated and difficult to articulate. We seem to have some understanding of them (enabling us to identify cases) but our understanding is neither very precise nor very well articulated. We all recognize an ordinary chair when we come across one. But how might we answer the question "What is a chair?" Suppose we think of chairs as man-made objects designed for sitting upon. Such an account covers most of the cases we are familiar with, but it both lets too many things count as chairs, and perhaps at the same time, includes too few things. Are sofas and stools then chairs? What if we found objects that looked like and functioned like our ordinary chairs growing on trees and harvested for the purposes of sitting? Wouldn't these also count as chairs even though they are not man-made? Our initial account of what it is to be a chair was both not exhaustive (by not allowing the "natural chairs" to count) and not restrictive enough (by allowing sofas to count). Precision is hard to come by!

We seek an account of philosophy (of its questions, methods, value) that is both exhaustive and restrictive. That won't be easy since there are so many different issues that confront philosophers and so many different ways in which philosophers contend that philosophy ought to be done.

Love of Wisdom

One standard way of coming to grips with what philosophy is is to look at the etymology of the word "philosophy," which tells us that, early in its history at least, philosophy was understood to be the Love of Wisdom (*philein*, "to love" and *sophia*, "wisdom"). If we find it plausible to think that all and only philosophers are lovers of wisdom, we have still to ask what ideas of love and of wisdom are being used here. In what way do philosophers love wisdom and what does love have to do with the practice of doing philosophy? What is it to be wise in the sense intended here? Does this in any way restrict the range of questions or methods we might want to call philosophical?

Without trying to give a complete account we can say this much. To speak of love in this context is to speak of a desire for wisdom in which wisdom is valued for its own sake, not because it is useful as a means to get something else. It is out of this desire that one pursues wisdom. To love wisdom in this way is to display an intellectual curiosity and sense of wonder according to which no question is too deep or profound or difficult or complicated to be worth exploring.

What of wisdom? We frequently reserve the attribution of wisdom for the aged or for ancestors or for gods. Occasionally one is said to be wise in the ways of the world or wise about matters of the heart. In these examples, wisdom requires a certain amount of knowledge, which displays itself in sound judgment and careful analysis. The wise person is good at governing his or her own actions and good at counseling others. To be sure, there is then some practical benefit implied here, but that is not why the wisdom is valued. The lover of wisdom values it for its own sake.

Let us continue to explore this idea that the philosopher, as a lover of wisdom, pursues knowledge of a certain sort for its own sake. What sort of knowledge is relevant here? Insofar as one is seeking knowledge as a philosopher, one is interested in questions that are at once profound, fundamental, general and important. The question we are now considering—"What is philosophy?"—is itself a philosophical question largely because it concerns the nature of a discipline in a context too general for other, more specific disciplines, to address. Suppose a biologist were to ask the question "What is biology?" To answer this question she would not do more biology. And if she asks "How ought I do biology in order to achieve the knowledge biology aims for?" she could not do more biology to find an answer. Instead she must think as a philosopher, evaluating the methods biologists use in light of the goals that define biology. These questions are more general than questions of biology, or of any other specific science. And they are more fundamental since anyone engaging in the science must presuppose answers to them. But there is no discipline that studies questions more general than philosophy's questions. "What is philosophy?" must be addressed by the philosopher, as must "How ought we do philosophy?"

Other general topics of interest to the philosopher include the ultimate nature of reality and the distinction between appearance and reality, the general and abstract character of justice, of beauty, of truth and of knowledge, and the meaning and value of human existence. In none of these areas of inquiry can an empirical science—a science that relies on observation and experiment—address the issues with a sufficiently broad perspective.

We considered above a question that asks how one ought to do something. Questions involving "oughts" are *normative* questions and these also are generally reserved for the philosopher. We see questions like these arise when considering the appropriate methodology for a scientist. And we see them most explicitly in the field of ethics, where one asks how we ought to act in order to be morally good, or just, or right. In logic we ask how we ought to reason in order to preserve the truth from the premises of arguments to their conclusions. And in epistemology we are concerned with how we ought to establish our belief systems in order to arrive at knowledge.

We have been talking of philosophy as a special discipline, as an area of intellectual territory within which philosophers methodically explore fundamental questions well outside the territory of other disciplines. But the adjective "philosophical" should not be confined to this narrow circle of specialists. Someone who is not a professional philosopher can have philosophical thoughts or approach an issue philosophically. We've already considered the biologist who asks, philosophically, about the nature and methods of her particular science. Consider also a mathematician who has spent his life uncovering mathematical truths—lawful truths about square roots or different orders of infinity. It is not surprising that a person so involved in the "science of numbers" should one day ask himself what a number is. It is not a physical object nor is it simply an idea in his head. Is it no more than a piece of conventional notation? Is a number an abstract object? These are not merely questions within mathematics but philosophical questions about the subject matter of mathematics. Or consider the neuro-physiologist who has researched the workings of the brain. Now she asks whether physical events inside the brain could be identical with mental events such as hoping and fearing and believing. Could these mental events take place within a computer? Can we account for consciousness in strictly physical terms? These are philosophical questions to which nonphilosophical investigation might naturally lead. But, we must point out, these are not questions which the methods of neurophysiology can be used to answer. They demand reflection on the concepts of consciousness, mentality and mechanism, among others.

The philosopher, then, values and seeks answers to questions of a very fundamental or ultimate nature, questions that lie outside the domain of specific sciences and that those sciences presuppose. But we should not be led to think that philosophy simply takes what science leaves behind. Historically speaking, it is out of philosophy that the other sciences first came to light. Men and women first came to wonder generally about their universe and their place in it. Only gradually did questions become specialized and an articulated scientific method arise. The questions and problems that remain are the vestiges of age-old curiosity that no particular empirical science is equipped to satisfy.

Section 2: HOW IS PHILOSOPHY DONE?

A misleading model

One common image of a philosopher is that of a sage or an oracle who, through some divine inspiration or intuition, has attained wisdom. Upon request, this sage might dispense that wisdom in the form of aphorisms or conandrums or paradoxes, the proper reflection on which will yield those important truths the disciple seeks. The common conception of an Eastern philosopher is perhaps most closely associated with this model. But the model of a divinely inspired oracle is really too simple-minded to do that conception justice (for example, the important ideas of self-knowledge, resignation and one's relationship with nature are missing). This model is even farther removed from the proper conception of the Western philosopher. The philosopher of this tradition is not someone who sits on a mountaintop and dispenses wisdom that was mysteriously attained but someone who continually and actively seeks wisdom through careful, rigorous and rational reflection. The philosopher is someone who approaches fundamental and profound questions methodically, formulating hypotheses and critically examining objections and alternatives.

Consider the question of whether we have a free will. This question is a philosophical question insofar as no particular empirical science will suffice to provide an answer. Neither elaborate laboratory experiments nor sophisticated polling techniques will serve to inform us. To be sure, we might find out what most people think about whether we have free will, but we will not in this way be able to find out whether they are correct. To find out whether we do have free will we must subject carefully formed hypotheses to critical examination.

The gauntlet of objections

How will a philosopher proceed to investigate the nature and possibility of free will? We will look at this particular question in some detail later in the text but for now it will suffice to point out the role hypothesis and critical examination play in the philosopher's method. Much as in the empirical sciences, the philosopher will set out the most plausible hypothesis (or hypotheses) available to her. She might begin with a hypothesis that takes into account what most people do think about free will, a hypothesis that handles most of the actions we would normally count as acts of free will and excludes those that we might commonly regard not to be free. Other hypotheses are also likely to be suggested. To select one over another we must be prepared to submit all contenders to critical examination.

Philosophers are deeply concerned with rational arguments. What arguments can be offered for each hypothesis? Given the methods that logic provides for evaluating arguments, can the arguments themselves withstand criticism? And will they be convincing to anyone who attends to them? To be convincing an argument's premises must provide appropriate support for its conclusion and it must be clear to all that the premises are true. That is a tall order. More often than not arguments are found to be deficient, demanding either revisions that will avoid a particular difficulty or else complete abandonment. If our hypothesis is that we have no free will, then we must provide reasons for thinking this is correct. We might argue that Determinism is true and that if Determinism is true, then we cannot have free will. While the reasoning itself looks impeccable here, one might still ask what Determinism is exactly and whether there are any reasons for thinking it is true. Are the arguments offered for Determinism sound? Also, why should we think that Determinism and acts of free will are incompatible? It is easy to see that one question can quickly lead to others and that a careful examination of one argument can quickly lead to a consideration of others.

In addition to examining critically the reasons one might offer for thinking a philosophical hypothesis is true, the philosopher must also consider the consequences of her particular position. Are there consequences that lead to absurdities, telling us immediately that the original position is unacceptable? Does our hypothesis have consequences that conflict with other well-established beliefs? For example, if we contend that we have no free will, it seems to follow that we are not responsible for our actions, and consequently, we cannot be held morally responsible for our actions (that is, we cannot be the proper subjects of praise or blame). Are we willing to accept the consequence that no one is morally responsible for any act they perform? It may well be that we find it so intuitively plausible to think that we have free will that, given that acts of free will and Determinism are incompatible, we would rather accept the thesis that Determinism is false.

Hypotheses or arguments that face serious objections or which have unacceptable consequences may still be plausible enough to warrant revision. Sometimes a subtle change is all that is required to meet the objection or avoid the consequence. In such a situation the new hypothesis or argument must now face a new examination. This process of revision will be evident throughout the text.

In short, the philosopher must be willing to put his or her hypothesis to the test, running it through what Plato refers to as a gauntlet of objections. Only by passing such a rigorous examination will the philosopher's position be worthy of belief. The process is very similar to that found in the empirical sciences with the exception that the ultimate testing is done, not with laboratory experiments and empirical observations, but with careful reflection and thought experiments. Though all along the way we appeal to what seems intuitively correct after careful and rigorous reflection, no assumption can in the end be left unexamined.

Section 3: WHY DOES ONE DO PHILOSOPHY?

Capturing the average nonphilosopher's perception of philosophy, Bertrand Russell may seem to be portraying the enterprise as frustrating, confusing and worthless when he writes that ". . . the point of philosophy is to start with something so simple as to seem not worth stating, and to end with something so paradoxical that no one will believe it."[1] As Russell is well aware, the statement smacks of irony given that the philosopher is properly expected to begin with the paradoxical and end with clear, credible truths. How can we reconcile the manner in which philosophy often appears to proceed with its intended purpose?

To be sure, you may be left wondering why you should do philosophy when so much philosophical reflection seems to go in circles, from one question to a proposed solution and back to another, or even the same, question. You may get the feeling that the issues are only getting more muddled and more complicated after we subject them to philosophical examination. Our common everyday understanding of the world appears more serviceable and much easier to understand than the complicated views philosophers propose to account for the problems that their own theories seem to introduce.

The irony of Russell's statement arises precisely because, while the process of philosophy does appear to lead to paradoxical and incredible theories, in fact, if properly engaged in, it does no such thing. The fault is not with philosophy or its methods, but with those views that seem "so simple as to not be worth stating." What seem to be simple, credible and coherent beliefs before one starts philosophizing are found, upon closer scrutiny, to fall far short of the philosopher's high standards of credibility. Pre-philosophical views often earn their acceptance by ignoring, or failing to see, the paradoxes and problems that turn up under careful scrutiny. It is a mark of progress that the philosopher moves from unreflective complacency to a more sophisticated understanding of the world, even if that new perspective on the world lends itself to more questions than the old worldview. Those who naively find the pre-reflective opinions satisfactory are also likely to find the post-reflective opinions of philosophers to be paradoxical and incredible.

Philosophical progress is achieved through the process of questioning commonplace assumptions. The world is not so simple as our everyday beliefs would suggest, and penetrating questions lead naturally to more questions. Finding that something once held to be obviously true is really false or at least questionable might leave the philosopher feeling insecure and confused about what he should believe. And when a proposed explanation or theory does not survive critical examination you may feel as though you have gone in circles. But you are not back where you began if you have learned that one overly simplified view will not suffice and if, in the process, you have been led to consider other, more plausible hypotheses.

Section 4: WORKING WITH THIS TEXT[2]

As an introduction to philosophy, this text may differ from other texts you are familiar with. With that in mind you should be prepared to approach this text differently.

Before you read, consider what the authors intend for you to learn from the text. A large part of understanding what philosophy is is understanding how philosophy is done, and to do that you need to see philosophy being practiced and to engage in philosophizing yourself. Thus, the material in this text is presented in an order that someone philosophizing (maybe for the first time) will find natural. We start with theses or propositions that might seem to be obvious to the layman and, by introducing various difficulties or observations, work toward positions that are more sophisticated. To continue with an example we used above, we are not so much interested in telling you whether persons have free will as how a philosopher might go about defending or refuting the view that persons have free will. What considerations motivate a philosophical interest in the question of whether we have free will? And how can someone begin to answer those questions?

Reading the text

We recommend that you read each assignment at least three times. A first reading should be quick with the objectives of getting a rough idea about the general contentions and questions in the assignment, and noticing the key concepts and new vocabulary. During a second, more careful reading, examine each paragraph slowly noting key terms and definitions, checking to see how examples are used, and isolating arguments and their critiques. Taking notes either in the margin or on separate paper will be very helpful. Write down questions you have about the material whenever they arise. These may be questions about what a particular phrase or passage means, or they may be questions (or insights) you have about the issue itself. Do not refrain from taking part in the philosophical process.

Often, if you have carefully attended to an assignment paragraph by paragraph, you may find that you have lost sight of the entire project, or with the initial issue. Once you have gone through the assignment with great care, go back a third time and develop an outline of the assignment. Were you reading about an argument which was critically evaluated and revised? Or was it about two theories that were compared and evaluated?

Definitions

Key terms and concepts are defined in the context in which they are being discussed. Usually they are italicized in the sentence that introduces them. As you read, stay alert for these and take careful note of the wording. Attention to detail is essential. Misunderstanding a key concept when it is introduced might lead you to deeper misunderstandings later on. Also, definitions are often accompanied with examples. Check to make sure that you see how each example illustrates the concept in question. Considering examples of your own making is a useful way to test your understanding of the concept and a good device for remembering what you read.

Examples and counterexamples

Examples are used positively to reinforce your understanding of a new concept or term. But often examples are also used negatively as counterexamples to illustrate a weakness in a definition, a theory or an argument. If someone defines squares as four-sided closed plane figures, then we might refer to a rectangle as counterexample to the definition since it satisfies the given definition but is clearly not a square. Or if a philosopher were to attempt to define an act of free will as any act that is done because the person wants to do it, then we might cite as a counterexample an example of a person who acts because they wanted to act that way, but who is just the same clearly not acting of their own free will (perhaps because a mischievous scientist is controlling her mind).

Sometimes counterexamples serve to point out the weakness in a piece of reasoning. Consider someone who argues that a brain cannot be a conscious thinking thing because the parts of the brain (the neurons, cells, etc.) are not themselves conscious thinking things. A philosopher might easily challenge such an argument by pointing out that similar reasoning is used in the argument that water is not wet because the hydrogen and oxygen that make up the water molecules are not wet. Since the latter reasoning is clearly absurd, there is good reason to be suspicious of the former argument about the brain.

We should point out that counterexamples only need to be possible situations, and not actual. Philosophers often tell fanciful stories about mad scientists or martians or omniscient beings. Though they are not about actual situations, these stories may serve as forceful counterexamples if they are properly constructed. Philosophy, as discussed above, is concerned with the most general and fundamental features of the world. If she considers only actual situations, the philosopher would not be addressing issues that are appropriately general. Whether we are concerned with the nature of knowledge, or consciousness or free will, we will need to consider not only what it is for actual humans to have knowledge, be conscious or have free will, but what it is to have knowledge, be conscious and have free will in general, for any possible being.

Working with arguments

We have already said something about arguments and their role in doing philosophy. More can be found about arguments in Chapter 2 on logic and language. We will conclude this section, however, with some remarks about working with arguments when you come across them in your reading. Occasionally you will find that arguments are set out from the paragraphs in which they are introduced. In so doing we are isolating precisely the conclusion of the argument and the premises used to support that conclusion. Typically the premises and the conclusion are numbered for convenient reference later on. Arguments are set out in this manner to facilitate better understanding and evaluation. Consider the argument for the existence of God that we call "Causal."

(1) There are things that come into existence.
(2) Whatever comes into existence is caused to exist by something else.
(3) There cannot be an infinite series of past causes.
(4) So, there was a first cause (God).

Statements (1) through (3) are premises, which taken together provide support for the conclusion (4). The word "So" signals that a conclusion follows. Setting out the argument clearly in this form allows us to focus on each premise, examining its credentials and its contribution to the whole argument. For example, while premise (1) in this argument is uncontroversial, premises (2) and (3) require further argument. And, in setting out the argument carefully, we can also emphasize the important work that, say, (3) is doing in the argument. Without it we cannot conclude that the series of past causes is finite—a series of past causes that has a first cause.

When reading the section that contains this argument you will find that before we present the argument we discuss its motivation (what is this argument used to show and why would anyone consider it in the first place?) and explain why each premise is stated the way that it is. More discussion of the argument follows, including passages in which we attempt to defend the premises from objections that may initially seem devastating. Finally, we raise more serious objections, perhaps suggesting ideas for further revision.

Even when arguments are not set out in the ordered manner above you should try to isolate the conclusion (that which is being argued for) and the premises (whatever reasons are offered in defense of the conclusion). After reading a subsection of the text ask yourself whether an argument has been presented. If so, what is the conclusion and what reasons were offered in its behalf? Have the premises themselves been supported? What objections have been discussed and were any revisions in an argument or theory developed in light of those objections? The arguments we discuss in this text all have had their proponents and opponents. That we do not settle on any one argument as sound, or on any particular theory as correct, should not lead you to think that there are no good arguments or true theories. Philosophy is a difficult business with the highest of standards. It is not surprising that these complicated issues are still being discussed and that there is work remaining to be done. The many weaknesses in the arguments and theories that we discuss are evidence only of one kind of progress that a careful and critical method can supply. As well, we might expect that in contemplating the problems that plague these traditionally important arguments and theories, new insights will become available.

NOTES

[1]Bertrand Russell, *The Philosophy of Logical Atomism*, Ed. David Pears (La Salle, IL: Open Court Publishing Company, 1985), 53.

[2]For helpful ideas about how to read, write and study philosophy see David Oja's companion to this text: *Writing in Philosophy* (New York: McGraw-Hill, Inc., 1990).

RELATED READINGS

Gorovitz, S. and R. G. Williams. *Philosophical Analysis: An Introduction to its Language and Techniques*. Second edition. New York: Random House, 1969.

Oja, David E. *Student Writing in Philosophy*. New York: McGraw-Hill, Inc., 1990.

Rosenberg, Jay F. *The Practice of Philosophy: A Handbook for Beginners*. Englewood Cliffs, NJ: Prentice Hall, Inc., 1978.

Russell, Bertrand. *The Philosophy of Logical Atomism*. Ed. David Pears. La Salle, IL: Open Court Publishing Company, 1985.

_____. "The Value of Philosophy." *The Problems of Philosophy*. New York: Oxford University Press, 1969.

Woodhouse, Mark B. *A Preface to Philosophy*. Third edition. Belmont, CA: Wadsworth Publishing Company, 1984.

CHAPTER 2 | Logic and Language

Section 1: LOGIC

A. Arguments

Arguing without arguments

IMAGINE the following all too common scene. Larry and Clyde have squared off on the abortion issue and for the past half hour have been yelling back and forth. Larry, firmly attached to his position, has been loudly asserting "Abortion is wrong, definitely wrong" to which Clyde has consistently responded in an equally emotional and deafening voice "No Larry, you're wrong—abortion is okay."

The "dialogue" at the end of the half hour remains as it began: Clyde favors abortion and Larry opposes it. What we have in this scene is nothing more than a heated exchange of opinions. Without attempting to clarify or support anything, each party stands dogmatically and emotionally committed to his position. As a result there has been no progress. Surely, one or the other must be correct. Abortion is either right or it is wrong: there is no third, intermediate position and it cannot be both right and wrong (assuming, of course, that Ethical Relativism is incorrect). But there is no way for either person to assess the other's claim, and there is nothing by which a third party might decide between the two views. By merely gainsaying one another, Larry and Clyde have done nothing to further the debate.

If we suppose that, instead of disagreeing simply for the sake of disagreeing, or for some personal satisfaction in "winning," they are undertaking this debate in the true philosophical spirit, then we may expect that as a result, one party would come to see that he was wrong and the truth of the matter would be discovered. The aim of disputes between reasonable people ought not be to bludgeon or coax the other into accepting one's own position. It should be to arrive at the truth, and one cannot be expected to convince others of the truth, or even be sure of one's own possession of the truth, unless one does something more than merely assert a position.

Arguments and rational debate

What more can Larry and Clyde do to improve the quality of their discussion? Suppose we begin again with Larry claiming that abortion is "wrong, definitely wrong" and with Clyde opposing. This time, however, Clyde challenges Larry to support his position—what reasons does he have for thinking that abortion is wrong? "Why, clearly," Larry retorts, "abortion is the taking of a life, and since the taking of a life is murder and murder is always wrong, abortion must be wrong." Now Larry has supported his position, and Clyde can do more than merely deny the claim—he can assess the reasoning. Are his reasons good reasons? Do they really support his position? Are his reasons themselves true?

Furthermore, Clyde can offer reasons on behalf of his claim that abortion is okay. "I understand your reasoning," he might say, "but I don't think that the taking of just any life constitutes murder (stepping on a bug is not murder, for example). It is only the taking of a human life that is properly called murder and I don't think that human life begins until the fetus leaves the womb. So, I find your reasons to be faulty. I also happen to think that in some cases abortion is clearly a better option than giving birth to a child who might not have a healthy or happy life, or when the birth itself might endanger the mother's life." Continuing in this way, with one person offering reasons to support his position and the other critically evaluating those reasons and the reasoning itself (perhaps reasons might be offered to support the truth of other reasons and so on), the interlocutors may eventually find some point on which they can agree. From there, perhaps, they can reason to a common and, if all goes well, correct conclusion concerning abortion.

Of course, some issues—and abortion may be one of them—are very complex and not easily decidable. But no headway is made in the investigation or the debate if one merely asserts opinions without supporting them or critically evaluating what support is offered. The use of reasons and reasoning adds to the discussion between Larry and Clyde. What one must do is look carefully not only at the reasons one uses but at the way in which they support the position. It will not do to offer reasons for believing that something is true if they in no way support the claim. Notice that if Larry had supported his claim that abortion is wrong by noting only that abortions can be very expensive, one could easily reply that, although it may be true that the operation is costly, it is irrelevant to the moral status of abortion (whether it is good or bad, or right or wrong). Consequently, it is not a very good reason to think abortion is wrong. Larry's reason may be true but his reasoning is faulty—he has failed to find the right kind of support connecting his reason with the position he wishes to defend.

When someone offers reasons in support of a claim we will say he is offering an *argument* for that claim. More formally we can say that an argument is any series of sentences (or propositions), one of which is offered as the claim to be supported and is called the *conclusion*, the rest of which are offered in support of the conclusion and are called the *premises*. Logic is the discipline that studies the procedures by which we evaluate arguments; it is by logic that we determine what in general makes an argument good or bad. As noted above, we are not merely interested in the truth of the premises (although this surely must be a feature of any good argument), but also in the connection between the premises and the conclusion. Since truth is the ultimate goal, good arguments will be restricted to those that have the potential for preserving the truth from the premises to the conclusion.

In virtue of this important connection between premises and conclusion we can divide arguments into two kinds. Arguments that are intended to guarantee that truth will be preserved from the premises to the conclusion are called *deductive* arguments. These arguments are said to be proofs or demonstrations of their conclusions. What remain are arguments that do not guarantee the truth of the conclusion but are merely intended to render the conclusion probably true on the basis of the premises. These arguments we call *inductive*. The premises of inductive arguments are said to provide evidence for the conclusion's likelihood. We turn now to a closer look at deductive arguments.

B. Deduction

A good deductive argument for a particular claim is typically harder to come by than a good inductive argument, primarily because the deductive argument has the more difficult job. It must do more than just render its conclusion *likely* or *probable*: deductive reasoning is such that the premises are intended to provide *conclusive* reasons for why a particular claim is true. Because conclusiveness is preferable to mere likelihood, philosophers usually try to construct deductive arguments when they can.

What makes a deductive argument a good one? We have already seen what is wrong with simply asserting some belief of ours as true, without offering any reasons to justify or defend it. If we want our reasons to show conclusively that the conclusion is true we must provide reasons that together rule out every possibility incompatible with our conclusion. If we have done that, we can say that the conclusion *follows* from the premises. The idea of a conclusion following from a list of premises is the idea of validity: in a good deductive argument the premises and the conclusion must be related in a way that guarantees the truth of the conclusion given the truth of the premises.

Be aware that an argument's premises and conclusion may be related in the appropriate way to provide validity and yet the premises be false. This possibility arises because validity is strictly a matter of the form of the argument and guarantees only what would be the case *if the premises were true*. That the premises should actually be true is an additional requirement for a good argument. Let's now focus our discussion on the virtue of validity.

Validity

One requirement for a good deductive argument is that the premises follow logically from the conclusion. If the conclusion of an argument is related to the premises in this way, then the truth of the premises will guarantee the truth of the conclusion. Because we are accustomed to look closely at the truth of what is said, we tend to overlook the important connection between premises and conclusion. Consider the following two arguments.

(1) If George Berkeley is a vegetable, then George
     Berkeley is a fish.
     George Berkeley is a vegetable.
So, George Berkeley is a fish.

(2) If George Berkeley is human, then George Berkeley is
     an mammal.
     George Berkeley is human.
So, George Berkeley is an mammal.

(1), surely, isn't a very promising argument. We never have thought that a vegetable could be a fish or that George Berkeley, the famous philosopher, was a vegetable. And even though the conclusion is supported with reasons (the premises), we remain unprepared to believe that George Berkeley is, or was, a fish. But we mustn't settle with this judgment about how good or bad (1) is as a deductive argument: the relation of premises to conclusion is a *logical* feature of arguments, and we have so far only noted the *psychological* fact that we are unconvinced of this conclusion. To see this point more clearly, consider argument (2).

(2) is a perfectly good argument, partly because the conclusion is logically connected with the premises: we can easily see if George Berkeley's being human is sufficient for his being an mammal and that he is human, then we must conclude that he is an mammal. This logical connection between premises and conclusion is captured in the *structure* or *form* of the argument, and can be represented by using "p" and "q" as variables or place-holders for propositions.

(3) If p, then q
     p
So, q

Notice that (1) has this same form. Indeed, any argument of this general form is good in that its conclusion follows from its premises. That is to say, *if the premises are true, then the conclusion must be true.* Put otherwise, we say that it is impossible for the premises to be true and the conclusion false. Any argument structured so that the conclusion follows (conclusively, necessarily) from the premises is called a *valid* argument.

It is important to emphasize that validity concerns only the general structure of the argument, and not the specific content of its premises or conclusion. (1) and (2) are different in that one contains truths and the other does not. But (1) and (2) are similar in that they are valid arguments since each has the same valid argument form. This form is perhaps more obvious (3), where no content is made explicit at all. Any argument of valid form, regardless of content, is good at least in the sense that its conclusion must be true if its premises are. (*If* George Berkeley's being a vegetable were sufficient for his being a fish and *if* he were a vegetable, *then* in that case it would follow that Berkeley would be a fish.) Validity, then, is precisely what we seek in an argument when we insist that good arguments must preserve truth.

Invalid arguments will have a form that does not preserve truth: it will be possible for the premises to be true while the conclusion is false. Again, we are not concerned here with the specific content of the argument—we are not asking, "Are these premises true or false?" or "Is this conclusion true or false?" Rather we ask, "Is there any way of filling in this form that yields true premises and a false conclusion?" Consider, for example, that the following invalid argument has true premises and a true conclusion:

> (4) If George Berkeley is snake, then George Berkeley is a
>   reptile.
>   George Berkeley is not a snake.
> So, George Berkeley is not a reptile.

We can see that it is not valid by noticing that it has a form by which it is possible for the premises to be true while the conclusion is false. A *counterexample* can be used to demonstrate the invalidity of the form. A counterexample would be an argument with exactly the same form but for which it is obvious that while the premises are true, the conclusion is false. Here is the argument form of (4):

> If p, then q
> Not-p
> So, not-q

And here is a counterexample with the same form:

> If George Berkeley is whale, then George Berkeley is a
> mammal.
> George Berkeley is not a whale.
> So, George Berkeley is not a mammal.

Both premises of this argument are true, but the conclusion is false. The argument form, then, did not guarantee that truth would be preserved from premises to the conclusion. One possibility the premises did not rule out was that something could be a mammal in ways other than by being a whale.

Invalid arguments may come in any combination of true or false premises and true or false conclusion. (An invalid argument could even have true premises and a true conclusion, but the premises would be insufficient to guarantee the truth of the conclusion.) Valid arguments, on the other hand, have three possible combinations (true premises and a true conclusion, false premises and a false conclusion, false premises and a true conclusion) and one *impossible* combination: true premises and false conclusion.

Some examples of valid argument forms

Logic is primarily the study of the many possible relationships between premises and conclusion that render an argument valid. It provides us with a range of methods for actually showing when arguments are valid. All of us have an intuitive ability to recognize simple valid forms, but other valid forms are very complex and require more sophistication. Since this is not a logic text it is impossible to stop here and familiarize ourselves with enough logical apparatus to acquire that sophistication. There are, however, some common valid argument forms that occur frequently in philosophical discussion. These are listed below, along with examples.

modus ponens

Form: If p, then q
                   p
         So,   q

Example: If the apples are edible, then they are red.
              The apples are edible.
         So, the apples are red.

modus tollens

Form: If p, then q
              Not- q
         So, not -p

Example: If the apples are edible, then they are red.
              The apples are not red.
         So, the apples are not edible.

disjunctive syllogism

Form: Either p or q
                 Not- p
        So, q

Example: The apples are either red or green.
                 The apples are not red.
        So, the apples are green.

hypothetical syllogism

Form: If p, then q
                 If q, then r
        So, if p, then r

Example: If the apples are red, then they are ripe.
                 If the apples are ripe, then they are edible
        So, if the apples are red, then they are edible.

There are two additional sorts of arguments that are of special interest. One is the *dilemma*, that may take several forms, and the other is called the *reductio ad absurdum*. These ways of arguing are particularly useful in rhetorical contexts in which one wishes to employ the most powerful tools of persuasion. In the case of the *reductio ad absurdum*, as its name indicates, one attempts to reduce the opponent's view to some logically absurd position. If the opponent's view validly leads to something absurd, then the opponent should see that his view is false. There are two elementary facts about logic that we need to mention here before saying more. First, a false proposition cannot validly follow from a true proposition. So, for example, if I show that something false *does* validly follow from a proposition p, then I have shown that p is also false. Second, a contradictory proposition—something of the form 'q and not-q'—cannot be true. It is necessarily false. So, if I can show that a contradiction follows from some proposition, p, then I have shown that p is false. And that is how a *reductio* works. To show that an opponent's view is false, begin by assuming that his claim or claims are true, and then derive a contradiction. Since something undeniably false follows validly from a statement of his view, that statement must be false. Here is the best way to abbreviate this form:

reductio ad absurdum

Suppose p

·

·

·

q and not-q

So,   not-p

A simple example of a *reductio ad absurdum* might run as follows. Suppose I claim that there are four-sided triangles. You might
argue:

Well, suppose that's so. Suppose there is some figure (call it
"Fig") that is a four-sided triangle. We know what a triangle is:
it's a closed figure with exactly three angles and three sides. So
Fig has exactly three sides. But since our figure is, by supposition, a four-sided triangle, it follows that Fig both has and does
not have a fourth side. And that is a contradiction: it is
impossible for something to both be a certain way and also
not be that way. Since a contradiction follows from the
assumption that there are four-sided triangles, the assumption
must be false.

(Notice here that you had to add a premise to the initial assumption:
the contradiction did not follow *directly* from the single assumption
about there being four-sided triangles. Typically that is how such
arguments work. If we have some set of, say, three claims, two of
which we already know to be true on independent grounds, then upon
deriving a contradiction from this set, we will have proven that the
third is false.)

The dilemma is also a useful way of showing that some favored
view of an opponent is in jeopardy, this time by showing that he must
choose between only two alternatives, each of which require the denial
of the favored view. In one common form of the dilemma, then, it is
used to show that a particular proposition is false.

dilemma

Either p or q
If p, then not-r
If q, then not-r
So,   not-r

Here is a simple example to which we'll return later.

Either you dislike being in my company or you enjoy my company. If you dislike being around me, asking you to be with me a lot is of no use (you'll simply not want to be around me a lot); but if you enjoy being with me, then asking you to be with me a lot serves no real purpose (since you already wish to). Therefore, asking you to be with me a lot is of no purpose.

Soundness

So far we have been discussing an important quality of deductive arguments—*validity*. Valid arguments are those whose form guarantees that if the premises are true, then the conclusion will be true. But the valid argument just noted (the dilemma) reminds us again that there are other qualities an argument may have or lack that make it good or bad. However valid the dilemma above is, surely something is wrong with it. And recall arguments (1) and (2): each was of the same valid form, but argument (1) about vegetables being fish clearly was not as good an argument as (2) about humans being mammals. The difference was one of content, not form: the premises of (1) were false, while those of (2) were true. We do want arguments to be valid, of course, but we also want them to contain truths. Another important quality of deductive arguments, then, is called *soundness*. A sound deductive argument is valid and has only true premises. Notice that, since a sound argument is valid and has true premises, its conclusion must be true as well. That's what makes a sound argument particularly nice. It not only incorporates good reasoning (i.e., good form), but it also contains truths (i.e., good content).

Convincingness

There is one final measure of the quality of an argument worth noting here. Recall that arguments can be used to make progress in a disagreement: they are often tools of persuasion. In such cases, what an argument does is to genuinely *show* us something we had not already seen. Now someone might offer you a sound (hence, valid) argument which altogether fails in this respect. What might happen, for example, is that your seeing that one or more of the premises is true depends on your having already agreed that the conclusion is true. An argument such as this would not be *convincing*: it is altogether unhelpful as a persuasive tool, as a means of progress in a dispute. Suppose, for example, that you and I are beginning zoology students and that you are behind in your reading. We disagree about the zoological classification of your cat, and I offer you the following argument:

(5) Your cat is of the genus *Felis*, and two is half of four.
So, your cat is of the genus *Felis*.

It is impossible for the premise of (5) to be true and the conclusion false (it's valid), and the premise is true ((5) is sound). But in the context of a dispute about zoology, (5) is not very convincing: I haven't started with premises with which you already agree and *shown* you, by argument, that your cat belongs to the genus *Felis*. The best deductive lines of reasoning, then, are sound arguments that are convincing.

Fallacies

Just as we saw earlier that there are common good ways of reasoning, so there are common bad ways of reasoning as well. These bad arguments are sometimes called *fallacies*. Not surprisingly, most fallacies affect one of the three qualities of deductive arguments at which we have looked. One mistaken way of arguing is called *affirming the consequent*.

affirming the consequent (invalid)

Form: If p, then q
                 q
     So,   p

Example: If it is raining, then the street is wet.
                The street is wet.
         So,   it is raining

This is invalid because it is possible for the premises to be true and the conclusion false. Suppose it is true that if it is raining then the street is wet, and suppose also that the street is wet: it may still be false that it is raining. A counterexample here is, perhaps, a case in which the fire hydrant has broken on the streetside during a sunny day.

Another fallacy, which we saw a few pages back in argument (4), is called *denying the antecedent.*

denying the antecedent (invalid)

Form: If p then q
                Not-p
         So,   not-q

Example: If it is raining, then the street is wet.
                It is not raining.
         So,   the street is not wet.

The counterexample just offered, involving the broken fire hydrant, shows why this argument could have true premises and a false conclusion.

A different sort of mistake arises when an expression appearing in more than one premise shifts its meaning mid-argument. This shift in meaning, called *equivocation*, sometimes occurs with vague or ambiguous expressions, and usually renders the argument invalid. Here is an example:

(6)   All cancer is potentially harmful to one's health.
      Sally is a Cancer.
So,   Sally is potentially harmful to one's health.

The second premise in (6) is meant to indicate Sally's astrological sign, and so in that use of it 'cancer' means something quite different than it does in the first premise. Superficially, (6) appears to have this valid form:

      All Fs are Gs
      s is an F
So,   s is a G

In our example, however, (6) actually has this invalid form:

All Fs are Gs
s is a H
So, s is a G

We have already seen one interesting example of a fallacy affecting the soundness (not validity) of an argument. The argument about asking you to be in my company contains what is sometimes called a *false dilemma*. The first premise "Either you dislike being around me or you enjoy being around me" seems quite false, for surely there are more than just two attitudes you may take about being in my presence. If, for example, you are thoroughly indifferent about it—if it really doesn't matter one way or the other whether you are with me—, then my encouraging you to be with me might be of some consequence after all. The argument is valid, then, but since it has (at least) one false premise, it is not sound.

One final bad way of arguing that frequently affects the convincingness of an argument is called *begging the question*. In this case, the arguer presupposes the truth of what is to be proven. Here is an example.

In Enrico's autobiography he claims that he is an honest man. This claim is true, since Enrico wouldn't lie. Therefore, it is true that Enrico is an honest man.

While this argument may be sound, it is not convincing since one of the premises states what is found in the conclusion. If the object of presenting an argument is to persuade, or to make the conclusion reasonable to believe, then the argument should not include premises that are just as doubtful as the conclusion. One obvious way of making this mistake is to offer some claim as a reason for believing that very claim. The question-begging premise is relevant to the conclusion, but it isn't relevant to establishing the conclusion, or to showing that it is true. In our example, if the premise "Enrico doesn't lie" is acceptable entirely on its own, then we certainly don't need an argument to show that Enrico is an honest man.

The study of deductive arguments—how they work, what makes them good or bad—constitutes only a part of logic. Logic also investigates how inductive arguments work, and what makes them better or worse. Let's look now at these.

C. Induction

Characterizing inductive arguments

We can characterize induction by noting how it differs from deduction. First, recall that in any argument the premises are intended to support the conclusion. In cases of deduction the argument is purported to preserve truth from the premises to the conclusion. That is, the relation of support that holds between the premises and the conclusion of a good deductive argument will be strong enough to *guarantee* the truth of the conclusion given the truth of the premises. In cases of induction, however, although the premises are intended to support the conclusion, they are intended to do so only to a certain degree—it is not guaranteed that truth will be preserved. Consider the following examples.

(D) If Mel is not feeling well, then Mel ate the chili.
Mel is not feeling well.
So, Mel ate the chili.

(I) Mel is not feeling well.
Whenever Mel got sick in the past he had just eaten some chili.
So, Mel ate the chili.

Argument (D) is a valid deductive argument: if the premises are true, the conclusion must be true. Certainly one might question the premises (for example, what reasons are there for thinking that, as stated in (D), if Mel became ill, he ate chili?), but such questions would not affect the argument's validity. Validity is strictly a matter of form. Turning to argument (I), however, it should be evident that the premises could all be true, yet the conclusion false. Simply knowing that in the past eating chili was invariably connected with Mel's ill health, we are not thereby guaranteed that this time Mel's sickness is connected with his eating chili. Argument (I) is, by the deductive standards outlined above, invalid. Still, we cannot deny that the premises of (I) appear to provide good reasons for thinking that the conclusion is (probably, at least) true. Given the premises, we might say, it is likely that Mel at the chili. So, whereas deductive arguments are intended to guarantee the truth of the conclusion given the truth of the premises, inductive arguments are only intended to render the conclusion probable.

Second, validity plays no role in inductive arguments. The form of a deductive argument can be assessed as either good or bad depending on whether it is valid. There are, clearly, no degrees of validity, and hence, no range of assessment beyond good and bad. Inductive arguments, on the other hand, can be assessed by degrees—they are better or worse depending on how well the premises support the conclusion. To return to our example above, argument (D) is a valid argument and, consequently, can be considered good on that score (although there is still a question as to whether the premises are true). In assessing (I), however, we need to consider how likely it is that Mel ate the chili, given that he is now not feeling well and that in the past his eating chili was connected with his ill-health. Many factors are relevant to this assessment, including how often he was sick in the past, whether there are any alternative explanations for his illness, and whether he has eaten chili in the past without getting sick. Different answers to these questions will assign different values to the argument.

Finally, in a good inductive argument the conclusion has more content or information than can be found in the sum of the premises, but in a good deductive argument this is not possible. Consider again arguments (D) and (I). If in the deductive argument (D) the conclusion follows from the premises, then the conclusion will tell us nothing more than the premises do (although it might make the information more concise or explicit). To say that if Mel is sick, then he ate the chili, and indeed he is sick, is just to say (in a cumbersome, perhaps roundabout way) that Mel ate the chili. But the story is different in (I), which is an inductive argument. To say that Mel is presently sick and that *in the past* eating chili has been connected with his ill health is *not* to say that *in the present case* his sickness is connected with eating chili. It is likely, of course, given the evidence we have (his eating the chili appears to be a good explanation for why he got sick), but the conclusion still goes beyond the evidence. The information found in the conclusion about Mel's recent encounter with chili is not found, either explicitly or implicitly, in the premises; they only inform us about past connections between Mel's state of health and chili—and that's why, given the premises, the conclusion is only probably, not necessarily, true.

The importance of inductive reasoning

In spite of the fact that inductive arguments do not guarantee the truth of the conclusion given the truth of the premises, they are important. Much of our everyday reasoning is inductive. We infer that it is likely to rain given the presence of dark clouds above us; you think it probable that you will pass the course since you have studied hard and whenever you studied hard for a course in the past you did well; you suppose that the car you bought today will probably get good gas mileage because, of the many people you know who have a car like this, none get less than 28 miles per gallon; you believe there is a good chance that your life is in danger because you see a tiger that has just escaped from the zoo charging you and you know that charging tigers are often fatal.

Induction is also of great importance in the field of science. It is the scientist's job to gather data that will count as evidence in support of certain hypotheses he is considering. Thus, if his hypothesis is that all swans are white, he will attempt to observe a relatively large number of swans. If all of the many swans he observes are white, he may have good reason to think that all swans (including the ones he has not observed) are that way. Or it may be that the scientist has encountered certain phenomena and posits the existence of an unobservable entity to explain those phenomena. Electrons, for example, are thought likely to exist given that they best explain the results of certain cloud chamber experiments and other phenomena. The experiments do not guarantee that these entities exist, they only make it probable that they do.

Philosophy, too, sometimes makes use of inductive reasoning. The claim that God exists is often thought to be supported by certain evidence found in nature and experience. The claim that God does not exist might also be inductively supported. Are there minds other than my own? Is there a physical reality beyond mere appearance? Does every event have a cause? These are philosophical questions that have been discussed by some philosophers using inductive methods. One fascinating philosophical issue concerns whether induction itself is a good or reliable method of reasoning. Should we continue to trust inductive arguments? Although there have been many different answers to this question, one interesting line of response is to say that induction has worked well in the past, so it is probably a good reasoning practice. This, of course, is to give an inductive evaluation of induction and, consequently, is highly controversial. But it illustrates the fact that philosophers have not ignored the importance of induction.

Some key notions

So far we have only mentioned some key notions related to the method of induction. It is to several of these that attention must now be drawn. First, the premises of an inductive argument express what has been called *evidence* for the truth of the conclusion. The notion of evidence is one with which we are all familiar but which is difficult to define. Suppose that upon hearing a gunshot, we rush into the room to find Larry holding a smoking gun and Clyde lying dead on the floor. When investigating this apparent homicide, we would consider the fact that we found Larry holding a smoking gun to be evidence for the hypothesis that he murdered Clyde. Of course, this evidence does not guarantee that Larry is a murderer. Perhaps he entered the room just moments before we did, found the gun on the floor alongside the unfortunate Clyde and picked it up unthinkingly. Or perhaps he only accidentally fired the gun so that it was not strictly speaking murder. In similar fashion we may say of our inductive inference (I)—regarding Mel and his chili—that our observing the connection between Mel's ill health and his eating chili in the past counts as evidence for the conclusion that he has recently eaten chili (given that he is now not feeling well). Again, the evidence does not guarantee that the conclusion is true.

Generalizing from this, we might say that evidence is whatever may be used to provide support for an hypothesis or conclusion. Of course, there may be evidence for both sides of an issue. My observing 100 white swans with no exceptions may provide evidence for the hypothesis that all swans are white. But it is easy to find evidence to build an inductive argument for the opposite conclusion. For example, almost every variety of bird we know of has members differing in color; swans constitute a variety of bird; so, probably, swans have members differing in color (i.e., not all of them are white). In both of these arguments we have evidence that supports a conclusion. Of course, some evidence is better than other evidence, and consequently, some inductive arguments are better than other inductive arguments. What makes some arguments better than others is a question we will address shortly.

We have mentioned the notion of support but have, so far, left it rather vague. One thing we can say is that evidence supports an hypothesis or conclusion to the extent that it makes the hypothesis or conclusion *probable*. What is it to make something probable? Generally we think of probability as coming in degrees and we frequently assign numerical values to these degrees. But it is not at all clear what it is that degrees of probability rank. There are many theories about this but for our purposes we will not need to decide upon any particular one; we can rely on what might be called our "pre-theoretic" understanding of probability. Even if we do not have a theory about what probability is we can still meaningfully and significantly use the notion. This much will suffice: the degree to which the conclusion is probable varies with the degree to which the premises support the conclusion.

Inductive generalization

There are several important kinds of inductive argument; we will look only at two. Consider first *inductive generalization* (also called "argument by enumeration"). Here we start with a sample of cases in which some individuals of a certain kind have been observed to have a specific feature in common (without exception). These can provide evidence for the conclusion that all individuals of that kind have the feature in question. We are, in effect, simply generalizing over several known cases. We used this form of reasoning in arguing that all swans are white. There, by noting that without exception every swan we observed was white, we concluded that (probably) all swans are white. The following schema illustrates the general form of inductive generalizations.

inductive generalization

    Every F we have observed so far was G.
So, all Fs are Gs.

In other words, we argue from a claim that everything we have examined in the past having property F has, without exception, also had property G, to a claim that (probably) all things, including those we have not examined, that have property F also have property G. By way of another example let F be the property of being a person who has eaten a poisoned muffin and G be the property of dying. We might then encounter the following argument: person a was observed eating a poisoned muffin and dying; people b and c were observed doing the same (and perhaps many others were similarly examined); nobody has been examined who has eaten a poisoned muffin and not died; so, probably, all those who eat poisoned muffins die.

There are a number of factors by which we may evaluate inductive generalizations. Suppose we have examined only two white moths. We have found both to have a black spot on one wing, and since these are the only two moths we have examined, we have no counter-instances. Should we conclude that all white moths have a black spot on one wing? Surely, this would not be a very good inference. There are many white moths and we have examined only a very small fraction of the total population. If, however, we were to examine many more white moths (perhaps looking at hundreds) and find no counter-instances, then our argument would be improved. The *size of the sample* relative to the size of the total population of the items to be considered is sometimes an important parameter by which to evaluate inductive generalizations. The greater the sample size (relative to the size of the total population), the greater the support offered by the evidence.

To illustrate another parameter let us imagine that we want to show that *all* moths have one black spot on their wings. Is the fact that we have observed hundreds of *white* moths in this condition (without exception) good evidence for our hypothesis? Not really. Our hypothesis would be better supported if we had observed many different kinds of moth. After all, we want to make a claim about moths in general. Our sample, then should represent as well as possible the total population of moths, which includes many kinds of moths other than the white-winged variety. Also, our sample should reflect the various subgroups in the same proportion in which they belong to the total population. If only a third of all moths are of the white-winged variety, then our sample should include only one-third white-winged moths. *The representativeness of the sample* determines to some degree the value of the generalization. A random sample is the best means to insure that our sample reflects the diversity, in the correct proportions, of the total population.

Argument by analogy

Another important kind of inductive argument is the *argument by analogy*. Analogies, of course, mark a similarity between two things or groups of things. They can be used to illustrate or emphasize certain features of an object, as when we illustrate the function of the heart by saying that the heart works in the way a pump does. But we can also construct inductive arguments using analogies. The idea is simply to show that a certain object probably has a certain feature since other objects analogous to it in relevant ways have that feature. Once again we can focus on the general form of arguments by analogy by looking at the schema for the argument.

argument by analogy

    a has F, G, and H
    b has F, G, and H
    a has J
So, b has J

Let's consider several examples of this form.

(A) Mars is a planet not much further from the sun than the earth; it receives sunlight like the earth; and it revolves on its axis and so has both days and nights as does the earth. Since there is life on earth, it is likely there is life on Mars.

(B) Just like Samantha, Alison has been renting from Mr. Smith for about seven years, has always paid the rent on time and sends Mr. Smith a Christmas card every year. Now when Samantha asked the landlord to install a hottub, it was done within the month. No doubt when Alison requests a hottub she will have no trouble getting one.

Arguments by analogy are not unrelated to inductive generalizations. Consider argument (B). Both Samantha and Alison have been renting from the same person for a number of years, pay their rent on time, and send Christmas cards to their landlord. It is also claimed that Samantha received a hottub upon request. The point of the argument is that the analogy between Samantha and Alison will continue to hold and Alison too will receive a hottub if she asks. Why does the argument seem to be a reasonable one? Presumably the qualities of being a tenant of longstanding, of paying one's rent on time and sending Christmas cards to one's landlord are intended to suggest the idea of a conscientious tenant. It is further suggested that getting a hottub is in some way generally related to being a conscientious tenant of Mr. Smith—anyone who is a conscientious tenet of Mr. Smith will get a hottub upon request. This is a generalization that is illustrated by

Samantha's case and that appears to be at work when we go on to infer that Alison, too, will get her hottub.

Notice that, given only Samantha's case, we do not have much support for the generalization. But this need not be seen as a flaw. The argument may not be intended to support the generalization, but only to suggest or illustrate what is tacitly assumed to be a reasonable claim. If the assumed generalization—"all conscientious tenants of Mr. Smith will receive (things like) hottubs if they request them"—is correct, then naturally Alison can expect to get one if she asks.

An assumed generalization can also be seen to be at work in argument (A). The fact that the planet earth is capable of sustaining life is presumed to be relevantly connected with the facts that it is a certain distance from the sun, gets light from the sun, and revolves on its axis. The suggested generalization is that any planet that is within a certain distance from the sun, etc. (in roughly the same way as the earth is) will be capable of sustaining life. Consequently, we are asked to conclude that Mars will also be capable of sustaining life. Once again, only one case is appealed to (the earth) but that is not so much for support as for the purpose of suggesting or illustrating the generalization.

Since arguments by analogy and inductive generalizations are related in this way, it is no wonder that the parameters by which we evaluate inductive generalizations will also apply to arguments by analogy. Recall that the size of the sample relative to the size of the population of items under consideration affects the strength of the argument. Suppose in argument (B) we consider not only Samantha's case but several others: perhaps Ernie, Nan and Hubert also have been renting from Mr. Smith for seven years, pay their rent on time and send Christmas cards to their landlord every year. In addition, Mr. Smith has installed a hottub for each one shortly after being asked. When we add this information to the premises of (B) the argument becomes stronger; not only is the generalization suggested, it is explicitly supported as well.

We noted above, however, that it is not only the size of the sample that matters, but also how *representative* it is. If we are to observe a large number of "conscientious tenants," we want to check an assortment of people who vary in other ways. If the implicit generalization is that *all* conscientious tenants of Mr. Smith will receive hottubs upon request, then it will not do to restrict our observations to conscientious tenants who are closely related to Mr. Smith, or conscientious tenants who are between the ages of sixty and sixty-three.

There are other factors that may affect the value of an argument by analogy. *Increasing the number of relevant respects of analogy* between the individual mentioned in the conclusion and the items referred to in the sample will typically improve the argument. Suppose in argument (B) that the only thing that Samantha and Alison have in common is that they each sent their landlord a Christmas card. That by itself would not be a good enough reason to think that Alison will get a hottub given that Samantha did. But the more we say about the analogy between Samantha and Alison, the better the argument becomes. If we add to the analogy suggested in (B) that both women are nieces of the landlord and that both have often received gifts from him, then the conclusion begins to look more probable.

We must note that one can not simply increase the number of respects of analogy to improve arguments by analogy: the features upon which the analogy is based must be *relevant to the conclusion* . In the case of (A), the argument does not seem to be a reasonable one because the number of respects of analogy is limited and perhaps not as relevant to the capability of sustaining life as, say, having a gravitational system that supports an atmosphere of a certain kind and having minerals of a certain (life-sustaining) kind. Of course, to add that both planets are analogous in that they are both spherical or have been photographed at some time or other would not help the argument since these are respects of analogy that are completely irrelevant to the possibility of supporting life. Or, turning again to Samantha and Alison, if we include in the premises the fact that both women enjoy bowling, we have added another respect of analogy but have not increased the probability that the conclusion is true since bowling appears to have nothing to do with likelihood that Alison will get a hottub.

Finally, it is important to *limit the number of relevant disanalogous respects* between the sample cases and the case in the conclusion. If, unlike Samantha, Alison has just insulted Mr. Smith's wife, it is not so clear that Alison will get a hottub when she asks for one. This is one respect in which Alison and Samantha are not analogous and it appears to be relevant to whether Mr. Smith puts in a hottub for Alison as he did for Samantha. Certainly in argument (A) we can see that since Mars is disanalogous to the earth in that it fails to have the right kind of atmosphere or environment that is required for the support of life, the argument must be considered a weak one.

Induction and explanation

So far inductive arguments have been discussed roughly in terms of their structures. Some arguments work as generalizations over specific cases, while others seem to work on a principle of analogy. There are, however, other useful ways of thinking about inductive arguments. A particularly instructive way is to consider the sorts of things we mean to *accomplish* when we argue inductively. Inductive reasoning is frequently used within particular kinds of contexts to play quite specific roles.

One interesting role inductive arguments play is that of an *explanation*. The concept of explanation turns out to be rather complicated and controversial. But we can sneak up on the connection between explanation and inductive arguments in a fairly simple way. We are all quite familiar with situations in which we encounter something unusual or puzzling in an otherwise normal course of events. On such occasions we desire some account of *why* things are this particular way: we wish to discover some other facts that can account for the facts giving rise to our puzzlement. In short, we desire an explanation. This doesn't mean that only puzzling or unusual facts have explanations, of course. But often it is those features that lead us to ask "why?"—to seek an explanation. Thus a child may ask why the match lighted (perhaps on the first occasion he sees this common event), while you may ask about something less obvious even to adults. In any such case, however, the task of seeking additional facts to account for those in question is a familiar one.

Not just any facts will do, of course. There are better and worse explanations, and at least one quality worth demanding of good explanations is *relevance*. It will not do to answer the child's inquiry about matches with a statement of what day of the week it is. Rather we say that the match lighted because it was struck in a certain way. And in this case our intuitions probably suggest that we can say even more, for surely it is not just truths about this match that explain its lighting, but truths about matches generally—say, that all matches light when properly struck.

The point here is that explanation is an idea that is familiar to us, and that we possess certain intuitions about their being better or worse. But what now is the connection between explanation and inductive arguments? Recall for a moment that inductive arguments too can be better or worse. One especially interesting way of appraising inductive arguments is simply to ask whether or not the conclusion explains the premises. Indeed this turns out to be a useful way of understanding what it is we mean to accomplish when reasoning inductively. Inductive arguments are often just explanations, or more precisely, *good inductive arguments are often inferences to the best explanation.* So, for example, a good explanation for why all the metals we've looked at conduct electricity is that it is a fact about all metals that they conduct electricity.

We said earlier that many uses of inductive reasoning occur within particular kinds of contexts and hence play quite specific roles. It is in the context of science that induction is perhaps the most obvious in its role as explanation. Consider, first, that one task of science is to discover observable facts about the physical world, and to describe these phenomena in a systematic way. To keep our simple example, science discovers that mercury conducts electricity, that gold conducts electricity, and so on. But surely science does much more than this. The real power of science is that it goes beyond what we have observed in specific instances to advance general *hypotheses*— typically hypotheses involving what has not been (and perhaps cannot be) observed at all. And that is precisely the role of inductive reasoning: to reason beyond observed facts (premises) to some general hypothesis (conclusion) that will account for the specific cases we've observed so far. These hypotheses serve to *predict* future observations. One can imagine, for example, the inference 'Therefore, all metals conduct electricity' to have prompted experiments with other as yet untested metals. When an experiment involving a particular instance of the general hypothesis turns out to be as the hypothesis predicts, we say that it helps to *confirm* the hypothesis. This idea of confirmation, then, coincides with our earlier discussion of *support*: premises of an inductive argument support or help confirm, to a greater or lesser degree, the general hypothesis that we conclude from them. They provide evidence for it. The more confirming instances (the larger the sample size, to use earlier terminology) we have, the stronger the evidential support.

One important kind of generalization in science is a *causal law*. Recall again the simple example about matches. We infer inductively from the premise 'all observed instances of correctly striking well-made matches were followed by the matches lighting' to the general hypothesis that all well-made matches light when properly struck. This generalization is a kind of causal law, because it justifies us in saying that striking matches cause them to light. Consequently, some explanations are called *causal explanations*. When we ask why the match lit, we seek the cause of its lighting: we answer "Well, because it was struck, and all well-made matches light when properly struck."

What makes an explanation better or worse?

If many cases of inductive reasoning are appropriately viewed as explanations, something still needs to be said about what makes an explanation better or worse. We've suggested, after all, that on the present view good inductive arguments are inferences to the best explanation. One criterion noted already is *relevance*. But there are others. To introduce them, it is helpful to emphasize a point made earlier. Most hypotheses—most conclusions to inductive generalizations—cannot be *directly* verified in the sense that we cannot by some simple observational means see if they are true. One reason for this, of course, is the universal nature of such hypotheses: even a simple conclusion about all matches has this difficulty, for inspecting all matches is something we cannot do. But a second, more important, reason is that many of these conclusions are not about observable entities at all, and so are not *directly testable*. The scientist cannot directly see electromagnetic waves or gravitational forces or electrons. Such items are sometimes called *theoretical entities*. How these entities come to be posited by theories should by now be clear. A certain body of phenomena involving *observable entities* (say, deflections of meter needles or bubble-paths in an ion cloud chamber) is taken to be best explained by the existence of such unobservables. So we clearly needn't demand direct testability: we shall be willing to accept observable phenomena as indirect evidence for the existence of certain unobservable entities posited by the hypothesis.

There is a sense in which every inductive generalization is testable if it is inferred from premises about observable entities. Those premises, we say, *support*, or help *confirm* that conclusion. Consider, then, two explanations for why different elements emit different wavelengths of light. One explanation refers to transitions of electrons within atomic orbits of varying radii, the other refers to an invisible genie acting on our eyes (or on photographic plates, etc.). Hypotheses about electrons and genies are not directly testable because electrons and genies are unobservable, but each might be claimed by its proponent to have observational consequences—the *same* observational consequences as far as emitted light goes—and so to be testable by such predicted consequences. What should we say here?

One thing this example shows is that different hypotheses can be offered for the same data. An important criterion to consider in such cases is how well the hypothesis fits in with the rest of the theory—how easily it can be reconciled with other hypotheses that are already well-confirmed. Evaluating the *coherence* of an explanatory generalization is not an easy matter, but we can note several important components of this criterion. Sometimes two explanations will be equivalent only with respect to a small part of the total observational data to be treated by the theory. In this case, they might turn out to differ in other observational consequences. If the theory can more readily accommodate the consequences of the one hypothesis over the consequences of the other, then we have good reason to prefer the former over the latter.

Suppose, for example, the genie-hypothesis predicts not only that different elements will emit different wavelengths of light but also that Eskimos sneeze in July and September. The electron-hypothesis, of course, does not have this other consequence, though it does predict the different wavelengths of light. Here the electron- and genie-hypotheses agree of *part* of the phenomena predicted by the theory, but they differ with respect to Eskimo-sneezing. Since the general theory cannot easily accommodate the phenomenon of Eskimo-sneezing, we prefer for reasons of coherence the electron-hypothesis over the genie-hypothesis.

We also need to consider the number and nature of commitments accompanying the hypothesis in question. If we need electrons and atomic orbits (etc.) elsewhere in the theory, for example, then by adding the genie-hypothesis we are thereby committed to more entities than the electron-hypothesis. Moreover, in requiring that we admit a whole new *kind* of entity, it requires that we have some account of its nature as well, and (in the case of genies, anyway) that will frequently require adding quite a lot to the theory, simply for the purpose of accommodating the hypothesis. Unless this extra baggage makes the theory more powerful, adding it to maintain equal power with a rival is something no good theorist would do.

Finally, it is important to see that explanatory hypotheses should be open not only to evidential support, but also to evidence counting against it. Recall that when an experiment involving a particular instance of a general hypothesis turns out to be as predicted, we say that the hypothesis is confirmed. An experiment might, on the other hand, disconfirm a hypotheses—as when, say, we test a metal and find that it fails to conduct electricity. In this case the hypothesis that all metals conduct electricity would be disconfirmed. Good hypotheses will be such that it is clear what sort of evidence would disconfirm them: they are, we say, *falsifiable*. Now in the example of electrons vs. genies, as we originally set it up, the rival hypotheses had identical observational consequences in the sense that the body of confirming evidence was the same in each case. But unlike the electron-hypothesis, it is not at all clear what could ever count as evidence *against* the genie-hypothesis. If disconfirming evidence is impossible, then the hypothesis is being offered as true regardless of what possible evidence is available, and so it is no explanation at all. No genuinely explanatory hypothesis (for data that might have been different than it is) will be such that it is true *however* the data might turn out, *however* the world might be.

Conclusion

Explaining why we have the sensory experiences we do, or why the universe exhibits signs of order and design, or why you behave like I do when I'm in pain—these are only a few of the tasks for which philosophers have employed induction. In such cases, the philosopher seeks to account for some range of data in a way that best explains that data. Both inductive and deductive arguments, then, are frequently used by the philosopher, and hence logic, as the study of inferences and good reasoning in general, proves to be vital to the task of doing philosophy. In this section these tools of reason have been discussed; their application to specific philosophical topics will appear frequently in later sections of this book.

Questions: What is an argument? How do deductive arguments differ from inductive arguments? What is it for an argument to be valid? Sound? What is an inductive generalization and what makes such an argument better or worse? What is an argument by analogy and what factors affect the value of such an argument? What is an inference to the best explanation?

Section 2: LANGUAGE

A. Meaning

Recall the earlier dispute between Clyde and Larry about abortion. What we have learned in our discussion of logic is that arguments are the best vehicle for presenting reasons for beliefs. If we would like to settle disagreements in the spirit of arriving at the truth, offering arguments to justify our views is the only dependable way of advancing the dispute. Of course, this may not immediately resolve matters: an opponent can attempt to show that our argument is invalid, or that one of our premises is false. Consider the last of these. To be in a position to judge the truth or falsity of a premise, one must understand it: one must know what it means. Thus, meaning is central to assessing arguments generally, and to using argument for resolving disputes in particular.

We can speak of meaning as it applies either to sentences or words. For our purposes, a sentence has its meaning partly in virtue of the meanings of the words making it up. To understand a premise, then, we must understand the meanings of the words appearing in it.

Informative and emotive content

The concept of *meaning* is a difficult one. Indeed, contemporary philosophers of language disagree about how the concept is to be understood. For our purposes it won't be necessary to spell out rival theories of linguistic meaning. It will suffice to get clear about the general features of meaning in order to avoid certain common mistakes. By getting clear about this, however, we will also go some distance toward learning what constitutes good critical reasoning.

Let's begin by considering the following sentences, (A) and (B).

(A) Tom is a maintenance engineer, and his father has been a government official since serving in the military conflict in Vietnam.

(B) His old man was a soldier in the Vietnam war, and then became a bureaucrat; Tom's a janitor.

What is noteworthy about these sentences is that, while the same information is conveyed by both (A) and (B), each is associated with a kind of emotional "overtone" not shared by the other. Sentence (B), for example, uses the derogatory 'old man' to pick out what the neutral 'father' picks out in (A); sentence (A) employs the euphemism 'maintenance engineer' in place of 'janitor', and so on. What this example illustrates is that sentences sometimes contain words which, in addition to having their usual literal or *informative content*, may also have *emotive* meaning. Words possess this last feature if they are emotionally charged in ways that express attitudes of favor, disapproval, and so on. While sentences (A) and (B) mean the same in terms of their informative content, sentence (B) has an emotive overtone that is negative where sentence (A) uses emotively favorable words.

The emotive element in language is both natural and useful. Communication would be altogether boring without it; poems would lack their distinctive aesthetic qualities, and advertisements would have little persuasive appeal if there were no emotive side to language. But it is important to emphasize here that we mustn't confuse emotion with reason. Remember that arguments present reasons in support of a claim, reasons meant to justify the belief that some claim is true. Premises employing words charged with positive or negative overtones may supply a certain *motive* for believing a claim (Larry gets us to pity poor helpless babies, or fear the monetary sacrifice required by expensive abortions), but emotive meaning contributes nothing to the *reasons* serving to justify our belief that (say) we shouldn't abort human fetuses. Emotionally charged language may be persuasive in certain contexts, precisely because it does conjure up feelings like pity or fear. But emotions can easily get in the way of good reasoning, and if our goal when disagreeing is to resolve matters in favor of the truth, then we must learn in those contexts not to heed emotional appeal. That is simply because the only feature of meaning relevant to the truth or falsity of a sentence is its informative content. Abortion is right or wrong quite independent of whether we refer to it as pre-natal termination or the killing of helpless unborn lives, and it is true or false that Tom's father works for the government whether we call him a bureaucrat or a civil servant. Hereafter, then, when we talk about *meaning*, we will be speaking of the informative content of a word or sentence.

Ambiguity

We have seen that two (or more) *different* words or expressions may have the *same meaning*. 'The undertaker is in the graveyard' means what 'The mortician is in the cemetery' means. But it also turns out that one and the *same* word can have *different meanings*. 'Spring', for example, can be used to pick out the sudden leaping action of your cat on a mouse; or it can variously pick out a source of water from the earth, a season of the year beginning in March, a device that operates wind-up clocks or watches, and so on. A word that is standardly understood to have more than one meaning is said to be *ambiguous*. This is a common linguistic phenomenon, and there is nothing really "defective" with ambiguous expressions. But they *can* be troublesome in certain cases. Recall, for example, that we aren't in a position to assess the truth or falsity of a sentence unless we understand what it means, and then consider that contexts may arise in which it isn't clear which meaning of a particular word is being employed.

Not surprisingly, then, in the context of arguments we must be especially alert to ambiguity. Typically a particular word or expression will appear more than once in an argument, and if such expressions are ambiguous, we cannot decide on how good the argument is until we know what these expressions mean. It may turn out that, when we try to understand the premises and conclusion of an argument in a way that makes them all true, we end up being forced to give different readings to the same word—which isn't much good, of course, since that's very like changing the subject in the middle of an argument. In such cases it will generally turn out that, if we insist on the same reading for these expressions throughout the argument, certain sentences in which they appear will end up false.

The fallacy of *equivocation* is committed in arguments in which an ambiguous word or phrase is allowed a subtle shift of meaning, rendering the argument invalid. Sometimes this can be very difficult to notice, and in such a case we mistake a bad argument for a good one. Here is a relatively easy example, offered by a clever young urchin to spite his sister: "Man is the only rational animal, and you're no man, so you're not a rational animal!" Clearly the only hope of getting both premises to come out true here is to understand 'man' in the first premise to mean 'humankind' and in the second to refer to the male gender; but from the facts that (i) humans are the only rational animals and (ii) Missy is not male, it hardly follows that Missy is not a rational animal. The argument is invalid. If, on the other hand, we understand 'man' to mean the same thing in both premises, then one or the other of them must end up false, and so the argument will be unsound.

There is another caution about ambiguity to offer here: it can disguise a merely verbal dispute as a genuine one. If you and your roommate are involved in a genuine disagreement, then you disagree about some real facts-of-the-matter: you say matters are this way, and your roommate says matters are that way. Depending on how the real facts-of-the-matter *are*, either you or your roommate (or perhaps each of you) is wrong. We know that disputes aren't always easy to settle, but that however we settle them—by good argument, by empirical observation, or some other means—, we do so by agreeing on what really is the truth about the matter.

To indicate how some disputes can be merely verbal, consider a disagreement in which no amount of argument or empirical observation *could* settle the matter. Here's a simple example. Suppose I tell you that there is a spring in my back yard and you return from looking to inform me that there isn't. I insist that there is, and perhaps we even go take a look. There in the yard we stand, each insisting that it's obvious that the other is wrong. The "dispute" here stems from my intending by 'spring' to mean the coiled apparatus that my neighbor extracted from beneath the cushions of my old sofa, and you're understanding me to indicate that some natural source of water could be found in the yard. It turns out that we don't disagree about any facts-of-the-matter at all. The only thing we must do (and in this case it will dawn on us pretty quickly) is realize that a lack of verbal clarity has led us each to think that the other is wrong about my yard. And, of course, neither of us is: you're right that no natural source of water exists in my yard, and I agree; I am right that the old sofa-springs are there against the fence, and you agree.

There is one final warning. Some people think that, as long as two people "define their terms," there can *be* no real disagreement. They think that all disagreements are merely verbal, that anyone who engages in argumentative dialogue is merely "arguing semantics." This of course is not true. It is possible for people to disagree without simply saying the same thing with different words. Moreover, from the discussion above it should be clear that, if the present suggestion were correct, there would be no facts-of-the-matter in virtue of which someone says something false or in virtue of which someone has a false belief about the world. Indeed, the concepts of truth and falsity would be *empty*, and that, surely, is something we should like to avoid saying.

Vagueness

We have seen that an ambiguous expression may present us with a certain *lack of clarity* about its meaning. But even for words that we already understand the meaning may be unclear. These are cases of *vagueness*, where there is no definite boundary between objects to which the word does and does not apply. Many common expressions are vague: 'tall', 'flat', and 'middle-aged' are examples. Unlike the question 'Is Joel married?' to which we believe there is a definite answer (and we're clear on what sort of information would provide it), questions like 'Is Joel tall?' or 'Is Joel middle-aged?' may be questions for which there is no definite answer (questions that no amount of information will resolve).

As with ambiguity, we mustn't suppose that vagueness necessarily points to something defective in our knowledge of the world or about the vague expression itself. Just as you and I agree about the occupants of my back yard, so we can be perfectly clear on Joel's height (in feet and inches) or Joel's age (in years). Vagueness is a naturally-occurring feature of the meaning of some words; some words are fitted only for an unspecific range of application. Indeed, where their applicability is uncontroversial (if Joel is a midget or is 91 years old), or where imprecision is desirable, vague expressions are particularly useful items of language. For example, in the latter case, it is sometimes helpful to make assertions with as much precision as possible, although our evidence does not allow complete specificity. Thus it may be a psychological fact about humans that they tend to exhibit kinds of behavior in crowds which they don't otherwise exhibit: the vagueness of 'crowd' here allows us to offer an important fact of human behavior, in the absence of any knowledge of exactly how large a group must be before the behavioral difference is observed.

There are times when we can reduce the lack of clarity by stipulating definitions of vague terms, making it clear whether they apply or not. This is frequently done in medical and legal contexts, for example, where certain decisions require it and where there exists a tacit authority behind the stipulated definition. 'Death', for example, is vague; more determinate criteria for 'brain-' or 'biological-' death (especially in light of new abilities to maintain signs of life) may be offered by medical authorities in place of the vague concept. The lesson here is obvious: if there are more determinate concepts available in which to conduct our discourse, then we should employ them whenever it is helpful to do so.

Of course, it will not always be helpful to do so. In ordinary conversation, for example, attempting to clarify every instance of vagueness would be virtually impossible. Furthermore, in some cases clarifying vague terms would be impractical. Consider that if we stipulate that only groups over 100 people are a crowd, we can no longer offer with any assurance the psychological fact about humans that they tend to exhibit behavior in crowds that they do not otherwise exhibit.

Definition and dictionaries

Assessing the strength of a piece of reasoning often comes down to deciding how various expressions in the argument should be understood. We have seen that clarifying the meaning of a term or expression can be an important part of this procedure. Now it is sometimes suggested that there is a very simple and sure-fire way of doing this: simply consult the dictionary. Dictionaries define words, after all, and when we are unclear about what a word means, the dictionary will tell us.

There are several mistakes lurking here, some more obvious than others. First, insofar as dictionaries contain definitions, they cannot help much with ambiguity or vagueness. Many entries in a dictionary report how words in a language are actually used by speakers of that language (these are sometimes called *lexical* definitions). It may well be that uncovering the use of a word in this way will reveal more than one candidate for what the author of an argument intends by a word; *that* a word is ambiguous between several meanings does not, however, decide for us *which* meaning the author intends. And of course a vague word does not have its vagueness somehow removed by its dictionary definition: words expressing vague concepts have vague definitions. 'Flat', for example, is defined by one dictionary as 'having an even horizontal surface, or nearly so', and clearly 'having a nearly even surface' is just a vague as 'flat'.

The second mistake is to suppose that dictionaries always supply meanings of words. Of course they never do exactly *that*: they supply *more words*. But often the words making up an entry is not a definition at all if by 'definition' we intend something like 'other words that are synonymous with, or have the same meaning as' the entry word. Thus, unlike a definition such as 'unmarried adult male', which explains the meaning of 'bachelor' by offering words that do pretty much the same work in language as 'bachelor' does, consider the following entry for a different sort of word.

> **and**: a particle expressing the general relation of conjunction or addition

Here, we are given words that *describe* the work 'and' does in language, not words that do pretty much the same work because they have pretty much the same meaning. One could replace 'bachelor' with 'adult unmarried male' in the sentence 'Joel is a bachelor and a lousy cook'; but one could not replace 'and' with 'a particle expressing . . .' while still preserving its role in the sentence.

Not all words in the dictionary are ordinary run-of-the-mill words. Many of them are technical expressions that belong to the vocabulary of specialized practices or disciplines of study such as economics or medicine or philosophy. Many other words that *are* run-of-the-mill have nevertheless come to be assigned meanings by practitioners of those specialized disciplines. (Entries in dictionaries that do not report the ordinary use of a term are sometimes said to give *stipulative* definitions.) Most entries of this sort are drawn up by experts working in the relevant field.

These facts signal a final warning about consulting a dictionary. Dictionaries are not magical super-books or infallible volumes written by God (always edited and updated, perhaps, as we sleep). This is particularly crucial to keep in mind when we are trying to settle a philosophical dispute. What is at issue in such cases are philosophical matters like, Do we have free will?, What is the relation of mind to body?, Can we have perceptual knowledge of physical objects?, and What is the nature of linguistic meaning? What is primarily at issue is exactly *what these concepts* (of freedom, mind, perception, knowledge, meaning, and so on) *come to*. To consult the dictionary in such a case, then, is simply to beg off from doing the philosophical work and let someone else—the author of the entry for 'freedom' or 'mind' or whatever—hand us a verdict by fiat. The author of such definitions is proposing his (or perhaps, the favored) conclusion to the same philosophical problem we are confronting for ourselves. And clearly we should not be prepared to accept uncritically a dictionary proposal if we think that the matter is open to debate in the first place.

As an illustration consider for a moment the concept of (linguistic) *meaning*. What constitutes the meaning of a word is a longstanding philosophical issue, and philosophers are divided on it even today. According to *referential* theorists of meaning, for example, the meaning of a word is that to which the word refers, or perhaps the relation between the word and that to which it refers. According to *ideational* theorists, meaning consists in the idea for which the word stands as a written or spoken symbol—say, the idea I have in my mind (and that I want to call up in your mind) when I use the word 'dog'. According to *use* theorists, the meaning of a word consists in the contribution it standardly makes in sentences capable of performing some distinctive linguistic act (like asserting, ordering, or promising).

Now clearly we cannot, when confronted with a philosophical dispute over the concept of *meaning*, resolve or make much advance in matters by accepting straight off a dictionary definition as what that concept "really" amounts to. Consider:

meaning (n): that which is meant

mean (v): to have in mind as the object of a linguistic symbol

If in a philosophical dispute of the sort described we are led to conclude that the "true" definition of the concept of meaning must be essentially spelled out in these terms (of that which one has in mind...), then we shall have already accepted an account of meaning according to which other philosophical terms (like those of use theories, say) are inadmissible. But as we have seen, *deciding* that issue is what such disputes are all about, and no dictionary can take the place of good hard philosophical thought.

B. Conceptual Analysis

Concepts and arguments

Judging the soundness of an argument can be relatively easy in some cases, and very difficult in others. The easy cases are those in which we can readily determine the truth or falsity of premises. A premise like 'Stewart believes that lead bricks are mostly empty space' is easy enough: we go ask him if he believes that lead bricks are mostly empty space. Something like 'Sheldon has a brain' is tougher only in practice: we can use new-fangled imaging techniques of medical technology, or simply go and open Sheldon's head. These are easy cases because, in principle, all we need to do is "go look." But other cases seem to be much tougher. Consider the claim that Stewart knows that lead bricks are mostly empty space, or the claim that Sheldon has a mind. How do we assess the truth of these claims? Asking Stewart if he knows that lead bricks are mostly empty space is no help unless we accept the premise that as long as one believes something, one knows it. How would we discover that Sheldon has a mind? Opening his head helps only if we suppose that whatever has a brain has a mind. And how should we assess the truth of that?

Assessing claims like these latter ones isn't so simple as just going and looking. We do something quite different in such cases—something that can turn out to be very difficult. We ask ourselves what is involved in the concept of *knowledge* or of *mind*, and try to make headway by thinking. So, for example, we might reason as follows.

> If someone believes something, does it follow that he knows it? It doesn't seem so. There have been lots of things I believed in the past that I later came to discover were just *false*—as when I thought that the sun really did move around the earth while the earth remained stationary. That was something I believed, but it wasn't something I knew.
>
> So my knowing something requires both that I believe it, *and* that it be true. But hang on, now: that isn't enough, is it? I might believe something for who knows what reason, and it just so turns out that it's true. Bill pulled that stunt on me last year when he said that he knew Peter would be elected this year. After that runoff vote between me and Peter, Bill said "I told you I knew he'd win." But he's such a fan of Peter's he would believe anything in Peter's favor. He couldn't have *known*, even if he did believe it and it turned out to be true. If that's all there were to knowledge, we could end up knowing all sorts of things just by accident, which makes no sense. We have to believe them for the right reasons.

Analyzing concepts in this way is an important skill and the backbone of good philosophical reasoning. Claims that can't be assessed by just looking around us require this sort of evaluation: it's what philosophers do when confronted with difficult concepts like mind, freedom, perception, meaning, and so on. This method of *conceptual analysis* isn't restricted to traditional philosophical concepts like the ones just mentioned, of course. You can engage the same sort of procedure with notions more familiar and perhaps of more immediate consequence, such as abortion or pornography or sexual discrimination.

Definition—a topic discussed earlier—and conceptual analysis are closely connected. Both attempt to answer the question 'What is (an) F?' for any concept **F**. Good definitions of 'dog', 'pornography' and 'knowledge', will answer the questions 'What is a dog?', 'What is pornography?' and 'What is knowledge?'. Often the answers to such questions are implicit in premises of arguments, and in the case of philosophical arguments, it is generally helpful to see these premises as based on theories about what constitutes such concepts. Theories of knowledge, for example, have been around a long time, and much of what epistemologists do is work at offering a conceptual analysis of knowledge.

Even in a nonphilosophical argument one may find oneself implicitly committed to particular analyses of concepts that figure in the premises one employs. Suppose the Provost of the college argues that, since pornography shouldn't be allowed on campus, this particular magazine shouldn't be sold in the bookstore because it explicitly portrays sexual activity. This argument leaves implicit the premise that something is pornographic if it explicitly portrays sexual activity, and that signals a commitment to a particular analysis of pornography. As in the case of the concept of knowledge that we illustrated above, if we pause here to analyze the concept of pornography, we'll discover that the premise in which it figures is questionable. Just as it can't be enough for knowledge that one have a true belief (that lets too much count as knowledge), so it can't be enough for something to count as pornography that it contain explicit representations of sexual activity. For on the Provost's argument, we must also forbid the bookstore and library to have special medical or educational books or films. Analyses of concepts, then, can also have legal and administrative consequences.

Necessary and sufficient conditions

In what exactly does a conceptual analysis consist? When we offer an analysis of a concept **F**, we specify the precise conditions (a list, usually) $c_1, c_2, \ldots$ that must be satisfied if an object is to fall under that concept. If we offer an analysis of the concept of a square, for example, we will specify the set of conditions that all and only squares meet. Anything that *is* a square will satisfy those conditions (a four-sided regular closed plane figure), and anything that *isn't* a square will fail to satisfy them.

This supposes that we offer a good analysis of the concept. If it is a bad one, the set of conditions we specify might be *too strong*—it might rule out things that count as perfectly good squares—, or it might be *too weak*—it might rule in things that clearly don't count as squares.

Before we can say more clearly how to spell out a conceptual analysis, we need to pause and learn a bit of terminology. It isn't difficult terminology, and it turns out to be useful for discussions in later parts of the book.

First, then, we need to say something about what are called *conditional* sentences. A conditional is any sentence of the form 'If p, then q' in which the variables p and q are filled in with sentences. The sentence 'If Frances is my aunt, then she is a woman' is a conditional. The left-hand sentence of a conditional—the "if" part—is called the *antecedent*, and the right-hand sentence—the "then" part—is called the *consequent*. So, in the conditional just offered, the sentence 'Frances is my aunt' is the antecedent and the sentence 'She is a woman' is the consequent.

Look again at that conditional sentence. Another way of saying "If Frances is my aunt, then she is a woman" is to say that Frances is my aunt *only if* she is a woman. And we can also say that Frances is a woman, if she is my aunt. All of these equivalent expressions preserve the meaning of the original sentence. The following forms, then, are all equivalent.

If p, then q

p only if q

q if p

Be careful to note that the sentence 'If Frances is my aunt, then she is a woman' is to be distinguished from 'If Frances is a woman, then she is my aunt'. The latter sentence is the *converse* of the first. Every conditional has a converse: the converse of 'If p, then q' is simply 'If q, then p'. Of course, converse conditionals are generally not equivalent. It is true that Frances is a woman if she is my aunt, but it may be false that she is my aunt if she is a woman. So, where p and q pick out specific sentences, we must distinguish the list of formulas given above from the following list of equivalent conditional forms.

If q, then p

q only if p

p if q

Conditional sentences help us spell out what are called *necessary and sufficient conditions*—two notions indispensable for understanding conceptual analysis. A necessary condition is something that is *required* for falling under the concept **F**. When we say that a necessary condition is a condition required for x's being an F, we mean that if the conditions are not met, then x doesn't fall under **F**. So, if being a woman is required for someone's being an aunt, then clearly if Frances is not a woman, she cannot be my (or anyone's) aunt. Notice that this argument has the valid argument form *modus tollens*.

If p, then q	If Frances is my aunt, then she is a woman.
Not-q	Frances is not a woman.
So, not-p	So, Frances is not my aunt.

What this teaches us about necessary conditions, then, is that *the consequent of a conditional specifies necessary conditions for the antecedent.* So, if we let '**nc**' signify any condition that is necessary for something's falling under the concept **F** (i.e., for something's being an F), then all of the following are equivalent.

nc specifies a necessary condition for being an F

If something is an F, then **nc**

Something is an F only if **nc**

A *sufficient* condition is something that would be *enough* for x's falling under **F** (or being an F): if the conditions are satisfied, then x is an F. To return to our example, if being an aunt is sufficient (or enough) for someone's being a woman (since only women can be aunts), then if Frances is an aunt, she will also be a woman. Here too we have an argument with a valid form (in this case, *modus ponens*) that helps illustrate this.

	If Frances is my aunt, then she is a
If p, then q	woman.
p	Frances is my aunt.
So, q	So, Frances is a woman

What we've learned about sufficient conditions, then, is that *the antecedent of a conditional specifies sufficient conditions for the consequent*. So, if we let 'sc' signify any condition that is sufficient for something's falling under the concept **F**, then all of the following are equivalent:

sc specifies a sufficient condition for being an **F**

If **sc**, then something is an **F**

Something is an **F** if **sc**

Let's compare necessary and sufficient conditions briefly, with a couple of examples. *x's being an animal* is a necessary condition for *x's being a dog*, because it is required that x be an animal in order for x to be a dog. But it isn't sufficient, that is, it isn't enough for being a dog that x be an animal, since x might be an animal and a duckbilled platypus. If we wanted to give a conceptual analysis of the concept 'dog', then, our offering the (necessary) condition 'x is an animal' wouldn't do, because it is too weak: it lets in things that clearly don't count as dogs.

x's being a dog is a sufficient condition for *x's being an animal*, because it is enough for x's being an animal that x be a dog. But it isn't necessary: that is, it isn't required for being an animal that x be a dog, since there are lots of things—like the duckbilled platypus—that count as perfectly good animals but aren't dogs. If we wanted to give a conceptual analysis of the concept 'animal', then, our offering the (sufficient) condition 'x is a dog' wouldn't do, because it is too strong: it rules out things that count as perfectly good animals.

Conceptual analysis

Recall again what a conceptual analysis of a concept **F** is: it is a specification of the conditions $c_1, c_2, \ldots$ that must be met if an object is to fall under that concept. We now know that offering conditions that are merely necessary is too weak (it lets too many things count as an F), and that offering conditions that are merely sufficient is too strong (it lets too few things count as an F). What we want, then, are conditions that let in exactly the right number of things, conditions that let in all and only Fs. We want a set of conditions A that turn out to be *necessary and sufficient* for being an F. If A specifies an analysis of F (i.e., specifies necessary and sufficient conditions for being an F), then the following are (equivalently) true:

If A, then something is an F; and *if* something is an F, then A.

Something is an F *if* A; and something is an F *only if* A.

Something is an F *if and only if* A

Typically, though, we just write 'Something is an F *iff* A' for short-hand. That's our model for conceptual analysis. We must come up with an expression (it might be pretty long) that says that something is an F (that something counts as pornography, knowledge, an aunt, a dog, or whatever) if and only if the following conditions hold (and then we spell those conditions out).

Let's run through a fairly easy example. Suppose that we want to offer a conceptual analysis of the concept 'square'. What we need to do is fill out the blank in the statement form

x is a square iff _____ .

That is, we need necessary and sufficient conditions for *being a square*. For the sake of illustration, consider the following geometric figures (call them 'Larry' and 'Curly').

Larry   Curly

Suppose one were to offer as a conceptual analysis of 'square' the following:

x is a square iff x is Larry.

Now, *being Larry* is certainly sufficient for being a square: if x is Larry, then x is a square. But that isn't necessary for being a square. It's too strong, because it leaves out objects that are perfectly good squares—Curly, say. This mistake is like offering 'x is Rover' as an analysis of 'dog'.

Here is a much better effort at completing the analysis of 'square'.

x is a square iff c_1:   x is a closed plane figure, and
c_2:   x has four sides.

This certainly give us necessary conditions for being a square: x can't be a square unless x is a four-sided closed plane figure. But that isn't sufficient for being a square. It's too weak, because it lets in objects that aren't squares at all—Moe, say.

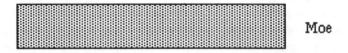 Moe

We must *add* the necessary condition x has equal sides; or, we can simply build that into c_2.

x is a square if c_1:   x is closed plane figure, and
c_2:   x has four equal sides.

But this isn't enough (isn't sufficient) yet either for it lets in things like Shemp that aren't squares.

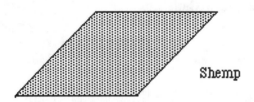 Shemp

We need to strengthen our attempt by adding the necessary condition that x has four right (interior) angles. And that should do it. According to a good conceptual analysis of 'square', something is a square if and only if it is a closed plane figure with four equal sides and four right interior angles.

"Paradoxes" of analysis

The analysis of concepts is rarely as easy as the example just offered: in the case of 'square', we're already perfectly clear on what is built into the concept. But this suggests something rather odd. If we *already know* what's built into a concept, we don't need an analysis of it; yet if we *don't* know what is built into a concept, how shall we ever be able to recognize a correct analysis when we see it?

That is an old puzzle, and there are various versions of it. Let's consider a slightly different formulation in a bit more detail, alongside an example. Suppose our concept **F** has as its correct analysis A. (**F** might be the concept of a bachelor, and A the correct analysis given by 'adult unmarried male'.) Put generally, no one could verify that the concept **F** applies to an object without verifying that A applies to the object, and any word or phrase that expresses the concept **F** must be synonymous with any word or phrase that expresses A. Thus we say that 'adult unmarried male' means what 'bachelor' means; to say that a person is a bachelor is to say that that person is an adult unmarried male; to be a bachelor is (the same thing as) to be an adult unmarried male.

The puzzle can be put this way: if the statement 'to be a bachelor is the same thing as to be an adult unmarried male' is true, then it seems identical with the statement 'to be a bachelor is the same thing as to be a bachelor'; if the latter is uninformative, then so is the former. And yet, surely the former is an analysis of the concept of a bachelor, while the latter isn't.

Generally, if a word or phrase to be analyzed (say, 'F') is merely synonymous with the analyzing expression (say, 'A'), then no information is conveyed and the analysis is trivial. Yet, if 'A' means something different than 'F', then the analysis is false. And since 'F' and 'A' either are, or are not, synonymous, every analysis is either uninformative and trivial, or false.

In wondering what we should say about this puzzle, we can learn quite a lot more about analysis and meaning. In particular, the puzzle can help us get clear on a distinction between two different senses of the informative content—the *meaning*—of a word or phrase. First, though, we need a quick lesson in the concept of *identity*.

Identity

We sometimes speak of "identical" twins, suggesting that (monozygotic) twins often look very much alike. In these cases we are calling attention to what might be called *qualitative similarity*: twins are similar insofar as they possess many of the same properties or qualities.

When philosophers talk about identity, they usually have in mind something different from qualitative similarity. Consider what we call an *identity expression* of the form 'a=b', where the symbol '=' is the *identity sign*. When doing sums, for example, we write expressions such as '2+2=4'. Now we don't mean by this something like 'Two plus two is very much like four', or 'Two plus two is qualitatively similar to four'. Rather, we say that two plus two *is* four, meaning that the number we pick out (refer to) with the expression '2+2' is *the same number as* what we pick out with the expression '4'—that is, the number four. Or, when you say that Mark Twain is Samuel Clemens, you mean that the fellow you refer to with 'Mark Twain' just *is* (the same guy as) Samuel Clemens. You aren't talking about two persons here (as when you spoke earlier of "identical" twins): to say that Mark Twain is identical with Samuel Clemens is to talk about *one* person. Philosophers generally refer to this concept of identity as the concept of *numerical identity*, to highlight the fact that true identity expressions are expressions about one object, not two.

Sense and reference

Words like 'dog', 'Mark Twain', 'pornography', 'mind' and so on pick out things: 'dog' applies to many things (Rover, Benjie, lots of mutts without names, and so on), and 'Mark Twain' applies to just one. In a fairly obvious sense, then, what we mean by such words is *what we're talking about* when using them. We're talking about all the dogs when we use the word 'dog' (so that, if I say "Dogs are four-legged," part of what I may intend to say is that Rover is four-legged, etc.), and so the collection of dogs constitutes the meaning of 'dog'; this fellow here (the guy who wrote *Huckleberry Finn*) is what I mean by 'Mark Twain'; and so on. As we saw earlier, 'bachelor' means what 'adult unmarried male' means, insofar as both expressions apply to the same group of persons. The objects that a linguistic term picks out or to which it applies is sometimes called the *extension* of the term (and this is said to constitute its *extensional meaning*). We'll call it the *reference* of the term.

Recall what we said about numerical identity expressions. What is expressed by such sentences is that the object picked out by 'a' is the same object as what the term 'b' picks out. So, when we say that 'Mark Twain is identical with Samuel Clemens', what we express by this sentence is that the terms 'Mark Twain' and 'Samuel Clemens' pick out the same person. Now consider sentences of the form 'a=a' and 'a=b'. Sentences of the first sort are uninformative and trivial (it is altogether unhelpful to tell someone that the evening star is identical with the evening star). But then, if 'b' in 'a=b' picks out *the same thing as* 'a' in 'a=a', how can 'a=b' be informative? Indeed, if meaning consists in reference, these expressions say the same thing: it should be no more informative to say (1)

(1) The morning star is identical with the evening star.

than to say (2).

(2) The morning star is identical with the morning star.

But of course, (1) *is* informative: that (1) is true is a genuine discovery (the morning star and the evening star are actually the planet Venus), but (2) is no discovery at all.

This puzzle should remind us of the paradox of analysis. Let's restate it quickly. If the word or phrase to be analyzed ('F') is synonymous with (means the same thing as) the analyzing expression ('A'), then no information is conveyed and the analysis is trivial (where meaning is reference, it's like writing 'a=a'). Yet, if 'A' means—refers to—something different from 'F', then the analysis is false.

If sentences like (1) are to be informative in a way that sentences like (2) are not, then it seems as though there is more to meaning than reference. Otherwise, I could know that the morning star is identical with the evening star just by understanding the meanings of the terms: (1) would say no more than (2) because they would have the same meaning (and I can know (2) easily enough). The concept of *meaning* that goes beyond reference is sometimes called the *sense* or *intension* of the linguistic term. Notice that you can perfectly well understand a word insofar as you understand how to apply it correctly, without having to know all the objects to which it may actually be correctly applied. What you know in such cases is it's sense. So, for example, the sense of 'equilateral triangle' corresponds to the property of being a plane figure enclosed by three lines of equal length, while the sense of 'equiangular triangle' corresponds to the property of being a closed plane figure whose three sides intersect to form equal angles. These expressions have different meanings, then, even if they apply to exactly the same objects. Similarly, 'the morning star' differs in meaning from 'the evening star' insofar as they have different senses, just as 'the author of Huckleberry Finn' means something different from 'Sheldon's favorite writer', even though the expressions within each pair have the same reference.

What we have learned, then, is that very often there seems to be an element of informative content that distinguishes the meanings of expressions having the same reference. An analysis (A) of the concept **F** can be informative even if A applies to the same thing, and (1) is not trivial because, unlike (2), the informative content figuring in it is not redundant. This mustn't be understood to suggest that no difficulties remain. It is unclear, for example, whether proper names like "Mark Twain" really do have a unique sense associated with them in addition to their reference. A separate issue arises when some philosophers take treatments like those offered above to suggest that *no* two expressions can be genuinely synonymous, while others believe that two expressions could have exactly the same meaning. Those favoring the latter position believe that sentences like 'Bachelors are unmarried adult males' specify instances of synonymy and consequently, since their truth depends only on the meanings of the terms occurring in them, these sentences cannot be false. Of course this is denied by those taking the former position. Most philosophers, even those in the anti-synonymy group, will agree that sentence like the 'Bachelors . . .' sentence are special. The difficulty lies in explaining how they are special in the face of the paradoxes discussed above.

C. Propositions and Sentences

As ordinary speakers and writers we seldom concern ourselves with how our (or any) language works; we simply go about speaking and writing without ever questioning how the use of certain words or sentences enables us to call our audience's attention to particular features of the world. But in our philosophical moments we may indeed wonder at how language relates to the world, at how sounds or ink marks can be used to mean something or to refer to something. Is there such a thing as a *meaning*? What is it for a word or sentence to have meaning? How shall we account for the difference between saying something true and saying something false? What is it for two people to *say* the same thing but *mean* something different? Or to *say* different things but *mean* the same thing?

These are difficult questions and certainly we shall not attempt to address, much less answer, them all in this text. We have looked already at some of the issues concerning word meaning. Perhaps further discussion with respect to sentence meaning will help us avoid some confusing matters that are otherwise likely to arise in the course of our study.

Propositions and sentences

When José, pointing to the German shepherd in the bushes, utters the sentence "That's my dog over there," he is obviously saying something different from Catherine when she utters the same sentence pointing to the dachshund standing by the fire hydrant. They are, clearly enough, referring to different dogs. But there is a sense in which they said the same thing: they each said (or uttered) the same sentence.

Now consider the case in which José is heard to say of his dog, "Heinrich is a better watchdog than a pet," and Catherine, also referring to José's dog, says "He is a worse pet than he is a watchdog." In this case both José and Catherine said (in one sense of 'said') the same thing about José's dog, Heinrich. They did that, however, by saying (in another sense) different things, i.e., they uttered different sentences. Or, to consider another example, suppose José exclaims "Mein Hund ist gross" and Catherine says "Heinrich is large." José said something in German and Catherine said something in English, so there is a sense in which they each said something different. But there is also a sense in which they said the same thing, namely, that José's dog, Heinrich, is large.

How are we to keep these two senses of 'said' straight? One way that philosophers typically find helpful is to distinguish sentences from propositions. In the first case, José and Catherine both said the same thing in uttering the same sentence: they made the same kind of noise, with the same words and the same grammatical construction ('That's my dog over there'). But they said different things by referring to different situations or by *meaning* different things. The things they meant we will call "propositions." José used the sentence 'My dog is over there' to mean that his dog, the German shepherd, was over by the bushes. Catherine used the very same sentence to mean that her dog, the dachshund, was by the fire hydrant.

Just as the same sentence can be used to express different propositions, so different sentences can used to express the same proposition. This was the case when José said "Mein Hund ist gross" and Catherine said "Heinrich is large." Notice that if we are asked to report what José *said* it is unclear whether we are to give the exact *words* he used (the German sentence), or the *proposition* he expressed with those words. That is, depending on what the inquirer wants to know we could say either "He said 'Mein Hund ist gross'" or "He said that his dog is large."

This last point illustrates a convention we have for distinguishing sentences from propositions when we talk about what is said. Sentences are put in quotation marks, as in the following.

José said "Heinrich is a better watchdog than a pet."

Catherine, referring to José's dog, said "He is a worse pet than a watchdog."

We can indicate the common proposition expressed by those sentences if we drop the quotation marks and use a 'that . . . ' clause as in

José and Catherine both said *that José's dog, Heinrich, fares better as a watchdog than he does as a pet.*

If you are told that José said *that his dog is large*, you cannot tell just from this which sentence he used to express the proposition. He could have expressed that proposition by uttering any of these sentences: 'My dog is large', 'Heinrich is large', or 'Mein Hund ist gross'.

In summary: we can express the same proposition by using different sentences and we can use the same sentence to express different propositions. We must distinguish *saying* something in the sense of uttering a sentence from *saying* something in the sense of expressing a proposition.

Some further differences

Sentences are uttered, or written in ink on paper or in chalk on the blackboard; they are heard or seen, or perhaps even felt if written in braille. Thus they take up space (if written), and can come into existence as well as go out of existence. The sentence you are reading right now is nothing more than an organized set of ink symbols on paper—it has both spatial and temporal dimensions.

What that sentence means, i.e., the proposition expressed with it, is something quite different in nature. You really don't *see* the meaning or the proposition (although you may be said to *understand* it); it isn't something that exists in space or in time as is the sentence. Moreover, the proposition didn't come into existence when the sentence did and it wouldn't go out of existence were the sentence erased or whited out.

We can say that a particular sentence is a *physical* phenomenon (made of ink or chalk marks, or perhaps of sound waves if spoken); a proposition is best regarded as an *abstract* object. It is important to note that by saying that propositions are nonphysical or abstract we are not saying that they are mental items; a proposition is not simply the thought one has in one's head when using a sentence. It is more accurate to say that the proposition is what we are *thinking of*, not the *thought* itself. Just as there can be the same mind-independent island resort of which we are all thinking (or dreaming), so there can be the same mind-independent proposition (say, that José's dog is large) of which we are all thinking, or expressing with our sentences.

We must mention one further way in which sentences are distinguished from propositions. Suppose José says "My dog is a German shepherd" and someone else remarks, "What he said is true." Now what exactly is it that is claimed to be *true*? We noted above that 'said' has two senses: one in which what is said is a sentence and another in which what is said is a proposition. Is it the sentence or the proposition that is claimed to be true?

If we were to take the sentence to be what is true in this case, we would find ourselves in difficulty when Catherine uses the same sentence and, referring now to her dog, says something false; the same sentence would be both true and false. Perhaps more important is the fact that physical things like spots of ink or sound waves don't seem to be the right *kinds* of things to have *truth values* (i.e., having the value of true or the value of false). It would be better to say that it is what the spots of ink or the sound waves signify or express that is true or false. So if what José said is true, then it is the proposition he expressed that is true, not the sentence he uttered.

Propositions are the bearers of truth values; and they are true or false depending on the way the world is. If the world is really such that José's dog is a German shepherd, then the proposition *that José's dog is a German shepherd* is true; otherwise it is false. This proposition could be expressed by many different sentences: José could say "My dog is a German shepherd," Catherine could say "José's dog is a German shepherd," or someone could write on a slip of paper "José has a German shepherd for a pet." In all these cases a common truth is expressed, hence, it is not the sentence which is true but the proposition expressed.

Finally, there are two important principles of logic to keep in mind. First, every proposition is either true or false. There is no third truth value and every proposition must have some value. Second, no proposition can be both true and false. If it is true that Heinrich is a German shepherd, then it cannot also be false—dogs cannot both be and not be German shepherds.

Two common mistakes

1. Someone might think that propositions can change their truth values over time. Isn't it the case that the proposition *that Heinrich is large* is true now but was false once, when he was a puppy, for example? Back when Heinrich was a puppy, if José said "My dog is large" he would be expressing a false proposition. But if José utters the sentence today, he will be expressing something true. Hasn't the proposition José expressed changed its truth value as Heinrich has grown?

The answer is no. The explanation is that although the *same sentence* was uttered by José both then and now, there was a *different proposition* expressed each time. Suppose José says on January 1, 1982 (when Heinrich was still a small puppy) "My dog is large." What he means (that is, what he expresses) is *that Heinrich is now (on January 1, 1982) large.* That proposition is false, and it will always (eternally) be false. In twenty years (in 2002) the proposition *that Heinrich is/was large on January 1, 1982* will still be false. But notice that this is a different proposition from the one expressed when José utters the sentence "My dog is large" on October 20, 2002. At that time the proposition expressed is *that Heinrich is now on October 20, 2002 large* and it is true—it always has been, and always will be, true.

2. Someone might think that a proposition can be true for one person and false for another. Such a claim often occurs in a debate over evaluative judgments. Suppose Catherine says "José, your dog Heinrich is a lousy watchdog" and José, defending his best friend, responds "Actually Heinrich is a very good watchdog." Now the debate continues for some time until Catherine, tired of arguing,

remarks "Well, I guess it's true for you that Heinrich is a good watchdog but false for me."

Catherine's final remark is terribly misleading. Remember that propositions are true or false depending on the way the world is. Either José's dog is a good watchdog or he is not—that will depend on what it takes to be a good watchdog and we may suppose that there are certain things that determine whether a watchdog is a good one or not.

It may be that José and Catherine (whether they realize it or not) are simply arguing about the proper criteria for determining good watchdogs. If that is the case, then they are probably not arguing over the same proposition after all—their disagreement is only a verbal one. Catherine may just be saying that Heinrich is not aggressive enough, presupposing all along that being aggressive is what it takes to be a good watchdog. And José may be saying that Heinrich is a loud barker, presupposing that this is what makes a good watchdog. Both may be correct in what they are saying about Heinrich, but they are saying different things, i.e., expressing different but non-conflicting propositions.

Should they both agree on a criterion for being a good watchdog, say, that it must be alert, then there may be a genuine disagreement and they both cannot be correct. (The correct position depends on the way the world, or in particular, on the way Heinrich, is.) It cannot be that the same proposition is true for one person but false for another. At best we can say that one person *believed* (perhaps incorrectly) that the proposition was true and the other *believed* (perhaps incorrectly) that the proposition was false. So we can say that it is true of José that he believed the proposition to be true but false of Catherine that she believed it to be true. But the proposition itself was either true or false (not both) independent of what the interlocutors believe.

Questions: How do informative and emotive content differ? What is it for an expression to be ambiguous? vague? What are necessary and sufficient conditions and how are they relevant to analyzing concepts? What is the sense of a term? the reference of a term? What are propositions? How do they differ from sentences?

Section 3: MODALITY AND POSSIBLE WORLDS

Propositions, we noted earlier, are either true or false depending on the way the world is. And very often we are interested in finding out whether certain propositions are actually true or false, i.e., we want to know how the world is. Such is the case, say, for the scientist who works by hypothesis and experiment to uncover the workings of the universe; his concern is the way things *actually* are. But as philosophers we may not only want to know how things actually are, but how things *could be* (what is possible), how things *couldn't be* (what is impossible), and how things *must be* (what is necessary). With these interests in mind, we should then inquire into what it means to say not only that a proposition is *actually* true (or false) but into what it could mean to say a proposition is *possibly* true (or false) or *necessarily* true (or false). Possibility and necessity are called "modal" notions, and it is with these that we shall be concerned in this section.

Necessarily true propositions

We can start with some fairly clear-cut examples of how things must be and of necessarily true propositions. First, consider whether someone could be a bachelor but not be an unmarried adult male. Surely not: being unmarried is just what it is to be a bachelor. This is one way the world *must* be: *if* there are any bachelors, then they are unmarried adult males. We can say then that the corresponding proposition *that all bachelors are unmarried adult males* is necessarily true. Notice we are not saying that there must be bachelors in the world or that the proposition *that there are bachelors* is necessarily true (suppose every adult male got married tomorrow—that's possible). Our comment is conditional: on the condition that someone is a bachelor, he must also be an unmarried adult male.

Second, in mathematics we make certain statements about numbers and the connections between them. Two added to three equals five and nothing else. It's not that they just happen to add up to five some days and not others, nor can we even conceive of what it would be like if they added up to some other number. What would it be like for two and three to equal twenty-seven, or for someone to have twenty-seven pieces of fruit in virtue of having only two apples and three oranges? Such nonsensical things cannot be. So here is another way the world *must be*: two plus three equals five. And the corresponding proposition *that two added to three equals five* is necessarily true.

Finally, some philosophers claim that objects have certain properties necessarily, i.e., the objects couldn't exist without these properties. John F. Kennedy was the child of Rose and Joseph Kennedy, but could he have had different parents? Many philosophers claim he could not: different parents (your parents, for example) could have had a son who was very much like John F. Kennedy (looked like him, was given that name, became President, etc.) but it would not *be* John F. Kennedy. Being the son of Rose and Joseph we say is an *essential* part of being John F. Kennedy. Or to take an example from mathematics, could the number two be anything but even? Certainly not. Being an even number is part of what it is to be the number two, just as being the child of Rose and Joseph Kennedy is part of what it is to be John F. Kennedy. Consequently, it is necessarily true *that if John Kennedy exists, he is the son of Rose and Joseph Kennedy* (supposing, of course, that Rose and Joseph were actually his parents) and *that if there is such a thing as the number two, it is an even number*.

In sum: necessarily true propositions are propositions that must be true or, to put it another way, that could not be false. They correspond to ways the world *must* be.

Necessarily false propositions

If there are some ways the world *must* be, then there are also ways the world *can't* be. It is impossible that two be an odd number; it is impossible that John F. Kennedy should exist but have different parents than the ones he actually had; it is impossible that a bachelor be married; and it is impossible that two added to three equal twenty-seven. Any proposition that corresponds to one of these impossibilities is *necessarily false*. In general, any proposition that *denies* or *negates* a necessarily true proposition is necessarily false.

Contingently true propositions

Aside from questions about the way the world must be, the philosopher will inquire into the various ways the world could be (or could have been, could become—tense is irrelevant here): what is possible? Let's first consider the way the world *actually* is in order to ask whether it could be otherwise. As things actually stand, it is true (1) *that Bertrand Russell had five fingers on his left hand*, (2) *that you are now less than ten feet tall*, and (3) *that the sun will rise tomorrow*. None of these propositions is necessarily true since each of them could be false—each of them is possibly false. We shall call any proposition that is actually true but not necessarily so a *contingently true proposition*. The idea is that although (1), (2) and (3) are indeed true, they don't have to be. Russell didn't have to have five fingers on his left hand—he still would have existed otherwise; you would still exist if you were more than ten feet tall; and even if the sun does rise tomorrow, there is no necessity in this. These are contingent states of the world.

We sometimes say that these alternatives are *logically* or *metaphysically* possible (metaphysics being the philosophical study of the ultimate nature of reality). This is to say that no logical or metaphysical laws or principles would be broken by them were they the way things actually are. (1), (2) and (3) are logically possible propositions, as are the denials of (1), (2) and (3). Notice that there is something logically wrong with the necessarily false proposition *that some bachelors are married*. To say that there is a bachelor that is married is in effect to say that there is a bachelor that is not a bachelor. But of course that is contradictory and so logically impossible: a fundamental principle of logic—nothing can be said to both have and not have the same property—is broken.

Contingently false propositions

Just as some propositions that are true are contingently true, so some propositions that are false are contingently so. To say that a proposition is contingently false is to say that it is actually false but possibly true. George Washington was not an astronaut, but that is not an impossibility. Russell didn't have six fingers on his left hand, but he could have. And the sun won't break into a million pieces tomorrow, but this is a way the world could be. Once again, to say that something is possible is just to say that if it were actual (or actually true), it would not break any laws of logic or metaphysics.

Notice that the proposition *that there are round squares on the moon* is false but not contingently false. This is so because it is not possibly true. If things were actually that way, laws of logic would be broken—nothing can be both round and square at the same time on pain of contradiction.

Some important distinctions

Now there are some very important distinctions to be made here. When we ask whether Russell could have had six fingers on his left hand, we are not necessarily implying that we might have gotten the historical facts about his digits wrong or that we are ignorant about what is actually the case. Or when we say that your being ten feet tall is a possibility we do not imply that for all we know you only appear to be under ten feet. There is, of course, a sense of 'could' or 'might' or 'possible' that we use when we are unsure about what the facts are. "I don't think it was Larry who shot Clyde, but it could (or might) have been." "It's possible that Jupiter has three moons, but I really don't know." Or, to take a more elaborate example, just glancing at the problem, someone might be inclined to say that 57,988 is possibly the product of 327 and 174; but since $327 \times 174 = 56,898$ is a truth of mathematics, it is logically impossible that the product be anything but 56,898. In these cases the sense of 'could' or 'might' or 'possible' is the same as 'for all I know it is the case'. This is what philosophers call the epistemic sense of possibility. But this is not the sense we are using when we talk of what is logically or metaphysically possible. So, 57,988 is possibly the product of 327 and 174 in the epistemic sense but not in the logical sense.

There is yet another sense of possibility that we are not particularly interested in here. This is the sense in which we refer to the existence of a certain *potential*. So, for example, one might say "I am actually six feet tall but I could be seven feet tall" to suggest that I have a potential for becoming seven feet tall in the future. But the sense we are interested in is not used to suggest that a change is in the offing. We want to suggest something like "Although I am actually now six feet tall, my being seven feet tall now is a logical possibility" or "There is nothing logically wrong (contradictory) with the proposition *that I am seven feet tall.*"

Finally, we must add that we do not mean *probability* either. That is, to say that something is possible is not to say that it is probable. Probability, unlike possibility, has to do with likelihood; and whereas probability comes in degrees, possibility does not. It is not very likely that you will spontaneously burst into flames in the next two minutes, but such a thing is logically possible. Notice how odd it sounds to say "I know George Washington was not an astronaut, but it's probable that he was"; on the other hand it is acceptable to say "I know George Washington was not an astronaut but it's possible that he was." More generally, any event that is probable is also possible (it makes no sense to think that an impossible event like there being a round square on the moon could nevertheless be likely), but not all possible events are probable.

So, what are we interested in when we ask whether Russell could have had six fingers on his left hand, or whether John F. Kennedy could have had different parents than one ones he actually had, or whether you could be ten feet tall and blue? We do not wonder at the extent of our ignorance of the way things actually are ("For all I know it's true"), we are not wondering whether these things have certain potentials ("He's a lousy cook, but he could get better"), and we do not wonder what the odds are that these propositions are true ("Probably it will come up heads"). Rather, we are interested in what properties are accidental (contingent) and what properties are essential (necessary); we are wondering in what ways the world (or perhaps the objects we say are "in" it) could be different and in what ways it must be the way it is.

Modality and propositions: A summary

Let's summarize what we've done so far.

(1) A *necessarily true proposition* is a proposition that is actually true and can't be false. For example, the proposition *that all bachelors are unmarried adult males* is necessarily true since it is impossible for something to be a bachelor and fail to be unmarried; the proposition *that two added to two equals four* is necessarily true since it is impossible for two added to two to equal anything else.

(2) A *necessarily false proposition* is a proposition that is actually false and can't be true. For example, the propositions *that some bachelors are married* or *that two added to two equals six* or *that there are round squares on the moon* are necessarily false. The world couldn't be any of these ways: a bachelor couldn't be married, two and two couldn't equal six, and round squares can't exist on the moon or anywhere else.

(3) A *contingently true proposition* is a proposition that is actually true but could be (or is possibly) false. It is actually true that Bertrand Russell had five fingers on his left hand, but as we discussed above, the proposition could be false. It is not that for all we know Russell didn't have five fingers on his left hand, only that there is nothing logically wrong with the proposition *that Russell had more or less than five fingers on his left hand* (Russell could exist without five fingers).

(4) A *contingently false proposition* is a proposition that is actually false but could be (or is possibly) true. The proposition *that George Washington was an astronaut* is actually false but could be true. Once again this is not to say that we might be wrong about the history of the space program, or that George Washington could come back to life and become an astronaut (surely that's impossible!). Our point is simply that although Washington was not an astronaut, this is only accidental or contingent, and that there is nothing logically or metaphysically wrong with his having the property of *being an astronaut* in the way that there would be something logically or metaphysically wrong with a bachelor being married or a square being round.

Determining necessity and contingency

Now that we understand what it is for a proposition to be either necessarily or contingently true (or false), we must look at how we tell when a particular true (or false) proposition is necessarily or contingently so.

In some cases we can know a proposition is true not by looking to the world but by considering the meanings of the words in the sentences we use to express it. Take the sentence 'All sisters are female siblings' that we may use to express the proposition *that all sisters are female siblings*. Now we would not have to look at a number of sisters to see whether or not they are all female siblings. Instead, we only need to know the meanings of the words 'sister', 'female' and 'sibling'. If one understands these words, then one knows that 'sister' simply means the same as (is synonymous with) 'female sibling' and so anything that is a sister will also be a female sibling. As long as the meanings of the words stay the same, the sentence 'All sisters are female siblings' will express a proposition that is true. A sentence that expresses a proposition known to be true in this way is sometimes called an *analytic* sentence (one only needs to *analyze* the sentence to see that the proposition expressed with it is true). Other examples include the sentences 'All bachelors are unmarried adult males', 'A triangle has exactly three sides' and 'If something is red and square, then it is red and square'.

Any sentence that is not analytic is *synthetic*; the true propositions that are expressed by synthetic sentences must be known to be true in some way other than by attending to the meanings of the sentence's words. Take, for example, the propositions expressed with the sentences 'This page is white' and 'Bertrand Russell had five fingers on his left hand'. Knowing the meanings of the words alone will not enable one to tell whether the propositions expressed are true. One also has to check (by looking) to know that the page at which one is now looking is white. And one has to do some work to find out whether Russell had five fingers on his left hand: perhaps by looking at a photograph, or by asking someone who would know.

Propositions expressed by analytic sentences are necessarily true. A sister could not fail to be a female sibling; a bachelor couldn't fail to be unmarried; a triangle must have exactly three sides. So one way we can tell when a particular proposition is necessarily true is to see whether it is expressed by an analytic sentence: if it is, the meanings of the terms tell us that the proposition expressed cannot be false.

But even though all analytic sentences express necessarily true propositions, this is not to say that all necessarily true propositions can be expressed with analytic sentences. Some philosophers hold that some synthetic sentences express necessarily true propositions as well. Consider the sentence 'Every event has a cause'. Does it express a necessary truth or not? Although many philosophers say it does, it is not by the meanings of the words that they can tell: it is not part of the meaning of 'event' that an event must have a cause (although it may be part of the meaning of 'effect' that an effect has a cause). Or, if Rose and Joseph Kennedy *are* the parents of John F. Kennedy, then the sentence 'If John F. Kennedy exists, Rose and Joseph Kennedy are his parents' is not analytic but does express a necessary truth.

So, if a sentence is analytic, it expresses a necessary truth. But if a sentence is synthetic then we cannot tell straight off whether it is true or false, much less whether it is necessary or contingent. Of course, to tell whether a synthetic sentence expresses something actually true or false, we look to the world (Is the page white? Did Russell have five fingers on his left hand?). Unfortunately we cannot tell whether the proposition expressed is necessary or contingent simply by looking to the world. To get a grip on the answer to that question we must think about the proposition in a broader context.

Suppose we are wondering whether the false proposition *that George Washington was an astronaut* is necessarily false or just contingently so. Nothing appears to be logically wrong with the proposition—it doesn't seem to be self-contradictory, for example, as does the proposition *that there are married bachelors*. So there is no immediate reason to think it is necessarily false. And if we think about how the world would be if George Washington had been an astronaut, it seems there is nothing inconsistent or incoherent in such a world so long as we are able to allow for other changes as well (the space program would need to have started earlier, or Washington would have had to have been born later, etc). In other words, what we must do is think not just about the individual proposition in question but about the bigger picture into which it might fit—would it entail or lead to logically improper consequences? We have good reason to think that the proposition, though *actually* false, is possibly true and so contingent, if it can form part of a larger story that is both consistent and coherent.

Consider what would happen if we tried to fit a necessary falsehood into a larger story, or if we tried to tell a story in which a necessary truth is false. Such stories lead to inconsistency and incoherence. Try to create an *intelligible* (i.e., coherent and consistent) story in which bachelors are married; either you will use the words 'bachelor' or 'married' to mean something other that what they conventionally mean (that's cheating), or your story will contain some logical absurdities, such as particular individuals being both married and unmarried at the same time.

The general strategy is this. When considering whether a particular proposition is contingently true (or false) or necessarily true (or false), first see whether it is true in virtue of the meanings of the words used to express it, i.e., expressed by an analytic sentence. If so, then it is a necessary truth. If not, then consider it in the context of a whole world or story. Could the world consistently and coherently accommodate the changes that would occur if this proposition were true. If the answer is yes and the proposition in question is actually false, then it is only contingently false. But suppose the proposition in question is actually true? Then we ask: Could the world consistently and coherently accommodate the changes that would occur if that proposition were false? If the answer to this question is yes, then the proposition is contingently true.

Possible worlds

To make this procedure clearer and more precise, we need to say a little more about the notion of a *world*. When we talk about the world as it actually is we do not mean to restrict ourselves to the planet earth. We want to consider the way the entire universe is. And we are not necessarily interested in the universe at any particular time, but for all times. So when considering whether a proposition is true (that is, *actually* true), we must look to the world (universe) as it actually is, i.e., the *actual world*. It is natural to think then that when considering whether a certain proposition is possibly true (either contingent or necessary), we should consider that proposition in relation to what philosophers have called *possible worlds*. What is a possible world?

Consider once again the notion of the actual world. Instead of thinking of it as the entire universe at all times, think of a complete story that describes in minute detail every fact about the entire universe at all times—all the goings on of every atom and every planet and every animal, etc., covering every event and all times. The story will no doubt be a long and complicated one. We can think of our story as a list of propositions: no proposition is missing from the list and every proposition is labeled either true or false depending on how the universe is. We will put this infinitely long list of correctly labeled propositions into a book (we won't actually write this all down; think of it as an abstract or imaginary book) and entitle it "The Actual World." This book will tell us whether Russell had five or six fingers on his left hand and whether the sun will rise tomorrow.

When we think about worlds in general, we will be thinking of lists of propositions very much like the one we called "The Actual World." But note: those worlds that are not actual will differ from the actual world in some ways and so the stories will be different. But this is just to say that some propositions that were labeled 'true' on the actual world list will be labeled 'false' on other lists, and of course some propositions labeled 'false' on the actual world list will be 'true' on other lists. So, for example, when we say that the proposition *that George Washington was an astronaut* is actually false but possibly true, we simply mean that on the list of propositions in "The Actual World" (the list that describes the way things actually are) that proposition is labeled 'false' but on other lists (lists describing the ways things could be) it is marked 'true'.

We must place two restrictions upon our notion of a world as a list of propositions. First, the list must be complete in that *every* proposition is included and labeled either 'true' or 'false'. It is in this way that every fact and falsehood about the universe, in very minute detail, is represented in "The Actual World."

Second, the story "told" by a list must be consistent. By this we simply mean that no proposition will be both true and false; no proposition will contradict another. Thus we cannot have the proposition *that there are married bachelors* on any list, nor can we have the both the propositions *that Bertrand Russell had only five fingers on his left hand in March of 1903* and *that Bertrand Russell had six fingers on his left hand in March of 1903.* It is easy to see that a universe (or as we say, a world) could not be like this.

Let's summarize. A *possible world* is a complete and consistent story or list of propositions describing in minute detail a way in which a universe could be. The *actual world* , then, is one of the infinitely many possible worlds; it is the story that describes a way the universe could be, but what is more, it describes the universe as it is.

Necessary and contingent truths and falsehoods

We now have another way of defining necessary and contingent truths and falsehoods.

A *necessarily true proposition* is a proposition that is (i) true at the actual world, but moreover, (ii) true at *every* possible world.

A *necessarily false proposition* is a proposition that is (i) false at the actual world, but moreover, (ii) false at *every* possible world.

This should make perfect sense. The denial of a necessary truth is a necessary falsehood. For example, consider the necessarily true proposition *that all triangles have exactly three sides,* and the denial of the this, *that not all triangles have exactly three sides.* Every complete list of propositions must contain these propositions and label them as either true or false. But the latter could not appear *as true* on any list of propositions that counts as a possible world since that would make the list inconsistent—it is self-contradictory to say that a triangle had more or less than three sides. If the latter must appear as false on every list, then its opposite must appear as true on every list. So, the proposition *that all triangles have exactly three sides* is on every list as true, i.e, it is true at all possible worlds, and the proposition *that not all triangles have exactly three sides* is on every list as false, i.e., it is false at every possible world.

A *contingently true proposition* is a proposition that is (i) true at the actual world but (ii) false at *some* possible world.

A *contingently false proposition* is a proposition that is (i)
false at the actual world but (ii) true at *some* possible
world.

The contingently true proposition *that Bertrand Russell had five
fingers on his left hand in March of 1903* is, of course, true at the
actual world—that is the way things actually were with Russell in
March of 1903. But things didn't *have* to be that way: this is only a
contingent fact. So we say it is possibly false, i.e., there is a complete
and consistent list of propositions (a possible world) on which that
proposition is labeled 'false'.

Or consider the contingently false proposition *that Bertrand
Russell had a nose the size of a trumpet*. This is false at the actual
world—fortunately for Russell—but since there is nothing logically
inconsistent with it, and since one could incorporate it into a complete
and consistent story, i.e., since there is a complete and consistent list of
propositions that includes it labeled as 'true', it is said to be possibly
true. Thus, although it is false at the actual world, it is true at some
possible world, and we call it contingently false.

This possible-worlds approach to modality provides us with a
useful method for determining whether certain proposition are necessarily or contingently true. It is not foolproof, however. Since possible
worlds are infinitely long "lists" of propositions, they are not places to
which we can travel and observe things as they would be, and we cannot peer into them from the actual world. Moreover, the lists are too
long for us to be able to consider the whole of one. What we must do
is consider as much of a total possible way things could be as will
satisfy us that the proposition in question will either "fit" or "not fit"
into some complete and consistent list. We are thus invited to let our
imaginations roam, but only within the confines of what is logically
proper. The possible-worlds approach helps keep us from accepting
as possible the inconsistent and absurd.

We must add one final note. Sometimes we want to confine our
thinking about possibilities not just by the laws of logic, but by the
laws of nature or physics. So, for example, we might ask whether
Peter's jumping to the moon is possible. Now this is logically possible
since there is nothing contradictory about it and supposedly there is a
possible world at which Peter does jump to the moon. But that possible world, it is important to notice, will not have the same laws of
nature as the actual world. Given the laws of nature as they actually
are, it is impossible that anyone jump to the moon—the proposition

that Peter jumped to the moon would contradict certain laws governing the forces of attraction between bodies. So we shall say that while someone's jumping to the moon is *logically* possible, it is not *physically* possible. Although we will sometimes have occasion to speak of physical possibility or necessity, we will for the most part restrict our discourse to the wider logical sense of these modal terms.

Questions: How do necessarily true (or false) propositions differ from contingently true (or false) propositions? How does epistemic possibility differ from logical or metaphysical possibility? How is the notion of possibility different from the notion of probability? What is it for a sentence to be analytic? synthetic? What is a possible world? How does the idea of a possible world help us define necessary and contingent propositions?

RELATED READINGS

Copi, Irving M. *Introduction to Logic*. Sixth edition. New York: Macmillan Publishing Company, 1982.

Hurley, Patrick J. *A Concise Introduction to Logic*. Fourth edition. Belmont, CA: Wadsworth Publishing Company, 1991.

Weston, Anthony. *A Rulebook for Arguments*. Indianapolis: Hackett, 1987.

CHAPTER 3 | Rationality and the Existence of God

Section 1: INTRODUCTION

Philosophy and religion

THE PURPOSE of this chapter is to consider in a philosophical light the claim that God exists and to assess the grounds one might have for believing this claim. We are primarily concerned to see if there can be any rational grounds for believing that God exists. By restricting our study to "rational grounds" we are purposely ignoring the possibility that one could hold such a belief simply as a matter of faith. While this possibility is an interesting one, we shall not take it up here. The bulk of this chapter is devoted to analyzing critically several traditional arguments that have been set forth to demonstrate or prove that God exists. We will also look at several arguments for the opposite conclusion—that God does not exist. In addition, we will consider whether an argument is the only kind of ground one could have for a rational belief in God. (If there are no good arguments for the existence of God, could one still be rational in believing that God exists?) It should be emphasized, then, that our topic does not merely concern the question of whether or not God exists, but it also bears heavily on questions of rationality and belief.

Although our focus throughout will be strictly philosophical, it is quite obvious that our topic has religious import. In order to capture the true philosophical spirit of our investigation and to keep it distinct from a more religious approach, it will be helpful to distinguish the two domains.

While religion is difficult to define, it can be roughly characterized. Religion, we might say, is an institutionalized system of special kinds of beliefs and practices. Typically these systems involve a belief in a supernatural and divine being, a commitment to various rituals, doctrine and worship, and the authorization of a particular moral and cosmological worldview. It is to be admitted that this description is only marginally adequate—not all religions incorporate exactly these elements and practically all religions include much more. Our intent, however, is only to capture a certain attitude—an attitude by which the claim "God exists" might be considered to have great significance, yet which is distinct from a purely philosophical stance. The religious person will indeed consider questions about the existence of God, but the character of his concern (as religious) will differ from the character of ours (as philosophical) in the following ways and for the following reasons.

First, the philosophical attitude must be objective, detached and independent of any particular religious position. This is not required for the religious stance, which might involve an emotional and personal commitment to certain doctrines and practices. This kind of commitment might even be viewed as essential to the religious attitude.

Second, questions such as What is rationality? When is a reason a good reason? and How can we demonstrate the existence of anything? are questions that most assuredly are philosophical in nature. Specifically, they are epistemological questions in that they deal with issues of knowledge and rationality. The question, Does God exist? is itself an important philosophical question, being just a special case of the more general metaphysical question, What is there? These philosophical questions lie at the heart of the present chapter and the specific questions we will examine, namely, Can the religious believer rationally believe in God? Can one construct an argument that proves (or possibly one that disproves) the existence of God? and How well do these arguments stand up to rational criticism? While these questions have religious significance, addressing them will demand philosophical attention. The philosophical perspective is especially geared to handle issues of this kind.

Finally, not withstanding the religious import found in such questions, the spirit in which they will be addressed must remain philosophical, since in addressing them we want to be looking at general and fundamental features of religion itself. When we evaluate the methods by which religious practitioners arrive at their beliefs, when we assess the grounds they have for their beliefs, when we investigate the presuppositions of religion in general, we are undertaking a project that has religion as its subject matter. In this sense we are looking at meta-religious issues. Because it is the philosopher's task to investigate matters that are either too fundamental or too general for other particular disciplines to investigate, the issues we will be discussing fall quite naturally into the hands of the philosopher. Just as the philosopher of science will seek to understand the nature of science in general—perhaps by taking a close look at the goals, presuppositions and methods of science—so too will the philosopher of religion look to the goals, presuppositions and, perhaps, practices of religion to understand better the nature of that enterprise. When the scientist asks whether the experimental method is the best one by which to find out what the physical universe is like, he is not asking a scientific question but a philosophical one. And similarly, when the religious devotee asks whether his reasons for believing in God are good ones, whether his arguments are sound, or whether his beliefs are rational, his questions are not religious but philosophical.

Our topic—rationality and the existence of God—is but one topic among many investigated in the philosophy of religion. There is also the question of the immortality of the soul (What is a soul? Could such a thing exist eternally?), the nature of religious language (Are religious statements meaningful?), the status of religious experience (Is religious experience like perceptual experience in any significant way? Do mystical experiences lead to religious knowledge?), the nature of the divine attributes (What is it for something to be omniscient or omnipotent?), and the nature and role of faith and revelation in religion. Given the scope of this chapter, we will not be able to address all of these topics.

The concept of God

It should be evident that the concept of God will be central to our discussion. In looking at arguments for or against the existence of God, it is crucial that one know exactly what is being argued for or against.

First, a word of caution. It is a frequent worry of students that saying what we mean by 'God' is somehow illegitimate. "Who is to say what God is like? Everyone has his own idea about God, and it isn't reasonable to suppose that you could really say that *this* is what 'God' means. Besides, we don't even know if there is a God—deciding that question is what needs to be done first." Now this sort of worry turns out to be frightfully unhelpful and it is important to see why. When a Philosopher asks what is meant by 'God', he isn't prejudging the question of God's existence. Rather, the question he asks is conditional: "On the condition that God exists, what is this being like?" or "What would God be like, if there were such a being?"

Consider that when asking if there are any extraterrestrial beings, we pose a sensible question only so far as we offer some fairly well-defined notion of an extraterrestrial, long *before* we have any answer. Indeed—and this is the important point—we cannot address the question of a thing's existence, or offer grounds for believing that it does or doesn't exist, without first being clear on what that thing must be like. Remember that we shall be constructing and assessing rational arguments for the existence of God. Suppose then, for a moment, that I ask you to construct an argument for the existence of Yeti. What would you do? Likely you would ask me what or who this 'Yeti' is. And only after I tell you what is meant by 'Yeti'—it is said to name the huge beast of Tibetan lore believed by the highland tribes to yet inhabit the eastern Himalaya—can you hope to get on with the job of offering rational grounds for claiming that Yeti exists.

Before going on to address the problem of alternative conceptions of God, it is worth briefly attending to some objections to the project of developing a clear notion of what God is like. Some existentialist philosophers of religion, for example, frequently deny the legitimacy of any objective, conceptual analysis of 'God', particularly in the context of arguing for His existence. Their motivations are both religious and linguistic. Other philosophers have worried about whether God can be meaningfully characterized. Suppose one claims that God is personal insofar as he possesses attributes similar in kind to ours, like (moral) goodness, though He has these to a much greater degree (He is, say, infinitely good). Some have held that it is inappropriately demeaning to God to say that He has goodness (in *any* amount) in the same sense that you or I do. And since the only sense of 'good' we understand is as it applies to humans, it is meaningless to say that God is good—or that he is any other way that we can specify or understand at all. Finally, a similar conclusion about the meaninglessness of religious language stems from a separate philosophical view sometimes called "verificationism." On this view, sentences in a language are meaningful only if they can in principle be verified or falsified. It is difficult, however, to imagine how one would ever go about checking to see if most religious claims are true or not.

These objections do touch the present task of specifying the concept of God to be used in this chapter. But as we have already noted, they are problems making up other topics in the philosophy of religion (the meaningfulness of religious language, for example), separate from our examination of rational arguments for the existence of God. The primary concern now is to see that some particular concept of God must be offered if we are to begin treating these arguments.

What concept, then, are we to employ? Clearly, there are alternatives (each of us does have a favorite idea about what God would have to be like on the supposition that He exists). An important strain of Deism views God as creator but otherwise disconnected from the workings of the universe and from human experience; traditional Judeo-Christian Theism holds God to be the transcendent yet personal creator and final judge, whose properties are possessed without limitation (e.g., He is all-powerful, all-knowing, etc); Pantheism takes God to be all there is—the whole of the universe conceived as one thing; and so it goes, for many alternative views of God.

The concept of God used in this chapter is that of the Judeo-Christian tradition. There are several important reasons for settling on this choice. First, most of us were raised and trained within a western culture and so have lived closest to this tradition. It has influenced our thinking more than other traditions, whether we are particularly religious or not. Second, the most famous and philosophically important arguments for the existence of God (hence, the ones in which we shall be interested) have been endorsed by philosophers operating within the Judeo-Christian tradition. And third, this concept of God is undeniably interesting: it is more philosophically engaging than, say, the view that God is a head of cabbage, and has proven to offer meatier substance for good argument than the view that God is all there is.

For the purposes of this chapter, then, the core of the Judeo-Christian view is that God is all-powerful, all-knowing, and perfectly good: we will say that God is, respectively, omnipotent, omniscient and morally perfect. There are other attributes, of course, and some of them may be noted along the way. The most important of these include eternality, incorporality and immutability. These, however, will play only a minor role in our discussion.

Prudential and epistemic rationality

It will be useful to say a few words early on about the general concept of rationality. We often find ourselves talking about people being rational or irrational, which is an idea closely related to that of rational or irrational actions and beliefs. We can perhaps say that people are rational to the degree that they tend to perform rational actions or hold rational beliefs (or irrational to the degree that they tend to perform irrational actions). Our focus will be on the specific activity of believing something (some proposition, viz., that God exists) to be true. We will be asking whether it is rational to hold a belief in the existence of God or to come to believe in a certain way that God exists. We can also put our inquiry in terms of the justification of belief, asking whether belief in the existence of God could ever be justified (or whether someone could be justified in believing in God). Thus, following many contemporary discussions, we will be treating issues surrounding justification and rationality together.

One can be said to be rational in believing something in a variety of senses. When we ask whether it is ever rational to believe in God we are asking whether it is ever *epistemically* rational to so believe. This is the sort of rationality most closely related to the concept of knowledge. To say that someone rationally believes something to be true in the epistemic sense is to say roughly that they came to believe in the kind of way that tends to produce knowledge or that they have support for their belief strong enough to qualify that belief as a piece of knowledge.[1]

Exploring a contrasting sense of rationality might be helpful. Consider an argument the French philosopher and theologian Pascal offers for believing that God exists. Lacking any knowledge of whether God does exist, imagine you are forced to place a wager on the question of God's existence. How would you bet? If we limit your options to two (to believe that God exists or to not believe this) and the relevant states of affairs to two (God either does or doesn't exist), then we find there are four distinct outcomes. You might begin the decision procedure by considering the consequences of the four alternatives. It may be argued that correctly believing that God does exist is more beneficial that any of the other options and incorrectly believing that God doesn't exist promises the most harm. Compared to these consequences, the consequences of the remaining two alternatives are negligible (let us suppose there are no noteworthy gains or losses). It should be clear what the prudent decision would be. Believing in God will result in either a large gain or at least no great loss, but not believing in God stands the chance of suffering a great loss and at best no great gain.

While the decision matrix offered above might suggest that it is rational to believe that God exists, the concept of rationality employed here is *prudential* rationality, rationality aimed at one's practical benefit or at self-interest. To wager with Pascal on the basis of his decision procedure that God does exist does not take us any closer to knowing whether God exists. So if we are rational in believing that God exists based on Pascal's wager, it is not a case of epistemic rationality.

For our purposes in this chapter, when we ask whether it is ever rational to believe that God exists (are we ever justified in believing that God exists?), we are not interested in whether the practical consequences of believing in God are better that the practical consequences of not so believing. Instead, we are asking how we might set our methods of inquiry and adjust our beliefs with the goal of knowledge in mind. We can also ask, Is there any way to tell whether God exists? Is there some way of coming to know whether God exists?

One way to become epistemically rational in believing something is to have a good argument for it. Using valid deductive methods one might *deduce* one's belief that God exists from premises that one knows, or has good reason to believe, are true. Alternatively, one might infer the proposition that God exist from evidence that, by *inductive* standards, makes it likely that it is true. In either case, one is considered epistemically rational in believing that God exists because one bases one's belief on other propositions—the premises of the arguments—that would be considered good support for his or her belief.

Under these circumstance we would normally require that the premises of the arguments we use be themselves propositions that are rationally believed. Our being justified in believing the conclusion depends in part on our being justified in believing the premises. Suppose a friend of yours believes that philosophy majors tend to graduate from college and become wealthy. She bases her belief on another belief about a survey in which nine of ten graduated philosophy majors have high paying jobs with large corporations. Normally we might consider this a pretty good argument and judge that her belief in the prospects of philosophy majors is rational. But suppose we add that her belief that there is a survey showing that nine out of ten philosophy majors have high paying jobs is not rationally held. Suppose we note that she believes that there is such a survey because she had a dream about this one night, and that in fact she has in her course work come across very reliable statistics that reveal that very few philosophy graduates get jobs at all? Suppose she simply refuses to believe what she has learned in class and stubbornly accepts the "evidence" she has dreamed about. Now it is no longer clear that her belief in the good prospects for philosophy majors is rational since it is based on support that is irrationally held.

So sometimes we are rational in believing something because we have a good argument for it and because we are rational in believing the premises of that argument. But there also seem to be times when we rationally believe something without argument. For example, isn't it rational for you to believe you're seated in a chair reading a book when you have the experience of sitting in a chair reading a book? We wouldn't ordinarily say that you have an argument for your belief that you're sitting and reading, but your belief does seem to be reasonably supported by your *experience*. So we need to consider the possibility that one might be rational in believing that God exists because one has had experiences of a certain kind (sometimes called religious experiences).

Furthermore, there is the possibility that one might not have any support for belief in God, yet believes anyway, lacking any reason to believe to the contrary. Is a person rational in a belief for which they have no support, provided they have no evidence against their belief? This possibility also needs to be explored.

Outline of the chapter

With respect to any proposition—but in our case, to the proposition that God exists—one may either affirm it, deny it, or simply confess ignorance. A *theist* affirms the proposition that God exists; the *atheist* believes the proposition is false; and the *agnostic* withholds belief about it. As has already been noted, the theist might hold his belief that God exists simply on faith or on the basis of some rational ground or grounds, perhaps offering an argument to support his position. It is the latter alternative—especially as it concerns the presentation of arguments—that will serve as the primary subject of this chapter.

Arguments can be classified in a number of ways. For our purposes it is useful to employ two classifications. The first of these distinguishes arguments as being either *a posteriori* or *a priori*. An argument is said to be an *a posteriori* argument if at least one of its premises can be known to be true only via sense experience; otherwise it is said to be *a priori*. A second distinction concerns not the way in which we come to know the truth of the premises, but rather concerns the relation the premises bear to the conclusion. An argument is inductive when its premises are intended to support the conclusion as probably true; and argument is deductive if it is intended to guarantee the truth of the conclusion given the truth of the premises.

In Section 2 below we look at an *a posteriori* inductive argument for the existence of God called a teleological argument. Section 3 examines what are called cosmological arguments: these are deductive *a posteriori* arguments for the conclusion that God exists. Two deductive *a priori* arguments are treated in Section 4: these are called ontological arguments and attempt to establish God's existence simply on an understanding of the concept of God.

The atheist too, of course, may offer rational grounds in the form of arguments to support his denial that God exists. In Section 5 we will look at a deductive and an inductive argument for the conclusion that there is no God. These arguments are based on what is called the Problem of Evil.

The job of these sections, then, is to understand the sort of reasoning underlying the argument in question, to construct such an argument, and then to evaluate it critically. This last task requires both a careful look at the content of the argument (in particular, the premises) and at the form of the argument, since the strength of any argument depends primarily on each of these two features.

Finally, the theist may admit to having no argument for his view. It might emerge that he nevertheless is rational in believing that God exists. The final section of this chapter, Section 6, considers this possibility, looking both at the idea that one might have an experience that supports their belief and at the idea that one might be rational in believing in God providing one has no good reason to think otherwise.

Questions: How does a religious attitude differ from a philosophical attitude? What is difficult about defining "God"? What sort of being will we referring to in this text? What is Pascal's wager? How does epistemic rationality differ from prudential rationality? How do a priori arguments differ from a posteriori arguments?

Section 2: TELEOLOGICAL ARGUMENTS

A. Developing the argument

An inductive a posteriori argument

Perhaps the most common kind of argument for the existence of God is the Teleological Argument. Also called "the Argument from

Design," it is initially striking both in its simplicity and in its convincingness. The Teleological Argument is an example of an *a posteriori* inductive argument. It is *a posteriori* in that it has at least one premise which can only be known to be true by appeal to sense experience. And it is inductive, rather than deductive, since its premises, if true, are only purported to render the conclusion probably true; in good inductive arguments the premises provide strong enough evidence to support the likelihood of the conclusion. Consequently, there is no guarantee that the conclusion will be true given the truth of the premises: it is possible that the premises be true yet the conclusion false.

What is the point in trying to show that a certain proposition is probable? After all, if one can really prove something to be true, one has obviously done something valuable. If the conclusion of an argument, however, is not certainly true, but only probable, what good is the argument to us? While a thorough answer to this question would take us away from our current task, this much can be said in response to it. We often find that the reasons we have for holding our beliefs are in no way conclusive. This does not, of course, mean that such reasons are worthless. By serving to make our beliefs likely to be true they do enough to show that our beliefs are rational—and this certainly is of some value. So, if the Teleological Argument does succeed in making it probable that God exists, it will have shown that belief in God is—or at least can be for one who uses the argument—rational.

The main idea

There are many complex things we are aware of that display marks of design. Their parts are arranged in such a way as to serve a certain purpose or to meet a particular end. Many of these objects we know from past experience to have been designed by some intelligent designer (an architect or an engineer), who intentionally specified that arrangement of parts in order to achieve a desired goal. Other objects are so analogous to these known cases that we can reasonably infer that they, too, had a designer.

Cameras, for example, are very complicated instruments that we know to be designed with a particular purpose in mind. Ground glass lenses move to focus an image on light-sensitive film, the aperture adjusts to allow for various depths of field, the shutter opens for the precise amount of time to let in the right amount of light, and there are various buttons, knobs and levers to make all the appropriate adjustments. Any object we might come across that is like the camera in these ways can reasonably be thought to have been designed just as the cameras with which we are already familiar are. Suppose, upon exploring the planet Mars, we were to come across some object that, while unlike ordinary cameras in outward appearance, was very like a camera in the ways its parts were arranged and could be used to take take pictures just like an ordinary camera. We would be perfectly reasonable in thinking that this otherwise strange object had an intelligent designer.

The proponent of the Teleological argument would carry this idea farther to suggest that the universe itself is an object like the camera in that it, too, has parts that seem to be purposefully arranged. By analogy it would be reasonable to think the universe, too, has an intelligent designer (namely, God).

Does the universe display marks of design?

Does the universe show the marks of design we discussed above? Certainly various parts or subsystems of nature do. Most animals do seem to fit in very well with the environment in which they live. There are, for example, varieties of bottom-dwelling fish that blend in with the ocean floor so that they are not easily spied by their enemies. Some of these fish even have both eyes on the same side of their bodies so that, as they swim on the bottom, their entire field of vision is above—no sight is wasted scanning the ocean floor. Obviously, this makes catching prey much easier than it would be if they were more like conventional fish.

More generally, consider the tenuous balance of the ecosystem. One cannot help but be impressed by the way that the parts of the system are arranged and interrelated to work together. In order to maintain a well-balanced ecosystem, populations of the various animal types must stay within a certain range. When a particular population becomes too large, the population of its predators typically increases, thereby setting off significant changes throughout the system. Consider, too, how dead vegetation decays to become fertilizer for new plant life that in turn becomes food for the wild life, and so on.

Finally, and perhaps here we can find a strong analogy with the camera, notice how well the parts of the human eye—the retina, rods, cones, etc.—work together to serve the purpose of providing the possessor visual access to the world around her.

There certainly do seem to be features of design exemplified in nature. Can we say, then, based on our observation that various parts and subsystems of the universe display features indicating purpose and design, that the universe *as a whole* has such features? Our intention, recall, is to construct a teleological argument that supports the claim that God exists in the role of an intelligent designer. Perhaps, though, we do not need to make the extra claim about the whole universe to get a teleological argument off the ground. Instead, we could argue that since various parts and subsystems of the universe display marks of design, it is reasonable to think that there is some designer for these things. What does it matter whether we argue that there is a designer for the universe or for the eye? In either case God is the likely candidate for the job and, after all, the existence of God is what we are trying to support.

Our argument, then, might look like this.

(1) There are objects, like cameras, that have parts that seem to be purposefully arranged.
(2) We know (from past experience) that intelligent beings designed these objects.
(3) Parts of the universe, like the eye, have parts that seem to be purposefully arranged.
(4) So, (analogously) an intelligent being (God) designed these parts of the universe.

An initial problem

Until the middle of the nineteenth century, teleological arguments of this kind were thriving. The reason for this is that science was far enough advanced to show us just how complex the world was, and how well things were arranged and ordered. Science, however, had not advanced far enough to give us an account of just how all this complexity, interrelatedness and apparent purposefulness had come to be. Thus, it seemed to many that the most plausible explanation of this design was that the universe was created by an intelligent designer. In 1859 this changed dramatically when Charles Darwin published *The Origin of Species* in which he offered an alternative explanation. According to Darwin, the apparent design is brought about merely by chance mutations coupled with the way particular changes affect the survivability of the species. Consider the case of animal species. Over the course of time, small, random changes in the genes bring about changes in the structure of a given species. If the change is one that is advantageous to the animal (e.g., if it helps it move faster to escape predators, or makes it more efficient at getting food), then the animal will survive better than its predecessors and will be able to reproduce more of its kind. If the change is harmful to the animal's chances of survival, then it will die quickly and so not reproduce effectively. Thus, over a long period of time, animals adapt to their environment: the better they adapt, the better the survival rate.

Since the time Darwin introduced evolutionary theory, we have available to us an alternative explanation for the design we find in the parts and subsystems of nature: the explanation is natural, not (what theists call) supernatural. Hence, it is not so clear that the existence of an intelligent designer is the reasonable inference to make given that this same data—the features of design displayed in nature—may be equally well explained by an appeal to Darwin's scientific theory.

Revising the argument

This consequence need not be seen as the final word on teleological arguments, however. For we might simply return to our initial idea that the universe *as a whole* displays marks of design and so, (probably) had an intelligent designer. On this view, we may treat the Darwinian explanation of design found in subsystems of nature to be just a *part* of the larger explanation for design found in the universe as a whole. Here we can use evolutionary theory to our advantage. That a universe should be geared to run in this mutation-adaptation cycle with survival as a goal is an incredible fact that itself may be viewed as a mark of intelligent design.

With this in mind, let's construct a more formal version of the Teleological Argument that captures the reasoning we have until now only discussed informally. We will appeal to our past experiences with artifacts (man-made objects—for example, power saws, tables, and television sets) as objects displaying marks of design and that we know to have a designer. Of equal importance in our version of the argument is the claim that the universe itself has features indicating design. If the universe as a whole is analogous to artifacts in that it exemplifies design, then we should be able to extend the analogy and claim that *the universe, like artifacts,* must have a designer (in the case of the universe it is thought to be God). Consider, then, the argument we will call *DESIGN*:

DESIGN:

(1) There are objects, like cameras, that have parts that seem to be purposefully arranged.
(2) We know (from past experience) that intelligent beings designed these objects.
(3) The universe has parts that seem to be purposefully arranged.
(4) So, an intelligent being (God) designed the universe.

As a teleological argument, *DESIGN* has premises that are known *a posteriori* (only through sense experience) and is inductive. The question we must ask, then, is not whether the argument is valid (for that is a virtue attributed only to good deductive arguments) but whether the premises provide good reasons for thinking the conclusion is true—do they make the conclusion probable?

The structure of the argument

Before assessing *DESIGN* it is helpful to notice that it is what may be called an *argument by analogy*. (Inductive argument by analogy is discussed in Chapter 2, Section 1C.) It attempts to support its conclusion by suggesting that there is an analogy between the class of objects referred to in the conclusion and another class of items referred to in the premises. By way of illustration, consider an argument that is very much like *DESIGN* in form.

> Joan worked hard on her first research paper. She spent long hours in the library examining the relevant texts; she carefully outlined her paper; and she wrote three separate drafts before turning in the final version. The hard work paid off because Joan received an A for the paper. Now she has worked just as hard on the second paper, spending much time in the library and extensively revising her work. She will likely receive an A on this project as well.

The idea behind this argument by analogy seems to be that the circumstances relevant to Joan's earning an A on her first paper are analogous to the circumstances in which she hopes to earn a second A. That she should receive an A on the second paper seems reasonable in this case because the respects of analogy mentioned—her hard work in researching and writing the paper—are clearly relevant to her receiving a good grade. We can strengthen the argument by adding more respects of analogy. Suppose that the same teacher evaluates both papers and that in both cases Joan has received helpful comments on her drafts from an expert in the field. These facts can only make the conclusion more probable.

On the other hand, relevant respects of disanalogy weaken an argument. If we add that the teacher will be more demanding on the second paper than on the first, or that Joan will not be as careful citing her sources in the second paper, then it is no longer as reasonable to think that Joan will receive the same excellent evaluation on the second paper.

Irrelevant respects of analogy or disanalogy will do nothing to either strengthen or weaken the argument. That Joan takes notes for each paper using a blue pen is irrelevant to what grade she receives and will not affect the strength of the conclusion. In general, the more relevant we see the analogy to be, the more it is likely to help the argument and the more relevant we see the disanalogy, the more likely it will weaken the argument.

What makes a respect of analogy relevant? This is a difficult question to answer completely, but it does seem that relevant respects of analogy indicate a causal or explanatory connection between events or facts mentioned in the two sets of circumstances. Joan received an A on the first paper, and can expect to receive an A on the second, *because* she worked hard in the ways mentioned. Relevant respects of disanalogy work in similar fashion. If Joan fails to get an A on the second paper, it may well be *because* she didn't properly or carefully cite her sources in that paper.

Let's return now to *DESIGN*. The respects of analogy include the fact that both the universe and artifacts like the camera have parts that seem to be purposefully arranged. In light of this analogy we are asked to infer that the universe, like a camera, has an intelligent designer (which, in the case of the universe, we take to be God).

B. Assessing the Argument

A first important objection

Is *DESIGN* a good inductive argument? Is the analogy between the objects mentioned in the first premise and the universe as described in the third a good one? Should we expect the analogy to hold even further, making it reasonable to conclude that an intelligent designer produced the universe? Answering these questions will require us to consider several parameters by which arguments by analogy are evaluated. We will approach it by considering an objection David Hume makes in his *Dialogues Concerning Natural Religion*.

Hume appeals to a principle which states that in order to infer legitimately from a particular effect to a particular cause, one must have experienced that *same type* of cause and that *same type* of effect "associated" in the past. We can reasonably infer that a person has passed along the beach recently because we see a set of footprints in the sand. But this is only reasonable because we have previously witnessed footprints as the effects of people walking in the sand. The new effects are of the same type as the old: they are footprints in the sand. And the causes we can also expect to be the same: people have walked by.

We can see a similar sort of principle at work in the case of Joan's term papers. We can reasonably infer that Joan's hard work will yield an A on her second paper because in the past we have experienced the same type of cause (careful researching and writing) leading to the same type of effect (an A quality paper). Here we infer from a cause to an effect; in the footprint case we infer from an effect to a cause.

What about *DESIGN*? In this argument by analogy we are inferring from an effect (the various marks of design apparent in the universe) to a cause (an intelligent designer or God). Hume, employing the principle mentioned above, objects that the universe is not of the same type as the camera and other artifacts that we know to be designed by man. We have not experienced the designing of other universes in the past and so we are not entitled to infer anything about the cause of this universe. More precisely, what we observe when we claim there is apparent design in the universe is not the same as what we observe when we claim there is apparent design in, say, the martian camera. If Hume is right, then one can reasonably infer that an intelligent being designed the martian camera because we have past experience with the design of that sort of complex instrument. But we cannot reasonably infer that the universe had an intelligent designer because we have had no past experience with the design of *that type of thing*.

Hume's objection seems to depend on what type or types of things we are taking about when are talking about cameras and universes. A proponent of the Teleological argument might respond that the universe is of the same relevant type as the camera. After all, we said in the premises that both the universe and the camera were the type of thing that has parts arranged in such a way as to achieve a specifiable end. Cameras take photographs and universes evolve (or contain cycles of genetic mutation and adaption). And that, the proponent of the argument will say, is just the type of thing we have previously experienced to be associated with a designer.

The controversy that is brewing here is difficult to assess. On the one hand our argument has been constructed so that the universe and the camera are described as falling under the same type (things that have parts that seem to be purposefully arranged). Yet, on the other hand, one suspects that Hume is addressing an important concern. In many ways the universe is disanalogous with cameras (and other artifacts we might use as examples). The question we must ask is "Are these disanalogies relevant to the issue of whether an object is designed?" For example, the objects we know to be designed are all man-made, yet the universe is clearly not the product of human design. Is this a relevant respect of disanalogy? The strength of the argument hinges on the answer to questions such as this.

It is generally agreed that inductive arguments allow their conclusion to "go beyond" the premises in the sense that the conclusion has more content or carries more information than the sum of the premises. So, for example, to say that *all* cameras are man-made is to say something more informative (contentful) than that *every camera I've ever seen* has been man-made. The question we need to ask when evaluating inductive arguments is whether the conclusion goes *too* far beyond the premises: do the premises support the conclusion given the amount of information that it contains? Hume can be understood as claiming that the conclusion of an argument like *DESIGN* contains more information than the premises can support. Since we have never observed an event like the design of a universe, merely observing the "design" of artifacts like cameras and cars will not be enough to support the conclusion that the universe too was designed by an intelligent designer. The proponent of the argument, on the other hand, can be seen as claiming that arguments like *DESIGN* are reasonable, the conclusion does not go beyond the premises to the degree that it becomes unreasonable.

The above discussion marks a genuine difficulty in assessing inductive arguments. There is no easy rule to tell us when a conclusion contains more information than the premises can support. The value of an inductive argument is assessed by degree—there is no hard and fast measure like "valid" or "invalid"—and so perhaps it is to be expected that some arguments admit of opposing evaluations, as we have just witnessed in the case of *DESIGN*.

An objection against the conclusion

In evaluating *DESIGN* we have been looking primarily at whether the premises, if true, support the conclusion that the universe had an intelligent designer. But suppose we grant the proponent of this teleological argument that the conclusion is adequately supported. We might still question the conclusion itself. Does the argument show that the existence of *God* is probable? Concluding that there is an intelligent designer entails that there is something other than the universe itself that was responsible for the existence and arrangement of the universe. Consider for a moment what the traditional theist takes God to be: a single omniscient, omnipotent, morally perfect, and—it is typically added—everlasting and omnipresent being. Now, even if we ignore all the other objections mentioned so far, we should ask whether the "intelligent designer" mentioned in the conclusion must have these attributes. Must the designer really be *a single* designer rather than *many* designers? It doesn't seem so. Just as many objects of human design have more than one designer (consider how many designers are needed to plan an automobile), it is perfectly consistent with *DESIGN* that there are many designers. There is nothing in the argument to rule out the conclusion that the universe is the product of an intelligent committee. The argument, then, supports Polytheism as well as it supports Monotheism. Must the designer be everlasting or eternal? That doesn't seem to be necessary either. Perhaps the designer was produced by something else and perished soon after creation. Nothing in *DESIGN* precludes this. Again, must the designer be omniscient and omnipotent? It would seem not. To be sure, the designer would have to be greatly superior to us as far as "brains and brawn" are concerned, but this does not entail omnipotence or omniscience. Finally, must the designer be morally perfect? This question raises more problems for the defender of *DESIGN* than any other. It is often alleged, however, that given the evil in the world, the world just can't be the product of a completely good (and powerful) God. More will be said on this problem in section 5 of this chapter.

Let's briefly summarize what we have accomplished in this section. *DESIGN* is a teleological argument and, consequently, an *a posteriori* inductive argument. It is meant to support the claim that God exists. We have evaluated the argument on several grounds of assessment relevant to inductive arguments by analogy (of which *DESIGN* is an instance). Finally, even if the universe is the product of an intelligent designer, we are given no reason to think that this designer must have the attributes that traditional Theism has claimed to be God's.

Questions: What is an argument by analogy? Why is a camera compared with parts of the universe in the first version of the Teleological Argument? Why does the Theory of Evolution present a problem for this version? How is the argument revised? What is Hume's principle and how is it used to evaluate the final version of the argument? What objection can be raised against the conclusion of the argument?

Section 3: COSMOLOGICAL ARGUMENTS

Characterizing cosmological arguments

What is today called a *cosmological argument* came to have that name because its original defenders sought to account for the "cosmos" or the universe. Beginning with what are agreed to be obvious truths about the existence of a universe or of particular kinds of things in it, the argument proceeds from a need to explain why there is this universe (or why there are things of some particular kind in it at all) to the conclusion that there must be a God. Thus, like teleological arguments for the existence of God, cosmological arguments depend in part on certain empirical truths—truths known by our experience of the physical world. It is, again, a purported *a posteriori* proof of the existence of God. But unlike a teleological argument, whose premises (if true) only *support* its conclusion inductively, cosmological arguments are deductive: the premises, if true, genuinely *establish* the truth of the conclusion.

For our purposes, then, a cosmological argument is a deductive *a posteriori* argument for the existence of God. It turns out that there are three or four historically famous kinds, offered in some form by Aristotle, Aquinas, Descartes, Leibniz, and others. We will discuss two particularly interesting kinds that differ mainly in what sort of principles they invoke, alongside their empirical premise, to argue for the existence of God. One argument, which employs a principle about causation, is called the Causal Argument; the second uses a principle of explanation or "sufficient reason" and is called the Contingency Argument.

Before looking at these arguments individually, it must be noted that in fact we'll be looking at only *parts* of them. A completely filled-out cosmological argument consists of two parts. The first part argues for the existence of a particular kind of being—say a necessary being or a first cause. The second part would show that such a being has the properties traditionally associated with a God of Judeo-Christian Theism—say an all-powerful or eternal God. Historically, the philosopher has been mainly concerned with the first part, while the second part has received most attention by scholars concerned to treat Theism within primarily religious contexts. More recently this second half has been viewed as a task for both philosophers and theologians. In any case, since the first half engages the most philosophically interesting and important task of cosmological arguments, and since the success of the second half is parasitic on the first, we will attend to just the first parts of causal and contingency arguments.

A. The Causal Argument

Some initial attempts to develop the argument

In keeping with the motivation that originally gave cosmological arguments their name, we might begin thinking about the Causal Argument by simply looking at the cosmos around us. This huge physical universe with all its planets and stars and people and plants and mountains and atoms must have come from somewhere. Things don't just pop into existence. Rather, something else brings them about, as when you were conceived and born or when a volcano's erupting forms a new mountain. If you found a huge mountain outside your room one morning that was absent the previous night, you would reasonably ask "What caused *this*?" But of course that question can be asked of anything that happens, not only of the extraordinary. Thus we might reason more generally as follows: "The physical universe does exist, and so it must have a cause. That cause is God. Therefore, God exists."

Now there is an interesting line of thought lurking here, but, expressed as an argument, it stands in need of revision. Notice first that the claim "Therefore, God exists" is offered as the conclusion. What precedes this, then, are premises. But surely, stating "That cause is God" as a *premise* isn't legitimate, for it presupposes what we are trying to prove, that there is a God. Since that claim doesn't follow from anything preceding, employing it as a premise just begs the question.

Second, notice that the contention ". . . so it must have a cause" also requires support. One reason we might be inclined to hold that the universe must have a cause is that we believe that *everything* has a cause. That presupposition might be plausible, but then we certainly should include this causal principle explicitly as a premise. Indeed, we saw earlier that what distinguishes the Causal Argument from other kinds of cosmological arguments is its appeal to a principle about causation, and nowhere in the argument sketched above is that appeal made explicit.

So the argument above isn't a good one as it stands; it simply goes much too quickly. To see how one might preserve its basic line of thought without making either of the errors just noted, consider the following very old argument Aristotle offered about motion:

> If we look around us, we see that there are things in motion. Now whatever is in motion must be moved by something else. But there can't be an infinite series of previous movers, each moved by another. So, there must have been a first unmoved mover.

This interesting bit of reasoning has two features we should like a good causal argument to have. First, it argues for a being of a certain very special kind, without simply presupposing the existence of that being. And second, it includes a universal principle (the second sentence) that does seem true but which needs to be made explicit if the conclusion is to follow from the premises. A defender of the Causal Argument, then, might reason analogously to the argument about motion:

> If we look around us, we see that there is a physical universe. Now whatever exists has a cause, that is, something else which caused it. But there cannot be an infinite series of past causes,

each the effect of a previous cause. So, there must have been a first uncaused cause. (This being we take to be God.)

Remember that it is the second part of cosmological arguments, with which we are not concerned here, that engages the task of demonstrating the parenthetical claim at the end.

This is a far more promising argument than the one originally suggested. Indeed, it seems very compelling. No one wishes to deny that there are planets and stars and mountains and people and so on, making up the physical universe. And of this universe we may reasonably ask, "What *caused* it?" The general principle that everything has a cause makes that a reasonable question. Having offered an answer, we may of course ask for the cause of *that* cause as well. But now, we can't just keep asking the question over and over. The series of past causes cannot go backward in time infinitely; it must finally terminate somewhere. So, there must have been a first cause, i.e., a cause that is not itself caused (God).

(1) The universe exists.
(2) Everything that exists has a cause.
(3) There cannot be an infinite series of past causes.
(4) So, there must have been a first, uncaused cause (God).

A problem with this initial version

To say that an argument is compelling is to report a psychological fact, and of course it is with *logical*, not psychological, facts about an argument that a philosopher is primarily concerned. If what at first appears compelling can be shown on second (and better) thought to contain logical problems—an inconsistency, say—, then we must be prepared to reconsider the argument. To see that an inconsistency exists in this argument consider the following claims taken from the argument above. In the second premise we said that

(2) Everything that exists has a cause.

And in the conclusion we said

(4) So, there must have been a first, uncaused cause (God).

These are clearly inconsistent claims. If (2) is true and everything is caused by something else, then it applies to God as well. But in that case, there can be no *first, uncaused* cause, and (4) is false. To say that everything is caused is to deny that anything is uncaused. On the other hand, if (4) is true, there was a first, uncaused cause. But in that case not everything that exists was caused, and (2) is false. To say that something is uncaused is to deny that everything is caused. If the premise in question is true, the conclusion is false; if the conclusion is true, then that premise is false.

No defender of the Causal Argument can leave matters as they stand. What options are there for avoiding this charge of inconsistency? (4) is the conclusion, something a defender of the argument very much wants here. Premise (2) seems to be the place to focus our attention. One maneuver is to back off from (2) a bit and say, not that *everything* has a cause, but that everything except God has a cause. This revision of (2) is consistent with (4).

But surely this will not do. First, if we amend (2) explicitly in this way, we shall be guilty—as we were earlier—of *presuming* the existence of the being whose existence we are trying to *prove*. By claiming that God is the exception, we will have presupposed that God exists. And second, there seems little reason (save desperation) to demand causes for everything in the series except God. Why stop the demand for causes there rather than elsewhere? Indeed, why not lift the demand much earlier, say, immediately with the physical universe itself? In other words, why not make the universe the exception? But of course if we did this, the argument would never get started. Unless the defender of the Causal Argument can offer good independent reasons for stopping precisely where he suggests, we are left with no good reasons for accepting his proposed salvage of the argument.

A second maneuver is to say, not that everything is caused by *something else*, but rather just that everything is caused by *something or other*. In this case we may still conclude (4) that there was a first cause, where now God is regarded as self-caused. But introducing the notion of a self-caused being will only make matters worse. The only immediately obvious sense to make of "x is self-caused" is that x causes—and so exists prior to—x. But surely a thing cannot exist before itself. Yet suppose that's wrong. If x did exist before itself, then x already exists and there would be no causing of x left to be done. Either way, the second maneuver must fail.

A final version of the Causal Argument

The futility of emending premise (2) to recover from the objection of inconsistency suggests that something might be fundamentally wrong with the causal principle as we've stated it in the first place. Thinking a bit more carefully about causation might help us reformulate the principle more suitably. Upon reflection we see that physical *objects* (like planets and stars, etc., or the universe they make up) aren't caused at all. Rather, *events* or *states* of things are caused. An event is a happening of some kind; a state is a way a thing is. So, for example, your falling is an event and your being tanned is a state. When we say simply that you were caused, or that the mountain or the universe was caused, what we are really saying is that you (or the mountain or the universe) were caused *to come into existence*. Strictly speaking, then, we shouldn't speak of physical objects being caused, but rather of their coming into existence being caused.

This more careful reflection about causation suggests that our general principle ought to be about things being *caused to come into existence*, not about things being *caused simplicitor*. And now we're prepared to formulate a revised argument that is not inconsistent as we saw the first one was.

If we look around us, we see that there are physical things like people and trees and so on which were caused to exist. Now whatever is caused to exist is caused to exist by something else. But just as we saw in the case of motion, where something unmoved must initially *begin* the motion of a thing, so it is here that no series of past causes can stretch infinitely far back in time. So, an infinite regress of past causes is impossible; so, there was a first cause. This first cause cannot be something that comes into existence (for then it would need some prior cause) and it cannot be self-caused (that is incoherent), so it must be something that has always existed, causing other things to exist and yet not itself being brought into existence.

Here then is a much-improved version of the Causal Argument, which we shall call *CAUSAL.* (Notice how the first and second premises have changed.)

CAUSAL

(1)　There are things which came into existence.
(2)　Whatever comes into existence is caused to exist by something else.
(3)　There cannot be an infinite series of past causes.
(4)　So, there was a first cause (God).

An objection to the third premise

Earlier we saw how discovering logical problems with an argument forces us to give up favorable psychological judgments of it. *CAUSAL* has no internal logical difficulties of that sort. If the argument is valid, then, shouldn't we be compelled by it to agree that there is a God, or at least that there was a first cause? Not necessarily. Not every valid argument is sound. Thus we might remain unconvinced by *CAUSAL* because we think one of its premises is false. Now it seems clear that there *are* things which are caused to come into existence, and that such things don't cause themselves to exist. If premises (1) and (2) seem obviously true in this way, the source of any uneasiness would appear to rest with (3). Is it true that there cannot be an infinite series of past causes in time? What can a defender of *CAUSAL* offer in defense of (3)? There are a number of reasons one might give for endorsing the third premise, some of which have their origin in historically famous views of philosophers like Aristotle, Aquinas, Ockham, and Kant. Four defenses of (3) are discussed below. The first defense of (3) is fairly intuitive: it distinguishes the notion of an actual infinite series from that of a potential infinite series; it finds its earliest statement in Aristotle's distinction between describing a collection as infinite *per se* or as infinite *per accidens*. The last two are slightly more difficult.

A first defense of premise three

(a) A first defense of premise three might go like this.

> Premise (3) looks straightforwardly true, because it seems obvious that there can't be an infinite number of anything. That an actual collection or series of things could be infinite is simply incoherent. For example, suppose there were actually

an infinite number of red and white marbles in some huge expanse of space, the red ones corresponding with the odd numbers, say, and the white ones corresponding with even numbers. If all the white marbles were to be taken away, it would leave a collection of marbles no smaller than that with which I began. But it is absurd to speak of an actual collection of things, a subset of which is the same size as the whole set of them. We can make sense of there being a "potential infinite," in the sense that, one could just keep on counting out numbers—though of course however long one might count, one would have only enumerated finitely many numbers. It seems clear that cannot make sense of an actual infinite number of anything.

Now this last claim is very strong indeed. If something is impossible, then it fails to obtain at any possible world. Are we then to understand the proposition that *there is no actual infinite collection of anything* as a necessary truth? It certainly is not obvious that it is necessary. Or anyway, it isn't obvious that a contradiction follows from denying it. Moreover, many mathematicians and philosophers contend that we have a genuine *science* of an actual infinite collection, namely mathematics. We all know that the series of integers is infinitely large: for any number n, there is a larger number n+1. If such an infinite series has been treated by mathematicians without internal contradictions, then there is no reason to think that an infinite series of past causes can be ruled out on the conceptual grounds that "there can't be an actual infinite number of anything." No logical considerations count against an infinite series of past causes.

   (One might wonder, with all this in mind, how a theist of the traditional strain—a potential defender of *CAUSAL*—could actually endorse a view like (a). He says, after all, that God is *infinitely* powerful or good or knowing. Perhaps that is just a way of speaking, though it is not clear that it *can* be in every case. Suppose a theist endorses (a) to the extreme point of even denying that there are numbers. He still claims that God is all-knowing and the only candidates for what God knows are true propositions. God knows, for example, that 1+1=2. God also knows that 1+2=3, that 1+3=4, and so on. But there are infinitely many such true propositions. And since no talk of a potential infinite will be useful here (the theist will not wish to say that God knows only potentially), the theist seems committed to there being an actual infinite number of things God knows.)

A second defense of premise three

(b) A second argument on behalf of premise three is the following.

> Everybody agrees that an infinite series doesn't have an end—
> doesn't have a terminus or point of completion. But the series
> of past events does terminate, namely at the present moment.
> So that series can't be infinite.

If we isolate the premises and conclusions of this defense of premise
three we find:

(i)   By definition an infinite series doesn't have an end or
      point of completion.
(ii) So, any series which does have a terminus cannot be an
      infinite series.
(iii) But the series of past causes in time does have a ter-
      minus, namely, *now*.
(iv) So, the series of past causes in time cannot be infinite.

The argument is valid, but our earlier considerations show why it
is not sound. Think of the positive and negative integers as ordered
along the familiar number line. The series of positive integers (1, 2, 3,
. . .) does not, we might say, have a point of completion or a terminus:
but it does have a beginning, that is, a boundary at its first element.
Now consider the negative integers (. . . , -2, -1, 0). This series has no
beginning, that is, no boundary which is its first element; but it *does*
have a terminus or point of completion—a boundary which is its last
element. So (i) and (ii) in the above argument aren't correct. Indeed,
the simplest way to make sense of an infinite series of past causes in
time is to think of matching the present moment with 0, the previous
moment (or hour or day or whatever you choose) with -1, the moment
(hour, day) before that with -2, and so on infinitely far back. Since we
can make perfectly good conceptual sense of the infinite series of
negative integers, we can make perfectly good conceptual sense of the
infinite series of past causes in time.

A third defense of premise three

(c) Consider a third line of defense for the claim that there cannot be an infinite series of past causes.

> In any series of past causes, there will be an earlier, an intermediate, and a last element. Now if one eliminates a cause, one eliminates its effect. So, if one eliminates the first element of a series, one would eliminate the intermediate elements; and so, thereby, eliminate the last element too. Thus, in a beginningless series, there would be no first element, and hence no intermediate elements, and so no last element either. But that just means that there would be *no* elements of the causal series, which is absurd. Hence, a series with no first, intermediate, or last elements is no series at all.

The reasoning here is interesting, but it includes a subtle mistake. Consider carefully the sentence beginning "So if one eliminates the first element of a series, ..." No one will deny that, in a causal series which *does* have a first element, if one eliminates that first member one eliminates the subsequent ones. But that is not to the point. The worry is not how we can manage to eliminate the first member of a series and still have a (now beginningless) series, but rather why we *need* a first member in a causal series at all. The argument in (c) simply presumes that any causal series with intermediate and last members must have a first, but that is precisely what is at issue here. Someone objecting to premise (3) of *CAUSAL* wishes to offer a consistent picture of a causal series with intermediate and last members yet *without* a first member. One cannot show this is impossible with an argument requiring at the outset a series *with* a first member.

Indeed, the infinite series of negative integers embodies the sort of consistent picture needed to disarm the argument here in (c). Such a series is a beginningless series with only intermediate and last members. It is not true that a series with no first element can have no intermediate elements: all that is required for an element to be intermediate is that it be preceded and succeeded by some elements of the series, and *that* requirement will never ensure a first element.

A fourth defense of premise three

(**d**) Finally, one might defend premise three with the following argument.

> If the series of past causes were infinite, we would have to go through infinitely many of them to reach the present moment. But it's impossible to go through—to complete—any infinite series in time. So, were the series of past causes in time infinite, we should never have reached the present moment. Since we have reached it, the series of past causes in time must be finite.

This argument is, in a way, even more subtle than the defense of premise (3) offered in (c). By reminding ourselves of the picture modeled after the negative integers, however, we can see where it fails. Again, match the present moment with 0, the previous moment with -1, the moment before that with -2, and so on. Notice that *no* integer in this series is infinitely far from 0. Or, on the picture under consideration, no past moment is infinitely far from the present. And so it is *never* the case at any point in the infinite series of past causes in time that there were infinitely many elements yet to go through to reach the present.

When the argument in (d) suggests that "we would have to go through infinitely many of them to reach the present moment" it asks us to envision precisely what is impossible. It says something like this: "Go to the beginning—way down to the very front—of the infinite series, and notice that, from there, you've got infinitely many elements to go through to get to the end." But of course, the infinite series we are considering is the *beginningless* series of past causes in time, and so there is no beginning, no "very front," at which we are infinitely far removed from the present.

It seems clear that the weak spot in *CAUSAL* is its third premise, which states that there cannot be an infinite series of past causes. According to the objection to (3) we have been considering for several pages now, there seem to be no good reasons for believing that (3) is true. Unless the defender of this causal argument can disarm the present objection, the soundness of the argument remains in question.

Objections to the conclusion

In addition to evaluating the validity or soundness of an argument, one might also consider the challenges that could be raised against the conclusion as it is stated. Objections of this sort might be offered against CAUSAL. Consider then (4), the conclusion: 'There was a first cause (God)'. As stated, this isn't exactly what we should like to conclude. Even if we grant that we can identify the first cause with God, it is yet consistent with this conclusion that God does not now exist. If somehow I managed to prove that there was a Sahara Forest (where now there is a giant desert), I wouldn't have thereby proved that there is a huge forest in Africa called the Sahara Forest. If we should like to prove that there is a God, the argument must be appropriately reformulated.

But now suppose we do have the conclusion "There is a first cause (God)." Something is still quite wrong here. Recall that objects aren't caused, but rather events (i.e., happenings involving objects, like your falling) or states (ways objects are, like your being tan) are caused. Similarly, however, neither do objects cause. Causes of states or events are other states or events. Your falling (the effect) is caused by your tripping (a previous event which is the cause). Happenings, or things being a certain way, can cause other occurrences or things to be a certain way. So when we say that x causes y, the cause x and the effect y are events or states.

Clearly, then (and this is a second objection against the conclusion), we do not wish to identify God with the first cause: that would be to make Him an event or state. God is not a happening or a way something is, but rather an all-powerful (and so on) being. Indeed, it does not seem that (4) concludes with the existence of a being of the sort we wanted at all.

Some final considerations

These last two objections against the conclusion (4) suggest how we might construct a kind of cosmological argument taking a considerably different line. Perhaps talking about causation in this contemporary sense of events or states causing later events or states is wrongheaded as a context for an argument. After all, temporal entities like events occurring at times just don't seem to fit easily into our concept of God as an eternal but timeless being. Indeed, early proponents of cosmological arguments understood its causal versions atemporally (timelessly). God, and other members of the causal series, were understood to be what they called "efficient causes," where here the idea is not that objects are caused to come into existence, but rather that objects are sustained—objects are caused to *continue* existing.

Suppose we have some objects x, y, z, . . . etc. x's being the way it is now might be causally dependent in some way on y's being the way it is now; and y's being the way it is now might in turn depend on z's being a certain way now; and so on. As a rough illustration, consider that my existence now is somehow causally dependent on there being an atmosphere of an appropriate oxygen content at some appropriate temperature (etc) surrounding me now, which is itself causally dependent on the earth's spinning and being some distance from the sun now, which is in turn dependent on the mass of the sun and the earth (etc.) now, and so on. Or consider the relation of links in a chain to other links above it, where the chain hangs vertically from some support. Here, then, the "causal" sequence is not stretched temporally backward from event to previous *event*, but rather is meant to be stacked atemporally "upward" from object to "causally" or metaphysically prior *object*.

While this picture is not so easily formulable within our familiar contemporary way of thinking, one can easily see how reformulating *CAUSAL* along these lines would avoid our latest criticism of the conclusion about saying that there *was* a first cause, where causes were understood not to be *objects* at all. Such a reformulation would also avoid one's having to defend the claim that the world had a beginning in time—a claim which we also saw was problematic.

It turns out that the next kind of cosmological argument we consider has many of the features just sketched. In particular, it leans heavily on the notion of dependence, and is an atemporal version in the sense just noted above. Instead of offering a new version of the Causal Argument, then, we can see how those features are employed by moving on to this new kind of argument.

B. The Contingency Argument

Motivating the Contingency Argument

Remember that cosmological arguments are generally divided into two parts, and that we are concerned here only with the first of these. The first part begins with some obviously true empirical premise about the universe or about the existence of certain objects in it, and proceeds by way of a generally accepted principle to a conclusion about the existence of a particular kind of being. The Causal Argument attempted to show, by way of the principle that every event must have a cause, that a first (uncaused) cause must exist. In a similar fashion, the Contingency Argument attempts to show that there must exist a self-dependent being whose existence not only explains itself— i.e. its own existence—but also explains why there is a universe. We shift, then, from the question, How did the universe come into being?, to the question, Why is there a universe at all?

Let's begin with the obvious fact that a variety of beings exist. The kinds of beings that come most quickly to mind—planets, stars, people, plants, mountains—depend for their existence on the existence of other beings. As a living organism, for example, your existence depends on the existence of carbon and other elements, an atmosphere with oxygen, the sun, food and water for nourishment, and so on. And each of these items in turn depends on yet other beings for their existence. Notice that we are concerned with "dependence" here, not in the sense that the origin of x depends causally upon some earlier occurrence y, but rather in the logical sense that certain other facts or conditions y, z, ... are enough to guarantee that there is such a thing as x.

Now beings like these which depend on other beings for their existence are called *contingent beings*. In the framework of possible worlds, which often helps us understand better the notions of necessity and possibility, we can say that contingent beings exist at some but not all possible worlds. Plants actually do exist, but if things were otherwise than they are such that there were no sunlight, for example, or more drastically no carbon and nitrogen, then there would be no plant life as we know it.

We can contrast the idea of a contingent being with that of *necessary being*. A necessary being doesn't depend on other beings for its existence; it is completely independent or self-sufficient. Since beings of this sort don't depend on other beings for their existence, they would exist no matter how different the world was. Thus, we say they exist at every possible world. Many philosophers take numbers to be necessary beings. The number 39 exists, and it exists at every possible world because it is independent of the many possible ways things could be. If one were to ask why there exists such an object, it would do no good to answer by citing the existence of other objects or facts about other things: it isn't as if numbers exist only so long as something else does. One can only respond that the number exists by its own nature. More relevant to the Contingency Argument we're about to formulate, God is sometimes thought to be a necessary being. Traditional theologians have held that God depends on no other beings for His existence. God exists by virtue of the kind of being God is; it is by God's own nature that God exists.

Necessary and contingent truths and beings

An important parallel can now be drawn with contingent and necessary propositions (see Chapter 2, Section 3). Propositions are the sorts of things that are true or false. And not all truths are of the same sort. Consider first what we call contingently true propositions. A proposition p might be true, but (we say) possibly false, meaning that it is logically possible that not-p. In the language of possible worlds, p is true at the actual world, but it is false at some possible world.

A proposition p is a contingent truth just in the case that (if and only if)
    (i) p is true, and
    (ii) p is false at some possible world.

Consider what it takes to explain why contingently true propositions are true. Suppose someone says:

(C) It is snowing outside now.

What explanation might be offered for why (C) is true? One might reply: "Why is it snowing outside now? Well, because certain atmospheric conditions obtain: there is just enough moisture in the air and the temperature is sufficiently cold, to mention only a few of the conditions." (C) here just so happens to be true, then, because something else is the case, but it needn't be that way. (C) isn't true by its own nature, but rather depends for its truth on other things being true.

The main point here should be clear. Some propositions depend for their truth on something else's being the case: when we supply the reason for their being true, we must appeal to something other than that very truth itself.

A proposition p is a contingent truth just in the case that the
reason for p's truth is found in something else.

Now let's look at necessary truths. A proposition p may be true,
and (we say) not possibly false. In the language of possible worlds, p
is true at the actual world and it is true at all possible worlds.

A proposition p is a necessarily truth just in the case that (if
and only if)
(i) p is true, and
(ii) p is true at all possible worlds.

Consider what it takes to explain why necessarily true propositions
are true. Suppose someone says:

(N) Bachelors are unmarried.

What explanation might be offered for why (N) is true? One might reply: "Why are bachelors unmarried? Well . . . because bachelors are
unmarried! That's what it is to be a bachelor. What else can be said?"
In this case it doesn't just *happen* that (N) is true. Bachelors are by
definition unmarried, and so N's being true doesn't depend on
anything else's being the case: it is true by its own nature, and there is
no other way things could be that would make a difference.

A proposition p is a necessary truth just in the case that the
reason for p's truth is found in itself.

(There will, of course, be contingent and necessary falsehoods. A
proposition is contingently false if it is actually false but true at some
possible world; a proposition is necessarily false if it is actually false
and false at all possible worlds.)
 With the notion of explanation before us, return again to the ideas
contingent and necessary beings. We have discussed contingent beings
in terms of their existence at some but not all possible worlds:

b is a contingently existing object just in the case that (if and
only if)
(i) b exists, and
(ii) b fails to exist at some possible worlds.

But we also said that these objects depend for their existence on something else. Their existence can be accounted for only by appealing to something else.

> b is a contingent being just in the case that the reason for b's existence is found in something else.

Necessary beings were also characterized in terms of their existing at every possible world, existing no matter what the world was otherwise like.

> b is a necessarily existing object just in the case that (if and only if)
> (i) b exists, and
> (ii) b exists at all possible worlds.

We understand necessary beings to exist at every possible world because their existence is independent of the existence of anything else. The existence of such a being is accounted for by its own nature: it is "self-dependent."

> b is a necessary being just in the case that the reason for b's existence is found in itself.

Explanation and the Principle of Sufficient Reason

Now that we have characterized the nature of necessary and contingent beings, as well as necessary and contingent propositions, we can formulate the general principle that gives the Contingency Argument its force. To begin, notice that our two-fold distinction between contingent and necessary truths and beings is exhaustive: *every* truth is either self-explanatory or explained by other facts, and *every* being either exists by its own nature— is self-dependent—or depends for its existence on some other being. There is no third category of truths or beings that are neither contingent nor necessary. The implausibility of suggesting that there might be truths having no explanation (even ones we don't know about), or that there could be beings whose existence is without any explanation whatsoever, recommends an important general principle called the *Principle of Sufficient Reason* (PSR). For any truth, the principle tells us, there is some sufficient reason or explanation for its being true. And we can add that for any being, there is a sufficient reason or explanation for why it exists, something (perhaps itself) on which its existence depends.

In demanding a *sufficient* reason for some truth or the existence of some being, this principle demands a complete account. An account is complete whenever its being true is enough to guarantee the truth or existence of what it explains. So if one were to attempt to explain the fact that it is snowing by saying only that the temperature is now below 32 degrees Fahrenheit, the "explanation" as it is given would not be complete. This fact about the temperature alone would not be enough to guarantee that it is snowing. One would have to add that there is a certain amount of moisture in the air, as well as mention other facts about the atmospheric conditions (and about the general laws that govern such weather patterns), in order to provide a complete account—a sufficient reason for the fact that it is snowing.

This understanding of sufficiency is fairly rigorous. Ordinarily we might seem to demand less of a good explanation. But ordinary explanations will often fit this model, since we frequently presuppose some of the facts required for a proper explanation and ask only about others we're unsure of. Suppose, for example, I know it's cold enough to snow and that there is enough moisture in the air but still I ask why it is snowing. You might then reasonably explain why it is snowing by some of the general principles that govern this sort of precipitation. The information I already have and the information you supply would then be a complete account (or at least close enough to being complete to satisfy us).

In sum, the Principle of Sufficient Reason (PSR) asserts that

for every truth there is some sufficient reason (or set of reasons) for why it is true and for every being there is some reason for its existence, some being (or beings) on whose existence it depends.

A version of the Contingency Argument

We are now in a position to make an attempt at constructing a contingency argument. Like the causal argument discussed earlier, we aim to demonstrate that God exists by showing the need for a special sort of being. With the Causal Argument we tried to show that there must exist a first cause. Our particular aim in the Contingency Argument is to show that there must exist a necessary being on which the existence of our universe depends—a being whose existence is self-explanatory and whose existence also explains the existence of the universe. That necessary being we will take to be God.

We begin by noting the existence of our physical universe. In contrast to the Causal Argument, however, we now ask *why* this universe exists. By asking this we needn't be seeking a causal explanation: we are not asking how the universe came into being. Instead we are asking what sufficient reason can be given for there being this physical universe at all. Surely our universe is a contingent being, since it doesn't have to exist. None of the physical objects making up the universe has to exist, and so there are possible worlds drastically unlike the actual world, wherein many or all of these contingent objects fail to exist: indeed it is possible than no such objects exist, and there be no physical universe whatsoever. Thus, given that there is a contingent universe, and given PSR, it follows that the universe must depend for its existence on some other being or beings. Our universe does not exist by its own nature.

If the universe depends upon something else for its existence, what sort of thing might this be? It seems unlikely that it would be another contingent being. Such a being would itself depend upon some other being, and this being, if contingent, would likewise depend upon something else again, and so on and on without any final explanation unless we stop with something necessary. If this is correct, then the contingent universe must ultimately depend for its existence upon some necessary being. As a necessary being, it would be self-dependent and would explain its own existence. Such a being is reasonably thought to be God.

We have then the following argument that we will refer to as the Contingency Argument.

CONTINGENCY

(1) There is a contingent universe.
(2) For every truth there is some sufficient reason (or set of reasons) for why it is true and for every being there is some reason for its existence, some being (or beings) on whose existence it depends.
(3) An infinite collection of contingent beings cannot explain its own existence.
(4) So, there must be a necessary being (God).

In the previously mentioned *causal* version of the Cosmological Argument, objections based on temporal worries arise in several cases. Recall, for example, the difficulty in conceiving of a self-caused object: since causes are earlier than their effects, a self-caused object would seem to be a thing that exists at some time before it exists, and that hardly makes good sense. With the Contingency Argument, however, it appears that nothing particularly worrisome accompanies the notion of a self-explanatory being: like a self-explanatory proposition whose truth we can explain without appeal to any other truth, so a self-explanatory being exists by its own nature, without depending for its existence on any other thing. Remember too that we are asking why there is a physical universe, and not how the universe came about. Even if the physical universe turned out to have always existed, so that the question of its origin in time does not even arise, we should still like to know why this eternal universe exists rather than not.

What can be said in favor of *CONTINGENCY*? Are its premises true?

Defending premise (1)

As we have seen, premise (1) seems reasonably straightforward. It is implausible to suppose that our physical universe of past and present and future stars and mountains and phone booths *must* exist, by its own nature. That we must thereby regard the universe as a contingent thing follows from our acceptance of PSR, according to which every being must have some explanation for its existence. Since the universe does not exist necessarily, by its own nature, as a self-dependent being, it must depend for its existence on something else: it must be a contingent being.

Now it is tempting to understand this intuitive defense of premise (1) as an argument, to the effect that the contingency of the universe as a whole *follows from* the contingency of the parts making it up. This defense of (1) invites an important criticism from an opponent of the *CONTINGENCY*, who may properly object that the defense involves a logical fallacy: from the fact that every member of a collection is contingent, we cannot infer that the collection is contingent. This sort of inference, sometimes called the "fallacy of composition," is of the following form:

(a) Every member of U is thus-and-so;
(b) So, U is thus-and-so.

From the fact that every brick composing my house is two inches by five inches by three inches, it does not follow that my house is of those dimensions. Or consider that every member of the set of odd numbers is a number, but that collection is neither odd nor a number.

While it may be true that one cannot infer (b) above from (a), this does not mean that both cannot be true. It is true that each of the bricks composing my house takes up space, and it is true that my house takes up space. Thus, while it may not be a matter of logic that the second fact deductively follows from the first (perhaps laws of nature provide the connection), there nevertheless remains something to recommend the intuition that, since bricks take up space, a house composed of them will also. Suppose we agree that a single brick takes up space. Is there anything about adding another brick to the first which suddenly makes it the case that we now have two bricks taking up *no* space? Surely not. Consider, then, some simple contingent object like (say) a single atom or a speck of dust. It is perfectly easy to imagine that every other contingent object turned out never to have existed at all. The physical universe in this case would just *be* that single contingent atom or speck of dust. And should it have turned out that there were *two* atoms, that slightly more populated universe would also be contingent. Nor should the universe suddenly become necessary if we added one more atom, or a phone booth, or a mountain, or a star.

(Consider a slightly different analogy, very much akin to our earlier parallels between contingent or necessary truths and contingent or necessary beings. Suppose we have a contingently true proposition p. Conjoining it with another contingent truth q does not suddenly give us a necessary truth. We simply get the conjunction 'p & q' which is possibly false (contingent) since both p and q are. For example, let p stand for the proposition that Mitch went to the store, and let q stand for the proposition that Buffy has red hair. Each of these is a contingent proposition. Now to say that Mitch went to the store *and* Buffy has red hair—that is, to assert the conjunction 'p & q'—is just to assert another contingent proposition. It is possibly false because at least one of the conjuncts is possibly false. So, the analogy consists in this: just as no conjunction of contingent propositions is necessary, so it would seem no object composed of contingent objects is necessary either.)

It is fortunate that we did not need to deploy the fallacy of composition in defending premise (1). Our defense is simply that it is implausible to think of the universe as a being that exists by its own nature, necessarily: surely a different universe could have existed, or there might have been no universe at all, and whatever intuitions can be brought to bear in deciding—as we all surely do—that the things in the universe needn't exist, these same intuitions apply to the universe itself. Since the universe is not a self-dependent necessary being, and since PSR tells us that it's existence must have some explanation, it follows that the universe depends for its existence on something else: it is a contingent being.

Defending premise (3)

Let us move on to premise (3) of the Contingency Argument.

>   (3) An infinite collection of contingent beings cannot explain its own existence.

The intuition behind (3), recall, was that the whole of reality cannot consist of beings each of which depends for its existence on another being, because in that case we would fail to have an adequate explanation of the universe as a whole. But is this correct? Can't we respect the requirements of PSR and still deny (3)? By way of an objection to the Argument, suppose we try to account for the existence of the universe merely by accounting for each contingent being in the universe. Each of those contingent beings will presumably depend on some other contingent being or beings, these depending upon others, and so on. We might then have an infinite collection of contingent beings, each dependent on and explained by the existence of another. (As an illustration, suppose that your existence now is in part dependent on the existence of oxygen, which is dependent on the existence of an atmosphere around the planet, which is dependent on there being gravity, and so on.) Now even though our collection makes up an infinite sequence of dependent beings, there would seem to be no harm in this: PSR requires simply that everything have a sufficient reason—that for each contingent being there exist some other being(s) on which it depends. Supposing the universe is nothing more than a collection of all the contingent beings there are, if *each* contingent thing is explained, nothing seems left unexplained. Doesn't this suffice as an explanation of the universe as a whole?

Appearances aside, this objection fails: we would not have satisfied tPSR if we settled for this account of the universe's existence. For even if we explain the existence of each contingent being by reference to some other contingent being(s), something still lacks an explanation: we still have no explanation for *why there are any contingent beings at all*. In order to explain this fact, it seems clear we shall have to go *outside* the collection of contingent beings. Nothing *in* the collection explains why there is this collection (the universe) as opposed to nothing. Nor could it: if something in the collection explained the collection, the collection would be self-explanatory. But we already know from our discussion of premise (1) that the physical universe is not a self-explanatory, self-dependent necessary being. And so it must follow that, given the contingency of the universe and PSR, there exists a necessary being on which the existence of the universe depends.

Clearly our acceptance of premises (1) and (3)—and so *CONTINGENCY* itself—leans heavily on the Principle of Sufficient Reason. We turn now to a discussion of PSR, which is premise (2) of the argument.

Do we know that PSR is true?

Suppose we agree for the sake of the argument that the Contingency Argument is right about the contingency of the universe. Let's agree also that something remains unexplained if the whole of reality were a collection of dependent beings. An opponent could still refuse to agree that there is some necessary being on which the universe depends for its existence. "Why," such an opponent will ask, "should I agree that everything must have an explanation? Why couldn't the existence of this contingent physical universe be an unexplained, brute fact? In short, why believe that the Principle of Sufficient Reason is true?"

Like many general principles, including the principle at work in the Causal Argument that every event has a cause, the Principle of Sufficient Reason is at once difficult to defend and yet *prima facie* plausible. In this vein, some defenders of the Principle contend that it has the status of a necessary truth (and axiomatic for us), in the sense that it is known intuitively by reflection and not provable from something else more fundamental or more certain. There are of course propositions of this kind: "The whole is greater than any of its proper parts" and "Nothing can be red all over and also not red all over" express such propositions. But it is unclear that PSR has this status. As our objector illustrates above, it is hardly correct to say that PSR cannot be denied without contradiction, or that no reasonable person can doubt it. And even if the Principle is something we naturally find ourselves presupposing as true, we cannot infer from this that it is *thereby* true: presuppositions can be false. In short, we do not seem to be in the position of knowing that PSR is true. Thus, while *CONTINGENCY* might turn out to be sound, and anyone accepting its premises as true must rationally accept the conclusion, we can hardly say that the argument succeeds as a proof. Failing to provide compelling rational grounds for why we should accept PSR as true, we fail to give compelling rational grounds for believing the conclusion it is said to support.

Perhaps we can go even further in judging the reasonableness of believing PSR. One way that philosophers assess the acceptability of a fundamental principle such we are discussing is to consider carefully the *consequences* of accepting it. If those consequences conflict with other propositions we already find it reasonable to accept, then we know something has gone wrong. In these circumstances one might well decide the price to be paid for accepting the principle is too high. Of course, one might find the conflicting proposition more suitable for rejection if there is more riding on the principle than on the conflicting proposition. Either way, we cannot properly judge principles such as PSR unless we first consider their consequences. Let's look more closely at the work PSR does in *CONTINGENCY*.

PSR presents a problem

Recall for a moment what it means to say that x is a sufficient reason for y (as discussed above and in Chapter 2, Section 2B). First, remember that a condition which is *necessary* for y is distinguished from a condition's being *sufficient* for y. Its being 32 degrees or less is necessary for its snowing: if the temperature weren't at least freezing, then it could not snow. But freezing temperatures are not sufficient for snow—that is, freezing temperatures aren't enough to guarantee that it is snowing. Surely it is false to say "If the temperature is freezing or below, then it is snowing," since these temperatures could obtain in the presence of clear skies. Thus if x is a sufficient reason or adequate explanation for y, the truth of x will be enough to guarantee the truth of y. In short, y must be true whenever x is true.

With this view of sufficient reason in hand, consider now what the proponent of *CONTINGENCY* claims. According to her, PSR is true and everything has a sufficient reason, including all contingent facts about the universe; from this it emerges that a necessary being N is the sufficient reason for the existence of the physical universe U. As a necessary being, N exists at every possible world: "N exists" is a necessary truth. But then it must follow that U exists at every world too, for on our understanding of "x is a sufficient reason for y," y must be true whenever its sufficient reason x is true. In the present case, the sufficient reason for the existence of the universe U can be found at every world, since N is necessary. "U exists" is thus necessary as well: contrary to our best intuitions, the physical universe apparently is not contingent after all.

PSR looks to have demanded too much of us. In requiring that nothing contingent be unexplained, including the fact that there are contingent things at all, we cannot avoid locating the sufficient reason in something necessary. This in turn seems to render false our initial belief that the universe itself is contingent.

A response to the problem

In response to the difficulty outlined above it might be argued that something is amiss with our understanding of what a sufficient reason can be like. God is indeed a necessary being, but it is not God alone, or simply the necessary truth "God exists," that is sufficient for the existence of the physical universe. We must consider the idea that God freely chooses or wills that our physical universe exists, and not some other exists or none at all. This act of willing was a contingent fact, not necessary as God's existence is supposed to be. Consider the following fanciful analogy:

You are sitting in your room, and suddenly you notice a kangaroo standing next to you that you hadn't noticed before. A heavenly host of angels appears and says: "Fear not. For behold God has (ex nihilo) made it the case that there is a kangaroo for you in your office. Enjoy it." You look at your marsupial roommate and find her apparently indistinguishable from those now roaming the outback. After making arrangements to have her removed, a philosophically-minded kangaroo catcher arrives to say: "Look, this kangaroo seems to be just like all her down-under cousins. But in respect to her contingency, that must be wrong, because in this case it is a necessary being, God alone, which is the sufficient condition of her existence. Since God exists in every world, waltzing Matilda here must be a necessary being and so exist in every world as well."[2]

Clearly our kangaroo is not a necessary being, even if God does exist at every possible world. What the analogy seems to recommend is that, although God is indeed a necessary being, it is not simply the existence of God alone but also God's willing to make this or that world actual that should be cited as the sufficient reason for its existence. God may thus exist at every possible world, yet as a genuinely free agent, His willing to actualize our world instead of actualizing some other is a radically contingent fact. And this is what we should expect: if the physical universe is contingent, then the sufficient reason—the complete, adequate explanation—for "U exists" must consist not *only* in the necessary "God exists" (else U would then be necessary), but also in some contingent fact about God's willing as He did rather than otherwise.

This response does appear to salvage our intuition that the physical universe is contingent, and it seems to do this while still preserving the result that God is a necessary being. But it does so at the cost of re-introducing a new element of contingency into the picture, namely an act of God's willing. If PSR is true, there must be a sufficient reason for God's willing as He did, and here we face again the prospect of an infinite sequence of contingent explanations.

Questions: What is the initial version of the Causal Argument? Which inconsistent claims present a problem for the argument? How is the argument revised to meet the objections? How might someone defend the third premise? What objections can be raised against the conclusion? How does the Contingency Argument differ from the Causal Argument? How are contingent and necessary truths defined? contingent and necessary beings? What is the Principle of Sufficient Reason? What is the Contingency Argument? How might someone defend its premises? In what respect is the Principle of Sufficient Reason problematic?

Section 4: ONTOLOGICAL ARGUMENTS

What are ontological arguments?

The Ontological Argument has been a popular subject of philosophical debate since 1077 when St. Anselm first formulated it. The argument is important for us here in many respects. In the first place, it is a fine example of philosophical reasoning. The argument relies essentially on deductive inference and attempts to establish the truth of its conclusion *a priori*, through reflection on particular concepts, without any appeal to empirical premises. In this latter respect it differs from cosmological arguments. Second, although the Ontological Argument is not exempt from difficulties, the objections that have been offered against it provide important lessons for any student of philosophy. Progress in philosophy, as in any discipline, depends to a large extent on what can be learned from mistakes. By attending carefully to some traditional objections raised against the Ontological Argument we will become familiar with some important philosophical insights.

Just what is the Ontological Argument? In this section we will look at several different versions of the argument, though all are similar in crucial respects. The primary notion behind all ontological arguments is the view that we cannot be said to have properly apprehended the concept of God without acknowledging that it entails God's existence. Our understanding of God is of a being of a very special sort, a being that is maximally perfect, greater than any other being could possibly be. All ontological arguments attempt to lay bare this concept in such a way as to show that God's existence deductively follows from it.

A. Anselmian and Cartesian Versions of the Ontological Argument

Concepts and existence

That one should be able to derive the existence of anything from a concept alone is a very startling suggestion. To see this, it will be helpful to say more clearly what a concept is. Two quite different ways of thinking about concepts recommend themselves. First, there is a sense in which concepts are mental entities. Our individual conceptions of what a dog is might be different in certain respects; you might, for example, think of them as good pets and I might think of them as ferocious carnivores. Still, there is another sense in which it is correct to say that there is only one concept of a dog, a core concept, which we both share and to which we each have added our little idiosyncrasies. A dog, we can agree, is any animal belonging to the family *Canidea*. On this second view, a concept is not understood as private, subjective, mental entity, but rather as single objective, perhaps abstract, entity that we can all understand and share. Concepts are much the same as numbers and propositions in this regard: there is a single proposition that each of us understands when we understand that *All humans are mortal,* a single number we are considering when discussing among ourselves whether 37 is prime.

It is this latter view of an objective concept that concerns us most here. When understood in this way, concepts serve as objective criteria for picking out things of a certain specific kind, or discriminating it from other kinds of things. For example, the concept of a dog mentioned above serves to distinguish that sort of object from any other sort in the world: all dogs fulfill the criteria of being an animal of the family *Canidea* and nothing but a dog could satisfy the conditions. We call these necessary and sufficient conditions. They are necessary because an object *must* satisfy them in order to count as a dog, and they are sufficient because satisfying these conditions is *enough* to qualify that object as a dog.

Consider another example. What are the necessary and sufficient conditions for something's being a triangle? One necessary condition is that the object be a closed plane figure—nothing can be a triangle without being a closed plane figure. But this is not sufficient, that is, this is not enough: more must be added to rule out squares, circles and other closed plane figures from qualifying as triangles. Another necessary condition is that the object have exactly three angles (having exactly three sides would do here as well). This, together with the first condition, constitutes a set of necessary conditions which together are sufficient. Thus, a set of necessary and sufficient conditions for a thing's being a triangle includes its being a closed plane figure with exactly three angles. (We sometimes say that something is a triangle if and only if it is a closed plane figure with exactly three angles. The 'if and only if' construction is used to indicate that the conditions specified are necessary and sufficient.) This we will say is our concept of triangle. (For more on concepts see Chapter 2, Section 2B.)

We began a moment ago by noting how extraordinary is the suggestion that by simply reflecting on the concept of a thing, one might derive the existence of that thing. This strikes most of us as implausible. For even though we have the concept of a dog (say), we are not *thereby* guaranteed that there are dogs in the world: it is surely possible that dogs should fail to exist—perhaps they are suddenly eradicated from the face of the earth for some unknown reason, or never evolved—and yet we would still have the concept of a dog. So we would know what it would be for something to qualify as a dog even though nothing in fact does qualify as a dog. Likewise we have the concept of a river flowing with molten gold, or of a jolly fat man with a white beard living at the North Pole (except in late December). So the existence of a thing cannot be determined *a priori* by reflection on concepts: whether there are dogs, or rivers flowing with molten gold, or jolly fat inhabitants of the North Pole are empirical questions, to be answered by *a posteriori* means.

It is interesting to reflect briefly on the possibility of the opposite conclusion. Could the concept of a thing guarantee that the thing does not exist? Can we derive the *non*existence of an object from its concept? There are two sorts of cases to consider here. First consider the concept of a round square. The necessary and sufficient conditions for being a round square are that the object or figure be both round and square. Since it is obvious that this concept includes contradictory criteria and we know that nothing can exist which satisfies these conditions—that is, nothing can exist which is both round and not round at the same time—, we can be quite sure there are no round squares. Concepts that include contradictory criteria cannot be satisfied by anything.

We should also consider concepts that do not include contradictory criteria but which might nevertheless guarantee that nothing of that kind exists. Perhaps our concept of a unicorn is one. It seems correct to say that we typically consider unicorns to be mythical creatures or creatures of the imagination which resemble a horse and have a single horn in the center of the forehead. If its being a mythical creature is part of the concept, that is, if being mythical is one of the requirements for a thing's being a unicorn, then even if we find an animal which looks exactly like what we would expect a unicorn to look like, we can be sure that it is not really a unicorn. For if it is a flesh and blood animal, then it is not mythical. By requiring unicorns to be mythical, we seem to be guaranteeing that none exist. How we should think about mythical creatures, or creatures of fiction, is by no means a simple question. It remains a topic of philosophical debate. But the issue does yield interesting cases for our topic at hand, namely the relationship between the existence of a thing and the concept of that thing.

The Cartesian version

As a general objection against ontological arguments, the view expressed above—that existence claims cannot be determined *a priori* but must be answered by *a posteriori* means—should not deter us from moving ahead. We can, at the very least, cast reasonable doubt on this objection. Perhaps you can know *a priori* that you exist (since knowledge of your existence hardly requires, beyond recognition of the fact that you are presently thinking, any sort of empirical investigation); and surely no amount of looking and sniffing and listening will show us that there exists an odd number smaller than three. Let us see then how one relatively simple ontological argument proceeds.

Our discussion of God's properties has thus far been restricted to omnipotence, omniscience and moral perfection. This account of God's properties needs to be slightly expanded for the Ontological Argument. If God must have those three traditional properties specifically, it is because He is considered generally to have all perfections. According to Anselm, Descartes and traditional western Theism, God is the greatest, most perfect being possible: as such He must have all perfections. In the remainder of this section we will think of omniscience, omnipotence and moral perfection as perfections—properties that the most perfect of all beings would have. As we shall see, what motivates ontological arguments is the view that another property is required to make a thing perfect, a property that a being must have if indeed it is to be the greatest, most perfect being possible.

The simplest version of the ontological argument has more affinity with the argument René Descartes formulated in the seventeenth century than with the version Anselm presented, but it is helpful in elucidating some central themes. Descartes writes this, in the fifth of his *Meditations on First Philosophy*:

Certainly, the idea of God, or a supremely perfect being, is one which I find within me just as surely as the idea of any shape or number. And my understanding that it belongs to his nature that he always exists is no less clear and distinct than is the case when I prove of any shape or number that some property belongs to its nature.

. . . it is quite evident that existence can no more be separated from the essence of God than the fact that its three angles equal two right angles can be separated from the essence of a triangle, or than the idea of a mountain can be separated from the idea of a valley. Hence it is just as much of a contradiction to think of God (that is, a supremely perfect being) lacking existence (that is, lacking a perfection), as it is to think of a mountain without a valley.[3]

The main idea here is relatively straightforward. If anything is God, it must be perfect. Those perfections, which we commonly regard as necessary for a thing's being God, include omniscience, omnipotence and moral perfection. But it is further claimed that existence is a perfection, a perfect-making property. It follows, then, that God must have the property of existence. To say that God has the property of existence is just to say that God exists. Hence, God exists.

We can formulate the argument in the following way:

CARTESIAN VERSION

(1) God is understood as a being with all perfections.
(2) Existence is a perfection.
(3) So, God has (the property of) existence.
(4) So, God exists.

Like Anselm before him (as we'll see shortly), Descartes thinks that we all "have within us" the concept of God, even if some may not agree that such a being exists. So his first premise is available even to the unbelieving atheist: to assert that God does not exist still requires an understanding the concept expressed by 'God'. And once we understand this concept as properly including the notion of supreme perfection, Descartes thinks that we cannot withhold the property of actual existence to God. In this respect our concept of God is special, quite unlike our idea of a triangle (which can exist but needn't) or of a chimera (which cannot exist):

> . . . possible existence is a perfection in the idea of a triangle, just
> as necessary existence is is a perfection in the idea of God; for this fact
> makes the idea of a triangle superior to the ideas of chimeras, which
> cannot possibly be supposed to have existence.[4]

The notion that one sort of thing may be superior to another, in respect to whether or not it actually exists, figures in a slightly different way in St. Anselm's formulation. Having seen a relatively simple version of the Ontological Argument, we are in a position to look at Anselm's own rendition, saving our assessment of both until later.

Anselm's version of the argument

The CARTESIAN VERSION of the ontological argument has the form of what we call a *direct* argument: the conclusion follows directly from the premises without any additional assumptions. The version

Anselm formulates is somewhat different. This second formulation is said to be an *indirect* argument; more precisely, it is what we call a *reductio ad absurdum* argument. All such arguments attempt to show that an objector's denial of the conclusion can be reduced to an absurdity. We begin by assuming, for the sake of the argument, that our opponent is correct. We then try to demonstrate that a contradiction or some obviously false statement follows from this assumption. If so, we may then conclude that the initial assumption—the opponent's position—is false. Thus, by showing that the denial of the conclusion is false, we have indirectly shown that the conclusion itself is true.

For example, suppose someone contends that a round square exists. One might try to show her that she is wrong by following this line of reasoning: "Let us assume you are correct and that there is a round square. Since this thing is square and all squares have four corners, the object in question must have corners. Since it is also a round object and all round objects lack corners, we can be sure that the object in question has no corners. So, we have shown that this object which you claim is a round square *both has and lacks corners*. But surely this is contradictory: nothing can both have and also not have a certain property at the same time. Since a contradiction follows from your assumption, that assumption is false. There is no round square." (For more on *reductio ad absurdum* arguments see Chapter 2, Section 2B.)

St. Anselm's version of the Ontological Argument begins by assuming the thesis of the atheist that, although we understand what a thing must be like if it is to qualify as God, there is so such thing. The argument then proceeds to show that a contradiction follows from this assumption. Hence, the assumption is false and God exists.

Let us take a more detailed look at the reasoning. First, we can all agree that the concept of God is the concept of the greatest possible being: God is the sort of being than which none greater could be conceived. The atheist of course understands this concept, and indeed accepts it as expressing what a being must be like if it is to be God: if something is God, then nothing else is conceivably greater. Still, the atheist denies that any thing *is* God: like Santa Claus and the river flowing with molten gold, we can acknowledge that God exists in the understanding, insofar as we can understand what such a being would be if it were God, without acknowledging the existence of God in reality. Thus Anselm begins:

> And so, Lord, . . . we believe that thou art a being than which nothing greater can be conceived. Or is there no such nature, since the

fool hath said in his heart, there is no God? (Psalms xiv.1) But, at any
rate this very fool, when he hears of this being of which I speak—a
being than which nothing greater can be conceived—understands what
he hears, and what he understands is in his understanding; although he
does not understand it to exist.[5]

Beginning in this way, Anselm's objective is to show that this claim
of the atheist is absurd or even self-contradictory. If this is not immediately evident, it seems easy to demonstrate. Suppose (for the sake
of the argument) the atheist is right: suppose that God exists only in
the understanding, and not in reality. Now certainly existence in
thought (the understanding) *and* in reality is better than existence in
thought alone: in Anselm's view, really existing is a property that
makes a thing greater than it would otherwise be (in thought alone).
Compare that purely imaginary river of gold with an actual flowing
river of precious molten metal, or the purely fictional Santa with a real
fellow visiting real children in late December. Anselm wants us to see
that what exists in reality is greater than what exists only as an idea: an
existing river of gold is boundlessly greater than the mere idea of one,
which has no monetary value whatsoever, and the Santa of our imagination can do nothing so great as delight real children on Christmas
eve. So we can say that God, too, would be better or greater if He
existed in reality and not in thought alone, as the atheist presumes.

Now even if the atheist is right in asserting that God does not exist
in reality, we can at least conceive of a being like God existing in reality. But to do this would be to conceive of a being greater than God,
which on our atheistic assumption exists only in thought and not in
reality. And so it now emerges that, given the atheist's assumption, we
can conceive of a being which is greater than the greatest conceivable
being. Surely that is a contradiction. Anselm concludes from this absurdity that the atheist's assumption is wrong: God must exist, not
merely in thought but also in reality.

> Therefore, if that than which nothing greater can be conceived,
> exists in the understanding alone, [then] the very being than which
> *nothing* greater can be conceived, is one than which a greater *can* be
> conceived. But obviously this is impossible. Hence, there is no doubt
> that there exists a being, than which nothing greater can be conceived,
> and it exists both in the understanding and in reality.[6]

Anselm's Ontological Argument for the existence of God can be spelled out more precisely, following the informal statement of it just now given. As in the informal sketch, we will first state the concept of God (1) and assume for sake of argument that the atheist is right: God, the being than which none greater can be conceived, exists only in thought and not in reality (2). Then, we will offer the greatness principle: whatever exists in reality as well as in thought is greater than it would be existing in thought alone (3). Finally, we will add the obvious premise that we can at least conceive of God existing in reality, that is, we can think of a being that exists not only in thought but in reality as well (4). But then that being we are now thinking of is greater than the being we initially called "God." Thus it will follow that we can conceive of a being greater than God—greater than the atheist's view of God existing in thought alone (5)-(6). But that is contradictory: nothing can be greater than God. We conclude that the atheist's assumption is false: God doesn't exist in the understanding alone, but in reality also (7).

ANSELMIAN VERSION

(1) A being is God if and only if it is the greatest conceivable being.

Assume for the *reductio ad absurdum* argument:

(2) God exists in thought but not in reality.
(3) Existence both in reality and in thought is greater than existence in thought alone.
(4) We can conceive of God's existence in reality and in thought).
(5) So, we can conceive of a being which is greater than God.

Given the concept of God specified in premise (1), it follows from (5) that:

(6) We can conceive of a being which is greater than the greatest conceivable being.

But (6) is contradictory. So, the assumed premise (2) must
be false. It then follows that:

(7) God exists in reality as well as in the understanding.

The main idea behind the Ontological Argument is that we cannot
be said to have properly apprehended the concept of God without acknowledging that it entails God's existence. This is explicit in the indirect form of the ANSELMIAN VERSION of the argument, where
Anselm attempts to show that the atheist's view cannot be the proper
account of God: by assuming that account, we find ourselves in a
contradiction. Once we see that the concept of God is the concept of a
being that is maximally perfect, greater than any other being could
possibly be, we will see that the property of actual existence cannot be
withheld from God. In the Cartesian idiom, existence must be one of
the perfections God has. To say we understand the concept of God
while denying that God exists is like saying that we understand what it
is to be a triangle but denying that triangles have three sides or an in-
terior-angle sum of 180 degrees. In that case, as in the case with God,
either we have said something self-contradictory or else we have not
properly understand the concept after all. And so, like the
CARTESIAN VERSION, God's existence is in this way deduced *a
priori*, without any recourse to empirical premises.

Despite the appeal and cleverness of these arguments, scarcely any
student of philosophy has escaped the vague feeling that something
must have gone awry in them. It is time to see what might be said by
way of critical assessment. Since Anselm's argument is fresh in our
minds, let's begin with a famous objection to it.

The Perfect Island Objection

Not long after Anselm first formulated his argument, a monk named
Gaunilo offered a response. Gaunilo's objection was, in a way, that
Anselm's argument either does not work at all, or else it works too
well. The dilemma is an interesting one: certainly Anselm should not
choose the first of these options, but as we'll see the second would be
equally disastrous.

All of us can imagine a beautiful island. Presumably there are
many beautiful islands, most of which we have never seen. But might
there be an island somewhere out there that is not merely better than

any of the others, seen or unseen, but better than any possible island? Suppose we take an argument that is exactly like the *ANSELMIAN VERSION* in form and content with the exceptions that 'the greatest conceivable being' is replaced with 'the greatest conceivable island' and the name 'God' is replaced with 'Isle of Perfection'. The conclusion to this argument will be that the Isle of Perfection exists. In other words, if Anselm's argument works for the perfect being it should work for perfect islands (and perhaps even for the perfect dog-catcher and the greatest conceivable professor). As long as perfection requires existence in reality, then we can prove the existence of anything whose concept includes perfection. In the case of the Isle of Perfection we get the following argument (formally analogous to the *ANSELMIAN VERSION*):

(1) An island is the Isle of Perfection if and only if it is the greatest conceivable island.
(2) (Assume:) The Isle of Perfection exists in thought but not in reality.
(3) Existence both in reality and in thought is greater than existence in thought alone.
(4) We can conceive of the Isle of Perfection's existence in reality and in thought.
(5) So, We can conceive of an island that is greater than the Isle of Perfection. [From (3) and (4)]
(6) So, We can conceive of an island greater than the greatest conceivable island. [From (1) and (5)]

But (6) is self-contradictory.

(7) So, The Isle of Perfection exists in reality as well as in thought. [From (2) through (6) by *reductio ad absurdum* argument]

The conclusion that Gaunilo undoubtedly wants us to draw is that there is no Isle of Perfection, no greatest conceivable island. To suppose that by mere *a priori* argument we can establish the existence of a very special island out there in the ocean is absurd. But the perfect island argument exactly parallels the reasoning Anselm uses: so, Anselm's argument, like the island argument, must be flawed.

Now Gaunilo hasn't said exactly what is wrong with Anselm's version of the Ontological Argument. But we can say this much on

Gaunilo's behalf. Given that there is no Isle of Perfection, some-thing—either formally in the structure of the argument, or in the con-tent of its premises—must be wrong with the perfect island argument. Either way, the close parallel between the two arguments seems to guarantee that Anselm's argument goes wrong. For on the one hand, if Gaunilo's argument has an unreliable form, then so does Anselm's. On the other hand, if the form is unobjectionable as it seems to be, then we can only suppose one of Gaunilo's premises is false. But, excepting the difference in subject matter—an island in the one case, God in the other—, there are no kinds of assumptions made in Gaunilo's argument that are not also kinds found in Anselm's argument. So, it would seem that if one of Gaunilo's premises is false, Anselm should have a corresponding difficulty.

What might a proponent of Anselm's argument say in response to this objection raised by Gaunilo? One way of replying to the objec-tion would be to show that the two arguments are not really parallel or analogous in relevant respects after all. If they aren't appropriately analogous—either formally or with respect to some premise—, then one could agree that Gaunilo's argument does not prove the existence of a perfect island yet avoid being thereby forced to say that the ANSELMIAN VERSION of the Ontological Argument fails to prove the existence of God. We consider now two such attempts, the first of which is more general than the second, and somewhat anticipates it.

A first attempt to save Anselm's argument

(a) There are many categories of beings. Some categories are very restrictive in determining a quite specific kind of being, while others are considerably more general. The concept of a thirty-nine foot co-conut palm tree with six coconuts is very specific, and perhaps there are only a few things of that kind; the concept of a living organism is very broad indeed because there are countless things of that kind. And of course the concept of a *thing*—an object, a being—is surely our most general concept, because it does not specify a *kind of thing* at all. Everything satisfies the concept of being a thing.

Now Anselm has argued for the existence of the greatest conceiv-able thing. Gaunilo, on the other hand, has argued for the existence of the greatest conceivable thing *of a certain kind*, namely an island. This is clearly a difference between the two arguments, and perhaps it is a relevant difference. For a defender of the *ANSELMIAN VERSION* is surely right to insist that arguing for the existence of the greatest possible thing, in any respects whatsoever that contribute to greatness, is quite different from arguing for the existence of the greatest possible island or dog-catcher, in whatever specific respects contribute to island greatness or a dog-catching greatness.

Indeed, one might well argue that, while we can make good sense of the greatest or the best possible as it applies across the board to things generally, we cannot make sense of what it means to speak of a thing of a certain kind being the greatest of that kind. This points the way to a second, related objection to Gaunilo's argument against Anselm.

A second attempt to save Anselm's argument

(b) It is claimed in the *ANSELMIAN VERSION* that we can conceive of the greatest conceivable being as existing in reality. This does not seem to be a particularly controversial claim. If we do have the concept of God, then we can conceive of such a being existing, that is; we can conceive of a being that does have all of the properties required for a thing's being the most perfect being. As we discussed earlier, these required properties include omniscience, omnipotence and moral perfection; and we have added the property of existence to this list. Now properties such as these are what could be called *determinate* properties, in the sense that it is clear whether or not an object has them and there are determinate answers to such questions as, How knowledgeable must God be?, How powerful must God be?, and How good must God be? In these cases, the answers will all be the same: to the greatest degree possible; infinitely. In short, the characteristic properties traditionally ascribed to God admit of a natural, upper bound.

But now, what shall we say about the Isle of Perfection? In Gaunilo's argument it is claimed that we can conceive of the greatest conceivable island as existing in reality. Is this true? Let's first ask what properties such an island might have, and whether they are determinate properties as in the case of God. Perhaps there will be some disagreement about the Isle of Perfection, but let us suppose that the perfect island will have to be a tropical island with white sands, beautiful blue lagoons, colorful wild flowers and palm trees with coconuts. Are these determinate properties? Is there a determinate answer to the question of how many coconuts an island must have in order to be the most perfect conceivable island, or to the question of how many grains of sand the perfect island needs? No one answer seems to be better than any other. Given this, the proponent of the *ANSELMIAN VERSION* wants to point out that it is not so clear, after all, that we really can conceive of *the* most perfect island as existing in reality. For given any island we care to conceive of, we can conceive of another that threatens to be better somehow or other, perhaps having slightly more exotic wild flowers or bluer lagoons or more waterfalls or .... Such properties as typically come to mind when thinking of the greatest conceivable island seem to admit of no natural, upper bound.

If these latest reflections are correct, then we seem to have uncovered an important difference between the argument for the most perfect island and the argument for God. The difference indicates that one true premise of Anselm's argument has a false counterpart in the perfect island argument: we can make sense of the greatest conceivable being existing in reality, but we cannot make sense of the greatest conceivable island existing in reality. And so it may be that Anselm's argument for God succeeds where the perfect island argument does not.

Is Existence a property?

Let us return now to the *CARTESIAN VERSION* of the Ontological Argument. Recall that Descartes, like Anselm before him, thinks that we have failed to properly apprehend the concept of God if we do not understand this concept to entail God's existence. If anything is God, it must be perfect. Among the perfections, none of which God lacks, is existence, and to say that God has the property of existence is just to say that God exists.

What is obvious here is that the argument presupposes that existence is a property a thing can have. There is a famous reply to this presupposition, usually associated with the eighteenth-century philosopher Immanuel Kant. According to Kant, being or existence is not a real predicate. Kant did not mean by this that in sentences of the form "x exists", the word 'exists' is not a grammatical predicate; rather he means that 'exists' does not pick out a property, in the way that 'runs' picks out the property of running in the sentence "Smith runs." But long before Kant, in the 1640's, a contemporary of Descartes named Pierre Gassendi objected along these same lines, in a much clearer fashion than Kant himself.

> . . . what does not exist has no perfections or imperfections, and what
> does exist and has several perfections does not have existence as one of

its individual perfections; rather, its existence is that in virtue of which both the thing itself and its perfections are existent, and that without which we cannot say that the thing possesses the perfections or the perfections are possessed by it.[7]

Gassendi's point is that existence should not be considered one property among others that a thing may have, but rather that existence is a precondition for there being something to have properties at all. We might look at it this way: in ascribing a property to a thing we purport to say something more about the thing, about ways that thing is and how it differs from other things. But to say that something exists does not tell us anything more than that *there are* the things—that there exists something to have properties, whatever they might be.

Suppose we were to place a "wanted" advertisement in the local paper for someone to fill a certain professional position. We might include among our desired qualifications that the applicant have a Bachelor's degree, be willing to relocate, have 2 years of experience, and so on. We would not need to add to our list of properties "and must exist." We cannot imagine someone satisfying all the requirements *except* existing: anything having the mentioned properties must exist in order to have them. It is in this respect that existence is not a property that a being could have or lack. (Indeed, Gassendi would encourage us to see that it makes no sense to say that there is a thing that lacks existence. To say that there is the thing is to say that the thing exists.)

All of this applies no less to a being that meets the conditions for being God. If a being has the properties of omniscience, omnipotence, and moral perfection, then that being must also exist. Nothing could *have* those properties and fail to exist. It is thus a mistake to think that existence is one property among others that God has. There is, in effect, no difference between the concept of a being that is omniscient, omnipotent and morally perfect and the concept of a being that is omniscient, omnipotent, morally perfect and existing. Anything that satisfies the former concept will also satisfy the latter concept and *vice versa.*

Kinds of existence and Anselm's argument

To what extent does Gassendi's "existence isn't a property" objection apply to the *ANSELMIAN VERSION* of the Ontological Argument? There are a couple of ways that Anselm's notion of "existing in reality" might be understood, and Gassendi's point is relevant to both of them. One plausible way to understand the phrase "x exists in reality" is as expressing the notion that x has the property of existence. Adding that x exists "*in reality*" is redundant on this account, since reality is the sum total of all that exists, and so to speak of something not existing in reality is simply to assert that it lacks the property of existence. This reading of Anselm is plausible, first because his greatness principle (premise 3) seems to imply that a thing having existence is greater than a thing which lacks it, and second because his reply to the atheist suggests that we can conceive of a being having all the properties our atheist locates in the concept of God *plus one more* (existence). Gassendi's point is that this is the wrong way to think about existence: whatever lacks the property of existence can hardly be less great, since it does not exist at all. There is nothing that lacks existence, hence nothing that is less great than something that exists.

A somewhat different way of understanding Anselm focuses on the distinction between existing in the understanding (thought) and existing in reality. What might it mean for a being to "exist in the understanding but not in reality"? Anselm says that to conceive of something, or to understand something, is to have that something "in the understanding." To use Anselm's own example, when a painter first conceives of his painting, before he does any of the work, his painting is said to exist in the understanding but not in reality. After the process of painting is completed the painting can be said to exist also in reality. This suggests a view according to which there are different kinds (or levels) of existence. For example, imaginary or fictional characters might be said to have a kind of existence unlike the kind enjoyed by nonfictional, "flesh and blood" individuals. There are at least two kinds of beings: real beings out there in the world and imaginary ones. All of them exist, but they exist in different ways. Thus unicorns and rivers flowing with molten gold and Santa Claus exist, but they do so in a way unlike horses and the Amazon and the Pope. Surely, it might be argued, when we imagine something or talk about Santa or unicorns, there must be something about which we are thinking or talking. If we say that unicorns are mythical beasts, or that round squares are impossible objects, we are saying something about something. These beings may not exist in reality, in the same way that you and I exist, but they exist nevertheless. They exist in the understanding, not in reality.

This may be the sort of thing Anselm has in mind when he says that the atheist holds that God exists in the understanding but not in reality. God has existence in one sense, for the atheist, but not in the sense that you or I or the Pope do.

Do we have to agree that there are kinds of existence?

There are several things to say about this account. First, we can of course agree that there are different kinds of *beings*, without also insisting upon different kinds of *being* (existence). Existence need not be different whenever there are different kinds of existents (existing things). Indeed, to say that there are ways of existing seems rather like saying that there are ways of being a car—being a Ford, being a Chevy, being a sedan, being a hatchback. Surely that isn't right. There are kinds of cars, not ways of being a car. And so, if there are imaginary or fictional or impossible objects, we can properly say that they exist, all in the same, single sense of 'exists'.

But second, perhaps there are no imaginary or fictional objects. It is, in any case, wrong to claim that whenever we properly describe our talk as "talk about imaginary or fictional or impossible objects," we are commited to the existence of such objects. Such a claim may stem from the mistaken belief that whenever we use a noun or apparent subject term in normal, everyday speech, there must be some existing thing of the appropriate sort answering to it. If you see a cat in the road and announce "I see Felix in the road," then there is an object (the cat) to whom you refer, whose presence in the road makes your claim true. But suppose the road is empty and you you see nothing. Is there something—a "nothing"—that you see?

Consider another example. It would be a mistake to suppose that "The average American family has 2.3 children" expresses a truth only so long as there exists some family out there which is the average American family, and indeed one that has 2.3 children. The truth we express with those words is actually a quite complicated one: it is not about any family and their children, but about all the families in America and a mathematical fact about the number of children relative to the number of families. In this case, the supposed subject-term "average American family" serves as a useful fiction to abbreviate something much more complicated.

Other cases differ in details, but share the same moral. When we speak of Sherlock Holmes or Santa Claus or Unicorns or rivers flowing with molten gold, we may speak truly without being commited to any such objects. We may be expressing a very complicated conditional (to the effect that if the world were different in such-and-such a way, then . . .), or we may be speaking in the context of a language game of pretense or make-believe (where participants only speak *as if* they are referring to some character of fiction). The moral is simply that linguistic practices are suitably complex enough to permit the rejection of imaginary or fictional objects.

Concepts and objects

This brings us to an important third point, immediately relevant to Anselm's Ontological Argument and his distinction between existence in reality and existence in the understanding. It is surely true that unicorns and Santa and the river of molten gold do not exist in reality. But there is something, namely the *concepts or ideas* of these entities, which do exist and which might be the implicit subjects of common talk that we describe as "talk about imaginary objects." These concepts or ideas are not at all like horses or the Pope or the Amazon, and so may be usefully described as existing—not in the world of flesh-and-blood animals and people and rivers, but "in the understanding." Thus when we say that unicorns don't exist, there needn't be a fictional unicorn existing in some special sense, about which I am talking; rather we can be understood to say that there is nothing in the world that satisfies the conditions specified by our concept of a unicorn. Similarly for Santa and the river flowing with precious metal. There are no such fictional or imaginary objects, but there are concepts of these, and we express the contents of such concepts when saying, misleadingly, that Santa is fat or that the river is priceless. (Such talk is misleading because no concept is fat, or flows, or has a horn. Rivers flow, but concepts of rivers do not.)

What this latest point recommends is that "existing in reality" and "existing in the understanding" should be seen to distinguish not kinds of existence which some thing might enjoy or not, but rather kinds of objects that one and all exist. The atheist may then be understood to agree that God is the greatest being possible. She agrees, that is, that this is our concept of God, treating that concept like the concepts of the unicorn and Santa and the golden river. All alike are fictional or imaginary insofar as nothing out in the world answers to them.

Can Anselm's version be repaired?

Suppose now that we consider the *ANSELMIAN VERSION* of the Ontological Argument in this light. The atheist says that God exists only in the understanding, not in reality, which is to say that we have the concept of God, but there is no being that satisfies this concept. Anselm's greatness principle asserts that a thing's existing in reality is greater than its existing only in the understanding. How are we to understand this premise (3)? What sort of thing does he have in mind which, though existing only in the understanding, would be greater if existing in reality? On the one hand, our present view suggests that it means that our concept of God would be better if it *were* God, which is silly. On the other hand, Anselm can hardly be talking *only* about the concept of God. Whether or not God exists, our single concept of God exists, and the concept can hardly be greater or less great than itself.

This reasoning suggests an alternative—that the atheist's concept of God fails to include the property of existence, which it must include if it is to be consistent with the notion of the greatest conceivable being. This accords nicely with Anselm's claim that we can conceive of a being greater than the being our atheist has conceived of. But as we noticed earlier, existence is not a property. There is in effect, no difference between the concept of a being that is omniscient, omnipotent and morally perfect and the concept of a being that is omniscient, omnipotent, morally perfect and existing.

It would appear that the efforts of Anselm and Descartes, to argue for the existence of God on purely *a priori* grounds by reflecting only on the concept of God, do not succeed. But we cannot yet say with much confidence that no Ontological Argument is successful. There remains one further version of the Argument, to which we now proceed.

B. The Modal Version of the Ontological Argument

Necessary and contingent beings

The notions of possibility, contingency and necessity have been discussed earlier, in a somewhat different context. Since these concepts are central to our present discussion, however, a brief reminder is in order.

Initially the terms 'possible', 'contingent' and 'necessary' were discussed in connection with *truth*, but we saw that there is also a use of these terms that applies to *existence*. A possible being is a being that could exist, i.e., exists at some possible world. (We will use the term 'being' to refer to objects of any kind. By our usage, then, not only are humans and other living things beings, but so are chairs, molecules and numbers.) Now there are two distinct kinds of possible beings. There are beings that exist at some but not all possible worlds. Hence, we may say of these beings that they both possibly exist and possibly do not exist. Anything that satisfies these conditions is called *contingent*. Perhaps a more natural way of describing contingent beings is to say that they are beings that either don't actually exist but might, or that actually do exist but might not have. Human beings are contingent beings, as are desks, mountains, stars and daffodils.

The other kind of possible being is called a *necessary* being and is such that it exists at every possible world; we might say that it is impossible that it fails to exist. At first we might not think we encounter many necessary beings, but indeed there are quite a few. Numbers, for example, are beings that must exist at every possible world. It is utterly impossible that, say, the number four should fail to exist at some possible world. (What would such a world be like?) Other examples of necessary beings include propositions and, perhaps, objective and abstract concepts as we discussed earlier.

Even if we are correct in saying, as we did above, that existence is not a property, this does not rule out the legitimacy of saying that necessary existence is a property. Necessary existence is the property of existing at every possible world. It is true that a being must exist to have this property, but such a property does indeed add something to the concept of a thing. To say that x exists is not to tell you anything about any of the properties that x has, but to say that x exists in every room of this building is to tell you something about x, namely, where x is. Thus, one of x's properties is the property of existing in every room of this building (suppose, for example, that x is an odor). Or to say that x exists at every moment in time is to say something informative about x: it is not just saying that x exists but that x is (or has the property of being) eternal. Similarly, to say that x has necessary existence is to say something informative about x: x exists at every possible world, or equivalently, x is a necessary being.

Consequently, if some concept of a thing includes its having necessary existence, then *if* a being that satisfies that concept exists, it will be a necessary being. That is, if it exists at all, it must exist in every possible world. And conversely, if nothing satisfies the concept, then in no possible world is there a thing of that kind (in this case we then call such a concept the concept of an impossible being). As we noted earlier, the number four is a clear example of a necessary being since all numbers exist at every possible world. On the other hand, round squares are impossible beings because we conceive them to have contradictory attributes. Such a thing doesn't exist at any possible world because nothing could satisfy that sort of concept.

A more detailed example might help. Consider the following hypothesis in mathematics (we will refer to it as "H").

H: Every even number is the sum of two prime numbers.

One might at first suspect that this hypothesis is true. It seems that for every even number we can think of there can be found two prime numbers that when added together equal that even number. Two is the sum of one and one; four is the sum of one and three; six is the sum of five and one; and so on. In fact, the famous mathematician Christian Goldbach conjectured that it is true. This hypothesis, however, has not been proved—it is difficult to see how it could be. Must we check every even number one by one? There are infinitely many of them; the task is seemingly impossible. Could we falsify this hypothesis? Yes, if we could find an even number that is not the sum of two prime numbers. Let us call such a number a "Goldbach number" and define it in the following way:

Something is a Goldbach number if and only if it is an even number that is not the sum of two prime numbers.

The idea is that if there is a Goldbach number, then our hypothesis, H, is false. The real question is whether or not there is a Goldbach number. We have not found one yet; but then we have not looked at all the numbers (we have not even devised computers to look at all the numbers—remember there are infinitely many of them). We also know something else about a Goldbach number: not only will it be an even number that is not the sum of two prime numbers, but, since it will be a number and all numbers are necessary beings, it will have to be a necessary being.

So, we have the concept of a certain kind of number (a Goldbach number), but we do not know whether there is such a thing. We do know that *if* it does exist, then it must exist at every possible world; and if it doesn't exist (if H is a true hypothesis), then at no world is there a Goldbach number. Since we do not know whether a Goldbach number exists, we can only say that it is either a necessary being or a impossible being (existing at no possible worlds); when it comes to the possibility of such a number, it is an "all-or-nothing" being.

God as a necessary being

How does this notion of a necessary being or of necessary existence relate to the concept of God? It has been suggested in connection with Anselm's Argument that the concept of God involves all perfections: if anything is God, then it must be omniscient, omnipotent and morally perfect. In discussing that argument we saw that it required existence in reality to be a perfection. This, however, was deemed inappropriate. But now we can add a slightly different perfection to the list, one that avoids the difficulties that arise when we think of existence *simplicitor* as a property but that nonetheless captures what is essential to any ontological argument. This is the property of necessary existence. Consider the following argument:

(1) If anything is God, then it is the most perfect being.
(2) Anything that is contingent cannot be the most perfect being.
(3) So, God cannot be a contingent being.
(4) So, If anything is God, it must be a necessary being.

It is not clear how good an argument this is. Although (1) is true merely because it states the concept we are using of God, (2) is questionable (at least it is not obviously true). Perhaps a better way to see the plausibility of the suggestion that the concept of God includes necessary existence is to consider two beings, one that is omniscient, omnipotent and morally perfect but only contingent (exists in some possible worlds but not in all) and another that has all the perfect-making properties and is a necessary being. It seems correct to say that the necessary being is better or more perfect than the contingent being. If so, then necessary existence should be included among the perfect-making properties.

It might be added in support of the second premise that traditionally it has been thought that a god worthy of worship must not be a being that is merely accidental or contingent. The God of traditional Theism is eternal and immutable and doesn't simply happen to exist but in some sense must exist if it exists at all. As Anselm has noted, one cannot conceive of God as possibly failing to exist.

A version of the argument

Given the above discussion of God and the property of necessary existence, we can construct a so-called "modal" version of the Ontological Argument for the existence of God. (It is called "modal" because it relies on notions like possibility and necessity that are sometimes considered to be *modes* or *ways* a thing can be true or exist). It is important to emphasize that it is an ontological argument, for it begins merely by considering the nature or concept of God. Most significantly, it employs the requirement that we have just argued for above: that if anything is God, it must be a necessary being, or equivalently, it must have the perfect-making property of existing necessarily.

The argument goes roughly as follows. Our concept of God requires that such a being be perfect. In addition to omniscience, omnipotence and moral perfection, the perfect-making property of necessary existence is required, for a being that is merely contingent or accidental could not be the most perfect being possible. But this is just to say that no being that exists in some possible worlds but not others could qualify as God. As we conceive of God, then, either He exists at all possible worlds or He doesn't exist at any possible worlds; He is an all-or-nothing being. Now if we go on to claim, as seems quite reasonable, that it is possible that God exists, what we are claiming is that there is some possible world at which God exists. But, as we noted above, given that God is conceived to be the kind of being that cannot exist at some possible worlds and fail to exist at others, it follows from our claim that it is possible that God exists that He exists at every possible world, that is, He exists necessarily. Of course, if God exists at every possible world, then since the actual world is a possible world, God must exist at the actual world. Hence, God exists.

In short, all we need to do is recognize that it is possible that God exists, for, given that our concept of the most perfect being requires such a being to have necessary existence, if it is even possible that God exists, then it must also be necessary that God exists. We can capture this reasoning in the following argument.

MODAL-I

(1) If it is possible that God exists, then it is necessary that
      God exists.
(2) It is possible that God exists.
(3) So, It is necessary that God exists.

In an effort to make the argument even more perspicuous, we will
attend to each premise separately. Premise (1) follows from the very
concept of God. If it is part of our concept of God that He exists necessarily if at all (that is, if the concept of God includes necessary existence as one of the required perfections), then it will be true that if it is
even possible that He exists, it is necessary that He exists. Now,
premise (1) does not claim that God does exist or that it is even possible that God exists. It merely states that if God is possible, then He
exists necessarily.

Premise (2) also seems unobjectionable. A proponent of the argument might defend it in this way. Surely even the atheist will want to
claim that it is possible that God exists; he just denies that God actually exists. So it is possible that God exists just as it must be admitted
by the theist that it is possible that God does not exist.

If we accept both premises, then since the argument is valid, we are
committed to accepting the conclusion. And if it is necessary that God
exists, then He exists in every possible world. Since the actual world is
one of those possible worlds, God can be said to exist in the actual
world. It seems we have proven that God exists.

Different senses of possibility

But we must not be too hasty in assessing the argument above. We
should first consider a distinction between different senses of possibility. Something is *logically* possible if it is possible given the laws of
logic; this is the broadest notion of possibility available to us.
Something is *physically* possible if it is possible given the actual laws
of nature. And something is *epistemically* possible if it is possible
given what we know. We must take a closer look at this notion of
epistemic possibility.

Suppose you are presented with an addition problem involving
several very large numbers—much too large for you to do the problem in your head; the problem $2,361,002 + 1,003,740 + 117,169 = ?$
will do. You are then asked whether the answer could possibly be

3,482,911. "Well, that's possible," you say, "without doing the problem I don't know of course, but given the size of the numbers to be added, and what I know about addition, etc., I would think that your suggestion is pretty close. I certainly wouldn't want to say that it is impossible for your suggestion to be correct. So, it must be possible." The interesting thing about this case is that the answer is a possible one given what you know about the size of the numbers to be added and the number of them, etc., but this need not mean that the answer is possibly correct given *the laws of mathematics and logic*. (For convenience we will lump together both mathematical and logical possibility.) Suppose the numbers in question in fact add up to 3,481,911 (they do). Of course, given the laws of mathematics no other answer is possible: the numbers involved can only add up correctly to one particular number, and the initially suggested number was not it. We might say there is no possible world in which those very numbers add up to 3,482,911—it is impossible (logically). In this case, then, what was appropriately said to be possible in the epistemic sense (given what you knew about the numbers before you added them together), was impossible in the logical and mathematical sense.

Look now at an example of a logical, and even physical, possibility that is epistemically impossible. One of the things you know right now is that there is a page of text in front of you. (Let's presuppose that skepticism is not an issue here.) It is logically possible that there is no page in front of you. The claim "There is no page in front of me now" is not self-contradictory (unlike the claim "There is a married bachelor," which is self-contradictory). Moreover, it is physically possible that there is no page in front of you right now. The laws of nature do not rule out such a possibility. But it is epistemically impossible. Why? Given what you know—namely, that there is a page in front of you right now—it is impossible. The claim that there is no page in front of you is inconsistent with (that is, contradicts) something you know. Hence, just as we previously saw that what is epistemically possible need not be logically possible, so here we see that what is logically or physically possible need not also be epistemically possible.

This distinction between the epistemic and the other notions of possibility can be applied to a case we mentioned earlier. Recall the mathematical hypothesis, H (every even number is the sum of two prime numbers), and the notion of a Goldbach number (any even number that is not the sum of two prime numbers) discussed above. Is such a number possible? Our immediate reaction might be to say "Yes, of course it is. Certainly we want to say it might exist, and it is just as correct to say it might not." But in what sense of possibility is this intended?

First consider the claim that it is logically possible that a Goldbach number exists. To say that it is logically possible that there is such a number is to say that there is at least one possible world in which a Goldbach number exists, just as the claim that, say, it is logically possible that blue horses exist means that there is at least one possible world in which there are blue horses. But there is an important difference. A blue horse would be a contingent being; so, it would exist at some but not all possible worlds. In other words, not only is it logically possible that a blue horse exists, but it is also logically possible that a blue horse fails to exist (indeed, that is actually the case). A Goldbach number, however, because it would be a number and all numbers are necessary beings, cannot exist at some possible worlds and fail to exist at others. If I claim, then, that a Goldbach number exists at *some* possible world, I have committed myself to the claim that a Goldbach number exists at *every* possible world. Hence, I cannot further claim that there is a possible world at which there is no Goldbach number. And, hence, I cannot further claim that it is logically possible that a Goldbach number does not exist. Note that this is all because numbers are necessary, not contingent, beings. As such, if it is logically possible that one does exist, it cannot also be logically possible that it doesn't exist, and *vice versa*. This marks no trouble for contingent beings like horses: it is both logically possible that they do exist and logically possible that they don't.

Now, however, we must address the question of whether it is logically possible that a Goldbach number exists. As we said when we first introduced the notion, we don't know whether it is true or not that every even number is the sum of two prime numbers (that was our hypothesis H). Consequently, we don't know if there is a number that is even yet not the sum of two primes (that was what we called a Goldbach number). This puts us in a position similar to the position we were in regarding the complicated addition problem above. There we said it was possible that the suggested answer was correct even though we hadn't done the calculation and so didn't know what the correct answer was. This we decided had to be the *epistemic* sense of possibility: nothing we knew about the problem ruled out that answer. But only one answer was the *logically* possible answer and since we hadn't done the calculation, we didn't know what it was. Thus, we couldn't say that the suggested answer was the *logically* possible one.

We simply didn't know and as it turned out it wasn't. Analogously, in the Goldbach number case, we don't know if it is logically possible for a Goldbach number to exist. If it is logically possible, then one does indeed exist (if a Goldbach number exists at one possible world, it must exist at all possible worlds including the actual world). We simply don't know. When we find ourselves claiming that it seems possible that there should be such a number (and perhaps possible that there isn't one), we can see that we must mean possible in the epistemic sense. That is, nothing I now know about numbers rules out the existence of such a number, and nothing rules it in. We may conclude, then, that it is epistemically possible that there is a Goldbach number and it is epistemically possible that there is not one. But with regard to the logical possibility of a Goldbach number, we just don't know. (For more on epistemic possibility see Chapter 2, Section 3.)

The dilemma of premise (2)

We are now in a position to look more closely at the modal version of the Ontological Argument (*MODAL-I*) presented above. What sense of possibility is being used? Recall that the first premise states that if it is possible that God exists, then it is necessary that God exists. Here we must mean that if it is *logically* possible that God exists, then it is *logically* necessary that God exists. Why? We are arguing for the existence of God and we want to conclude that it is logically necessary that God exists, i.e., that he exists in all possible worlds including the actual one. To use the epistemic sense here would allow us only to show that *for all we know* God exists necessarily; but we want to show that God *does* exist necessarily.

Now, if the argument is to be valid, the 'possible' in the second premise—stating that it is possible that God exists—must mean the same as the 'possible' in the first premise. To have it otherwise would be to commit the fallacy of equivocation (see Chapter 2, Section 1B). Consider the following example of such a fallacy:

(1) I put all my money in the bank.
(2) The bank is where I stand to fish.
(3) So, I put all my money where I stand to fish.

This argument works—that is, it can be guaranteed the conclusion is true—only if the premises are true and the argument is valid. But the argument will be valid only if the word 'bank' in the first premise means the same thing as the word 'bank' in the second premise. Suppose, as the most obvious reading suggests, I mean 'First National Bank' in the first premise and 'river bank' in the second. Even if both premises are true, it will not follow that I put all my money in the river bank. To use the same word in different premises with different meanings is to equivocate, and that renders the argument invalid.

The final version of the Modal Argument

Since in our ontological argument (*MODAL-I*) we use the word 'possible' in the first premise to mean 'logically possible', we must mean the same in the second premise. Consider, then, the revised version.

MODAL-II

(1)   If it is logically possible that God exists, then it is logically necessary that God exists.
(2)   It is logically possible that God exists.
(3)   So, It is logically necessary that God exists.

Now that we are sure the argument is valid, are we still sure that the second premise is true? Think back to the Goldbach number example. We had to say that we did not know whether there was a possible world where it exists (i.e., whether it is logically possible that it exists). But if such a number does exist, it exists at all possible worlds. God, too, would have to be a necessary being if He exists. And like the Goldbach number example it seems we do not know whether or not there is a possible world where God exists (i.e., whether it is logically possible that God exists). At least we would need another argument or some good reason to establish that point. Of course, if it is logically possible that God exists, then He exists in all possible worlds including the actual world.

   In short, we have not been given a good reason to think that (2) is true; and certainly, it is not obvious that (2) is true. If God does not, in fact, exist, then it is not logically possible that he does; for He has to exist in all worlds or none, and if He doesn't exist in the actual world, then He doesn't exist in any world. On the other hand, if God does exist, then of course it is logically possible that He does; for there is some world in which He exists, namely, the actual world. But which of these is correct? We are trying to *prove* God exists. Can we *assume* that it is logically possible that He does? No.

So, we have this dilemma. If we read the second premise of *MODAL-I* as: 'It is epistemically possible that God exists', then it is obviously true—for all we know it is possible that God exists. But then we are using a different sense of 'possibility' than the one we must use in premise (1). Consequently, we equivocate and the argument is invalid. On the other hand, if we make sure the argument is valid by using 'logically possible' in the second premise (as we have in *MODAL-II*), then we no longer have reason to think the premise is true. Hence, we cannot be certain the argument is sound.

The counter argument: an objection

To see how much trouble we have gotten ourselves into, consider an analogous counter-argument.

*MODAL-II**

(1*) If it is logically possible that God doesn't exist, then it is logically necessary that God doesn't exist.
(2*) It is logically possible that God doesn't exist.
(3*) So, It is logically necessary that God doesn't exist.

Premise (1*) is true for the same reason premise (1) of the former argument is true: it follows from the very nature of God. If God must be a necessary being, then if He exists in any possible world, He must exist in all. And if there is a possible world where He doesn't exist, then He doesn't exist in any world. (Remember He can't exist in some and not in others—that would make Him contingent.) So, if it is logically possible that God *doesn't* exist, then there is some possible world in which God doesn't exist. And if there is some possible world in which God doesn't exist, then God fails to exist in every world. But of course, to say that God fails to exist in every world is just to say that it is logically necessary that God doesn't exist.

What about premise (2*)? Just as with (2) above, we do not know whether it is true or not. In the epistemic sense it is possible that God does not exist: for all we know He doesn't exist (and for all we know He does). But that will not help us here. Is there a possible world where God doesn't exist? We simply don't know (at least we need another argument or some additional evidence to support it). So, we are in this situation: either (2) or (2*) is true, but not both. If one is true, the other must be false. Of course, this means that either *MODAL-II* or *MODAL-II** is sound, but not both—one of them is unsound.

If the Modal Argument for the existence of God is to work, then we must not only have a valid argument, but we must have true premises as well. In addition, we must have true premises that we can see are true or have to reason to think are true. Otherwise the argument will be unconvincing and uninformative. We might present the following argument:

(1) God exists.

(2) So, God exists.

Unfortunately, if this argument is sound we would not know it unless we already know the conclusion is true, for the premise is true only if the conclusion is true. So even if the argument is sound, it is not convincing or informative. And this is just the predicament our modal argument has put us in. Until we have some independent reason to think that (2) is true as opposed to (2*), the modal version of the Ontological Argument must remain unconvincing.

There is a further question as to whether a theist could be rational in accepting (2)—and consequently finding *MODAL-II* both sound and convincing—without having any arguments for the truth of (2) (or equivalently, for the falsity of (2*)). But we must reserve a discussion of this important issue for a subsequent section (see Chapter 3, Section 6).

Questions: What do all ontological arguments have in common? What is the Cartesian version of the Ontological Argument? In what sense is Anselm's version of the argument indirect? What is Anselm's version of the Ontological Argument? What is the Perfect Island Objection and what response might Anselm make? How do questions that arise about the nature of existence affect the Ontological Argument's (the Cartesian and the Anselmian) plausibility? How might the distinction between concepts and objects help us understand the argument's weakness? What is the Modal argument? What does it mean to say that God is a necessary being? What different senses of possibility are used? What is the chief problem for the Modal version of the Ontological Argument?

Section 5: THE PROBLEM OF EVIL

The bulk of this chapter is devoted to looking at various arguments for the existence of God. There are, however, some traditional philosophical considerations for the conclusion that God does not exist. Probably the most widely discussed and influential problem raised against Theism is the so-called "Problem of Evil."

There are actually several forms this problem can take: we will look at two. The arguments for the existence of God can be divided into the deductive arguments and the inductive arguments. Similarly, the Problem of Evil can be offered either in a logical form by which we attempt to use demonstrative reasoning to show that God does not exist, or in an evidential form by which we argue in an inductive fashion, offering evidence in support of the conclusion that there is no God. Both forms of the problem use the empirical fact recognized by theists and atheists alike that there is evil in the world.

A. The Logical Problem of Evil

A first look at the problem

The logical problem of evil attempts to demonstrate that the person who holds both that *God exists* and that *there is evil* has inconsistent beliefs. We can show this conclusively, it is claimed, merely by reflecting on the concepts of God and of evil. The problem can be illustrated with the following reasoning:

The theist holds both propositions (G) and (E) below.

(G) An omnipotent, omniscient and morally perfect God exists.

(E) There is evil.

These propositions, however, are inconsistent; either (G) or (E) must be false. So, if there is evil in the world, then it must be that God does not exist.[8] Since it is obvious that there is evil in the world, the theist must give up his claim that God exists.

From this simple statement of the problem the following argument may be formulated:

EVIL

(1)   If there is evil in the world, then God does not exist.
(2)   There is evil in the world.
(3)   So, God does not exist.

Logical inconsistency

The important claim motivating *EVIL* is that (G) and (E) are inconsistent. Since this claim may not be obvious, some discussion of it is required. We can begin by taking a closer look at the notion of *inconsistency* in general. Two or more propositions are inconsistent if it is impossible that they all be true at the same time. This will arise if the propositions are opposed to each other in either of two ways. First, a set of propositions is inconsistent if two of them are *contradictories*. Two propositions contradictories if it is impossible for both to be true, and it is impossible for both to be false; that is, one must be true and the other false. So, for example, the proposition that all men are mortal and the proposition that not all men are mortal (i.e., some men are not mortal) are inconsistent because they contradict each other. Since they are simply the negations or denials of one another, we say they are *explicitly contradictory*.

Sometimes, however, a contradiction is only *implicit* in the sense that the propositions in question are contradictories but neither is simply the negation of the other. In the case of the proposition that Jones is a bachelor and the proposition that Jones is not an unmarried male we need to add the premise that *bachelors are unmarried males* in order to derive the conclusion that Jones is not a bachelor. This conclusion makes the contradiction explicit because it is an explicit denial of the first proposition.

There is another way for propositions to be inconsistent. Even if two propositions are not contradictory, they might be inconsistent because they are *contraries*. Two propositions are said to be contraries if both cannot be true, though both could be false. Thus the proposition that the only figure on that page is a triangle and the proposition that the only figure on that page has six sides are inconsistent because they are contraries: both cannot be true yet both could be false (if, say, the only figure on that page is a rectangle). The reason they cannot both be true is that no single figure can be a triangle and also have six sides—this is logically impossible.

This kind of inconsistency makes it clear that two propositions do not actually have to be true in order for them to be consistent, but only that there is some logically possible way for them both to be true at the same time. Consider the propositions that George Washington was an astronaut and that Eleanor Roosevelt invented the wheel. Both of these propositions are in fact false, but they are still consistent. It only needs to be logically possible for them both to be true at the same time. In the language of possible worlds, we only require that there be some possible world in which Eleanor Roosevelt invented the wheel and George Washington was an astronaut. This world is very different from the actual world—perhaps even difficult to imagine— but it is still possible.

How do we tell when a set of propositions is inconsistent?

If the propositions are explicit contradictories, then we can simply see straight-off that they are inconsistent. In the case of implicitly contra- dictory propositions and contraries, this job is a little more difficult. The best method is to derive an explicit contradiction from them. We performed such a job above in the example about bachelors by using a necessary truth as an extra premise in order to derive a conclusion that was an explicit denial of one of the propositions. The proposition that all bachelors are unmarried males is a necessary truth which, to- gether with the proposition that Jones is a bachelor, entails that Jones is an unmarried male, explicitly contradicting the proposition that Jones is not an unmarried male.

We must remember that in saying two propositions are inconsis- tent, we are saying that it is *logically impossible* that they both be true at the same time. Given this, we must be careful that when deriving an explicit contradiction we do not use premises that are possibly false or contingent. We want it to be the case that in every possible world in which it is true that Jones is a bachelor it is false that Jones is a married male, and in every possible world in which Jones is an married male it is false that he is a bachelor. If the premise that all bachelors are un- married males were false in some possible world (that is, contingent), then it *could* be true in that world that Jones is both a bachelor and married. Because the premise is a necessary truth, that can't happen. An important rule we'll use in our reasoning is the following.

To demonstrate that two propositions are logically inconsistent (either contraries or implicit contradictories) derive an explicit contradiction from the propositions using only logically necessarily truths together with the propositions.

What would happen if we used a contingent premise in our argument? Suppose we have a scientifically sound study that shows that all bachelors are of higher than average intelligence. What of the two propositions that Jones is a bachelor and that Jones is of lower than average intelligence? Are they inconsistent in the logical sense we have been discussing? Someone might point out that we can derive the proposition that Jones is of higher than average intelligence from the facts that he is a bachelor and that all bachelors are of higher than average intelligence. And this conclusion explicitly contradicts our second claim. While all three propositions might add up to a logical problem, the two we are considering are not really logically inconsistent. That all bachelors are of higher than average intelligence is only a contingent fact that we supposed to be true for our example. Even if in fact all bachelors are of higher than average intelligence, this is not necessarily so (it is not a way the universe has to be). Consequently, there are possible worlds in which Jones is both a bachelor and of lower than average intelligence. To demonstrate logical inconsistency we must use premises that are necessarily true.

The Logical Problem of Evil

We can now return to the Logical Problem of Evil. The objective is to show that God doesn't exist by first showing that the existence of evil and the existence of God are inconsistent. If we can show this, it will follow that if evil does exist, then God does not. Since it is obvious that evil does exist, we conclude that there is no God.

Let's see if we can construct an argument. Given what we now understand about inconsistency, is it correct to claim that (G) 'An omnipotent, omniscient and morally perfect God exists' and (E) 'There is evil' are inconsistent? (G) and (E) are not contradictories of any kind since both could be false. But to be inconsistent it is enough that they be contraries, and we know how to show that contraries are inconsistent by deriving an explicit contradiction from them using only necessary truths as premises. Consider, then, the following reasoning:

If God exists and is omnipotent, then there is no evil that He cannot prevent; and if He is omniscient, then there is no evil He does not know about; and if He is morally perfect He will not allow any evil to exist that He knows about and can prevent. So, if God exists and has all these properties, then there could be no evil in the world, for there would be none of which He was ignorant, and He wouldn't permit any evil He knew about, and He could prevent any evil He knew about and wouldn't allow.[9]

If this reasoning is correct, then it should be clear that from the proposition that God exists we can derive the proposition that there is no evil. This proposition is, of course, an explicit contradiction of (E); and so, (G) and (E) are inconsistent as claimed. We can demonstrate the inconsistency more clearly in this way. The following three propositions appear to be necessary truths.

(a) If God exists and is omnipotent, then there is no evil He cannot prevent.
(b) If God exists and is omniscient, then there is no evil He does not know about.
(c) If God exists and is morally perfect, then He would not permit any evil He knows about and can prevent.

From these three claims it follows, by the reasoning offered above, that if an omnipotent, omniscient and morally perfect God exists, then there is no evil. And from this claim and our original proposition (G) it follows that there is no evil. But the proposition that there is no evil explicitly contradicts (E).

We have now shown that (G) and (E) are inconsistent by deriving a proposition from (G) which explicitly contradicts (E). We have used what appear to be necessary truths as premises. Recall now the argument for the nonexistence of God we called EVIL.

(1) If evil exists in the world, then God does not exist.
(2) Evil does exist in the world.
(3) So, God does not exist.

The first premise of this argument is based on the claim that (G) and (E) are inconsistent—if evil exists, then God does not. This we have just sought to establish. The second premise remains unargued for, but its truth is all too evident. Given that the argument is valid and all the premises are true, the conclusion must also be true—which is just to say that God does not exist. We have, in effect, given an abbreviated and formal rendering of the following argument, an argument that can be seen to incorporate the reasoning we used earlier to demonstrate the inconsistency of (G) and (E):

> If there is evil in the world, then either God permits it, in which case He is not morally perfect, or God does not know about it, in which case He is not omniscient, or He is powerless to prevent it, in which case He is not omnipotent. So, if there is evil, then nothing has *all* the God-making attributes. Consequently, the being which the theist calls 'God' must lack at least one of the God-making properties. It follows that the being he calls 'God' cannot really be God. If nothing has *all* the God-making attributes, then nothing is truly God.

The theist's response to the second premise

How should a theist respond to such an argument? Since the argument is obviously valid, the only thing left to do is deny one of the premises. Premise (2) 'There is evil' seems indubitably true, though some theists have thought it to be false. Typical explanations include the Augustinian claim that evil is simply the negation or absence of good; hence, there is only good and the lack of good. But this approach will not be of much help to the theist as a response to the Problem of Evil as we understand it. One merely has to replace 'evil' with what appears to be its definition—'lack of good'—and the argument is off and running. If there is a lack of good, then God does not exist: this is established by the same reasoning we displayed above. Or if they are troubled by our taking "lack of good" to be a "something," we might restyle the first premise by showing that if goodness is lacking or deficient, then God does not exist.

Some theists might argue that since we do not have a precise definition of evil, we cannot be sure there is any and so, cannot be sure the second premise of *EVIL* is true. But here we should note that merely failing to have a precise definition of something does not necessarily imply that we cannot recognize it when we come across it. One need not be able to give a precise definition of a tree to know that the thing in his yard is one. We will assume, then, that although it may be difficult to define evil, we all have some idea of what it is and recognize its existence. One only needs to think of the suffering of innocent children or the destruction of cities and loss of life brought about by floods or volcanos, and the many cases of torture and human indecency to understand the sort of thing the existence of which is claimed to be inconsistent with God's existence. (Indeed, most theists agree that the existence of evil plays an important role in traditional accounts of the relation of a perfect, sinless God to less-than-perfect, sinful man.)

The theist's response to the first premise

If the theist is willing to accept the second premise, then he must be prepared to deny the first. In effect, to deny premise (1) is to claim that (G) and (E) are consistent, that it is possible at least that they both be true at the same time. Now what reasons are there for thinking that God's existing and being omnipotent, omniscient and morally perfect are consistent with the existence of evil? The strategy will be the following. We used three premises to derive the conclusion 'If an omnipotent, omniscient and morally perfect God exists, then there is no evil.' According to our rule above, showing that (G) and (E) are not inconsistent requires only showing that at least one of these premises does not express a necessary truth. Consider now the following discussion in which theist argues that a morally perfect being might permit evil in order to create a world that had free will and was morally significant. This is to argue that the premise

(c) If God exists and is morally perfect, then He would not permit any evil that He knows about and can prevent.

is not a necessary truth, that is, it is possibly false.

It seems correct to say that a world in which the inhabitants have moral responsibility is a morally better world than a world in which there is no moral responsibility. But this requires that the inhabitants have free will, for if an action is not freely performed by you—if it is not up to you what you do—, then you should not be blamed or praised for doing it (you cannot be held responsible). So it seems that a morally perfect being would want to create a world in which there was moral responsibility and, consequently, free will. Now if these creatures are really free, then it must be possible for them to choose evil as well as good. If God caused them always to choose good, then their actions are caused and not free or up to them. At least something like this must be the case if the free will is to be morally significant. If this is even possibly true, then in such situations, God must permit some evil in order to create a world with moral responsibility and free will. And so, there is some reason to think that the existence of evil is consistent with the existence of God.

In the following discussion, the theist continues argue that (G) and (E) are consistent. As the argument goes, *possibly* in some situations evil is logically required to bring about some greater good. Since an omnipotent being cannot do what is logically impossible, even God could not prevent that evil if He wanted to bring about the greater good. Now this is just to say that the premise

(a)   If God exists and is omnipotent, then there would be no evil He cannot prevent.

is not a necessary truth (it is possibly false).

We can make the case even stronger by noting that it often seems as though some evil is required for bringing about a greater good. We are all aware of cases in which evil does bring about some greater good. Consider situations in which a few soldiers had to die or suffer in order to save a whole city or country from a greater harm, or in which a painful operation is required for continued health. And it is likely there could be cases in which it is *impossible* to bring about the greater good without first permitting some evil to occur (impossible, that is, in the same sense in which it is impossible for someone to die courageously without also dying or suffer magnificently without also suffering). We don't even need to suppose that this is the way the actual world is; all the theist needs to make his case is that it is at least possible that in some situations evil is logically required in order to bring about a greater good. Remember that the goal is to show that it is possible for (G) 'An omnipotent, omniscient and morally perfect God exists' and (E) 'There is evil' both to be true at the same time. Even an omnipotent being cannot do what is logically impossible, e.g., make 2+2=5 or make a round square. So, if it is logically impossible that a certain good exists without some lesser evil, then God could be omnipotent and still not be able to do away with all evil."

To summarize: earlier we said that two (or more) propositions can be shown to be inconsistent if we can derive an explicit contradiction from the propositions together with a few additional premises, which must be necessary truths. Two of the premises—(a) and (c)—we relied upon to derive the explicit contradiction between (G) 'An omnipotent, omniscient and morally perfect God exists' and (E) 'There is evil' do not seem to be necessarily true. Hence, the inconsistency of (G) and (E) has not been established. We have a situation much like that of the two propositions that Jones is a bachelor and Jones is not of above average intelligence. Since the premise we used to derive the explicit contradiction—that all bachelors are of above average intelligence—was not a necessary truth we have not demonstrated logical inconsistency.

If we cannot establish the inconsistency between (G) and (E), then it is not clear that the first premise of *EVIL*—the premise that states that if there is evil, then God doesn't exist—is true. This, naturally, takes all the force out of the logical Problem of Evil.[10]

Reformulating the problem

The above argument has been directed at the existence of evil in general. We have not been concerned with any particular kind or amount of evil. The atheist, however, might try to reformulate the problem by incorporating a more restricted notion. Suppose he agrees with the theist that some evil is consistent with the existence of an omnipotent, omniscient, morally perfect being: God might have a morally sufficient reason for some evil. We shall call evil that is required for a greater good or the consequence of free will "justified" or "proper" evil. The atheist might want to add, however, that not *all* the evil that exists is proper evil.[11] There are certain natural evils such as earthquakes and floods that clearly are not the result of free human choice. And it does not seem as though some evils such as the suffering of a small animal in a flood or the destruction of an orphanage in an earthquake are logically necessary for any greater good. So the atheist might argue that while (E) is consistent with (G) when evil is understood as proper evil, the following proposition, (E*), is not.

(E*) There is improper or unjustified evil.

It does seem correct to say that

> (f) If an omnipotent, omniscient and morally perfect God exists, then there is no *improper* or *unjustified* evil.

is necessarily true; for any evil that is compatible with the existence of such a morally perfect being must be justified or proper. And from (G) and (f) we can derive the conclusion that there is no unjustified, improper evil. This is clearly the explicit contradictory of (E*). We are now in a position to present an alternative to *EVIL*, which we'll call *EVIL**:

> *EVIL**
>
> (G*)   If there is *improper or unjustified* evil, then God does not exist.
> (E*)   There is *improper or unjustified* evil.
> (3)   So, God does not exist.

The theist's response to the reformulated problem

To this formulation of the Logical Problem of Evil it seems the theist has only one recourse. He does not want to deny (G), and (G*) seems highly plausible as a necessary truth, so he must agree that (G) and (E*) are inconsistent. What he must do to avoid conclusion (3) is demand of the atheist some independent reason for thinking (E*) is true. The atheist's reasoning presented above, however, will be unconvincing to the theist who claims that the *appearance* of unjustified evil to the less than omniscient mind does not entail the *reality* of unjustified evil. Merely because we do not find the purpose of the existent evil does not guarantee that it is unjustified. Moreover, given that we are substantially less than omniscient it might be expected that we do not see the significance of, or justification for, the evil that exists. For example, it is sometimes said that if God exists, then since He is morally perfect He must create the best of all possible worlds. Since He has created this world, this world must be the best. The existence of evil in this world is justified as being required to bring about the greatest possible good whether or not we can see the connections. And so there is no unjustified or improper evil in the world. It is something like this that the theist must hold. (Indeed, one finds a defense of this view implicit in the Biblical story of Job, on whom God allows Satan to inflict suffering and personal loss. That God should allow evils to be inflicted on a good man suggests either that God is not good or that evil is permitted for a greater good. As the Biblical story goes, the last of these emerges as an overwhelming moral.)

Conclusion

At this point we are going to leave the logical problem of evil. We have not been able to demonstrate the truth of the first premise of *EVIL* that states that if evil exists, then God does not. This, we saw, depended on whether or not God's existence was incompatible with the existence of evil, and this incompatibility was not established. We next tried to narrow our focus and consider the incompatibility between God's existence and the existence of improper evil. This incompatibility can be established, but a different question remains: Is or is not the evil in this world improper evil? If the atheist has some way of demonstrating that some existing evil is improper evil, then perhaps he is correct in claiming there is no God. But it is not obvious how such a demonstration should go. Until he has provided the appropriate reasoning, he cannot succeed in showing that no God exists by appealing to the logical Problem of Evil as we reformulated it. And unless he can show that the premises required for deriving a contradiction from (G) and (E) are necessary truths, the Logical Problem of Evil as initially presented (*EVIL*) will be without force.

B. The Evidential Problem of Evil

The argument

We now turn to a slightly different form of the Problem of Evil. Whereas in the logical form we were concerned with deductive reasoning, we will now present an inductive form of the argument that concludes that God does not exist. As with any inductive argument, the conclusion is not put forth as certain or guaranteed by the premises; rather, the premises are offered in support of the conclusion as good evidence that it is true, or as good reasons to believe it is true. If the inductive argument is a good one, then the conclusion is said to be probably true, and it is generally agreed that it is rational to believe what is probably true and irrational to deny it. The point of formulating the argument evidentially, then, is that even if we consider statements of God's existence to be consistent with statements asserting the existence of evil, there still may be reason to think that the existence of evil counts as good evidence against the existence of God, and so, renders the latter improbable.

The proponent of the Evidential Problem of Evil might reason in this way:[12]

No one can deny that evil exists in the world. It is all around us: wars, famine, pestilence, pain, and so on. Clearly, if God were morally perfect, He would not want to create a world that was not absolutely the best world possible; if He were omniscient, He would know which world was the best; and if He were omnipotent, He would have the power to create such a world. It also seems clear that the best possible world would be a world in which evil was minimized and goodness maximized; this is certainly morally necessary for the best possible world. Now surely it is possible that there be a world with less suffering and pain than the actual world. It is difficult to see what justification there could be for the suffering of a helpless animal, or the incessant hunger of a small innocent child, or the despair of a terminally ill cancer patient. Since it is highly unlikely that it was created and sustained by an omniscient, omnipotent, and morally perfect being, the existence of evil in the world, in the amount or to the degree it does exist, provides good evidence for the claim that God does not exist. Since there is good evidence for the conclusion that God does not exist, if one is rational, one ought to accept such a conclusion; in the face of such evidence, to believe that God does exist is to be irrational.

How should we assess such an argument? Three questions need to be addressed. Is the existence of evil *evidence* for the nonexistence of God? If so, is it *good evidence*? And, finally, if it is good evidence, then, in the face of such evidence, would it be less rational to believe in the existence of God than not to believe? The answers to these questions are not simple ones; some issues must be postponed until we reach the next section on rationality and religious belief.

The concept of evidence

What is it, in general, for something to count as evidence for something else? Although the notion of evidence is a fairly common one, this is no easy question. Suppose we are detectives investigating a murder. The Lord of Bentley Manor has been fatally shot and we have been summoned to uncover the fiend. Our job is to look for evidence—evidence that will "tell" us the identity of the guilty party. In what sort of things will we be interested? No doubt there are some things that are relevant to our case and other things that are highly irrelevant. The smoking gun, the fingerprints on the gun, the footprints outside the window and the victim's last words will all be relevant. What we had for dinner, what color the tile on the kitchen floor is, and the name of the family cat are all pieces of information that seem to play no role in the murder. Naturally, we will count the relevant things as evidence but not the irrelevant things. Why? Suppose the gun belonged to the butler, the fingerprints on the gun were the butler's and the footprints outside the window match the butler's shoes. Moreover, the victim's dying words were "He wasn't a very loyal employee, was he?" Now obviously this all seems to be very good evidence for the hypothesis that the butler did it. It is good evidence because it supports the hypothesis. It is not conclusive, of course, for it is still possible that (say) the doorman is guilty and has framed the butler. But evidence does not need to be conclusive to serve as evidence. It is the relation of support that is important here, and since the irrelevant information does nothing to support the hypothesis, we do not count it as genuine evidence for the hypothesis.

We can be a little more precise by saying that one proposition (we will throughout talk of propositions being evidence for other propositions) is evidence for another proposition only if the truth of the first makes the second more probable than it otherwise would be. So, in our murder case, the proposition that the fingerprints on the gun were the butler's is evidence for the proposition (our hypothesis) that the butler did it, since the butler's guilt is more probable given the information about the fingerprints. Of course, the proposition that the butler did it would no doubt be very probable even without the fingerprint information—after all, we have the footprints, the last words and the ownership of the gun. But the fingerprint information still adds to the probability of the hypothesis. Notice that the information we considered to be irrelevant—the color of the kitchen tile and the name of the family cat—does not seem to affect the probability of the hypothesis. So far as we can tell, that information bears no relation of support to the hypothesis, so we do not consider it to be evidence.

Evaluating evidence

When is evidence good evidence? Unfortunately, this is a misleading question. We should not think of good evidence as simply evidence for a proposition and bad evidence as evidence against it. Rather, we may have both good and bad evidence for a proposition as well as against it. And even so, it is not as though there is some well-defined criterion for determining when evidence is good and when it is bad. It is more useful to think of evidence as being better or worse. The fingerprints on the gun might be considered to be better evidence than the last words of the victim because the former has more of an effect on the probability of the hypothesis that the butler did it. So, we can judge better or worse evidence on the basis of how much the evidence supports, or makes probable, the proposition in question.

Indeed, this is already clear from the fact that inductive arguments can be better or worse. To see this in another light, consider the relationship between induction, explanation and evidence. Inductive conclusions serve as better or worse explanations of facts specified in the premises (see Chapter 2, Section 1C). Since the premises of an inductive argument are viewed as evidence for its conclusion, evidence will be better or worse to the extent that it receives a better or worse explanation from the conclusion. The butler's having committed the murder seems to better explain his fingerprints on the murder weapon than it does the dying man's last words.

When discussing the value of a piece of evidence, however, it is important to consider what other evidence is available. We noted that the fingerprints on the gun constituted good evidence for the hypothesis that the butler did it—that is, it makes our hypothesis highly probable. But suppose (for the moment) we also learn that it was another gun that fired the fatal bullet and that the gun with the butler's fingerprints was fired only to scare off the murderer after the crime had taken place. This new piece of evidence counts against our hypothesis concerning the butler's guilt. In fact, the new evidence greatly diminishes the import of the old evidence. No longer do the butler's fingerprints make it likely that the butler was the killer. To put this another way, the hypothesis that the butler committed the murder does very little to explain his fingerprints on a gun that, in light of new evidence, is not the murder weapon at all.

What we must do, then, when inquiring whether a certain piece of evidence is good evidence for another proposition, is to consider the total body of evidence. Is all evidence to be consulted or just the evidence we already know or have readily available? Suppose we don't know that in fact the butler was in the wine cellar at the time of the shooting and so couldn't possibly have committed the crime. Unfortunately, no one saw him there, so no one can attest to this. This is an important piece of evidence that would greatly change the strength of the other evidence we have regarding the fingerprints, the footprints, the victim's last words, and so on. Could the butler's fingerprints on the gun *still* count as good evidence even if there is this counter-evidence that we do not possess? For our purposes in this section, we take the answer to be affirmative. Since we will ultimately be concerned with the issue of rationality and justification, we will want to confine our discussion to the evidence either possessed by or readily available to the person or persons in question. Good evidence, then, will be determined relative to the total evidence known by or readily available to some person or persons. This seems especially appropriate given the familiar relation of evidence (as premises) to explanatory hypothesis (as conclusion). A person cannot explain evidence of which she is unaware, however relevant it might be.

Rationality and evidence

We can assume that a person is rational in believing something if she is justified in believing it. And of course the notion of justification, as we're concerned with it here, is intended to indicate that one has good reasons or evidence for the truth of the proposition believed (and perhaps, that one lacks enough good reasons against the truth of the proposition). In this way we connect up the notions of evidence and rationality. There are many important issues relevant to these notions, but we must reserve a more detailed discussion until a subsequent section (Chapter 3, Section 6). For now we need only emphasize that one may have evidence against a certain proposition and still be rational in accepting the proposition given one's total body of evidence. Consider again our murder case. Given that we know that the smoking gun is owned by the butler, the butler's fingerprints are on the gun, the footprints outside the window match the butler's shoes and the victim's final words were "He wasn't a very loyal employee, was he?", we seem to have excellent evidence for the hypothesis that the butler is guilty. Suppose, however, we discover that the cook hated the victim, had threatened to kill him and has no alibi concerning his whereabouts at the time of the murder. This is evidence for the hypothesis that the cook did it and against the hypothesis that the butler did it. (We will assume throughout that evidence for one proposition can also count as evidence against its negation.) Are we, as detectives, still rational in believing that the butler is guilty? Given our *total* body of evidence it would certainly seem so. The butler's guilt is still more probable than the cook's guilt even though there is some evidence that suggests the cook is our man.

Evidence against the existence of God

Having come to a better understanding of what constitutes evidence and the having of evidence, we can return to our central concern. Is the existence of evil evidence for the nonexistence of God? If so, is it good evidence? And finally, can one be rational in believing in the existence of God in the face of such evidence? Certainly it must be granted that the existence of evil—particularly the kind and amount of evil that actually exists—is relevant to and even supports to some extent the proposition that God doesn't exist. At least we can say that the proposition that God doesn't exist is more likely to be true given that there is evil in the world than it would be if there were no or even less evil. According to our discussion of evidence above, then, the existence of evil in the world counts as evidence against the claim that there is a morally perfect, omniscient and omnipotent being.

There is, of course, the further question of whether the existence of evil is *good* evidence for the proposition that God doesn't exist. Taken by itself, the proposition that there is evil might be seen to make the existence of God highly improbable. But this is difficult to assess. What other evidence do we have against the hypothesis that God exists? How does the existence of evil compare with that? More importantly, what evidence do we have *for* the existence of God? Remember that we assess the value of evidence by taking into consideration the total evidence possessed by the person and relevant to the proposition. What other evidence might the theist have? It might be that he notes the apparent order and purpose in nature and has found the Teleological Argument (see Chapter 3, Section 2) to be persuasive; perhaps he takes into account the existence of goodness and morality; and he may even consider himself to have had experience of the love and forgiveness of God. All of this counts as evidence for the existence of God, and if it were to be included in one's total body of evidence, the existence of evil might not greatly affect the probability of the proposition that God exists. In short, whether or not we consider the existence of evil to be good evidence against the existence of God depends on what other evidence one has. It certainly appears to count against the theist's position, particularly when we isolate it from other potential pieces of evidence. But given what else the theist might possess in the way of evidence for the existence of God, it is not at all clear that in his case the existence of evil should count strongly against the proposition that God exists.

With this in mind, we are prepared to address the question of rationality. Is the theist rational in continuing to believe in God in the face of the evidence under consideration? Suppose a believer in the existence of God takes a philosophy course in which the Problem of Evil is brought to his attention and explained. He indeed takes note of the evil around him and sees the force of the problem. It may be said that he now possesses evidence against his belief that God exists. Must he now give up his Theism in the face of this evidence in order to be rational? Given our discussion above, it does not seem that he must. No doubt our theist has some evidence for his belief in God; some potential reasons were mentioned above. Given his total body of evidence for and against the existence of God, it might very well be that the existence of God is something he may rationally believe. We may suppose the rational person is one who open-mindedly seeks and considers all readily available evidence relevant to the proposition or hypothesis in question, and then commits himself to hypotheses according to the overall strength of his evidence. The theist, then, could rationally commit himself to the hypothesis that God exists even if he recognizes the existence and import of evil.

In short, the theist can admit the existence of evil as evidence, even as good evidence in a certain sense, against the contention that God exists without having to admit that one is irrational to accept the existence of God in the face of such evidence. Of course, for the atheist who does not have the evidence brought about by religious experience, or who interprets it in a different way, it is not irrational to deny the existence of God. Considering the evidence possessed by and or available to him, that may very well be the rational thing to do.

We may conclude that the evidential form of the Problem of Evil does not succeed in showing that Theism is irrational given the existence of evil. Even if by itself the existence evil is a good reason for denying the existence of God, there may be other evidence that is available to the theist and that outweighs or at least balances the evidence against the existence of God.

Questions: *How does the Logical Problem of Evil differ from the Evidential Problem? What is it for two propositions to be inconsistent? What is the rule for determining logical inconsistency? How can a theist respond the the Logical Problem of Evil? Can the problem be reformulated adequately? What is the Evidential Problem of Evil? What evidence is there for or against the existence of God? What is the rational person to do with the evidence?*

Section 6: RATIONALITY AND RELIGIOUS BELIEF

Rational belief without argument

A thorough examination of traditional "proofs" of the existence of God shows that they are subject to severe criticism (Sections 2-4, this chapter). Similarly, the most significant argument for Atheism—the Problem of Evil—fares no better. It thus appears that while there is no proof of Theism, there is also no proof of Atheism. What should we then conclude with respect to the rationality of belief in God? Does the fact that none of the arguments for God's existence succeeds make it irrational for a person to believe that God exists? It is this latter question that will concern us in the remainder of this chapter.

It might be suggested that looking only to *arguments* to establish the existence of God leaves out something important. Many people, it is claimed, have experiences of God and it is on the basis of these experiences that they know, or have good reason to believe, that God exists. So even if the criticisms of traditional arguments for the existence of God are correct and there is no argument with the conclusion 'God exists' that we know to be sound, it still does not follow that no one could know, or at least rationally believe, that God exists.

The claim that we must consider is the theist's assertion that she can believe in God rationally even if she has no argument for God's existence. In order to get a good grasp on this claim, let's first think about whether one is ever rational in believing anything without having an argument for it. Suppose that your roommate comes back from a camping trip and tells you that he met and had breakfast in the woods with the President of the United States. Doubtful, you ask him for a good *argument* to show that this is true. Not surprisingly, your roommate has no such argument to offer. You ask him to offer some *reason* for believing his rather incredible story, but he can give you none. Your roommate obviously believes that he met and had breakfast with the president, but he has no argument whatsoever to support his belief. This raises an important question: Does your roommate rationally believe that he met the president? Is he being rational in holding this belief even though he can offer no argument for it? It is important to emphasize that the real issue here is one of rationality and not of belief.

As we remarked earlier, to say that one rationally believes a proposition is to say that one is justified in believing that proposition. The question that we are asking about your roommate's belief can be translated, then, into the question "Is your roommate *justified* in believing that he met the president?" We need, now, to move toward an account of what it is to be justified in believing something if we are to offer a satisfactory answer to this question.

Direct and indirect justification

It is commonly said that our beliefs can be justified in two ways, *directly* and *indirectly*. A belief is indirectly justified if its justification depends on the justification of other beliefs. You might believe that philosophy majors tend to become wealthy because you also believe that statistics show that most philosophy graduates get high paying jobs. To take another example, you might believe that a certain basketball team will do well in the NCAA play-offs because you also believe that this team is a better shooting and rebounding team than any other in the tournament. In this case, if you are not justified in this belief about your favorite team's shooting and rebounding ability, then your belief about how that team will fare in the tournament is not justified either. The justification of your belief that the team will do well is then dependent on the justification of your belief that this team is a very good shooting and rebounding team. Thus, the justification for the former belief is *indirect* since it depends on the justification of the latter belief.

On the other hand, some of our beliefs are justified independently of the justification that we have for other beliefs. For example, you are right now looking at a page of text and you have the belief that there is a philosophy textbook in your hands. On what do you base this perceptual belief? If we are asking what sort of argument is there for the conclusion that there is a philosophy textbook in your hands, it's not clear what we can say. It seems you believe that there is a philosophy textbook in your hands because you are right now *looking* at it. You haven't inferred this belief from any other beliefs that you hold. It seems that this belief, if it is justified, is *not* justified by virtue of its relations with other things that you believe. If it is based on anything, it is based on the experience that you are now having of seeing the philosophy textbook in your hands. So if the belief is justified, its justification is not indirect; if it *is* justified, it does not have this status because of the justification that *other of your beliefs* have.

Justification and perceptual experiences

Are you rational or justified in believing that there is a philosophy textbook in your hands? Intuitively it might seem very strange to say no. We form countless beliefs solely on the basis of what we perceive each day. As far as we can tell, beliefs of this kind are usually true, and there isn't, in typical cases, any reason to think that they are false. Thus, some of our beliefs we take to be *directly* justified; their justification is not had by virtue of other of our justified beliefs, but merely by being the kind of beliefs that are based on normal perceptual experiences. Though the discussion that takes place in Chapter 5 of this text (Perception and our Knowledge of the External World) might leave one suspicious about the justification of ordinary perceptual beliefs, for our purposes here let's assume that it is uncontroversial that these commonplace sorts of experiences are sufficient to justify our beliefs.

Let's recall the question that led us to the topic of justification: Is your roommate justified or rational in believing that he met the president of the United States in the woods? We are now in a much better position to provide an answer. Let's embellish the story a bit, and rather than have it be about your roommate's belief, let's have the belief be yours.

Imagine that one day, in the not too distant future, you decide that you have had enough of the hustle and bustle of college life, and you head off alone to "find yourself" in the Oregon wilderness. Not long into your trip, you come across someone else alone on the trail who you recognize to be the president of the United States. You and the president spend several days together, discussing politics and matters of national concern, before finally going your separate ways. Now suppose that some three months later, after returning to civilization, you tell your friends about your life in the woods. You tell them that although they won't believe it, you had several conversations with the president, whom you happened to meet in the Oregon wilderness. Your friends look at you in amazement. "Do you really expect us to believe you?" they ask incredulously. You have no convincing argument for your claim and it turns out that no matter what you say, you can't get them to believe you. Eventually, they conclude that you honestly believe that you talked with the president, but they still don't believe that you actually did have such a conversation. Instead they think that you had been out in the sun too long or had eaten a wrong sort of herb. No matter how hard you try, you just can't convince them that you are right.

Is it rational for you to go on believing that it was the president that you met even though you have no good argument for it? Are you justified in believing that you met the president? Does the fact that you can't convince others on the basis of your experience entail that you should no longer believe it? It seems obvious that you are justified, or rational, in believing that you met the president. Just because you have no argument to offer for your story does not mean that you shouldn't believe it. It is true, of course, that you are not indirectly justified in believing that you met the president. As we have seen, however, that does not mean that you are not justified in your belief. Your belief, we want to say, is directly justified. It is not based on any argument that you have; instead it is based on your experience of the president.

Justified theistic belief and religious experience

All of this impinges on the role of religious experience in justifying theistic belief. The theist might admit that she has no good argument for the existence of God. Yet she might nevertheless maintain that she is rational in believing in God. Perhaps we should understand such a theist as claiming that her belief in God is directly justified rather than, as we had previously been assuming, indirectly justified. Many religious believers do, after all, claim to have experience of God. But these believers, as far as we know, are never in a position to prove to others that they have had an experience of God. Might it be true nevertheless that they are justified in believing that they have experienced God? That is, might a theist be directly justified in believing that she has experienced God just as you, in the president example, are directly justified in believing that you experienced the president?

The sort of religious experience here claimed to be relevantly parallel to the perception of physical objects, includes, but certainly is not limited to, mystical experience. Generally, the type of experience that the theist has in mind when stressing the analogy that we are considering is much less spectacular than the visions had by the mystics. Examples of religious experience that the theist has in mind are, upon the theist's repenting, her seeming to have the experience of the forgiveness of God, and, when tragedy has struck, the theist's seeming to feel God's comfort. This type of religious experience is widely reported among people of faith and does not seem to be reserved only for the most spiritual of believers.

Are religious beliefs analogous to perceptual beliefs?

Let's quickly take stock of where we are. We are considering the claim made by some theists that religious beliefs are analogous to perceptual beliefs. In cases of perceptual belief, one's belief is directly justified, that is, the person's belief is rational and based solely on the experience of having the perception that she has had. Similarly, some theists maintain, belief in God is directly justified. Just as in cases of perception where one is justified by virtue of a certain experience, so in many cases of religious belief one is justified in virtue of religious experience. And this religious experience need not be dramatic or wildly out of the ordinary.

It is clear that there is an analogy between perceptual experience and religious experience. But to say just this isn't to say much at all; the theist needs a *strong* parallel between the two. We turn at last to a discussion of the strength of this analogy.

What reasons might there be for thinking that religious experience and perceptual experience are not analogous? The first apparent disanalogy between religious experience and perceptual experience is that, while beliefs formed on the basis of one type of perceptual experience can, to some extent, be checked by other types of perception, there seem to be no such methods of verifying religious experience. With respect to perception, suppose that I am at a friend's house and I see what appears to be an apple in a fruit basket. Automatically I form the belief that there is an apple in the basket. But then I get suspicious. Knowing that my friend does a very good job of making wax fruit, I pick up the object to make sure that it really is an apple. I feel the texture of the skin, squeeze the object, and even smell it in order to determine just what it is. In such a case, I have used other types of perceptual experience to check the belief that I originally had formed on the basis of a single type of experience. In cases of religious experience, it is hard to see what type of corroboration one can get from other types of experience. If, for example, I have a certain experience that I take to be God telling me that He forgives me, then, lacking arguments that might provide indirect justification, what other sort of experience could I have that would verify or support my belief? It seems as though there isn't any that can fit the bill. If this is correct, then there is an important disanalogy between perceptual experience and religious experience: while perceptual beliefs can usually be checked by other senses, no such check seems to be available for beliefs formed on the basis of religious experience.

Furthermore, with respect to the apple example, not only can I look at, touch and smell the apple but I can get someone else to do this as well. If I have a perceptual experience of a physical object, and if you are in the proper position to perceive it and if your senses are functioning properly, then you should have the same sort of experience that I have. Of course there will occasionally be disagreement (you might think a certain object in the distance is a rabbit, while I think it is a cat) but in the great majority of cases we will agree. So with respect to perceptual experience, not only can I attempt to verify an experience of mine via my other senses, but generally I can also verify them through the reports of other perceivers. On the other hand, in the case of religious experience, neither of these methods of verification seems to be available: there is no other type of experience that I can have that will, even in part, verify my religious experience, and others are almost never in position to "share" the experience.

A third point of disanalogy between the cases of religious and perceptual experience, concerns the universal acceptance of one and the basic lack of agreement about the other. Every normal adult reports having experience of physical objects; and the sort of experience that people report is, by and large, the same. But this truth about perceptual experience does not hold with respect to its religious counterpart. Although it is hard to know what percentage of normal adults claim to have religious experience, it surely is significantly less than the percentage of those who take themselves to experience physical objects. Furthermore, even among those who have religious experience, it is not clear that there is general agreement about what it is that is experienced. People with vastly different conceptions of God claim to have religious experience. Since such people disagree about what God is like, and since such experience is purported to be experience of God, it appears that those with religious experience are not in agreement about the nature of the object of their experience.

These points of disanalogy between religious experience and perceptual experience do count against the claim that religious beliefs, just like perceptual beliefs, can be directly justified. It is not entirely clear, however, how strongly these disanalogous features count against the strength of the analogy. For the theist will be quick to point out that we ought to expect certain disanalogies since the nature of the object of our experience is radically different in the case of religious experience than in the case of our perceptual experience of physical objects. In the religious case, God is said to be the object of our experience. And God is not thought to be an inert object, but rather a personal agent who is able to reveal Himself as He pleases. Moreover, since God is infinitely greater than other persons, it is no wonder, the theist will claim, that those who experience Him report their experiences quite differently.

So it is not absolutely clear just how good the analogy that we have been considering is. Although there are points of disanalogy, the theist seems to be right in claiming that we should expect such divergence. We will, for the sake of the argument, assume that there is a significant analogy between religious experience and perceptual experience. It should be remembered, however, that the depth of this analogy is controversial.

Defeaters of justification

Supposing that there is a significantly strong analogy between perceptual and religious experience, there is nevertheless a problem with the view that belief in God can be directly justified. In order to see this, let's again consider typical perceptual beliefs. If, in *ordinary circumstances*, I have the visual experience of seeming to see a dog, then I am directly justified in believing that I really am seeing a dog. This does not mean, however, that in *every* case that I have the visual experience of seeming to see a dog I am directly justified in believing that I really am seeing a dog. For example, imagine that I have been in a rather unfortunate car accident, and due to neurological impairments, I now am prone to hallucinate about medium-sized four-legged animals. Furthermore, suppose that I have no pets and that one day, as I sit at home reading the morning paper at my dining room table, I seem to see a rather large Saint Bernard walk slowly across my living room. I think that perhaps in my haste to get the newspaper, I left the front door open and a stray dog has wandered in. Accordingly, I get up, check my door and find that it is securely closed. Given that I know that I have no pets and I believe that there is no way for an animal this size to sneak into my house except through the front door, which I know to be closed, and given that I am prone to hallucinations, am I now directly justified in believing that I am really seeing a dog in the living room? It doesn't seem so. And why is this? Because there are *other* things I am justified in believing that, taken together, count heavily against there being a dog in my living room.

So we see that even beliefs that can be directly justified are, in a roundabout way, dependent on other things that I justifiably believe. For even though it is usually true that I am directly justified in believing that I see a dog when I have the experience of seeming to see a dog, if there are other things that I justifiably believe that make it unlikely that I am really seeing a dog, then my belief will not be justified.

Let's now return to religious belief. It has been claimed that if one has a certain religious experience, then one is directly justified in believing that that experience is an experience of God. But as we have just seen in the case of perceptual beliefs, one's having a certain kind of perceptual experience is not always enough to directly justify a belief formed on the basis of that experience. If the person has other justified beliefs that count heavily against the truth of the belief, then that belief will not be directly justified. In the case of the dog hallucination, I was not directly justified because I was justified in believing that no dog could have gotten into my normally dogless apartment. This, coupled with the fact that I am prone to hallucinate, is good reason to think that my belief that I was really seeing a dog was false. Good reasons, such as these, to think false a belief that otherwise would be directly justified are called *defeaters*, for they can defeat one's potential justification for a belief. (We might distinguish two sorts of defeaters. First, those that run against the fact in question (as when I might be justified in believing that there are no dogs in the apartment complex in which I live, a claim which is incompatible with there being a dog in by living room right now). Second, there are defeaters that run against the conditions in which the perceptual experience is had (as when there is reason to believe that my eyes aren't working properly or that there are dog hologram machines in the vicinity).)

The question with respect to religious belief is, Are there things that the theist justifiably believes that make it very unlikely that her belief that she is experiencing God is true? That is, does the theist have any defeaters relevant to her belief that she is really experiencing God? This question is difficult to answer. In fact it is likely that, as it stands, it just isn't a good question at all. It is not a good question because it presumes that all theists are the same with respect to what they believe and with respect to what would defeat their direct justification for believing Theism. Yet such a presumption is clearly unwarranted. There are tremendous differences in what people believe and, furthermore, in what people are justified in believing. That is, even if two people have exactly the same set of beliefs, it may nevertheless be that they don't have exactly the same *justified* beliefs. So we will have to proceed by recognizing that what we say will not be applicable to every theist. But we may be able to say some things that are generally true of theists, and being able to do that is significant enough. (One controversial issue is when a defeater is relevant. Must the person have possession of the defeater (believe it) or could there be defeaters that defeat justification even though the person is unaware of them? Are we culpable for our ignorance of some defeaters?)

Is the Problem of Evil a defeater?

The first and most likely candidate for a defeater arises from what is called the Problem of Evil (see Chapter 3, Section 5). Most people believe that there is a fair amount of evil in the world. Many atheists sense that evil is in some way incompatible with the claim that God exists. How could an omnipotent, omniscient, and completely benevolent being allow evil? If God is omnipotent then He should be able to prevent evil; if He is omniscient then He should know about it and how to prevent it; and if He is completely benevolent, then He should want to prevent it. Thus, it seems as though the recognition of evil gives the theist good reason to think that there is no God. In other words, the theist's justified belief that there is evil defeats the direct justification that she might have from her religious experience.

It may seem, then, that such a theist is not justified in her belief in God because her total evidence does not adequately support it. This gives us a hint as to what is required of the theist who knows the Problem of Evil and who wants to have her belief in God justified. What she needs to do in order to be directly justified is to learn new evidence that will make her total evidence (apart from her experience) at least neutral with respect to the question of God's existence.

Consider once again the example of the dog in the apartment. Knowing what I know (that there wasn't a dog in my apartment an hour ago, that my front door is closed, and that I am sometimes given to hallucinations), my belief that I am really seeing a dog is not directly justified. But let's add to the story and see what happens. Suppose that after checking the front door, my phone rings. As I go into the kitchen to answer it, I notice, to my great surprise, that my back door is wide open. I answer the phone, and it turns out to be my doctor. He tells me that he has good news for me, that the neurological exam I had last week shows that I am completely over my problems with hallucinations. I now have evidence that overrides much of the evidence I had against my belief that I was really seeing a dog, and so my belief that I was really seeing a dog may now be justified.

Similarly, if there is a good response that theists can make to the Problem of Evil, and if our theist learns this, then her total evidence will no longer support the proposition that God does not exist and she will again be directly justified in her belief. So what is the status of the theist's belief in God when she knows both the Problem of Evil and an adequate response? It seems that the reasonable thing to think is that the response in effect counterbalances the evidence against the existence of God that the Problem of Evil provides.

(It might appear that the theist, armed with an adequate response to the Problem of Evil, would not be directly justified since her justification depends not simply on her religious experience but also on her belief that her response to the Problem of Evil succeeds in showing that the problem is not devastating for theism. It might be thought, then, that her belief is *indirectly* justified. This, it turns out, is a point of controversy, but for our purposes it makes little difference. What is significant is that whether her belief is justified directly or indirectly, it is, either way, justified.)

Alternative explanations for religious experiences

As we have seen, unless its defeating potential can be neutralized by some adequate response, the Problem of Evil may serve to override the theist's direct justification for her belief that God exists. Another problem facing the possibility of directly justifying the theist's belief takes a more general form. Rather than question the justification of an individual's belief, we might question the legitimacy of religious experience as a whole. If an alternative explanation can be offered for the theist's "religious" experience, an explanation that is more reasonable and that does not include God as the object of the experience, then perhaps the theist would no longer be rational in believing that God exists on the basis of these experiences.

Two important alternative explanations for religious experience are found in the works of Marx and Freud. Both thinkers embed a re-description of religious experience in a much broader critique of the whole of religion; each pictures the religious believer as someone motivated not by veridical experience of God but by forces outside of their control. In the case of Marx, these are socio-economic conditions and, according to Freud, they are unconscious psychological processes. For our purposes it will suffice to discuss only one of these views.

Consider, then, the Freudian view that offers a psychoanalytic interpretation of religious belief and experience. Early in childhood, certain conflicts arise between the child and parents that result in repressed frustrations and distress. The male child, for example, will come to desire his mother and regard his father as a rival—a situation that is called the Oedipus complex. This leads to a conflict between the impulse to rebel against, and the desire to be loved by, the father. This entire range of conflict, frustration and emotion is repressed and remains in the unconscious. Belief in God provides an external object upon which to project a father image and release many of the unconscious frustrations. Religious practice in general supplies a socially acceptable means by which one may rid oneself of repressed guilt and distress.

On Freud's view, then, presumably what the theist takes to be an experience of God is nothing more than an expression of repressed guilt and anxiety. Now, if we take the Freudian explanation of the experience in question to be better than the religious explanation—perhaps because Freud's psychological theory is natural rather than supernatural and so is in principle open to scientific testing—, then the theist can no longer appeal to those experiences for the direct justification of her belief in the existence of God. Consequently, unless it is based on some good argument or set of reasons, the theist's belief will be unjustified.

Is the Freudian explanation better than the theist's explanation? Several points deserve mention. First, although the Freudian theory is intended to be a scientific one, very little evidence has been gathered to support it—many of its claims are today generally considered to be mistaken. There appear to be no good reasons to think it is true, and no reason to think it is more likely than the theist's explanation.

Perhaps we would do better to reject the Freudian theory in its specific form and consider some weaker, more general psychological explanation. We might simply say that it is likely that some psychological process or other is responsible for these experiences that the theist labels religious. A point against this move is that it leaves us very little by way of content. Exactly what are the processes involved? Is there any reason to think this account is true? A point in favor of the move, however, is that psychological theories—even quite general ones—are naturalistic, and so can at least offer the potential for scientific development and testing; supernatural theories or explanations like the theist's provide no such potential.

Second, even if Freud's or some more general psychological theory were correct, it would still be compatible with the claims of the theist. Given that psychological processes are at work in our experience, it does not follow that there is no God or that religious experiences do not have God as their object. It is still open to the theist to say that these experiences are God's way of revealing Himself, even though the immediate source of religious experience requires unconscious psychological mechanisms. God, it is sometimes said, works in mysterious ways.

Finally, a word about the rationality of the theist's belief in the face of alternative explanations. Since many psychological theories that could serve as alternative explanations for religious experience are either too general and underdeveloped or lacking in experimental support, and since psychological explanations are compatible with religious ones, there is no basis for the claim that the theist is being unreasonable or irrational in thinking that he sometimes experiences God. On the other hand, since for the nontheist there does not seem to be any public evidence for the theistic interpretation of religious experience and since psychological explanations have the advantage of being natural and scientifically testable, it would not be irrational to suppose that some psychological explanation is correct. It is not simply a matter of taste; it is a matter of what evidence one has at his disposal and the quality of the explanatory hypotheses being offered. The rational person should always seek the best explanation for the data, but assessing competing explanations is seldom an easy task. In the case of what we have been calling religious experience, neither the theist's explanation nor the nontheist's (psychological) explanation seems strong enough to rule out the other.

The rationality of religious belief not based on evidence

We have been considering a view of the justification of religious belief that allows such beliefs to be directly justified. One might be directly justified in a belief even if one has no arguments to support the belief. This does not mean, however, that the person will have no evidence for the truth of the belief. Surely, when I believe that there is a word processor on the desk in front of me because I have the visual experience of seeing the processor, I do have *evidence* for my belief—although I have no *argument* for it. As we have seen, if I then acquire some counter-evidence that cancels out my original evidence, my belief will cease to be justified.

A person can either believe that a proposition is true or not believe that it is true. Not believing it is true might take either the form of believing it is false or of withholding judgment about it altogether. The rational person surely will believe a proposition is true when the available evidence in its favor outweighs the available evidence against it. And the rational person will believe that a proposition is false when the available evidence against it outweighs the available evidence in its favor. But what should the rational person do when the available evidence is split or inconclusive? A person who is evaluating her beliefs with respect to the existence of God might very well find herself in such a position.

Let us examine two principles that yield different answers to the question about split evidence. In an essay entitled "The Will to Believe," James puts forth the following principle:[13]

> One should not believe what one has good reason to think false.

Other philosophers, however, W.C. Clifford being the best example, have offered a very different general principle.[14]

> One should only believe what one has good reason to think is true.

These two principles ("you should never believe what you have good reason to think false" and "you should only believe something if you have good reason to think it true") might sound as though they are saying the same thing. But careful attention will show that they are not. The first principle (call it the "Jamesian Principle") simply asserts that one should *not* believe what he has evidence *against*, while the second principle (call it the "Cliffordian Principle") says that you should *only* believe what you have evidence *for*. That these two principles are different can be seen by considering an example in which the evidence available to a person is inconclusive; it does not tell strongly for or against the proposition in question. For example, consider a certain astronomer's belief that there is an odd number of stars. Assuming that there is not good evidence one way or the other, his belief will be evaluated a bit differently by the two principles. According to the Cliffordian Principle, he should not believe the proposition, while the Jamesian Principle, in and of itself, leaves open the possibility that belief about the number of stars might be justified.

Clifford's principle

First let's look at the case for the Cliffordian Principle. Clifford argues that one has an intellectual and moral obligation to believe only what one has sufficient reason to believe. According to one argument, you are morally culpable for immoral actions that come about because you have formed false beliefs through hasty or sloppy investigation. Beliefs based on inconclusive and insufficient evidence stand a greater chance of being false, and false beliefs stand a greater chance of leading to harmful actions. You therefore have an obligation to seek out all available evidence and refrain from believing anything that is not sufficiently supported by that evidence. You must do all that is within your power to form true beliefs and avoid false beliefs.

Suppose that when designing and building a bridge I ignore evidence suggesting that my bridge will not withstand the weight that can be expected to travel over it. Perhaps I am told by a well-respected architect that the planned bridge cannot carry normal loads; or perhaps there are simple tests that can be performed on models that would indicate that the bridge's design is inadequate, but I refuse to perform these tests. I build the bridge and within a few months it collapses, killing several people. Aren't I to blame for these deaths? And wouldn't I be equally blameworthy if the evidence I had about the bridge's reliability was split, as much reason to think the bridge would hold up as there was reason to think that it wouldn't hold up? Clifford would conclude that I should refrain from believing that the bridge will work unless I have sufficient evidence in favor of the belief.

Two difficulties arise for Clifford's view. First, if Clifford contends that we ought to form beliefs in accord with certain obligations, then he must think that we can regulate our beliefs. But can we always decide what we will believe? Don't we, at least sometimes, simply find ourselves with beliefs that we have not chosen? James and others have argued that many, if not all, of our beliefs are outside of our immediate control. We do not seem to have direct or voluntary control over what we believe. If you now believe that there is a book in front of you because you see one in front of you, can you, by sheer willpower, decide to believe otherwise? Probably not.

In Clifford's defense, however, we might notice that even if we cannot directly control our beliefs, we perhaps can indirectly control them. We might, for example, train ourselves to be better evidence gatherers, to reason more logically, and to question what we find ourselves believing more carefully. I cannot lose weight immediately by willing that I should, but I can do things (exercise, eat less) that will, in the long run, bring it about that I lose weight.

A second difficulty concerns Clifford's goal of believing only what is true. If you want to believe only true propositions, then, as Clifford points out, you ought to believe only that for which you have very good evidence. But, as James asks, why should we think that the best epistemic goal is to have only true beliefs? If your goal is to believe only true things, then there will be many true things that you will consider and yet not believe because the evidence does not support them well enough. For example, if you really wanted to believe only true things, then the best way to make sure that you accomplish your goal is to believe only things for which you have completely conclusive arguments. If you follow this rule, then you will believe very few things outside of mathematical truths. And this doesn't seem to be desirable. James contends that the better goal is to attempt to believe many and mostly true things, and that the best way to do this, in many instances, is to believe even if the evidence for the proposition isn't overwhelming. If this is the goal, then believing a few falsehoods is not such a bad thing considering that the payoff might be rational belief in more and more important truths.

James's principle

James argues that it is, in fact, permissible to believe certain propositions even if one does not have good evidence for them. But believing without overwhelming evidence is not acceptable for any proposition—only with respect to those propositions that are "genuine options." An option is genuine for a person if it is momentous, living, and forced. *Momentous* options are those that have a significant impact on the life of the person. An option is *living* for a person if the person sees both sides or alternatives as real possibilities. And an option is *forced* if the two alternatives are mutually exclusive and there is no third option. One must take one of the two alternatives. According to James, certain religious hypotheses, like the proposition that God exists, are genuine options.

James contends that religious belief is just such a case in which it is rational for one to believe even if the evidence is split. But another qualification is required. We mentioned earlier that James thinks that believing is not something that one can just decide to do. Whether or not a person believes something is mostly beyond her control. Consequently, it is not that you are free to choose to believe if the evidence doesn't dictate what should be done. Rather, James is claiming that if the evidence is split *and you find yourself believing*, then it is rational for you to so believe.

A word needs to be said about what it means for evidence to be split. It might be thought that the evidence here is any evidence that a particular person has. Therefore, the claim might be interpreted as "Whenever the evidence that a person has for a proposition is split, then if that proposition is a genuine option and the person believes that p, then the person is justified in believing that the proposition is true." But this cannot be right. For suppose that the evidence available to humans was in fact very strongly against God's existence. Now imagine a certain person, Joe, who believes in God and who has not searched for evidence for the existence or non-existence of God. Suppose further that it just so happens that the evidence that Joe has relevant to the question of God's existence is split. Surely we don't want to say that Joe's belief is justified, since, by hypothesis, the evidence that Joe *could have had if he had worked at it a bit* would have supported the proposition that God doesn't exist. What James is saying, then, is not that whenever the evidence in one's possession is split, then if the options are genuine, one may justifiably believe either option. Rather, James's point is that with respect to religious questions, the *total amount of evidence available to us* is drastically inconclusive. Only when the total amount of evidence available to us is inconclusive will James's principle sanction belief.

James contends that in the case of religion, the evidence is not conclusive. Thus, if you find yourself believing, then it is perfectly fine and rational for you to continue believing so long as you do not have good reason to think that your religious belief is false. The only grounds upon which to object to the rationality of such belief is to accept a principle like the Cliffordian Principle. And such a principle seems to stem from an overly ambitious account of our intellectual goals. A more reasonable view of our cognitive goals would seem to be one that would give us the opportunity to believe rationally propositions of ultimate significance even if the evidence is split.

If James is correct, then the theist can be rational in believing that God exists even if the available evidence is not sufficiently in favor of that proposition. There is some reason, however, to think that James's position is misguided. One might question whether James really has epistemic rationality in mind when he says, for example, that Clifford's goal of believing only true propositions may not be suitable. If our epistemic goal is knowledge, then will the practical undesirability of believing only a few true propositions really be a worry? The utility of believing many true propositions (at the expense of permitting a few false beliefs to infiltrate the set) seems clearly to be a practical goal. Similarly, in what sense do we find it permissible to believe a proposition under the conditions that James places religious beliefs? Recall our discussion in Section 1 about Pascal's wager and the distinction between epistemic and prudential rationality. If the proposition that God exists is a genuine option (living, momentous and forced) and all the available evidence is inconclusive and we find ourselves believing it, are we now in an advantageous position with respect to *knowing* whether God exists? James's critics will think not. More is required for a belief to be epistemically rational.

Questions: How does direct justification differ from indirect justification? How might someone be rational in believing in God's existence without an argument? In what ways are perceptual and religious experiences analogous? disanalogous? What is a defeater of justification? What alternative explanations are there for alleged religious experiences and how good are they? Can someone be rational in their belief if they lack any evidence? How do the principles of Clifford and James bear on this issue?

NOTES

1When you know that a proposition is true you have more than a mere belief about the proposition. Your belief must be true and it must not be an accident that you are correct. What more there is to knowledge than there is to mere true belief remains open to philosophical debate. A short discussion of knowledge and belief can be found in Chapter 2, Section 2B. Perceptual knowledge is discussed more fully in Chapter 5.

[2]We thank Glenn Hartz for bringing this response to our attention.

[3]Rene Descartes, "Meditation V," *The Philosophical Writings of Descartes, Vol. II*, Trans. John Cottingham, Robert Stoothoff and Dugald Murdoch (Cambridge: Cambridge University Press, 1984).

[4]Descartes, "Fifth Replies," *The Philosophical Writings of Descartes, Vol. II*, 263.

[5]St. Anselm, *Proslogion*, Chapter II, *St. Anselm: Basic Writings*, Trans. S. N. Deane (La Salle, IL: Open Court, 1962).

[6]St. Anselm, *Proslogion*, Chapter II.

[7]Pierre Gassendi, "Fifth Objection," *The Philosophical Writings of Descartes, Vol. II*, 224-225.

[8]One could argue that what we have shown is that if there is evil, then either God is not omnipotent, not omniscient, or not morally perfect. We will assume that if God exists, then God is essentially omnipotent, omniscient and morally perfect. This means that if no being is omnipotent (or omniscient or morally perfect), then no being is God.

[9]See J. L. Mackie, "Evil and Omnipotence," *Mind* 64 (1955).

[10]Our discussion owes much to Alvin Plantinga's work in *God, Freedom and Evil* (New York: Harper and Row Publishers, 1974).

[11]See William Rowe's work in "The Problem of Evil" (Chapter 6), *Philosophy of Religion*, Second edition (Belmont, CA: Wadsworth Publishing Company, 1993); and "The Problem of Evil and Some Varieties of Atheism," *American Philosophical Quarterly* 7(1970).

[12]This sort of argument is discussed in William Rowe's work referred to in footnote 11.

[13]See William James, "The Will to Believe," *The Will to Believe and Other Essays in Popular Philosophy* (New York: Longmans, Green and Company, 1897).

[14]William Clifford, "The Ethics of Belief," *Contemporary Review* (1877), found in *Lectures and Essays: Volume II, Essays and Reviews* (London: MacMillan, 1879).

RELATED READINGS

Alston, William P. "Religion." *The Encyclopedia of Philosophy*. New York: Doubleday, 1965.
Pascal's Pensees. Trans. A. J. Krailsheimer. London: Penguin, 1966.

Rowe, William L. "The Idea of God" *Philosophy of Religion*. Second edition. Belmont, CA: Wadsworth Publishing Company, 1993.

The Teleological Argument
Hume, David. *Dialogues Concerning Natural Religion*. Ed. H. D. Aiken. New York: Hafner Publishing Company, 1948.
Paley, William. *Natural Theology*. Ninth edition. 1805..
Rowe, William L. "The Teleological Argument." *Philosophy of Religion*. Second edition. Belmont, CA: Wadsworth Publishing Company, 1993.

The Cosmological Argument
Aquinas, St. Thomas. *Summa Theologica (1a, 2, 3)*. *The Basic Writings of Saint Thomas Aquinas*. Ed. Anton Pegis. New York: Random House, Inc., 1945.
Clarke, Samuel. *A Demonstration of the Being and Attributes of God, Part II.* London, 1705.
Hume, David. *Dialogues Concerning Natural Religion, Part IX.* Ed. H. D. Aiken. New York: Hafner Publishing Company, 1948.
Rowe, William L. "The Cosmological Argument." *Philosophy of Religion*. Second edition. Belmont, CA: Wadsworth Publishing Company, 1993.

The Ontological Argument
St. Anselm. *Proslogion*. Chapters II—V. *St. Anselm: Basic Writings*. Trans. S. N. Deane. La Salle, IL: Open Court, 1962.
Descartes, Rene. "Meditation V." *The Philosophical Writings of Descartes, Vol. II.* Trans. Cottingham, John, Robert Stoothoff and Dugald Murdoch. Cambridge: Cambridge University Press, 1984.
Hartshorne, Charles. *Anselm's Discovery*. La Salle, IL: Open Court Publishing Company, 1965.
Malcolm, Norman. "Anselm's Ontological Arguments." *The Philosophical Review* 69 (1960).
Plantinga, Alvin. *God, Freedom and Evil*. New York: Harper and Row Publishers, 1974.
Rowe, William L. "The Ontological Argument." *Philosophy of Religion*. Second edition. Belmont, CA: Wadsworth Publishing Company, 1993.
The Many-Faced Argument. Eds. Hick, John and Arthur C. McGill. New York: The MacMillan Company, 1967.
The Ontological Argument. Ed. Alvin Plantinga. Garden City, NY: Doubleday, 1965.

The Problem of Evil
Adams, Robert Merrihew. "Must God Create the Best?" *The Philosophical Review* 81 (1972).
Mackie, J. L. "Evil and Omnipotence." *Mind* 64 (1955).
McCloskey, H. J. "God and Evil." *The Philosophical Quarterly* 10 (1960).

Plantinga, Alvin. *God, Freedom and Evil.* New York: Harper and Row Publishers, 1974.

Wykstra, Steven. "The Human Obstacle to Evidential Arguments From Suffering: On Avoiding the Evils of' Appearance'." *International Journal for the Philosophy of Religion* 16 (1984).

Rowe, William L. "The Problem of Evil." *Philosophy of Religion.* Second edition. Belmont, CA: Wadsworth Publishing Company, 1993.

Rowe, William L. "The Problem of Evil and Some Varieties of Atheism." *American Philosophical Quarterly* 7(1970).

Rationality and Religious Belief

Alston, William P. "Perceiving God." *Journal of Philosophy* 83 (1986).

Clifford, William. "The Ethics of Belief." *Contemporary Review* (1877). Found in *Lectures and Essays: Volume II, Essays and Reviews.* London: MacMillan, 1879.

Freud, Sigmund. *The Future of an Illusion. The Complete Psychological Works of Sigmund Freud.* Trans and ed. James Strachey. London: The Hogarth Press, Ltd., 1961.

James, William. "The Will to Believe." *The Will to Believe and Other Essays in Popular Philosophy.* New York: Longmans, Green and Company, 1897.

Plantinga, Alvin. "Is Belief in God Properly Basic?" *Nous* 15 (1981).

Rowe, William L. "Faith and Reason." *Philosophy of Religion.* Second edition. Belmont, CA: Wadsworth Publishing Company, 1993.

CHAPTER 4 The Mind-Body Problem

Section 1: THE TRADITIONAL MIND-BODY PROBLEM

Introduction

MOST of us, philosophers and nonphilosophers alike, have wondered whether there is life after death. After your body has died and decayed, what remains if anything? Do you still exist, conscious of the fact that you are now without a body and perhaps with fond memories of what your former life was like, or regretting that you never did take that trip to Europe? But the question "Is there life after death?" is poorly expressed. For we are not much worried about whether there is something that is *alive* after the body dies and decays. That does not seem very plausible; we are, after all, hypothesizing that the body has *died*. The interesting question is whether there is anything that remains conscious or thinking or feeling after death. The question we want to ask then is whether one can consciously survive one's bodily death.

If you think that it is possible to survive your bodily death, to exist even if you are disembodied, then you likely think that there is something more to you than your physical body. Whatever it is that thinks, feels, understands and perceives is not, then, merely physical; for once the physical stuff is gone, the thinking, feeling, understanding and perceiving supposedly remain. Perhaps it is the soul, the mind, or something spiritual that continues, but whatever you call it, it seems to be distinct from your physical being.

If, on the other hand, you are inclined to deny that you or anyone else could survive bodily death, then you likely think that being conscious—thinking, feeling, understanding, perceiving—is something that is ultimately a physical process, ceasing along with all the other physical processes of your body that cease when you die.

The question whether you could survive your bodily death leads naturally to the question whether it is possible that there exists a non-physical thinking thing. Now we might ask the question this way if we already believe that some physical things think. But of course that is a controversial position too. Consider a question with which cognitive psychologists, computer scientists and philosophers working in artificial intelligence are primarily concerned: Could a machine (e.g., a computer) think? We might put the question this way if we are already convinced that nonphysical things think (like minds or souls) and we are curious as to whether physical things can do so as well. But neither the question about disembodied conscious existence nor the question about thinking machines presupposes an answer to the other; we might simply wonder whether thinking is something that physical things or nonphysical things or both can do. This issue will be the primary topic of the present chapter.

We can begin by getting a little clearer on the question of whether a machine—more generally, a physical object—can think. By *thinking* we mean feeling, understanding, sensing, believing, willing, hoping, imagining and the like. (We can also cover this range of phenomena with the terms "mentality" or "consciousness.") Certainly there could be machines that make the sound "Ouch" whenever a blow is struck to a "sensitive" surface, and machines that respond through a speaker "I am thinking" whenever you ask into a microphone "Are you a thinking thing?" and robotic machines that reach out for a wrench whenever you say "Wrench, please." Machines like these are not merely possibilities—they actually exist. But we must not automatically conclude that machines like these think. For it is far from clear whether the machine *understood* what you asked when you requested the wrench or asked whether it was a thinking thing. And it is far from clear whether the machine *felt* anything that prompted it to respond "Ouch." And it is certainly not obvious that any of the machines was *conscious*. Thus, we need to distinguish responding in a thinking-like way from responding in a way that results from actually considering the matter, reasoning, feeling certain ways, or perhaps having an awareness of color, taste or an odor. Thinking must be understood in this more sophisticated sense.

By "material" or "physical" we could refer to whatever the physicist refers to with those words. But it will perhaps be easier to think of physical objects as objects that take up space, are publicly observable (directly or indirectly, with one or more of the five senses), have mass and are governed by laws of nature. Your brain is a physical object as are ducks, apples, Buicks, and those little scented, anti-static things you throw in the dryer.

Finally, in asking whether machines could think we are asking about the *possibility* of a machine—a physical object—thinking. We need to distinguish the question "Do—as a matter of fact—machines think?" from "Could—is it possible or coherent that—a machine think?" The latter is a philosophical question, for in asking about the possibility of a material thing thinking we want to explore the *concepts* of thought and matter; our answer to the question must arise from an understanding of that in which thinking (feeling, understanding, etc.) consists. Thus, we are not asking whether there were, are or will be machines that think. For even if the answer to this question is negative the more interesting question about the nature of thinking remains.

Dualism and Materialism

If you believe that a machine or physical object could not think, or if you believe that it is possible to survive bodily death or that one could be conscious yet disembodied, you may think there is some substance or kind of "stuff" (like a mind or a soul) distinct from physical substance. Those who contend that thinking can only be explained fully by an appeal to something distinct from the physical are *dualists*; their theory is called *Dualism*. The nonphysical substance that thinks, wills, understands, senses and feels is what the dualist will call *mental substance* or *mind*. As traditionally conceived, mental objects or states are nonspatial, i.e., they do not take up space and have no location. Your beliefs, pains and emotions, for example, have no sizes or shapes and you will not find them in any particular place as you might find a physical object.[1] Moreover, only you can experience your mental states; no one else can feel your pain, experience your sensation of red, or have your belief that your mother makes the best apple pie in the county (although someone might have feelings, experiences and beliefs very like yours). To say that only you can know that you are conscious is to say that you have *private access* to your mental states. In contrast, physical substance is *spatial* and *publicly observable*; it is often simply called body. According to the dualist, nothing can be both a mental thing and a physical thing, and everything that exists is either mental or physical.

The dualist will claim that only nonphysical, mental substance can think or be conscious. It is impossible, he will say, to explain fully the phenomenon of thinking solely in terms that refer to physical objects and their properties. In short, a complete *physical* description of the universe will necessarily leave something out. Such a description will not include those facts that refer to mental activity; it will not describe your experiencing a bright light in the sky, or Phil's belief that Martians are invading the Earth, or Emily's fear that Phil is correct.

The materialist is one who holds that what we typically single out as mental can be explained in terms of physical objects, states and processes. We need not talk about a distinct mental substance, for a complete physical description of the universe will include reference to your visual experiences, Phil's beliefs and Emily's fears. Thus, *Materialism* is the thesis according to which there is only one kind of substance in the world and it is physical substance.

We will proceed by contrasting dualist and materialist accounts of mentality. These are two very different theories each addressing the same set of issues yet clashing over very fundamental ideas about what it takes to treat the issues adequately. Dualist arguments for the existence of a distinct mental substance begin our discussion, with materialist responses interspersed. We then introduce two traditional problems for Dualism—the Relationship Problem and the Problem of Other Minds. Materialism is then given a chance to present its side of the story, moving in stages from a very crude form of Behaviorism to the Identity Theory. A brief discussion of Functionalism follows. We conclude the present chapter with a discussion of the Problem of Personal Identity.

This chapter presents a study of two theories, each one taking a different stance on the nature of consciousness and mentality. In deciding which theory is better, the philosopher needs to evaluate the arguments offered in behalf of each theory, the explanatory power of each theory, and the consequences of each theory. In many respects this chapter presents a running dialogue between Dualism and Materialism during which the strengths and weaknesses of both views are discussed.

Questions: What is being asked when you are asked whether you could survive your bodily death or whether a machine could think? What is Dualism? How does it differ from Materialism? How are mental things said to differ from material things, according to the dualist?

Section 2: DUALISM AND MATERIALISM
—ARGUMENTS AND OBJECTIONS

A. Arguments for the Plausibility of Dualism

The Argument from Disembodied Existence

The dualist claims that we cannot account for mentality solely in terms of physical stuff. Thus, if I am essentially a thinking thing, I cannot be merely a physical object. According to Dualism, then, I am neither my body nor some material part of it.

How might the dualist argue for this view? The seventeenth-century French philosopher Rene Descartes offered several arguments for Dualism. According to Descartes, we are essentially thinking things. Plausible as this may be, however, a further step is required to reach the central claims of Dualism. For it is one thing to say that I am essentially a thinking thing and quite another to say that I am not my physical body. Descartes offers the following reason for why I am not a physical thing.

> I know that everything which I clearly and distinctly understand is capable of being created by God so as to correspond exactly with my understanding of it. Hence the fact that I can clearly and distinctly understand one thing apart from another is enough to make me certain that the two things are distinct, since they are capable of being separated. . . . On the one hand I have a clear and distinct idea of myself, in so far as I am simply a thinking, non-extended thing; and on the other hand I have a distinct idea of body, in so far as this is simply an extended, non-thinking thing. And accordingly, it is certain that I am really distinct from my body, and can exist without it.[2]

Descartes' conclusion comes in the last sentence where he says that "it is certain that I am really distinct from my body, and can exist without it." How does he defend such a statement? Earlier in his *Meditations* Descartes has argued that God exists and that God would not deceive us when we reason carefully and properly. This contention about God guarantees that what we clearly and distinctly understand is at least possibly true, that is, "capable of being created by God" as we understand it. So if I can clearly and distinctly understand that my mind and body are distinct things, then it is at least *possible* that they are distinct things.

But Descartes wants to claim more. He wants to claim that my mind and body *are* distinct things. To defend this claim, Descartes might offer the following reasoning. If two things are *possibly* distinct, then they *must* be distinct. And if two things *must* be distinct, then, if they exist, they *are* distinct. This reasoning depends on the (perhaps obvious) idea that it is impossible for two things to be one thing. If you have two distinct things, perhaps you can put them together to make one new thing. But the two things you started with remain distinct as two parts of the new whole. On the other hand, what you cannot do is make the two things one and the same thing. If Eleanor Roosevelt and Karl Marx are two things, there is no way to make them one and the same thing. Now if it really is possible that my mind and body are distinct (two things), then it is impossible that they be one and the same thing. The second half of the reasoning adds that if the two things must be distinct, then they are distinct, if they exist at all. This reasoning is perhaps what lies behind Descartes' contention that "the fact that I can clearly and distinctly understand one thing apart from another is enough to make me certain that the two things are distinct, since they are capable of being separated."

Descartes then explains that he does have a clear understanding of himself as a thinking yet unextended thing and, also, a clear understanding of physical body (not just his, but any body) as an extended and unthinking thing. Since in thought (clear and distinct understanding) he (his mind) can be distinguished from a physical body, then he is distinct from his (or any) body. The Argument from Disembodied Existence looks like this.

(1) If I can clearly and distinctly understand that two substances are distinct things, then it is at least *possible* that they are distinct things.

(2) Substances that are *possibly* distinct *must* be distinct, if they exist.

(3) Substances that *must* be distinct *are* distinct, if they exist.

(4) So, substances that can be distinguished in thought are, if they exist, distinct in reality.

(5) I (a thinking thing) do exist and I can, in thought, distinguish myself (mind) from my body.

(6) So, my mind and body are distinct in reality.

We have already discussed to some extent premise (4) and premises (1)—(3), which are used to support it. What can be said on behalf of (5)?

The difficulty in defending premise (5)

Descartes has written about having a "clear and distinct understanding" of mind apart from body and of having "clear and distinct idea of myself as a thinking, nonextended thing" and a "clear and distinct idea of body, insofar as this is simply an extended, nonthinking thing." There are two different ways we might interpret his claims. On the one hand, he might mean that he can imagine what it would be like to be a conscious thinking thing without an extended body. Such would amount to forming a *mental picture* of what an experience of disembodied existence would be like. On the other hand, he might mean that he is considering two distinct concepts, that he can *conceive* of a difference between nonextended thinking mind and extended, nonthinking body. Let's explore each of these interpretations in turn.

First consider the premise that I can imagine myself disembodied. Can we imagine what it would be like to be disembodied? Many claim so. There are many stories about people who claim to have experienced disembodied existence when near death. They describe an experience of being separate from their bodies, perhaps looking down on their bodies from above, watching and listening while doctors work to revive them. If they are imagining what it is like to be disembodied, then premise (5) of the argument from disembodied existence has some support. They can separate themselves from their bodies in thought by imagining disembodied existence.

What would a materialist think about this argument for Dualism? Presumably she would challenge the dualist's contention that someone can imagine disembodied existence. That you can call up a mental image of your body is unquestionable, since that is no more difficult than *imagining what you look like,* or what your body looks like, as when we see pictures of ourselves or reflections in the mirror. But that, surely, is a far cry from imagining ourselves existing disembodied. What about putative near-death "out-of-body" experiences in which people claim to view their own bodies from high in a corner near the ceiling of the emergency room, say? Again, what more this amounts to beyond imagining what our bodies look like from this perspective is difficult to say. Moreover, if this high-in-a-corner perspective we have of our body is really a case of imagining ourselves disembodied, then it seems to require of the dualist more than he can readily allow since non-spatial immaterial souls cannot take up residence near the ceiling to see anything. Nor can the part of the story about looking at our body from high above our body fit cleanly into a mental *image*. Try to imagine your body as it might look from above. That's easy enough, and as we saw before it doesn't seem to amount to imagining yourself disembodied. Perhaps we are only imagining what it would be like for ourselves, fully embodied and positioned near the ceiling, to view a body below. We would "see" only the body below, not the body that perceives from above. The point is that what we *seem* to be imaging may not be what we are imagining after all.

So Descartes' argument is unconvincing if he is suggesting that he can imagine himself disembodied. What if he is saying, not that he can imagine himself distinct from his body, but that he can conceive of mind and body differently? Rendering premise (5) this way makes the argument more difficult to criticize, but it also makes the argument less likely to be convincing. A dualist like Descartes will naturally say that his concept of mind is that of a thinking and non-extended substance and his concept of body is just the opposite. But the materialist will not feel forced to adopt these concepts. Whether extended things (like computers or brains) can think is exactly the issue over which dualists and materialist debate. The materialist will claim that his concept of himself is of both a thinking and extended thing and that he cannot separate, even in thought, the idea of a thinking substance from the idea of a physical body.

The problem here is that the dualist has no leverage over the materialist if he merely states up front (presupposes) that the two substances, mind and body, can be distinguished in thought. For the materialist could respond that there is only one kind of substance (physical) which thinks, and while you may be able to consider the act of thinking without considering the extended object that thinks, you need not thereby be considering two different objects. Sometimes what seems to be two things is really one thing thought of in two different ways. So when Descartes claims that he can in thought distinguish his mind from his body and that these things are *possibly* distinct, does he mean only that it *seems possible* that mind and body are two things or that it *really is possible* that they are two things? If he means the first, then his argument will surely not work because he has not shown that what seems possible really is possible.[3] And if he means the second, then his argument is unconvincing because because it presupposes (without argument) the very distinction it attempts to show.

The Argument from Disembodied Existence fails to provide convincing proof that there exist minds apart from bodies and that consequently Dualism is true. Let's turn now to another Cartesian argument for Dualism.

The Divisibility Argument

In the Sixth Meditation Descartes says:

> The first observation I make at this point is that there is a great difference between the mind and the body, inasmuch as the body is by its very nature always divisible, while the mind is utterly indivisible. For when I consider the mind, or myself in so far as I am merely a thinking thing, I am unable to distinguish any parts within myself; I understand myself to be something quite single and complete. . . . By contrast, there is no corporeal or extended thing that I can think of which in my thought I cannot easily divide into parts; and this very fact makes me understand that it is divisible. This one argument would be enough to show me that the mind is completely different from the body, . . .[4]

Let's call this the *Divisibility Argument* for Dualism. Tidied up it goes as follows.

(1) My body is divisible.
(2) My mind—or myself, insofar as I am a thinking thing—is not divisible.
(3) So, my mind is distinct from my body (by Leibniz's law).

We've abbreviated this argument a bit. Descartes does believe that it is the nature of body that it be divisible, and the nature of mind that it be indivisible. Given that mind and body differ in this way, Descartes concludes that mind and body are distinct. The principle upon which this inference depends is a principle about numerical identity called *Leibniz's Law*: if x is identical with y, then x and y have exactly the same properties. In other words, if x just *is* y, then clearly x can't have properties y fails to have, or conversely. For example, although "Mohammed Ali" and "Cassius Clay" are different names, they name the same person. We can say that if Mohammed Ali and Cassius Clay are identical, then it follows that every property Mohammed Ali has Cassius Clay has too. Indeed, Cassius Clay has the property of being a former heavyweight boxing champion—the champion just didn't go by that name. Now, if someone makes a claim of the form "x is identical with y," then they are committed to the claim that x and y have exactly the same properties.

One way of arguing against an identity claim (x = y) is to look for a property x has that y doesn't have. Mohammed Ali was a professional boxer and Joe Namath wasn't. Joe Namath was a professional football player and Mohammed Ali wasn't. Consequently, they are not the same person. Descartes is arguing against the materialist idea that mind and body are identical and he does this by pointing out one way in which mind and body are different: the former is indivisible and the latter is divisible.

Premise (2) of this argument demands our attention. That a physical extended body can be divided into parts is uncontroversial. But what does Descartes mean when he says that the mind is indivisible? As Descartes is thinking of divisibility, if a substance is divisible, its parts have the same essential nature as the original whole. If we divide a material substance in two, each half will be spatial and located just as the whole substance was. And if we were to divide a mind in two, each half would be a conscious thinking thing just as the whole mind was.

But Descartes thinks that "the mind is utterly indivisible." Why? His explanation is that "when I consider the mind, or myself in so far as I am merely a thinking thing, I am unable to distinguish any parts within myself; I understand myself to be something quite single and complete." As with the Argument from Disembodied Existence, Descartes is using the first person perspective to generate support for his premise. He does not say that he cannot imagine what it is like for you to divide someone else's mind; rather he suggests that he cannot imagine what it is like to divide *his own* mind. He no believes that if you consider whether you can imagine yourself divided, you'll find that you appear to be indivisible, too. Descartes is also suggesting that because it is impossible for you to imagine this we can conclude that it is impossible for your mind to be divided. Mind, then, unlike body, is essentially indivisible.

The difficulty in defending premise (2)

If Descartes is correct in suggesting that I cannot imagine myself—insofar as I am a thinking thing—divided, then should his argument be convincing? Perhaps not. The materialist might criticize the move from what is *not imaginable* to what is *impossible*. Indeed, his doubts that imaginability is a sure-fire guide to possibility might emerge from something Descartes himself says.

> When I imagine a triangle, for example, I do not merely understand that it is a figure bounded by three lines, but at the same time I also see the three lines with my mind's eye as if they were present before me; and this is what I call imagining. But if I want to think of a chiliagon, although I understand that it is a figure consisting of a thousand sides just as well as I understand the triangle to be a three-sided figure, I do not in the same way imagine the thousand sides or see them as if they were present to me. . . . In doing this I notice quite clearly that imagination requires a peculiar effort of mind which is not required for understanding; this additional effort of mind clearly shows the difference between imagination and pure understanding.[5]

Let's shorten "pure understanding" to "conceiving." The point is simply that I cannot imagine a 1000-sided figure, but clearly such a figure is possible. That is, while I cannot form a *mental image* of a 1000-sided figure (as opposed to a 999-sided figure), clearly I can conceive of such a figure. Thus, from the fact that I cannot imagine something, it does not follow that this something is not possible.

We have been talking about whether being unable to imagine ourselves divided shows that we are indivisible. This inference seems to be implausible. Can we avoid the problem if we take Descartes to mean that he cannot *conceive* of himself divided? When we imagine something we must add sufficient detail to get a mental picture. But conceiving of a thing is quite different. The concept of a triangle doesn't have built into it a triangle of this or that size, or of one with equal angles, or any such detail as that. When I entertain the abstract *concept* of triangularity—when I conceive of a triangle—I am entertaining only the concept of a three-sided closed plane figure, and that is not my *imagining* a triangle. Similarly, the dualist may avoid the objections just noted about imaginability by saying, not that I cannot imagine my mind as divided, but that I cannot conceive of my mind as divided. Just as a triangle's being four-sided is inconceivable and, therefore, impossible, so my mind's being divisible is inconceivable and, therefore, impossible. In this case, inconceivability does seem to be a reasonable guide to impossibility.

So, is Descartes justified in claiming that his mind is indivisible? Given that a person's experience can only have one perspective at a time, Descartes' challenge is convincing. We cannot imagine or conceive what it would be like to be, say, a football team or a choir. That is like asking us to entertain what it would be like to think as two or more things at once. Perhaps we can pretend to be this person now and that person later, or perhaps we can have several personalities that take over at different times. But we cannot place ourselves in the position of being several "single and complete" conscious things at once. When we think (imagine, conceive or perceive), we can only take the point of view of a single thinker.

Descartes' argument may seem reasonable. He can't conceive of himself as being a divided thinking thing. But does this show that he is indivisible? The materialist will object: the dualist hasn't claimed that no mind is divisible. He has claimed that *his* mind is indivisible," and the reason he gives for this premise is that *he* cannot conceive of being only part (one-half, say) of a mind or of having half a mind. The dualist is clearly thinking about his own case, "from the inside" as we might say. From this first-person point of view—when I introspect about *myself* or *my* mind—I cannot make sense of the idea that my mind is composed of parts. That indeed is true, because from the first-person perspective, I cannot conceive of a number of distinct things somehow unified to compose my mind, unless *I* so conceive it. But then I'm back to a single thinking self. So it's impossible for me to think of my own mind as composed of parts since that very thought would already presuppose my mind doing the thinking about these many parts.

The materialist will then grant that I cannot imagine or conceive of my mind as composed of parts (or myself as halved), but he will deny the purported consequence that it is impossible that my mind be divided into parts. We can say that although it may be psychologically impossible for me to imagine or conceive of myself as divided, it might still be logically impossible that I be divided. Perhaps I cannot possibly learn in a direct, introspectable way that my mind has parts, but from this it does not follow that one could not learn—in an indirect, third-person sort of way—that minds have parts. If the materialist is correct, then science might uncover such parts. It is on just this point, of course, that the dualist and the materialist disagree. The dualist, therefore, must do more than appeal to psychological facts about the limitations of introspection (or imagination or conception) to show the materialist that minds are different from physical objects.

Introspection and knowledge of mental states

Let's now consider in detail another argument for Dualism that appeals to introspection. Some dualists have argued that by introspection you are perfectly well aware of your mind and its nature. When you attend to the contents of your conscious states, you're aware of thoughts and sensations and emotions; you are aware of how sadness feels, of dull aches, of sharp pains. But, the dualist continues, introspection reveals to us nothing whatsoever about electrochemical impulses along nerves. Mental states and their properties, knowable introspectively, are radically *different* from neural states and their properties. Similarly, by introspecting you do not experience the qualitative nature of the brain and events in it—a mushy grey mass, the firings of neurons at certain rates, the level of electric potential across a synapse—as the qualitative nature of your conscious states. Thus, your mental states are not electrochemical states in any mushy grey mass. The general upshot of these facts which introspection reveals is simply that minds and mental states have properties different from those physical objects and states possess. By Leibniz's law, the mental is not identical with the physical. The argument from introspection is the following.

(1) I can come to know about my mind (mental states) by introspection.

(2) I cannot come to know about my brain (brain states) by introspection.

(3) So, my mind and my brain or body are distinct.

The materialist will likely respond as follows. Suppose that Emily (a small child) claims to know of lightning that it precedes thunder, but she makes no claim to know that luminous electrical discharge in the atmosphere precedes thunder (she may even deny this last proposition). It does not follow from this that lightning is not luminous electrical discharge in the atmosphere. Or consider the following argument.

(1) I can come to know about Mohammed Ali by reading the Sporting News.
(2) I cannot come to know about Cassius Clay by reading the Sporting News.
(3) So, Mohammed Ali is not Cassius Clay.

Since Mohammed Ali and Cassius Clay are the same person, something is obviously wrong with the argument. For the same reason we can say that from the fact that I claim to have introspectable knowledge of mental states but not physical states, it does not follow that mental states are not physical states of my brain. Just as Emily either may not realize that lightning is electrical discharge in the atmosphere or is simply wrong in supposing that she knows something about the one but not the other, so I may falsely conclude that mental states are not physical states for exactly similar reasons. The materialist will say that, as a matter of fact, I do have introspective knowledge of my brain states. Introspection might perfectly well reveal some properties of mental states but not all of them. Why suppose that it should reveal all properties? And if it doesn't, then nothing follows from dualist arguments from introspection. Here is Paul Churchland's defense of a materialist position:

In discriminating red from blue, sweet from sour, and hot from cold, our external senses are actually discriminating between subtle differences in intricate electromagnetic, stereochemical, and micromechanical properties of physical objects. But our senses are not sufficiently penetrating to reveal on their own the detailed nature of those intricate properties. That requires theoretical research and experimental exploration with specially designed instruments. The same is presumably true of our "inner" sense: introspection. It may discriminate efficiently between a great variety of neural states, without being able to reveal on its own the detailed nature of the states being discriminated. Indeed, it would be faintly miraculous if it did reveal them, just as miraculous as if unaided sight were to reveal the existence of interacting electric and magnetic fields whizzing by with an oscillatory frequency of a million

billion hertz and a wavelength of less than a millionth of a
meter. For despite "appearances," that is what light is.[6]

Both the dualist and the materialist accept Leibniz's Law. But
whereas the dualist claims that mental and physical states (or objects)
differ in their properties and, hence, are distinct, the materialist (at
least one sort) claims that mental states are identical with physical
states, and so there can be no property differences. We cannot tell
from observing lightning that it is a luminous electrical discharge in
the atmosphere; we may be unable to tell by feeling heat that it is
identical with molecular motion; we may be unable to tell from introspection that mental states are identical with brain states. But for all of
that, such identities may hold nonetheless.

B. Materialist Considerations

Materialism

We have so far taken a critical look at several traditional arguments for
Dualism. We should now take a look at what can be said for
Materialism. What considerations motivate the materialist's opposition
to Dualism?

That there is physical stuff in the world seems pretty clear to most
of us. Both dualists and materialists agree about this. The question
then is whether there is anything else in the world beside physical stuff
and objects composed of it. Thomas Hobbes, a contemporary of
Descartes, thought that the answer was "no." According to Hobbes,
there is no need to posit that some other sort of non-material stuff
exists. His story was fairly simple. Surely we don't suppose that human
persons are *not* part of the natural world. One job of the natural
sciences is to describe and explain the natural world systematically,
and Hobbes hoped to use the physics of his day to describe and explain the nature of human persons. The universe consists of physical
bodies, and all change is accounted for in terms of motions of particles of matter, large or small. Sensible change—differences we're
aware of from moment to moment—are thus given a purely physical
account, and from this can be gotten a general account of the senses
and appetites of human persons. (According to Hobbes, all mental
content has its origin in the senses.) Thus:

Concerning the thoughts of man, I will consider them first singly, and afterwards in train, or dependence upon one another. Singly, they are every one a representation or appearance, of some quality or other accident of a body without us, which is commonly called an object. Which object worketh on the eyes, ears, and other parts of a man's body; and by diversity of working produceth diversity of appearance.

The cause of sense, is the external body, or object, which presseth the organ proper to each sense, either immediately, as in taste and touch; or mediately, as in seeing, hearing, and smelling; which pressure, by the mediation of the nerves, and other strings and membranes of the body, continue[s] inwards to the brain and heart . . . .

When a body is once in motion, it moveth, unless something else hinder it, . . ; so also it happeneth in that motion, which is made in the internal parts of a man, then, when he sees, dreams, etc.. For after the object is removed, or the eye shut, we still retain an image of the thing seen, though more obscure then when we see it. And this it is [one calls] imagination. . . . *Imagination* is therefore nothing other than decaying sense. . . This decaying sense . . . when we would express the decay, and signify that the sense is fading, old, and past, . . . is called *memory*.[7]

Hobbes goes on to explain the nature of willing, hating, deliberating, fearing, and so on in purely materialist terms. We can ignore the out-dated science and archaic language. That is irrelevant. Hobbes' general point is simply that the fundamental thesis of materialism is true: we can give an account of the mental features of human persons in purely physical terms, without any need to appeal to non-material substance. This physical story will of course be quite complicated— much more complicated than Hobbes' story. But that is irrelevant too, for the problem of accounting for mentality is a *complicated problem*. Since there is no reason to suppose that an account in terms of *non-material* substance will be any less complicated than the materialist's, objecting to the complexity of the materialist's account is without force.

But there are fairly intuitive reasons for believing that materialism is correct in any case. We have already noted the Hobbesian intuition that human persons are perfectly good inhabitants of the physical world, with perfectly good physical properties. We say, for example, "I weigh 127 pounds," "I am over five feet tall" and the like. Moreover, in denying that there are immaterial things called "minds," the materialist is not committed to the thesis that human persons aren't conscious or have no mental states. If your brain is functioning normally, you are conscious and able to think. Indeed, for that very reason we believe that your thinking and willing and deliberating and so on are events in your brain. You do not remain a conscious thinking thing when your brain is massively damaged. Is this not good evidence that my thinking—that the center of consciousness—is localized in my brain? Or consider that when your brain is altered in a certain way you lose your sense of taste, when altered in another way you vividly remember childhood episodes. In short, there seem to be plenty of good reasons for embarking on the materialist program. There seems to be much to be gained in explaining the nature of mentality in terms of physical properties of our nervous systems, while there seems to be very little explanatory power to be gained in positing the existence of immaterial substance for this purpose.

Leibniz's Mill

Could the inner workings of a purely material system account for, or serve to explain, the nature of mentality? If the materialist is correct, the answer is "yes." As we've noted, that account is likely to be a very complicated one, but this is beside the point. According to the dualist, however, no amount of complexity could be enough. A very close and detailed look at material parts and their motions and interconnections will never reveal the slightest evidence of consciousness or thought. Gottfried Leibniz, a seventeenth century philosopher, imagines himself shrinking and going into a complex Hobbesian physical structure—a sort of machine, perhaps, of pushing and pulling gears and strings and membranes and so on—to find there nothing that explains thinking or sensing.

> [P]erception . . . [is] inexplicable by mechanical reasons, that is by figures and motions. If we pretend that there is a machine whose structure makes it think, feel, and have perception, one could think of it enlarged yet preserving its same proportions, so that one could enter it as one does a mill. If we did this, we should find nothing within but parts which push upon each other; we should never see anything which would explain a perception.[8]

As before, the antiquated physics isn't important: replace these crude pictures with the more elaborate picture given us nowadays by neurophysiology—of complex networks of nerves and electrochemical impulses along them; imagine taking a fantastic voyage through the human brain. Leibniz's point is not merely that we don't see thinking going on in any such physical system, but rather that when we inspect the interior of a physical system we understand perfectly well what is going on, and *that isn't thinking*. The materialist is simply wrong, then, to suppose that thinking—consciousness, generally—is the sort of thing that physical systems and their properties could instantiate.

This sentiment is reminiscent of the attitude expressed earlier about the possibility of sophisticated machines thinking. What we have there, it seems, is simulated thinking in the sense that viewed from the outside we see the physical system perform in a way that simulates thoughtful behavior. But unless we believe that all there is to thinking is behavior, we have no reason to suppose that such systems are really thinking things. And the example of Leibniz's mill suggests that we have good reasons for believing that they aren't.

Immaterial substance and explanation

Now there is no question that *thought* is a difficult and mysterious phenomenon. The dualist has directed our attention to the problems of attempting to explain it in physical terms. But the materialist will point out that nothing seems to be gained by positing, as Dualism does, the existence of some non-physical thinking substance. If imagining how a physical object could have thoughts and sensations and so on is difficult, why is explaining how a non-physical thing could think and have sensations any less difficult? It won't do to say merely that the immaterial mind or soul is just *the sort of thing that thinks*, for this explains nothing about the nature of thought, or how thought is possible. Thinking is possible, but when we go on to ask what features of us make thought possible, we encounter the difficulty of explaining how bodies can think or how the qualities of mental states can be attributed to brain states. But supposing that there is *something else*—minds—that think, or that mental states are states of an immaterial substance does not clarify in the slightest those difficulties.

In short, the materialist will argue that no explanatory work is done by the dualist. Indeed, on that score, the materialist wonders if matters are not worse for the dualist than for himself. This non-physical stuff called "mind" is quite mysterious. What is it, and what is the nature of it in virtue of which the features of thought are explained? The task of accounting for mentality in terms of some non-observable, non-spatial stuff seems a considerably greater task than accounting for it by referring to things accessible to science, about which we possess a great deal of information, and about which we can reasonably expect to learn a great deal more.

Questions: What is the Argument from Disembodied Existence and why would a materialist find it unconvincing? What is the Divisibility Argument? What is Leibniz's Law and how is it used? What problem arises for the Divisibility Argument? How is introspection used to argue for Dualism? What objection does it face? How does Hobbes propose to account for thinking? How is Leibniz's Mill used to defend the dualist's intuition?

Section 3: DUALISM AND THE RELATIONSHIP PROBLEM

A. Interactionism

Mental events and physical events

We can't easily deny that our mental life has an effect on our physical life. Your being in pain, surely, has something or other to do with your outward gestures of discomfort; your deciding to leave the room has something or other to do with actually getting up and leaving; my feeling of sadness is not just accidently hooked up with my crying. The materialist, recall, is skeptical about Dualism's ability to provide a genuinely explanatory account of consciousness generally. A specific worry, now, concerns what sort of account the Dualist can offer by way of explaining how our mental life is hooked up with our physical life. For the materialist, clearly, this is not a special problem. The most likely place to look for the connection between events in my mental life and physical events is the brain, simply because the brain is the most likely place to look for the source of consciousness. That seems intuitively right, for your physical body moves to leave the room because something happens in your brain that eventually causes your body to so move. Again, that will likely end up being a fairly complicated story, in terms of (say) firings of neurons in the the motor cortex of the brain and so on. The important point is simply that we have a plausible and fully detailed causal story that explains this connection between your mental states and physical events.

The materialist challenge to Dualism, then, is to explain satisfactorily the relationship between mental events and physical events. On the surface that looks like a tall order. The dualist story will involve two radically different kinds of substances and events involving them—material and immaterial. Exactly what sort of relationship holds between the non-observable, non-spatial events of an immaterial mind and the observable, spatial events in our physical brains and bodies? We need some such story, clearly, because we do believe that our mental lives affect our physical lives and conversely.

A common sense view

That physical events can produce or change or affect mental states is a familiar fact. When a heavy object is dropped on your foot, for example, you feel pain, and were it to miss your foot altogether you would feel no pain; when light impinges on your retina you see shapes and colors, and, by closing your eyes those shapes and colors are no longer part of your visual content; if you ingest spoiled food you feel nausea; if you take certain drugs you may hallucinate giant magenta iguanas climbing up your pants, and so on.

An equally familiar fact is that your mental states can produce or change or affect physical states. Your being frightened may lead to trembling or perspiring or cries of fear, where in normal situations you would manifest none of these physical states; your decision to leave the room eventuates in the movements of your body in ways you would not move had you decided to remain seated; if you are happy you may smile; if you see an iguana on someone's leg you may shout loud warnings to her; and so on.

Nothing in the dualist's story seems to require a denial of such facts. When you have a pain, the doctor will prescribe a treatment that affects you physically, as a means of reducing the pain. A skilled neurophysiologist might even go into your body to treat you directly and relieve the pain. But of course he will never *see* your pain. Rather, he treats your physical condition in such a way that the pain is no longer produced. Likewise, behavior that we can observe accompanies your voluntary decision to leave the room. Clearly we do not observe your deciding to leave; no amount of looking and probing will uncover the mental event of your deciding. We uncover only the physical *effects* of your deciding—physical effects that we may observe in your behavior, perhaps effects in your neural states that eventuate in your body's moving so as to leave the room.

Interactionism is a dualist view that contends that the mind and the body interact. Events in your mental life may produce or bring about change of states in your physical life, and conversely, events in your physical life may produce or bring about changes in your mental life.

Causal interaction

What does it mean to say that the mind and body interact? According to the dualist version of the common-sense view, both physical and mental events can "produce" or "bring about" events of the other sort. The most obvious way of understanding interaction, then, is as a *causal* notion: the mind and the body causally interact. That, indeed, is our normal way of thinking about how the mind is related to the body. Though your brain is distinct from your mind, certain events happen in your body—but most importantly for our purposes, in your brain—that have causal consequences in your mind. Similarly, certain events occur in your mind that have bodily effects.

Notice that the interactionist is not suggesting that all physical events taking place in your brain or elsewhere in your body have mental effects, or that every mental event will cause some physical event. Surely, a nerve could fire in your brain without causing some mental state in you, or an idea might flash through your mind while you relax on your bed resting, without it causing some physical event to occur. The interactionist's claim is simply that mental events *can* cause physical events and conversely. We frequently do talk in this way, saying for example that what caused her trembling and perspiring was her being frightened, or that what caused her pain was her sitting on a tack. Indeed, we should be surprised if such events were uncaused, or if the relation between mental events and physical events of the sort noted by the common-sense view were, say, mysterious and inexplicable, or merely accidental.

In the cases we've been describing, what we take to be the effect wouldn't have occurred if what we take to be the cause hadn't occurred. This indicates that the relation between mental and physical events is indeed a causal one. We don't believe that your pain and your wincing are merely *both present*. Your wincing wouldn't have occurred if it hadn't been for your pain. *Given* your pain, you winced, but in the circumstances (when you're not play-acting or the like) you wouldn't have winced in the absence of pain. Thus, we see that the pain really does *bring about* the wincing, in a genuinely causal way. "What caused you to wince?" "I was in pain."

B. Problems with Interactionism

Causal connection

Before assessing the dualist's theory of Interactionism, let's review what we know about the causal relation. It isn't an altogether mysterious relation. We recognize it out in the world every day when we see, for example, a rock strike and break a window, or a match being scratched and lighting. But what exactly is it about these relationships between events that makes them causal? At least this much is obvious: whenever we've seen scratchings of a dry match we've seen lightings of the match, and similarly for strikings of windows and their breakings. This correlation, then—this "whenever we have the one we have the other" feature—goes into much of what we have in mind when distinguishing causal connections from merely accidental ones.

There is more, of course. We suppose that a cause must precede its effect in time. If the match's being scratched causes its lighting, then the lighting doesn't occur before the scratching, nor does the breaking of the window occur before its being struck if the striking causes the breaking. But even this is not enough. We're familiar with examples of temporally-ordered correlations between events that aren't causal connections. The rising of the sun invariably follows the sounding of reveille at summer camp; but we are not tempted to say that the bugle's sounding causes the sun's rising.

In the summer camp case, perhaps, one of our worries is that happenings at one spatial location can't directly cause happenings at a distant spatial location. In normal circumstances, something must actually strike the window if it is to break, or something must actually rub against the match if it is to light. There are causal chains, of course, running between spatial locations. But then it is still the case that what causes that event over there is *some event over there*, spatially contiguous with it, bringing it about. Very strong sound waves, for example, might travel from your enormously loud sneeze to that very fragile window.

Still, not just any two kinds of correlated, temporally-ordered, spatially contiguous events will be causally connected. There are always air particles striking the window, and hence, there are always air particles striking the window immediately before a window breaks. But those innocuous particles glancing off the window won't suffice to break a window. We suppose that a cause is *sufficient* for its effect in the sense that, given the circumstances, the cause-event is enough to guarantee the occurrence of the effect-event. Put otherwise, a cause is a necessary part of larger set of circumstances that, as a whole, is sufficient for the occurrence of the effect. Thus, given that the match is dry, that we're in the presence of oxygen, that the match is properly made, and so on, if we scratch the match then the match lights. And in the circumstances the match wouldn't light if we didn't scratch it.

Now that is a quite general way of characterizing the causal relation. In particular instances of one event's causing another, of course, we—or some properly-informed scientist at least—can add quite a lot of detail. Even in the simple case where one billiard ball strikes another and causes it to move, we can reconstruct a moderately complicated story drawn from our high school science classes. The cue ball has a certain mass, and given its velocity we know that it possesses a certain momentum; it strikes the eight-ball with some force, and the kinetic energy of one ball is somehow imparted to the other in sufficient degree to overcome a coefficient of friction, so that the eight-ball moves toward the pocket while the cue ball slows to a stop. Again, this is a pretty rough-and-ready story, but the point remains that there is detail to be had when filling in a particular causal story. It is the role of causal laws, discovered by science, to describe how these details figure in the course of events in the world. If an eight-ball moved across the table all on its own without being hit, we should have on our hands a mystery indeed, simply because none of the details figuring in typical causal stories like that above would be of any use in this strange case. We have no laws describing or predicting such phenomena.

Is causal interaction possible?

Let's return now to the interactionist's account of the relation between mind and body. According to this common-sense theory, mind and body causally interact, by which one means that mental events can cause physical events and physical events can cause mental events. Now despite the intuitiveness of this view, a little reflection shows that it is not straightforwardly true, if it is true at all. In fact, Interactionism may turn out to be unintelligible for the dualist.

To get an initial glimpse of the difficulty, recall that according to Dualism, mind and body are radically different things: one is spatial while the other is not, one is observable by the senses while the other is not, one is public while the other is not, and so on. Thus, the mind and mental events involving it are completely outside the domain of physical laws. These events involve no physical parameters like mass or velocity or momentum or the like; they cannot be spatially near or distant; they have no surfaces and cannot come into contact with physical objects; talk of kinetic energy or coefficients of friction make no sense in reference to them; and so on. What sort of story is there to tell, then, when claiming that mental events and physical events can affect one another *causally*? No physical laws could describe such relations. What details can the interactionist offer by way of filling out a story of such causal interaction? None of the details figuring in our familiar causal accounts will do. Our typical judgements about causal relations involve events of the same kind: the physical event of the rock's striking the window causes the physical event of the window's breaking. When the common-sense dualist speaks of an interaction between events of such radically different kinds, then, it isn't obvious that the relation could be a causal one at all.

Suppose you say that your pain was caused by the injury to your foot. Filled out, perhaps the story would go something like this. A heavy object falls and strikes your foot. Certain sensory neurons near the skin are affected in such a way that a so-called action potential—a sort of electrical impulse—is transmitted along a series of neurons in the peripheral nervous system to the spinal cord. Neurons in the cord shuttle the "pain" information up to the thalamus in the forebrain. From here it is transmitted to a specific region in the appropriate hemisphere of your brain, at which time you feel pain. True enough: at that moment you feel pain. But of course, that event of your suddenly feeling pain is suppose to be *caused*. By what? In this story, the entire process has been described in physical terms up to the very last step, at which point you say "and then I feel pain." Does this last physical event—this particular neuron's firing, say, at this particular spot—cause your pain? It is difficult to see how this makes any sense. For example, there is no point of contact between the last neuron that fires and the pain. There are no nerves running into the mind; no electrical impulses can affect further electrical changes at some spatially nearby region of your mind; your mental episodes do not occur at some particular spot your brain. In short, there seem to be no details available for filling in that part of the story between the firing of the last neuron and the part where you report "and then I feel pain." That part of the story remains altogether mysterious, and it is that part of the story at which, according to interactionists, a physical event causes a mental event.

The idea of a causal interaction between mind and body is perhaps even more mysterious when we consider how it is possible for a mental event to cause a physical event. We know roughly how physical events cause physical events: the billiard-ball story is an example, and we could easily tell a kind of rough-and-ready story for neurons too. In all such cases, at very least, we can specify a point of contact at which one object or event causally affects another object or event. But now we are to envision a mental event causing a physical event. We are to envision mind acting on matter with sufficient detail to understand how the firing of a neuron is caused, not by the firing of a neighboring neuron, but by some mental event. Some thought or feeling or doubt or fear, with no spatial location in or out of your head, involving nothing with mass or velocity, capable of possessing no electrical or chemical energy or the like, is supposed to make a neuron fire. Is that possible? We have plenty of detail available to us about how electrochemical states in one neuron can affect changes in a neighboring neuron. But none of *that* sort of detail is available for explaining how a fear can affect physical changes in a neuron such that an electrical potential suddenly exists within it.

Perhaps an analogy will help illustrate the strangeness of these sorts of claims. To envision a non-physical, non-spatial, non-observable mental event causing a physical event is very like imagining the eight-ball, resting quietly in the center of the table, suddenly moving in a trajectory toward the pocket. To envision a physical event causing a mental event is very like imagining the cue-ball, moving swiftly across the table, coming to a sudden halt without touching any other ball. The picture we've imagined here is very like the picture a neurophysiologist should get, according to Interactionism, were he able to watch the episodes in your brain with a special sort of cerebroscope. If your decision to leave the room causes your body to move in such a way that you walk from the room, the neurophysician should see a particular neuron, resting quietly in your brain, suddenly and spontaneously fire (without being caused to fire by any neighboring neuron) in such a way that your body eventually moves toward the door. That is indeed a remarkable story. It is no less remarkable than if someone were to tell you that the number four was moving the cue-ball. This, of course, sounds completely absurd. The number four is not something can push physical objects around. One obvious reason for this is that numbers, though they are not mental objects, are like mental objects in being nonspatial—they cannot come into contact with a billiard ball.

Conservation of energy

Thus far our misgivings have concerned the intelligibility of Interactionism. Given our understanding of causality and Dualism, it isn't obvious that mental events and physical events can be causally related at all. A different but related criticism of Interactionism concerns whether or not the theory is consistent with known principles of physical science. A principle in science is a law that our world obeys. The principle of inertia, for example, is a law that says that a body retains its state of rest or motion unless an outside force acts upon it. If we were to offer a theory entailing the claim that there are ordinary bodies not behaving in this way, our theory would be inconsistent with the principle of inertia. And to the extent that we take such a principle to be true—we actually find no bodies failing to obey it—we must suppose that our theory is false.

There is an important principle in physical science called the principle of *Conservation of Energy*. Energy is a magnitude scientists use as a measure of the amount of work that can be done by physical systems. According to this principle, the total amount of energy in the universe remains constant. It may take various forms, of course, as when the chemical energy in your body is transformed into, say, the kinetic energy of your moving limbs and the heavy object you throw, along with a certain amount of heat energy given off by your body. The general point, then, is that when events occur and bring about the occurrence of other events, energy is expended but not destroyed. The energy you expend when throwing a heavy object is not annihilated but rather changes its form in relation to other objects—the heavy object now moves and the surrounding air is warmer. When one billiard ball strikes another, clearly one ball loses some amount of energy (it stops moving) and another ball gains some (it starts moving). According to the principle of Conservation of Energy, the total amount of energy in the Universe remains constant. (Discussions of conservation of energy are frequently conducted in terms of "conservative systems"—physical arrangements or collections of objects in which the amount of energy remains constant or very nearly constant throughout all changes. The universe as a whole is a conservative system, but smaller systems are conveniently viewed as approximately conservative. A loaded but unfired cannon at one moment possesses the same amount of energy as the recoiling cannon, moving cannon-ball, etc,. a few moments later, even though the energy from the early moment to the later one has been radically redistributed in different forms.)

By the principle of Conservation of Energy, we know that when one event causes another event, the loss of energy accompanying the occurrence of the cause must be associated with some corresponding gain of energy in the effects. Consider now the interactionists' claim that mental events can cause physical events, and conversely. Suppose that you drop a heavy object on your foot. A string of causally-connected physical events occurs, running from your foot up to your brain, causing you to feel pain. The cause of your pain is some physical event. Accompanying the occurrence of that cause-event is a loss of energy. But now, where is to be found the corresponding gain of energy in the effect? The effect is a mental event that is not located in your head, nor even outside it. Indeed the effect is not part of the physical world at all. Thus, when a physical event causes a mental event, there is apparently some loss of energy in the physical world (on the "cause" side of the story) for which there is no associated gain of energy to be found in the physical world (since, the "effect" side of the story isn't physical). It is very like the billiard-ball story imagined earlier: the cue-ball loses its energy and suddenly stops, in the middle of the table, without having imparted its energy to anything physical in which we can find a corresponding gain. Again, suppose that you decide to raise your arm and as a result your arm goes up. The cause of this physical event is a mental event, nowhere to be found in the physical world. The gain of energy on the effect side of the story, required for your arm's raising, is thus associated with no corresponding loss of energy in the physical world. As before, it is very like the eight-ball suddenly being possessed of energy enough to roll toward the pocket, without having gained it from anything in the physical world wherein we can find a corresponding loss.

What we should expect to see, then, if Interactionism is true, are sudden losses and gains of energy in the world. If we imagined a kind of energy probe stuck into the world, it should register a sudden loss of energy, with no gain of energy corresponding to it, when a neuron's firing causes your pain, and it should register a sudden gain of energy, with no loss corresponding to it, when your decision causes your arm's raising. The principle of Conservation of Energy says that there simply are no such losses and gains of energy in the physical world. Indeed, no such losses—as we'd expect to notice when a physical event causes a mental event—or gains —as we'd expect to notice when a mental event causes a physical event—have ever been detected. In short, it seems that Interactionism is not consistent with a fundamental principle of science. If that is correct, and we accept the principle as true, then we must agree that Interactionism is false.

C. Parallelism

The common-sense dualist takes seriously the way in which we talk about familiar facts relating mind and body. We do indeed say things that suggest that mind and body causally interact: Lynn is in pain because she sat on a tack, and her pain caused her to jump and yell, and so on. But how we talk about things is not always a reliable guide to the way things in fact are. A closer look at Interactionism has shown that considerable difficulties are involved in the claim that mental events and physical events can be causally connected. An improved dualist account will avoid these difficulties by offering an appropriately non-causal story about the relation between mind and body.

Correlation without causation

What are the familiar facts we have in mind when speaking about the relation of mental events and physical events? Well, earlier we noted facts like these: when a heavy object is dropped on your foot you feel pain; when you decide to leave the room you move toward the door; when you take the right drugs you hallucinate giant magenta iguanas climbing up your pants; when you're fearful you tremble and perspire. Now what we have evidence for here is that certain of our mental events are correlated with certain physical events, and conversely. Thus, if we should like to avoid the difficulties arising for Interactionism, the best option is to build into our theory precisely this correlation between mental events and physical events, without going further to posit the existence of a causal relation between them. On such a theory, the events in our bodies are related to one another causally, following upon one another is an orderly way, in accordance with their own special laws. It may even be that mental events are causally related to one another, following each other in accordance their laws. But on this theory, it is incorrect to say that events of such different kinds could causally interact. Rather, the events of these separate realms operate—as it were—along parallel tracks, not causally related but correlated with one another in exactly the way our familiar facts above give evidence for. By way of an analogy, here is something Leibniz said:

> Imagine two clocks or watches which are in perfect agreement. Now this can happen in three ways. The first is by natural influence . . . The second way of making two clocks, even poor ones, agree always is to assign a skilled craftsman to them who adjusts them and constantly sets them in agreement. The third way is to construct these two timepieces at the beginning with such skill and accuracy that one can be assured of their subsequent agreement.
>   Now put the soul and the body in the place of these two timepieces. Then their agreement or sympathy will also come about in one of the three ways . . . .[9]

Leibniz goes on to say that the first way of "natural influence"—of causal connection—is impossible: Interactionism cannot work. The second way, representing a view called Occasionalism, would require divine intervention at every instant. But this is unacceptable. All that is left, then, is the Parallelist's option: our minds and bodies are simply made in such a way that mental events and physical (especially brain) events reliably correspond with one another in the way two synchronized clocks correspond in their readings of time.

> The souls follow their laws, which consist in a definite development of perceptions . . . , and bodies follow theirs, which consist in the laws of motion; nevertheless, these two beings of entirely different kind meet together and correspond to each other like two clocks perfectly regulated to the same time.[10]

D. Problems with Parallelism

Synchrony

Parallelists refuse to allow that an observable, spatially-located physical event could cause (produce, bring about) a mental event like a pain, or that a mental event could cause anything like an electrochemical changes in a neurons. By denying that causal relations hold between such radically different kinds of things as mental and physical events, parallelists can avoid the difficulties noted earlier in connection with Interactionism. This can be done without denying any of the familiar facts noted earlier, so long as Parallelism retains the sort of correlation between mental events and physical events that these facts clearly indicate.

Now it is one thing to claim that the order of your mental events inevitably concurs—remains in synchrony with—the order of physical events in your body (but especially, your brain); it is quite another to *explain why this synchrony holds*, or why it never fails. As a matter of fact, you never cry out in pain before feeling pain, nor do you feel the pain before dropping the object on your foot. There is no difficulty for the interactionist in explaining why this concurrence holds. Your crying out never precedes your pain, nor does your pain ever precede your injury, because effects never precede causes. But if, as the parallelist claims, there are no causal relations holding between mind and body, then in virtue of what does this synchrony hold? Again, it clearly *does* hold, but we should like some feature of the dualist's theory to explain this. There seems to be nothing in Parallelism ruling out the *possibility* that your mental life get—as it were—"out of synch" with your physical life. At best, the parallelist simply reports that as a matter of fact it does not, but this falls short of explaining why it cannot.

The difficulty seems to be that Parallelism rejects the causal relation between our mental lives and physical lives in favor of no relation at all. This theory allows relations between events of the same kind—between mental events or between physical events—that genuinely constrain their order of occurrence, but it also seems to permit no relations between mental events and physical events that guarantee synchrony. Each series of events is self-contained, and the order of neither constrains the order of the other. In short, that our pains never precede our injuries and that our cries never precede our pains is either a mystery or a rather odd kind of accident.

"Suppose there were no minds . . . ."

If Parallelism is correct about the relation between mind and body, then the episodes of your mental life in no way constrain the events in your physical life. Rather, physical events—those in your body and outside of it—happen in accordance with causal laws, these laws specifying the order of events in the physical world quite independent of any details about your mind. Thus, the explanation for any action of mine is properly given entirely in terms of a causal story about the physical realm, without reference to mental affairs.

This view is strange indeed. To see exactly how odd it is, imagine that God decides to annihilate all minds such that there simply are no mental events of any kind. (Never mind that, according to many dualists, this will entail the annihilation of all persons: the story will work just fine without persons. The story will work just as well, too, if you imagine that God annihilates all minds but your own. Perhaps that will make it easier to entertain the details of the story.) What will happen, as a consequence of this annihilation, to the way you and I, or our bodies, behave? Nothing whatsoever, if Parallelism is true. There will be no pains, but there will be cries of pain; arms will go up in response to questions in class, and answers will be vocalized, but there will be no thoughts and no decisions to raise one's hand. Since Parallelism entails that no mental event—no decision or pain or the like—constrains the order and occurrence of physical events, the order and occurrence of events in the physical world would remain exactly as it is whether there were minds or not. In our story, which is perfectly consistent with Parallelism, brilliant experiments in science would be conducted but there would be no brilliant ideas; painkillers would be in demand—and would have their calming effects—in the absence of all pain; and so on.

The point of this story is to emphasize that we do indeed believe our mental lives have genuine effects in the physical world. We do not think that it merely *so happens* that you raise your hand when you decide to raise your hand, but that your deciding somehow brings about your hand-raising. While Interactionism has been criticized for being too strong, the attempt to avoid its difficulties seems to render Parallelism too weak. It is too weak to explain successfully why our mental lives and our physical lives are correlated in the regular way that they are, and it is too weak to account for our conviction that the physical world would be drastically different were there no pains or thoughts or decisions or fears.

Explaining the occurrence of mental events

Fortunately, God isn't likely to annihilate all minds. But we needn't envision such a far-fetched example to appreciate a final difficulty with Parallelism. What explanation is given for why some particular physical event—a neuron's firing, say—actually occurs? Well, some preceding physical event or events cause it to occur. The parallelist does not deny regular causal connections between physical events. What explanation is given for why some particular mental event— your feeling pain now, say—actually occurs? The parallelist cannot say that some physical event caused it, as the interactionist might, because according to Parallelism such relations do not hold. There seem to be two possible remaining answers: either your feeling pain happened for no reason at all, but sheerly by chance, or else some preceding mental event or events somehow brought it about. The first of these options is not very satisfactory, for precisely the reasons we might say that the second option is just fine: we do have "trains of thought," for example, that don't fit into any story about mental events being entirely random or chance events. In some fairly obvious sense, our mental lives show patterns that we can predict, recognize, consciously alter, and so on. You may have some pain, and think immediately thereafter about the seriousness of it, and then consider its source, and then consider what action to take, and so on. Or perhaps you smell woodsmoke, and then think of home, and then think of your mother, and then think of home cooking. Sequences or trains of thought like these make it difficult to believe that our mental lives are randomly ordered and not regular. Indeed, as we characterized Parallelism earlier, and as Leibniz's analogy suggests, our conscious episodes are to be explained as following—perhaps even causally—in a lawlike way from previous ones, much as preceding states of the clock causally explain the successive readings on the clockface.

But how much of our mental lives show such obvious patterns of succession? On reflection, very little. The occurrence of many mental events—perhaps most of them—are not easily accounted for by referring to previous mental events. Consider the garden-variety experience of a sudden but mild pain, occurring abruptly in the course of normal affairs. There seems to be no obvious story about how the normal mental episodes you had a moment ago lead to or bring about or cause the sudden pain you now have. Do thoughts of mother or home-cooking cause feelings of pain? Not regularly, and not reliably. But that is what a lawlike, causal connection amongst your mental episodes would require.

There are more isolated cases that pose this same difficulty, perhaps in more striking form. Consider mental lapses. They seem at least possible: a person in a coma or a very deep sleep might experience no mental episodes. How are we to explain the occurrence of the first mental event following such a lapse? Suppose you fall asleep to quiet music and the thought of some pleasant memory, and suppose that you awaken from your deep sleep at 2:00 AM to the sound of a violent crash outside your window. If we deny either that physical events cause mental events or that mental events are purely random, but choose rather to explain their occurrence in terms of previous mental events, then we are committed to saying that last night's awareness of quiet music and a pleasant memory caused this morning's experience of hearing a loud crash. That is not a likely story. (If a coma were very long—many years, let's say—then the story becomes even more unlikely. That a mental event eleven years past can now cause the first conscious episode in the recovering patient is difficult to fathom.)

One might be skeptical about the possibility of mental lapses and the like. The present criticism of Parallelism doesn't really need them. For consider that, unless you have had mental episodes *forever* (into the distant past), the parallelist cannot explain at all your very first mental event.

There do not appear to be enough causal resources in the mental realm to explain the occurrence of every mental event. If there are not, then Parallelism has little hope of providing a successful dualist account of the relation between mind and body.

E. General Remarks about the Relationship Problem

Causation and science

The failure of Parallelism invites us to reconsider Interactionism. It seems clear that parallelists have posited too weak a relation between mental events and physical events (they have merely asserted the existence of a regular correlation between them): and there are no obvious candidates for a middle-strength relation—lying somewhere between correlation and causation—capable of doing justice to our belief that pains cause cries and injuries cause pains. Might our attitude against Interactionism have been too unyielding?

Many dualists, of course, will say that it has. Our understanding of the causal relation, they will suggest, was much too narrow. The A-acting-on-B version of causation, of the sort our billiard-ball examples capture handily, is oversimplified. Science is perfectly willing to countenance more elaborate and complicated cases of causal relations than this. Consider the gravitational affect of the moon on the sea: a distant heavenly body causes changes in the tides. Or again, electro-magnetism is a respectable sort of causal influence, capable of acting over a distance without some intervening objects striking one another. In such cases of gravity and electro-magnetism, of course, our picture is somewhat less refined than the billiard-ball cases. But they are not any the less instances of causal relations for all that. And since we know in such cases that A can affect B without being able to say exactly how, we should likewise be willing to admit that mind and body can affect changes in one another, even if we cannot say exactly how.

Still, there is an important disanalogy between these complicated cases in the physical sciences and the interactionist's thesis that mind and body causally interact. Both gravitational and electromagnetic phenomena represent the action of one physical thing on *another physical thing*. That is not so in the case of mind acting on body, and it is precisely this feature of Interactionism—the action of *non*-physical things on physical things (and conversely)—that makes it worrisome. However difficult it remains to explain gravity and electro-magnetism, we do not suppose that this is because such forms of action are not genuinely physical. These forms of action are difficult to explain because scientists have lots more to learn about them. But if Interactionism is correct, scientific investigation cannot completely resolve the difficulty of explaining how mind acts on body or body on mind, because the mental realm is not fully within the reach of physical science.

Theoretical disadvantages of Dualism

This last point, about the relative inaccessibility of mind to science, highlights an important theoretical advantage Materialism has over Dualism. We would like hypotheses of a theory to be *testable*, in the sense that they are open to being verified or falsified. (See Chapter 2, Section 1C.) Since much of the dualist's story is not open to empirical investigation, it is difficult to imagine what sort of evidence could falsify it. And insofar as Materialism refers only to objects and events that are spatially located and in principle observable, there is at least hope that many of its claims are testable.

A second theoretical disadvantage of Dualism concerns what we'll refer to as the *ontological commitments* of a theory. A fairly intuitive principle of theorizing is that one should not posit the existence of entities unless they are necessary for explaining the phenomena about which one is theorizing. Now the dualist has said that not only do physical objects and events involving them exist, but also that there exists some mental substance—mind—and countless mental events. The materialist, on the other hand, is committed to the existence of only some of these entities—entities that, unlike non-physical stuff, we already believe to exist in the first place. Thus, while both theories attempt to explain the nature of thought or mentality, Materialism does it with considerably less theoretical baggage than Dualism. And Dualism does not obviously provide better results for all this extra baggage. The payoffs seem slim when considered alongside the ontological commitments Dualism requires us to endorse.

There is another closely related theoretical disadvantage here as well. Dualism is not merely committed to more entities than Materialism is. As we've indicated, it seems to have done so without securing any more *explanatory capability*. Indeed, Dualism seems to be much worse off than Materialism on this score. The explanatory resources available to the materialist are considerable: we know that there are brains, and that they have a certain structure; we know something of how neurons are organized into systems for processing sensory and motor information; we know something of the electrochemistry of nerve cells; we know which parts of the brain are relevant to which sorts of behavior; and so on. And, of course, we will learn quite a lot more. But what explanatory resources can the dualist provide us about the structure and workings of the mind? Very little, it seems. The materialist will encourage us to agree that immaterial substance is altogether mysterious, and that by constructing a theory in terms of it, the dualist loses, not gains, explanatory capability.

Questions: How does the interactionist account for the relationship between mind and body? As we typically think of causation, what is required for one event to cause another? Why is a causal connection between mind and body problematic given the nature of a mental object. What problem does the interactionist face specifically with the Conservation of Energy Principle? What is Parallelism? How does it address the relationship problem? What objections might be raised? What disadvantages does Dualism have when compared with Materialism?

Section 4: THE PROBLEM OF OTHER MINDS

The materialist's objection

How do you know what it is to have a headache? The answer is obvious: you feel it. And how do you know when you have a headache? Again the answer is obvious: you feel it. Clearly in our own cases we can know that we have mental states because we experience them: we are aware of them in a very intimate and direct way. But now consider how we know that other people have mental states. We do, of course, think that other people have thoughts, desires, emotions and pains. Surely your neighbor felt angry when you backed the car over his shrubbery, the football player felt pain when the entire defensive line piled on his back, and your mother was happy when you bought her flowers for Mother's Day. That we all have these beliefs about the mental states of other persons is uncontroversial. But Dualism, as we shall see, seems to have difficulty in accounting for the fact that we do *know*—or that we are *entitled* to believe—that things other than ourselves have mental states.

A problem arises because the dualist has claimed that mental states are *private*: conscious persons can experience only their own mental states and no one else's. If you cannot experience another's mental states, then for all you know that other person is nothing more than a robot or automaton merely behaving according to a program, acting as though it had mental states without really having them. In virtue of what are you rational in believing that other persons are conscious— on what ground to you know that they are conscious—if you cannot tell by observation or experience whether something has mental states or not?

Imagine a cleverly made robot that looks and behaves exactly like a human being but that in fact has no mental life. It says "Ouch" when you hit it and answers "Yes, that hurt" when you ask whether it felt pain. Still, it is programmed to behave that way and feels nothing. Since you cannot experience any mental states other than your own, nothing you could do could determine whether it is conscious. You would likely believe that this robot was conscious upon observing it, but you would be wrong. On the other hand, suppose you do discover that it is a robot. Can you know—or are you justified in believing— that it is not conscious? This robot story indicates an apparent consequence of Dualism, that although you can know that you have mental states, you cannot know or be justified in believing that others have mental states.

Now the claim is not simply that you cannot know *what* someone else is thinking, or whether what they experience when they say they feel pain is what you experience when you feel pain. The claim is that you cannot know *that* anyone else feels, thinks, or believes anything at all; you cannot know *whether* that other being is even conscious. For all you know those other beings around you only act as though they have pains, think, etc.; for all you know they are devoid of consciousness. And this is true no matter how they behave.

Consequently, the materialist will be quick to point out that Dualism has skeptical consequences. If Dualism is true, we cannot know what we naturally take ourselves to know, namely, that other beings are conscious. The materialist's argument against Dualism might look something like the following.

(1)   If Dualism is true, we cannot know that other minds exist.

(2)   But we can know that other minds exist.

(3)   So, Dualism is not true.

It is up to the dualist to reject one of these premises. He could accept premise (1) and reject the otherwise plausible (2). The materialist would then not have succeeded in refuting Dualism, but the skeptical consequence of Dualism, indicated in the first premise, is a rather unwelcome one, and suggests we should think twice before accepting such a theory. On the other hand, if the dualist rejects premise (1), he must give some account how one can know about the existence of other minds given that mental states are private states. Let's take a look at how a dualist might attempt to support a denial of premise (1).

The dualist's response

Suppose the dualist denies that he has any problems in knowing that others have mental states. He will not deny that mental states are private. That is an important consequence of his theory. He will insist, however, that you can know that there are other minds even if you cannot know this in the way you know that you have a mind.

Let's distinguish two sorts of knowledge: weak and strong. Strong knowledge is the sort of knowledge you have when you are infallible with respect to what is believed—you can't be wrong. This is the kind of certainty you have of your own mental states because you have a very direct and intimate experience of them. You can't be wrong, for example, about your feeling a pain in your foot; having a pain and being aware of a pain are the same thing.

But consider your knowledge that the table in front of you is brown. You can't be fooled about the table's *looking* brown but you could be deceived about the table's *being* brown; the lighting might mislead you, or perhaps some mad scientist is playing with your brain making you think it is brown when it is not. Your belief that the table is brown is fallible since you could be wrong about it even though, as a matter of fact, you are not. This fallible sort of believing is "weak" knowledge. You have weak knowledge when, although you don't have absolute certainty, you do have good or adequate evidence (or reasons) for what you believe. The evidence needn't guarantee the truth of what is believed, but must make it (sufficiently) highly probable. You know, for example, that the sun is going to rise tomorrow even though you could be wrong. This is a very likely belief because your evidence for it—you've seen it rise every day in the past—is very good.

Now the dualist can claim that although we don't have strong, infallible, absolutely certain knowledge of the existence of other minds, we can have weak, fallible, evidentially supported knowledge. We do, after all, have certain behavioral evidence for thinking that others have minds. Consider the evidence you have for my mental states. My screaming when I sit on a tack tells you that I am feeling pain; my saying "What a nice day" tells you that I think it is a nice day; my crying at the funeral tells you that I am feeling sad. Similarly, your behavior tells me that you are conscious and have various mental states.

We can devise an inductive argument by analogy for the claim that others have minds. A person's behavior counts as evidence that he has mental states because we think that this is the way we would behave if we were in that situation, and we know that in that situation our mental states are connected with this behavior. Of course, more goes into our judgments about the existence of other minds than just behavior. We might also want to know that the other thing is pretty much like we are in certain ways. Even if a computer says it is feeling pain, we don't automatically conclude that it is feeling pain since it is not like us in relevant ways. We tend to think that having something like a brain and a nervous system are necessary for having mental states. Now what should count as a relevant similarity is all very controversial; the dualist after all thinks that mental states can exist independently of any physical body, and so it is not clear why having a brain or a nervous system should matter. But perhaps we can leave the controversial matters alone and say at least this much: the more the thing behaves like me in certain circumstances and the more it is like me in the ways specified above, the more likely it is (the better my evidence) that it too has mental states.

From the foregoing discussion we can devise the following argument by analogy:

    (1) Whenever I am in situation S (say I sit on a tack), I behave in manner B (I jump and scream).

    (2) Jones is in S and is doing B (and he is like me in other relevant ways (he has a brain and nervous system, say)).

    (3) I do B in S because I experience mental state M (pain, for example).

    (4) So, Jones is experiencing M, too.

Notice that this is an inductive argument. The conclusion does not follow necessarily from the premises, but they do support it to some degree or other. Jones' behavior (his jumping and screaming) is the *evidence* for the conclusion that he has mental states (that he is experiencing pain). We can also see that the conclusion *explains* the data (premises)—for example, Jones' feeling pain after having sat on a tack explains why he jumped and screamed. (Jones, of course, could be anyone, and S, M and B stand for any situation, mental state, behavior (respectively) that you want to use.) In particular, we are discussing an argument by analogy: Jones is like me in certain relevant ways and so he is analogous to me in this other related way, too. Recall that we used this same sort of reasoning when we argued in Chapter 2, Section 1C, that it was reasonable to think that Alison would get a hottub when she asks the landlord for one. This conclusion is reasonable because just like Samantha, who has already received one on request, Alison has been renting from this landlord for seven years, has always paid the rent on time, and sends the landlord a Christmas card every year. Because these girls are analogous in certain ways relevant to getting a hottub, we can reasonably expect them to be analogous in getting a hottub as well.

Evaluating the argument

A number of factors may affect the value of an inductive argument by
analogy. (a) The greater the number of respects of analogy the better
the evidence. (b) The more relevant the respects of analogy to the
conclusion the better the evidence. And (c) the fewer the number of
respects of disanalogy the better the evidence. We noticed in Chapter I
that arguments of this form always presuppose a generalization. The
hottub argument presupposes that *anyone* who is a long term renter,
pays the rent on time and is kind enough to the landlord to send
Christmas cards is going to get a hottub upon request, or perhaps better: anyone who is a conscientious tenant of this landlord will receive a
hottub on request. Certainly Samantha's case is an instance of this
generalization, and if it is true, Alison will get a hottub too.

What is the generalization that is presupposed in the dualist's
"Other Minds" argument? It is that *anyone who behaves in manner B
in situation S (and is like me in other relevant ways) will feel M*. My
situation is an instance of this generalization—I am someone who behaves in manner B when in S and consequently feels M—and if the
generalization is true, then Jones too feels M.

Notice that we can turn the inductive argument into a deductive
one:

(1) Anyone who behaves in manner B in situation S (and is
     like me in other relevant ways) will feel M.
(2) Jones is someone who behaves in manner B in situation
     S (and is like me in other relevant ways).
(3) So, Jones will feel M.

Now in the case of the inductive argument we know that the premises
are true and we are interested in whether the premises provide good
evidence for the conclusion. In the case of the deductive argument we
know the premises entail the conclusion, but we need to know whether
the first premise is true. If it is unclear whether the premises support
the conclusion in an inductive argument by analogy it is frequently
useful to find the implicit generalization—one that could be used in a
corresponding deductive argument—and question that.

In the case of the dualist's "Other Minds" argument, the generalization is a poorly supported proposition. Why should we think that
*anyone who behaves in manner B in situation S (and is like me in
other relevant ways) will feel M*? What evidence do we have for this

claim? Do we have enough evidence (how many sample cases support the generalization)? Do the sample cases represent the population over which we are generalizing? For example, consider the generalization that all swans are white. Suppose we base this conclusion on having observed 1000 white swans without exception. Clearly our sample of cases possessed the right features: all were swans and all were white. We also seem to have a reasonable number of cases. Of course, more evidence would make the case better, less evidence would make the case worse.

In the other minds case the evidential sample seems to be the right sort of thing. Our behavior is hooked up to our mental states in our own cases—I screamed because I felt pain; we have an adequately representative sample. But how many cases can I appeal to in order to support the generalization that *anyone who behaves in manner B in situation S (and is like me in other relevant ways) will feel M*? There is only *one* case to which I can appeal: my own. Only in my case have I observed that *someone who behaves in manner B in situation S (and is like me in other relevant ways) will feel M*. But this is only one case; the sample size is insufficient. Observing only a single case will not provide us with enough evidence to draw reasonable conclusions about a large population. Arguing in this way would be like arguing that all swans are white after having seen only one swan.

The extent of the problem

It looks as though the dualist's inductive argument and its deductive counterpart fall short due to insufficient evidence. There is no reason to accept the generalization and so we should not accept the first premise of the deductive argument. By the same token, the failure of the generalization shows that there is insufficient support for the conclusion of the inductive argument; a person's behavior is not adequate evidence for the existence of mental states. It seems we can't even know in the weak sense that other beings have mental states.

The dualist could argue that the existence of consciousness is a plausible hypothesis used for explaining the behavior of other beings. Thus, like the scientist who posits that certain unobservable particles exist in order to explain his experimental results, the dualist may claim that minds and mental states are theoretical entities, needed to satisfactorily explain behavior. (See Chapter 2, Section 1C for more on theoretical entities.)

Showing that Dualism has skeptical consequences doesn't *show* that it is false unless we accept the premise that we do know that others have mental states. The dualist may very well be willing to deny this initially plausible premise. This much we can say: even if we cannot refute Dualism with the Problem of Other Minds, we can insist that the problem provides an unwelcome consequence; we should think carefully before accepting Dualism.

Our discussion of the Problem of Other Minds does have some payoff for continued thought about mind and body in that it has forced us to see that we think behavior is closely connected with our mental life. In the following section we shall examine some alternatives to Dualism that take behavior very seriously and avoid the skeptical consequences of Dualism.

Questions: Why does the dualist have a problem knowing that other minds exist? How does the dualist respond? With what kind of argument? How is the argument evaluated?

Section 5: MATERIALISM ATTEMPTS TO EXPOSE THE CARTESIAN MYTH

A. Behaviorism

Ryle and the myth of Cartesianism

We have worked through a number of problems for Dualism. If Dualism is true, then we cannot tell, as we ordinarily think we can, that other beings are thinking and feeling. And, we seem to be left without a good account of the alleged relationship between our mental and physical lives. Apart from these problems, Gilbert Ryle has charged that substance Dualism is simply a myth. We are mistaken in believing that there is a separate substance involved in accounting for the activity of human thought; we are wrong to think of a person as "a ghost mysteriously ensconced in a machine." According to Ryle's diagnosis, we tend to assume that the mind, though different from the body, must nonetheless work somewhat like the body. We recognize that, as the Leibniz's Mill illustrated earlier, it is difficult to see how a purely mechanical story—a story about matter in motion—can explain how thinking arises. As a consequence we go on hastily supposing that there must be some corresponding nonphysical objects and processes. Thus, we finally posit some ghostly, mysterious mechanism composed of mental stuff "inside" the more familiar physical mechanism. Here is Ryle's account of the mistaken thinking:

Because, as is true, a person's thinking, feeling and purposive doing cannot be described solely in the idioms of physics, chemistry and physiology, therefore they must be described in counterpart idioms. As the human body is a complex organized unit, so the human mind is a complex organized unit, though one made of a different sort of stuff and with a different sort of structure.[11]

Let's see why this sort of thinking is mistaken. Imagine someone visiting a large University with many colleges. After being shown the various buildings and colleges, she asks "But where is the University?" Now this visitor is clearly mistaken in thinking that the University is yet another thing, something she has not yet been shown. She is mistaken in thinking that the University is not something that can be accounted for simply in terms of all the individual buildings and colleges she has already seen. We make a similar mistake if we take the mind to be some additional item or process distinct from the physical objects and processes making us up. Here again is Ryle, illustrating the mistaken thinking and then drawing an analogy to the University example:

Minds are things, but different sorts of things from bodies; mental processes are causes and effects, but different sorts of causes and effects from bodily movements. . . Somewhat as the foreigner expected the University to be an extra edifice, rather like a college but also considerably different, so the repudiators of mechanism represented minds as extra centres of causal processes, rather like machines but also considerably different from them.[12]

If we are led to think that "minds are things, but different sorts of things from bodies," we are misled. We can account for the mental life of humans without appealing to some mysterious mental substance. In particular, Ryle continues, we can account for our mental lives by looking closely at our physical behavior. On this Rylean-materialist picture, then, once we have a complete physical description of a person, we have all we need to understand what it is for a person to have fears and beliefs and pains. We will now look at some attempts to account for mental phenomena strictly in terms of physical phenomena.[13]

Radical Behaviorism

Suppose we are psychologists and want to study the conscious states of humans. What do we do? There is certainly no point in trying to examine the unobservable mental objects that the dualist posits. If there are such objects, they are not open to public inspection. We can, however, look at the behavior of others: we can consider responses to the various stimuli that affect the organism. Psychologists and philosophers who take this line will urge that we should not worry about some special mental object called pain; instead we should investigate the behavior that leads us to ascribe pain to someone. Indeed, on reflection that seems exactly the right line to take. If someone is not conscious, we expect that they will exhibit no behavioral response to stimulus; if they are conscious, we expect not only that they will respond, but that they will respond to particular kinds of stimulus with particular kinds of behavior. In general, then, we suppose that states of consciousness are precisely those states definable in terms of the sort of behavior one exhibits when subject to various stimuli. Thus, we needn't talk about Lynn's pain, isolated as an entity needed for filling in a special causal story, but only about her jumping and screaming in reaction to sitting on the tack. We have no need to postulate mental causes or any non-physical ghost in a physical machine.

The *methodological behaviorist* is one who holds that psychology should not be concerned with anything but the behavior of organisms. This sort of behaviorist remains mute on the issue of whether there are mental states or objects. Since mental causes themselves stand in need of explanation, telling a special causal story in which mental states play a central role gains us no ground. Psychology needs to focus only on observable behavior and to consider the likelihood of behavior given antecedent observable conditions. Here is B. F. Skinner:

> To what extent is it helpful to be told, "He drinks because he is thirsty"? If to be thirsty means nothing more than to have a tendency to drink, this is a mere redundancy. If it means that he drinks because of a state of thirst, an inner cause is invoked. If this state is purely inferential—if no dimensions are assigned to it which would make direct observation possible—it cannot serve as an explanation. But if it has physiological or

psychical properties, what role can it play in a science of behavior?[14]

Methodological Behaviorism represents a very narrow understanding of psychology, and has very little of interest to say about the questions we want answered —namely, questions about the nature of our mental life. Another kind of Behaviorism does address such questions. This is *Philosophical Behaviorism* and it takes two forms. *Radical Behaviorism* is the thesis that mental states such as pain, fear and belief can be identified with observable behavior of certain sorts. Thus, Frances's fearing the tiger is identified with her trembling, perspiring and making the noise "Yipes, it's a tiger!" Jonathan's being thirsty just is his getting a glass of water. And Lynn's pain is nothing more than her jumping up and down and screaming "Ouch!"

With Radical Behaviorism we seem to find a way of escaping problems inherent in Dualism. No non-physical substance is required by Behaviorism; no story needs to be invented for explaining the causal interaction of mind and body; our purposes in psychology are kept well on track merely in terms of behavior, without invoking mental causes; and, we can accommodate our intuitions that we know others are thinking things (recall that the dualist himself used behavioral criteria in the Problem of Other Minds). Notice here that Radical Behaviorism is a theory about what mental states *are*. The theory does not deny that there are pains, fears and beliefs; it simply identifies them with various kinds of observable behavior. Since we are talking solely about physical behavior, Radical Behaviorism is a materialist theory.

The problem with this form of Behaviorism is that psychology does more than catalogue stimulus-response connections. The psychologist, and certainly the philosopher of mind, is interested in what caused Frances's trembling, perspiring and shouting. Surely there is more to the cause of Frances's behavior than just the fact that light reflected off a tiger and struck her retinas. Between the stimulation of her retinas and the behavioral response stand mental states like fear (the belief that she had best run away, and so on). Contrary to the behaviorist, we say that her fear *mediated* the retinal stimulation and the behavior. Hence, the fear is not the behavior itself. Similarly, we think there is more to the cause of Lynn's screaming than just her sitting on the tack—she *felt* something. Jonathan's feeling thirsty is what brought about his drinking the water; we should not identify the feeling of thirst with the drinking.

There is another, related, problem for Radical Behaviorism. Isn't it possible to have mental states without having any behavior at all? Suppose you think that you see a tiger in front of you. You begin to feel a bit anxious, but then realize that there are no tigers in this country, and you remember that your neighbor received a tiger-hologram kit for Christmas and often tries to trick you into thinking there is a tiger in the yard. Finally you decide that you are mistaken about there really being a tiger in front of you. Now, couldn't all this mental activity take place even in the complete absence of behavior? Suppose that you are paralyzed and cannot move. It is still possible that you have all of the above thoughts. The radical behaviorist is clearly wrong to identify mental states with behavior. On such a theory there is no accounting for the inner causes of our behavior or the presence of thinking in the absence of behavior.

Logical Behaviorism

Still, Radical Behaviorism contains a grain of truth. Behavior isn't irrelevant to our inner states, and as we've noted before, one is entitled to predicate mental properties of things only insofar as they respond properly to stimuli. Can we concentrate on behavior and still maintain that there are inner causes, without committing ourselves either to a separate mental substance or to Radical Behaviorism? A different form of Philosophical Behaviorism claims that we can. According to *Logical Behaviorism*, to say that Frances is afraid of the tiger in front of her is to say something not about the behavior that actually occurs, but about the behavior that would occur if certain antecedent conditions are satisfied. And when we talk about the behavior that would occur under certain conditions we are talking about dispositions or tendencies of Frances that can be explained solely in physical terms. Thus, Frances's being afraid right now of the tiger is in part her being disposed to turn and run *if* the tiger gets any closer. Her current behavior—her trembling, perspiring and shouting—is a *manifestation* of her disposition to do such things when she is confronted with a tiger-like object.

Notice that this is a theory about what mental terms *mean*. Consider what we mean when we say "Phil believes the Martians are invading Earth." We mean that Phil is disposed to say "The Martians are coming" when asked "Who is invading the earth?" and he is disposed to run and hide when he sees unidentified bright lights in the sky. We needn't be committed to any occult entities or processes to think that what we say is true of Phil. And we needn't suppose our mental predicates *refer* to mental objects. Our description of Phil and his beliefs (as well as his fears and desires) can be given solely in physical terms. So, when we say that Phil believes the Martians are invading we mean to say something about the ways he would behave under certain conditions. And when we say Frances is afraid of tigers, we mean to say something about the ways in which she would behave when confronted with tiger-like objects.

Perhaps the Logical Behaviorist's most significant advance over Radical Behaviorism is that we can maintain our intuitive belief that a language with mental terms can still be used to explain behavior. What does it mean to say that Frances ran because she was afraid? It means that Frances is *disposed* to behave this way when she encounters certain stimuli (e.g., tigers), and she did encounter a stimulus of that sort. Frances's fear of tigers is no more than her being disposed to run, tremble, perspire, and scream whenever she encounters a tiger. Similarly, Phil ran and hid because he believed the Martians were invading; that is, Phil is disposed to run and hide whenever he sees unidentified bright lights in sky, and he did see unidentified bright lights in the sky. Thus, according to Logical Behaviorism we can understand statements about mental states to be sets of stimulus-response conditionals of the form 'if you were stimulated in such and such a way, then you would respond in such and such a way.' These will, of course, be very difficult to spell out in any great detail, for they must include all sorts of stimuli and responses. But in spite of this practical difficulty, the theory allows us to salvage the intuition that mental terms figure in explanations (perhaps even causal explanations) of behavior.

Dispositions

When we talk of the solubility of a sugar cube or the fragility of a crystal vase we are talking about dispositions. The sugar cube is disposed to dissolve when placed in liquids like water; the crystal vase is disposed to shatter when dropped on the floor or when struck with a hammer. We don't suppose that solubility is some mysterious state of the sugar cube. It is a property the cube has in virtue of having a certain physical structure. Thus, when asked why the sugar cube dissolved when placed in water we can properly say that it dissolved because it was soluble, that is, because it has a certain disposition to behave in that way when placed in water. The explanation for its dissolving is its having the particular physical structure it has. Furthermore, the sugar cube can have this disposition to dissolve in water even when it is out of the water. The disposition is not then being manifested.

When I say the vase is fragile I am not talking about its current behavior with respect to being struck. I am talking about what it would do (what would happen to it) if it were, say, dropped or struck with a hammer. As applied now to our mental life, then, to say that someone has a mind is just to say that they have certain dispositions or capacities or abilities. They have these dispositions, capacities or abilities in virtue of having certain physical properties. (We can let the physical scientist discover what the right properties are.) So, unlike the radical behaviorist, the logical behaviorist can account for the presence of mental states even in the absence of behavior. Beliefs, fears and thoughts in general are just dispositions to behave under the appropriate conditions. And rather than identifying mental states with the behavior itself, Logical Behaviorism identifies mental states with dispositions (capacities, propensities) to behave. Both Frances's confronting a tiger and her fear brought about her trembling, perspiring and shouting; her fear of tigers is her disposition to behave in these and other ways when confronted with a tiger-like object.

Problems for Logical Behaviorism

There are a number of problems with Logical Behaviorism that need to be addressed. First, it is incorrect to identify Frances's presently feeling frightened (of a tiger, say) simply with her disposition to run (tremble, perspire, shout) when she encounters a tiger. We need to include also that she experiences the tiger, that she believes it is a tiger that she sees and that it is potentially harmful, that she desires not to be mauled to death, and so on. The important point here is that frequently there is interaction among mental states: mental properties, we say, are *relational*, because relations sometimes hold among mental states themselves.

The logical behaviorist appears not to recognize this relational feature of mental states. An important feature of Behaviorism is that the stimulus-response conditionals used to cash out the relevant dispositions be spelled out in terms of *observable* stimuli and behavioral responses. The idea is to avoid unobservable nonphysical causes by explaining the mental in terms of physical dispositions. But treating mental states entirely in terms of dispositions to behave leaves no room for acknowledging their inner connections with one another: no room is left for explaining how Frances's sensory experience of the tiger causes her believing that there is a tiger and her deciding to run. Logical Behaviorism misses part of the story.

A second difficulty is that Logical Behaviorism is too liberal when it comes to attributing mental states. Imagine a perfect actor under local anaesthesia who is able to display consistently pain behavior in appropriate circumstances, but who (on those occasions) does not feel pain. In this case, although the actor is disposed to exhibit pain behavior under the appropriate circumstances, we are not inclined to say that he has pains in those circumstances. At very least, then, what Behaviorism isolates as the central feature of mentality needs to be restricted in some way.

Finally, although Logical Behaviorism might seem to be fairly plausible for states like being greedy, ambitious or conceited, where there is no "feel" associated with the mental state, it does not seem to work for states like being in pain or considering an hypothesis, where there is something it feels like to be in that state or something going on when one is in that state. Thinking is not just having a disposition to behave; there is something going on when I think. David Armstrong puts it this way:

> When I think, but my thoughts do not issue in any action, it seems obvious as anything is obvious that there is something actually going on in me which constitutes my thought. It is not simply that I would speak or act if some conditions that are unfulfilled were to be fulfilled. Something is currently going on, in the strongest and most literal sense of 'going on,' and this something is my thought.[15]

To review, whereas Methodological Behaviorism is silent on the nature of mental states, Philosophical Behaviorism is inadequate. Radical Behaviorism, a species of Philosophical Behaviorism, can account neither for cases in which thought is present but behavior is not, nor for cases in which there is some inner cause mediating the external stimulus and the behavioral response. Logical Behaviorism, on the other hand, avoids these problems, but fails to include the fact that other mental states are related to the stimulus and response. In addition, this form of Behaviorism cannot account for the nondispositional nature of mental states like pain, sensation, and thinking in general. We are left with the question of how we can account for mental states, in purely physical terms, in a way that isolates both its role in the production of behavior and it standing in relations to other mental states.

B. The Identity Theory

No mental objects

So, what is it for Lynn to feel pain, say after having sat on a tack? What is this pain? Clearly it is not to be identified with her jumping up and yelling; that is the radical behaviorist's position and we have seen that it is inadequate. But while her pain is not identical with her behavior, it is at least closely related to her behavior; she jumped and yelled because she was in pain. So, we must look for pain or her feeling pain amongst the causes of her behavior. That is, since her sitting on the tack caused the pain, and the pain in turn caused her jumping and yelling, it is reasonable to think of her pain as something that causally mediates the event of her sitting on the tack and the event of her jumping and yelling. What goes on in a person when this happens? Well, at least this much can be said: there are certain quite specific events taking place in Lynn's nervous system and brain, ones that wouldn't be taking place were she in no pain whatsoever. We would expect events of that sort to occur in Lynn's brain on any other occasion she's in that sort of pain, and we would expect those kinds of neural events to take place in the system of anyone else who sits on a tack and reacts as Lynn did. Why not, then, simply identify the pain with the neural events?

According to the *Identity Theory* mental states are identical with states of the brain or nervous system. This is not to say that we know exactly which states of the brain-nervous system are relevant—we shall let the neurophysiologists tell us that. This theory simply contends that there is an identity to be found. The Identity Theory is obviously a materialist theory. A complete physical description of the workings of the brain and the nervous system will tell us all there is to know about mental states.

There are some very good reasons to think that identifying mental events with brain events (or events in our nervous system) is the right move. That the brain is something intimately connected with our thinking and feeling seems obvious. After all, we know of cases in which damage to the brain results in the loss of some or all mental capacity, as when one suffers memory loss or becomes unconscious. Research in neurophysiology and work in artificial intelligence support to some degree the thesis that mental states are brain states.

Are we suggesting here that pains, fears, beliefs and desires are physical objects similar to or in the brain, that pains and fears are nothing more than neurons or pieces of brain? When discussing Dualism, speaking of mental *objects*, perhaps "composed" of mental substance, is natural. But the identity theorist urges us talk of mental *states* that he will then identify with brain states. States of things are not really objects in the usual sense of "objects," but rather *ways objects are*. An object is in a certain state, we say, when it has particular property. The distinction between objects and their states is important because frequently our use of language leads us into treating as objects what are better understood as states of objects. Consider that we say things like "Margie took a walk" or "The table has some redness in it." Now it may look as if we are claiming that, in addition to Margie or the table, there are also these objects called walks and redness. What sort of objects would these be? But we needn't suppose that when saying "Margie took a walk" there are two things to which we refer, Margie and her walk. Rather, we take ourselves to be referring to one object, Margie, and simply saying of her that she walked—that she had a certain property or was in a certain state, viz., the property or state of walking. The walk isn't a separate object. Similarly for the table. The redness needn't be viewed as some second, rather mysterious, object in addition to the table. Rather, the table is a certain way, or there is a state the table was in, namely, the state of being red. *Being red* is not another object.

Let's return now to claims we make about mental states. We frequently say things like "Lynn had a pain" or "Sheldon has a happy feeling" or "Phil has an odd belief in Martians." But in saying these things we needn't commit ourselves to the existence of special mental objects like pains, happy feelings, or odd beliefs. Rather, there is Lynn and she simply has a certain property or is in a certain state: she is hurting (is in a state of pain). Similarly, Sheldon is happy (is in a state of happiness) and Phil believes in Martians (is in a state of believing).

We must emphasize that, in contrast with the dualist, when the identity theorist speaks of mental states he is not speaking of them as states of mental objects. According to the Identity Theory, there are no mental objects, although there are mental states like believing, feeling, hurting and so on. These states are identical with physical states of the brain.

Identity statements

Suppose that the identity theorist is correct, and that being in pain just is being in some brain state, say brain state B. "Pain is identical with being in brain state B" can be compared with other identity statements found in science, e.g., "Water is identical with H_2O," "Lightning is identical with luminous electrical discharges in the atmosphere," "Light is identical with electromagnetic waves," "Heat is identical with mean molecular kinetic energy," and so on. In these cases the scientific theory is able to provide a better explanatory account (of phenomena like lightning or heat) than our common-sense theory does. Our naming the phenomenon "lightning" or describing it as a flash of light in the sky (consider the aborigine who calls it "fire from the gods") goes no distance toward explaining its nature. I pick out (refer to) with "lightning" the same phenomenon as you pick out when you refer to it as a luminous electrical discharge between clouds or between clouds and the ground. But clearly your means of picking it out discloses much more about is nature than does mine.

Now if lightning is identical with a luminous electrical discharge in the atmosphere, then nothing could be one without being the other. That follows straightforwardly from our concept of numerical identity. Since Cassius Clay *is* Mohammed Ali, no one could be Cassius Clay without being Mohammed Ali. But now, although the *reference* of "lightning" and "luminous electrical discharge in the atmosphere" is the same, we cannot conclude that the *meaning* of those linguistic items is the same. When the aborigine calls that flash of light in the stormy sky "fire from the gods," or when I call it "lightning," neither of us intend to communicate with our words anything about electricity, even though an electrical discharge in the atmosphere is in fact what we are referring to. As a matter of fact, the morning star is (identical with) the evening star, but the meaning of the "the morning star" (that last star I see in the east in the morning) is not the meaning of "the evening star" (that first bright star I see in the west in the evening).

Consider now "pain" and "brain state B." According to the identity theorist, they refer to the same neurological state; but they clearly don't mean the same thing. Jerry Fodor compares this feature of the Identity Theory with Behaviorism.

The chief advantage of the identity theory is that it takes the explanatory constructs of psychology at face value, which is surely something a philosophy of mind ought to do if it can. The identity theory shows how the mentalistic explanations of psychology could not be mere heuristics but literal accounts of the causal history of behavior. Moreover, since the identity theory is not a semantic thesis, it is immune to many arguments that cast in doubt logical behaviorism. A drawback of logical behaviorism is that the observation "John has a headache" does not seem to mean the same thing as "John is disposed to behave in such and such a way." The identity theorist, however, can live with the fact that "John has a headache" and "John is in such and such a brain state" are not synonymous. The assertion of the identity theorist is not that these sentences mean the same thing but only that they are rendered true (or false) by the same neurological phenomena.[16]

General features of identity claims are useful in comparing Identity Theory with Dualism. Recall that the dualist uses Leibniz's Law to argue that mental objects and physical objects must be distinct. According to these arguments, since the objects have different properties they must be two and not one. The identity theorist will reply, first, that it is best to conduct the discussion in terms of mental states and not objects, and second, that because mental states are identical with brain states, no differences are to be found between them. Like any physical states, mental states are spatial, public and observable. To say that Lynn is in pain is just to say that she is in brain state B, and we can in principle look and see (by opening up her skull) if indeed that is the state she is in.

Advantages of Identity Theory

The Identity Theory has a number of advantages over alternative accounts. First, if we identify our believing, fearing, hurting and other mental states with brain states, we needn't follow the dualist in positing that some mysterious immaterial mental substance exists. We can restrict our discussion of the mental realm to the brain and the nervous system. This is a particularly desirable feature if one is convinced that the explanatory resources available to physical science are capable of giving an account of consciousness.

Second, the Identity Theory avoids problems that plague Radical Behaviorism. By identifying mental states with behavior, the radical behaviorist cannot account for cases in which thinking is present in the absence of behavior. But the identity theorist is able to account for this possibility since thinking, on his view, is a brain state, that may or may not issue in behavior. Furthermore, the radical behaviorist is unable to accommodate our belief that our inner mental states cause our behavior. But the existence of inner causes is not a problem for the Identity Theory. Frances's trembling, perspiring and shouting "Yipes, it's a tiger!" are the effects of her being in a certain brain state—-the mental state of being afraid of a tiger. Frances's being afraid caused her behavior.

Third, the Identity Theory also improves on Logical Behaviorism. Recall that the identity theorist is not so much interested in the meanings of mental terms as in their reference. This is because identity statements are true or false depending on the identity of reference not identity of meaning. 'The evening star is identical with the morning star' will be true so long as 'the evening star' and 'the morning star' refer to the same thing, quite independently of the meaning of those referring expressions. Now the logical behaviorist implausibly holds that "Lynn feels pain" means the same as "Lynn would jump if she sat on a tack, and she sat on a tack." But the Identity Theory is not committed to this synonymy or to the synonymy of "Lynn is feeling pain" and "Lynn is in brain states B." Both of these last statements refer to the same mental state, even if they do not mean the same thing; and sameness of reference is all that is required for the identity claim "Lynn's being in pain is identical with Lynn's being in brain state B" to be true.

Moreover, since the identity theorist is identifying mental states with brain states, he is not confronted with the behaviorist's worry that because the anaesthatized perfect actor behaves as though he is in pain under the appropriate conditions, we must say that he is in pain. Surely, he doesn't feel pain, and as the identity theorist reminds us, that is because because the anaesthesia affects his brain and nervous system.

Finally, the identity theorist can acknowledge an important fact that the logical behaviorist cannot, namely that often our mental sates are interrelated. Frances ran from the tiger not just because she was *afraid* but also because she was *conscious* of the tiger before her, she *believed* that tigers are dangerous and that there was one before her, and she *desired* to escape the tiger, etc. Mental states are interrelated because brain states are interrelated.

Trouble for the Identity Theory

We need to distinguish between two versions of the Identity Theory. On one version the identity theorist claims that certain kinds or *types* of mental states, say believing or being in pain, are identical with *types* of brains states. Thus, if pain is identical with brain state B, then no one could be in pain without being in brain state B. And conversely, no one could be in brain state B without being in pain. Call this version *Type-Identity Theory*.

The identity theorist, however, might want to claim only that a particular person's mental states are identical with brain states; another person's mental states could be identified with some other physical states. Here we are talking not about kinds or types of mental states, but about particular states or *tokens* of mental states. A token is a particular instance of a type. Rocking chairs are a type of chair, but the rocking chair your grandmother sits in is a token of that type. The *token-identity theorist* holds that certain tokens or instances of mental states, say Lynn's feeling pain or Phil's believing in Martians, are to be identified with particular tokens of physical states, say Lynn's brain state B_{11} and Phil's brain state B_{27} respectively. For most of us with healthy brains, it is likely that some brain state can be identified with our being in pain or believing that Martians are invading the earth, but it remains possible that there be other creatures who feel pains and have beliefs about Martians even though they have no brains. A Martian's belief that Phil is paranoid might be identified with some state of the purple goo that is found in the Martian's skull in the absence of a human brain.

The problem with Type-Identity Theory arises from its quite strong claim that pains are the kinds of things that can be found only in brains. That seems too strong because it is at least possible that there be beings that feel pain but do not have brains. Suppose Martians do visit the Earth. They look slightly different from humans and we find that they do not have the same neurological apparatus that we have—they are constructed of purple goo and have no brains. But they behave in roughly the same ways as we do: they jump and scream when they sit on tacks, they tremble and finally run when they encounter tiger-like objects, they might even laugh at our jokes. Isn't it at least possible that these creatures feel pain, are afraid and experience happiness even if they have no brain states? The type-identity theorist must implausibly say that this is not possible.

The moral here is that we must be careful when we spell out identity statements. If it is true that water is identical with H_2O, then nothing could be water and not be H_2O. Suppose there is some liquid that is colorless, odorless and tasteless, fish swim in it and cooks boil potatoes in it. If it is not composed of hydrogen and oxygen, then it is not water but only something very much like water. But consider the statement "This desk is identical with this parcel of wood." Now it may be that nothing could be this chair and not be made of this parcel of wood, but this is not to say chairs generally must be made of wood. Analogously, it may be that *Frances's* being afraid is identified with *her* being in a certain brain state (B), but that is not to say that fear generally must be identified with that kind of brain state (or even any brain state).

As we have seen, the token-identity theorist does better than the type-identity theorist on the issue of whether brainless things can have mental states. But since Token-Identity Theory makes claims only about particular mental states (Frances's fear, Lynn's pain, Phil's belief), it has trouble accounting for the nature of types of mental states. We may know that Lynn's feeling pain is identical with her being in brain state B_{11} but what can this identity theorist say about being in pain generally? What can he say about that type of mental state? What do all things that feel pain have in common?

To answer this more general question about the nature of types of mental states, we must go beyond Token-Identity Theory. But we must do so without engaging anything so restrictive as Type-Identity Theory. In the next section we will look at an account that attempts such a project.

Questions: How does Methodological Behaviorism differ from Philosophical Behaviorism? What does the radical behaviorist say about mentality? What problems arise for the view? How does the logical behaviorist improve upon the radical behaviorist's theory? How might someone criticize Logical Behaviorism? What is the Identity Theory and how does it avoid referring to mental objects? What advantages does the identity theorist claim over Dualism? How does Type-Identity Theory differ from Token-Identity Theory?

Section 6: FUNCTIONALISM

A. The Functionalist Program

The theory

We want an account of *types* of mental states. What is it to feel pain, to be afraid of tigers, to believe the Martians are invading the Earth, to feel thirsty and want a glass of water? In addressing this matter we must be sensitive to problems arising for earlier attempts. We cannot identify mental states with behavior for, as we saw in connection with Behaviorism, Frances's being afraid of tigers is not merely her trembling, perspiring and shouting "Yipes!" But the mental states are related to the behavior. Frances trembled, perspired and shouted because she was afraid; Jonathan drank the water because he was feeling thirsty. In addition, we must acknowledge the fact that our mental states are often related to other mental states as well as to our behavior. Frances didn't turn and run just because she was afraid of the tiger. She wouldn't have run unless she also was conscious of the tiger, believed that tigers are dangerous and wanted to avoid bodily injury. There is, then, a certain relational aspect to our mental states: they are related to our behavior and to each other.

Our discussion of the Type-Identity Theory showed us that we cannot identify mental states generally with brain states, for there may very well be creatures (or machines!) that have mental states yet have no brains. We do, however, want to focus our efforts on devising a theory that permits us to identify mental states with some physical state or other. Restricting ourselves to Materialism seems to be the easiest way to account for the causal connections between mental states and sensory input, between mental states and other mental states, and between mental states and behavioral output (recall the difficulties that arose for the interactionist).

All of these considerations suggest that we should not worry so much about the particular material involved but about what the material does; that is, we should be primarily concerned with causal or functional roles of the material involved. Being afraid of tigers is whatever state causally mediates between having light from a tiger hitting the retinas, being conscious of a tiger, believing that tigers are dangerous and wanting to avoid bodily injury, and behavior such as trembling, perspiring, shouting "Yipes, it's a tiger!" Being in pain is whatever state causally mediates between sitting on a tack (for example), believing that one is in pain, and jumping and yelling (for example). Thus, we understand types of mental states *functionally*: they are whatever states take certain inputs (sensory stimuli), relate causally to other mental states, and yield certain outputs (behavior and/or other mental states). It doesn't matter what material has these relations—it might be a human's brain state or a Martian's purple goo state—so long as the proper functional roles are played.

The view according to which types of mental states can be understood in terms of the functional roles they play we shall call *Functionalism*. This theory provides us with the best of Behaviorism and the Identity Theory. As with Behaviorism, it acknowledges the fact that mental states have a relational nature. Your being in pain is something that *mediates* your sitting on the tack and your jumping and yelling. And as with the Identity Theory, Functionalism holds that mental states mediate *causally*; that is, they play a causal role in producing the behavior (and/or other mental states) and in being produced by certain inputs (say your senses being stimulated, perhaps in conjunction with your being in other mental states).

We should notice that strictly speaking Functionalism isn't a materialist view. Since what stuff plays the appropriate roles doesn't matter, this view is quite compatible with Dualism and the existence of states of a mental substance performing the appropriate functions. Most functionalists would no doubt want to claim that a materialist version of Functionalism is to be preferred because the idea of a mental substance remains mysterious and problematic. But Functionalism *per se* is not committed to this position.

Functional roles

Let's try to get clearer on the idea of a functional role. Generally speaking, to play a functional role is to be in a certain state, take inputs and yield outputs. A few examples may make this clearer. Being alive is a property that is defined in terms of the functional roles the parts of the living object play. At one time people thought of life as a substantial thing, as something distinct from the organism, but something that the organism in some sense possessed. (Recall, for example, the antiquated notion of a "vital fluid.") Biologists, however, no longer think of life as a distinct thing but as a property objects of many kinds can have provided their parts perform certain functions, such as repairing and sustaining themselves, and procreating. A thing is alive if its parts (no matter what kind of stuff they are composed of) engage in a certain specified activity or perform certain specified jobs.

Consider a soft drink machine that provides a bottle of soft drink for ten cents.[17] The machine has two states it can be in. If the machine is in state 1 and you insert only a nickle, then it goes into state 2. If the machine is in state 1 and you insert a dime, then it stays in state 1 and dispenses a soft drink. If, when it is in state 2, you insert a nickle, then the machine dispenses a soft drink and goes back to state 1. When the machine is in state 2, if you insert a dime the machine dispenses a soft drink and a nickle change, and returns to state 1.

	State 1	State 2
nickle input:	No output and go to state 2.	Dispense a soft drink and go to state 1.
dime input:	Dispense a soft drink and stay in state 1.	Dispense a soft drink and a nickle and go to state 1.

Notice that we did not need to say anything about what these states are states of, whether it be metal or plastic, organic or inorganic, physical or even mental substance. What is important is that the proper relations hold between the inputs (dimes and nickles), the outputs (soft drinks and nickles) and other states. We might think very crudely of state 1 as being the machine's desire for a dime and state 2 as being the machine's desire for a nickle. When you satisfy its desires, it dispenses a soft drink.

The soft drink machine is an example of something more generally called a *Turing machine*. A Turing machine is anything that can be specified in terms of a machine-table (like the one presented above for the soft drink machine) that, much like a software program for a computer, indicates what the machine will do (for example, go to a certain state and give a certain output) upon receiving a certain input and being in a certain state.

According to some influential forms of Functionalism, thinkers are a very complicated kind of Turing machine. Mental states are functional states that are defined according to their relations to sensory inputs, behavioral outputs and other mental states. As a result, functional states can be realized in many different sorts of material.

B. Critique of Functionalism

Functionalism is an attractive theory for several reasons. We have emphasized already its ability to capture the positive features of Behaviorism (the relational nature of mental states) and Identity Theory (the causal nature of mental states) without also inheriting their problems. In addition, the way is open for functionalists to employ the full range of explanatory resources available in the physical and cognitive sciences.

But it may appear to some that the functionalist characterization of mental states is too broad: coke machines, cigarette lighters, sausage grinders, and a whole host of things can be functionally characterized, but none of them has mental states like pains or doubts or desires. We need to specify some other feature of mentality that will suffice to distinguish functionally defined mental states from functionally defined non-mental states. There are two features for which we might want to look. First, many of our mental states are essentially *intentional*; that is, they are about (or *of* or *for*) something. For example, Phil has a belief about Martians, and Jonathan's desire is for water. Second, some of our mental states have *qualitative* features. There is, for example, some way it *feels* to be in pain; Jonathan notices that feeling thirsty is different from feeling hungry. We can say that both Lynn and Jonathan experience *qualia* in such cases—they are aware of a qualitative feel to their mental state. Some mental states have both intentional and qualitative features; for example, Frances's being afraid of the tiger is about a tiger and feels a certain way to her.

If we should like to avoid the worry that a functionalist characterization of mental states is too broad, it will be useful to capture these essentially mental properties that no state of a coke machine or cigarette lighter could possess. How can we account for the intentional and qualitative features of mental states? We shall see that to accommodate such features within a purely functionalist theory is difficult.

Absent qualia

When Lynn feels pain after having sat on a tack, her brain is in some state. This state is causally related to her behavioral output and to various states of her nervous system that are affected by her having sat where she did. Sensory-input neurons are sending signals to her brain, other neurons in her brain fire causing her motor-output neurons to fire sending signals to her muscles, etc., and these in turn cause her to jump and yell. Her feeling of pain (in Lynn's case, a state of her brain) plays a certain functional role in her overall neural system.

Now suppose that we have a robot that is just like Lynn from the outside, but on the inside things are quite different.[18] Connected to the sensory-input neurons are transmitters, and a series of receivers are connected to the motor-output neurons controlling behavioral output. This robot has no brain. Instead, we arrange all the inhabitants of China to do the jobs the neurons of Lynn's brain do. Now the remarkable abilities of the brain are due to the system of neurons that is in fact very complex and acts very quickly. But the job of each individual neuron, like the job of each Chinese worker, is really quite simple: it is roughly an input-output task, performable according to quite simple instructions. In our story, the people of China—all one billion of them—are wearing headsets and individually receive various signals sent via a radio transmitter either from the robot's sensory input neurons or from neighboring workers, just as Lynn's neurons—billions of them—received signals of some sort or other from her sensory system and from neighboring neurons. The Chinese, upon receiving whatever signal they receive, send out particular signals in response. If over the headset the person hears signal number 17, he will send out signal 27, if signal 11 is received, then signal 31 is sent, and so on. The particular signals eventually returning to the Lynn-like robot affect receivers at the motor-output neurons, causing the robot to behave in a certain way. Thus, when the robot sits on a tack, signals travel from its sensory nerves. These signals are transmitted to China where they are processed in a way functionally equivalent to the way a brain processes them. Other signals are then returned, causing the robot to jump and yell. Call this entire physical system of robot-connected-to-Chinese a "chibot."

Notice that as far as Functionalism is concerned this Lynn-chibot is in the same state as Lynn when Lynn is in pain. The relations between inputs, outputs and other states are the same in both cases. But something essential to pain is missing in the chibot—the *feeling* of pain. The robot behaves as though it is in pain, and there is a state (of the people in China) causally mediating the robot's behavior and stimulus, doing the same job as Lynn's pain state. Thus, according to the functionalist we should say this chibot is in pain. But clearly this is the wrong result. There is no pain in China, or in the Lynn look-alike, or in the robot-connected-to-China. In short, the functionalist cannot properly account for those mental states that essentially have qualitative features, for on functionalist criteria certain systems must be said to instantiate pains when clearly they do not.

We have presented one counterexample in terms of pain. Consider a slightly different situation in which we present the robot with the question, "Does two plus two equal four?" Upon receiving this input, certain signals are sent to the Chinese such that their instructions tell them to return certain other signals. The receivers attached to the robot's behavioral output mechanisms pick up the incoming signals and produce the sound "Yes." Suppose further that none of the Chinese understands English, nor do they know why they are sending the signals they do—they are just following the instructions. Here we have a story in which the state of the Chinese population is related to the incoming and output signals in the same way that Lynn's brain states would be if she were asked the question and responded accordingly. But of course, Lynn understands the English question and can calculate an answer, but presumably the chibot (or the robot, or the Chinese population) cannot. *Understanding* then, as well as being in pain, seems to require more than just being in a state that is functionally related in a certain way to inputs, outputs and other states.[19]

The dualist will emphasize at this point that even by considering the relational or functional properties of brains or of China, or by considering the relations among neurons or among the Chinese people, Functionalism remains unable account for the qualitative nature of mental states. Given Functionalism, we understand thinking no better than we could when, with Leibniz, we "walked" into a mill-like structure that supposedly was perceiving and feeling.

The inverted spectrum case

We can make a similar point with a slightly different story. Here is Ned Block's version of the *inverted spectrum case*:

> The special doubt about qualia can perhaps be explicated by thinking about *inverted* qualia rather than *absent* qualia. It makes sense, or seems to make sense, to suppose that objects we both call green could look to me the way objects we both call red look to you. It seems that we could be functionally equivalent even though the sensation fire hydrants evoke in you is qualitatively the same as the sensation grass evokes in me. Imagine an inverting lens which when placed in the eye of a subject results in exclamations like "Red things now look the

way green things used to look, and vice versa." Imagine
further, a pair of identical twins one of whom has the lenses
inserted at birth. The twins grow up normally, and at age 21
are functionally equivalent. This situation offers at least some
evidence that each's spectrum is inverted to the other's.[20]

The point of this story is that two people could be *functionally
equivalent*—such that the state each are in has the same relations to
inputs, outputs and other states—and yet have *different mental states*.
We would have different mental states because we have very different
qualitative experiences, that is, very different qualia. Clearly a mental
state like experiencing red has its qualitative features essentially: it
wouldn't be a sensation of red unless it looked a certain way. And if
you and I differ on what we are experiencing—qualitatively speaking—then we must differ with respect to mental states as well. Thus,
you and I could be in functionally equivalent states while having different mental states, and so mental states cannot be functionally defined. Once again Functionalism gets the wrong result.

Intentionality

An interesting feature of many mental states is their intentional character. They can be about something, stand for something, represent
something and have propositional content. You can believe that
Martians are invading the Earth; you can also doubt it, consider it, desire it, know it, regret it, fear it, or hope it. In all these cases what you
believe, doubt, desire, etc. is that a certain proposition is true. There
are other mental states that, although they do not obviously have
propositional content, are nonetheless about certain things. You can
have a mental image of Abraham Lincoln, have a memory impression
of the excellent dinner you had last Thanksgiving, be conscious of the
odor in the room, be suspicious of the man in the overcoat, and so on.

   Functionalism seems to have problems accounting for the intentional nature of some mental states. Fodor voices this difficulty when
he says that "the functionalist account of mental states does not by itself provide the required insights [about intentionality]. Mousetraps
are functionally defined, yet mousetraps do not express propositions
and they are not true or false."[21] Consider again a chibot—a robot
connected to the Chinese population via radio transmitters and receivers. The chibot could be arranged so that it is functionally equivalent to Phil when he believes the Martians are invading the Earth. But

even though the chibot is functionally identical with Phil, it does not seem to have a belief *about* Martians as Phil does. In fact it is difficult to see how we could account for the aboutness of Phil's belief with Functionalism alone. The functionalist story cannot be the whole story.

Functionalist philosophers of mind do make interesting attempts to deal with the phenomenon of intentionality. Some have suggested that since symbols can be about things, there may be some parallel between the intentional character of language, say, and thought. Here is Fodor:

> The basic concept is simple but striking. Assume that there are such things as mental symbols (mental representations) and that mental symbols have semantic properties [can be true or false]. On this view having a belief involves being related to a mental symbol, and the belief inherits its semantic properties from the mental symbol that figures in the relation. Mental processes (thinking, perceiving, learning and so on) involve causal interactions among relational states such as having a belief.[22]

An alternative effort to account for intentionality that predates this "language of thought" story involves mental representations that are about the world in the same way that pictures can be about the world—they in some sense *resemble* the world. But there is serious difficulty in saying in what sense "ideas" or mental representations can resemble the world. Moreover, we might ask how a mental "picture" of, say, Abraham Lincoln can be about his being president rather than his being bearded. The same picture illustrates both features: how then can it be about one and not the other?

We shall not spend any more time on the problem of intentionality. It is a difficult issue that currently breeds controversy among philosophers of mind.

Functionalism holds an initial promise of success. It avoids the failures of both Behaviorism and the Identity Theory and yet captures the advantages of each. In addition, Functionalism is compatible with both Dualism and Materialism. But it is not without serious problems. One disadvantage of Functionalism is that it makes no effort to address the difficult question of whether there is a distinct mental substance as the dualist contends. In particular, it remains unclear what we should say about *our* thoughts: are they instantiated in our neural systems, or in immaterial minds? The functionalist has told us what *kind* of thing our mental states must be, but he has not told us what in fact they are. Functionalism also has difficulty accounting for the qualitative and the intentional nature of our mental states. Unless these features of mentality can be treated in purely functionalist terms, it remains doubtful whether Functionalism has characterized mental states narrowly enough to exclude states of coke machines and cigarette lighters.

Questions: What does the functionalist say about mental states? How does it compare with Logical Behaviorism and the Type-Identity Theory? What is a functional role? Why are intentionality and the qualitative features of mental states problems for the functionalist? What are the absent qualia and the inverted spectrum cases?

Section 7: DUALISM OR MATERIALISM?

A. Consciousness and Subjectivity

The Mind-Body Problem is one of philosophy's most longstanding and difficult problems. We have seen that a primary source of difficulty comes in accounting for consciousness. Dualists have argued that no amount of physical detail can adequately capture this phenomenon, but their own treatment of it in terms of a non-physical substance seems altogether mysterious and devoid of detail. While acknowledging the difficulty of explaining consciousness, materialists have supposed that the complexity of physical systems like the brain offer recourses sufficiently rich to explain the phenomena of consciousness. Still, we are left with worries about whether the *qualitative* features of pains, feelings of sadness and the like, and the *intentional* aspect of many mental states, can ever be treated in purely physical terms.

Consciousness is a familiar phenomena. You and I have conscious experiences; we know what they are like. We might suppose that other living organisms have such experiences as well, and that there is something it is like for them to be conscious. That a thing has conscious experiences means, at least in part, that there is something it is like to *be* that thing, something it is like *for* that thing. It is this notion of *what it is like to be that conscious being* that we have in mind when we speak about the subjective character of conscious experience.

The dualist urges us to see that Behaviorism, Identity Theory, and Functionalism must all fail to treat mental phenomena adequately. An account of the mind-body problem will be adequate only if it captures the essential features of consciousness. And since each of these alternatives to Dualism is compatible with the absence of consciousness, and is thereby unable to capture the essentially subjective character of mentality, each of them must be judged unsuccessful.

Let's rehearse this general criticism in a bit more. It is charged that materialist programs cannot capture the phenomenon distinctive of consciousness—this subjective feature of what it is like to be that conscious thing. This is because the subjective phenomenon is connected with a certain "point of view" (the point of view of that conscious thing) that will not be included in any purely physical description of the universe. The distinction between the *subjective* element of consciousness and the essentially *objective* nature of physical treatments is nicely illustrated in Thomas Nagel's article entitled "What Is It Like to Be a Bat?"

> I assume that we all believe that bats have experience. After all, they are mammals, and there is no more doubt that they have experience than that mice or pigeons or whales have experience . . . I have said that the essence of the belief that bats have experience is that there is something that it is like to be a bat. Now we know that most bats . . . perceive the external world primarily by sonar, or echolocation, detecting the reflections, from objects within range, of their own rapid, subtly modulated, high-frequency shrieks . . . But bat sonar, though clearly a form of perception, is not similar in its operation to any sense that we possess, and there is no reason to suppose that it is subjectively like anything we can experience or imagine.[23]

What now should we say about this notion of *what it is like to be a bat*? Since a bat's form of perception is very dissimilar to our own, we must consider whether the subjective features of the consciousness of a bat can be understood in terms of our own inner experiences. It seems not.

> It will not help to try to imagine that one has webbing on one's arms, which enables one to fly around at dusk and dawn catching insects in ones mouth; that one has very poor vision .

. . ; that one spends the day hanging upside down by one's feet in an attic. In so far as I can imagine this (which is not very far), it tells me only what it would be like for me to behave as a bat behaves. But that is not the question. I want to know what it would be like for a *bat* to be a bat.[24]

It seems that we cannot understand what it would be like to be a bat in terms of our own case. The conscious experiences of a bat—the "what it is like *for the bat*" part—has a subjective character that is beyond our ability to conceive.

The point here is not simply that conscious states are private; rather it is the general point that the subjective features of consciousness are of necessity accessible only from a particular point of view. But now, if this is correct, it is strange indeed to think that this subjective feature of consciousness could be disclosed in the purely physical features of the conscious being. These features fall within the realm of paradigmatically *objective* facts—available to the senses, publicly observable, capable of being understood from many points of view (not just the human viewpoint, but the bat-viewpoint and the Martian-viewpoint too). Suppose we knew all there was to know about the physical workings of the bat—its neurological structure, its chemistry and its sonar capabilities. Still, we would not be able to find out what it is like to be that bat, that is, we would not know what it is like for the bat to experience the reflected high frequency sound waves its sonar produces.

One might wonder what sense can be made of the "objective" character of conscious experience. Wouldn't the genuinely objective features of experience be precisely those features that the point of view of the subject reveals? Surely there would be nothing left of what it's like to be a bat if we took away the viewpoint of the bat. In short, consciousness cannot be reduced to anything like physical features because it is not possible to understand its essentially subjective character in terms of purely physical facts about conscious things. Materialist alternatives to Dualism inadequately treat this most difficult part of the mind-body problem.

B. A Dualist Alternative: Epiphenomenalism

Property Dualism

Perhaps there is a way of capturing those features peculiar to conscious things, that materialists seem unable to capture, without running amuck on the mysterious non-physical substance that dualist accounts posit. All dualists will agree that *the nature of mentality*—of thought understood to encompass feeling, willing, sensing, doubting, imagining, and the rest—*involves something non-physical.* But this doesn't obviously require the dualist to posit that some non-physical stuff, beyond the physical body (brain), exists. A property dualist might suggest that properties like having a pain, believing that Martians are invading the Earth, feeling anxious at the thought of a dangerous tiger, and so on, are special kinds of properties that cannot be reduced to or accounted for in terms of purely physical features of the brain. They are *non-physical properties*, and we must appeal to them in giving an adequate account of mentality.

Epiphenomenalism is a version of property Dualism. According to this theory of mind and body, mental phenomena are not physical phenomena in the brain, nor are they genuine causes of bodily action. Instead, they are causal "by-products" of physical states of the body, a phenomenal upshot or *epi*phenomena ("epi" means "above") related to our bodies roughly in the way that your shadow is related to you. The phenomenon we call shadows are not any sort of physical stuff or shadow-stuff, but mere side-effects of the states of your body, quite different in kind from those physical states causing it, and unable to affect your body causally. The shadow's shape, for example, depends upon the body's being a certain way (its blocking light and being in a certain position), but the body's shape does not depend upon the shadow's being a certain way. Mind, similarly, is not a special kind of stuff, but rather a phenomenal consequence of states of our body emerging "over and above" matter when matter is suitably organized and active as our brains are.

These mental properties are not reducible to physical properties in the sense that when the physical scientist has done all his work, when he has offered a complete physical description of the universe, he will find that mental properties are left out of the picture. This is not to say that there are no mental properties, but rather that the complete physical story cannot be the whole story. The physical scientist does not have the resources to account for the existence and nature of mentality. The scientist can accept the thesis that mental states are the causal upshots of brain (or some physical) processes and yet acknowledge the property dualist's claim that it is impossible, within the confines of physical science, to explain the epiphenomenal mental properties.

Epiphenomenalists reason in the following way. Even a modest familiarity with physical science shows that it has the resources to explain human behavior. We can follow paths of purely physical influence back from behavior up along motor nerves to the brain. In the brain we find a complex structure with equally complex activity, all physical. No examination of it reveals (or could reveal) evidence of any non-physical substance; we seem able to explain behavior as a function of the structure and activities of the brain. Talk of such mysterious entities as souls or spirits or the like is thus both unnecessary and fruitless. None of this, however, leads us to deny the obvious facts about human consciousness, that we have doubts and desires and pangs of pain, that our mental states can have an intentional character, that there is something it is like "from the inside" to be the subject of these conscious episodes and to experience their qualities. We must therefore grant the reality of mental properties, different in kind from physical properties and not reducible to them, while granting too, as we just have, that behavior can be causally explained in purely physical terms.

Critique of Epiphenomenalism

The appeal of Epiphenomenalism resides primarily in its endorsing property Dualism. By denying that there is any special kind of non-physical substance, it avoids the most worrisome element of dualist theories discussed so far. But it is open to an objection to which Parallelism is subject as well. According to the epiphenomenalist, physical states of one's brain cause mental states and properties. Thus, my actions and my volitions are reliably correlated. But in no way is it correct to assert that mental states have effects. Thus, our typical explanations of human behavior are simply mistaken, for it is merely an illusion that our mental states cause our actions. Your deciding to leave does not cause your leaving the room; Jonathan's state of thirst merely accompanies—but does not cause—his drinking the water; why Frances shrieks and runs from the tiger is correctly explained without any reference to her fear; and so on.

There is nothing inherent in Dualism (understood generally now as neutral between substance Dualism and property Dualism) that forces property dualists to claim that mental properties can't cause physical events. If property dualists accept the thesis that mental states can effect physical states, we would have an interactionist property Dualism. But there remains, as one might expect, a worry that mental events might not be of the correct sort to causally interact with physical states anyway. Recall the serious difficulties that arose for the substance dualist who accepts Interactionism. (See Section 3B, this chapter.) Although in the present case we are not talking about two distinct substances, the property dualist is nonetheless claiming that mental properties fall outside the domain of scientific discourse. Such causal connections remain shrouded in mystery.

C. Why the Mind-Body Problem is Still With Us

There is a short answer to why the mind-body problem is still the subject of a lot of philosophical discussion. Consciousness (mentality, thinking) is a very complicated and difficult concept; no really simple theory is going to provide a satisfactory analysis of it. But moreover, the topic seems to be so difficult as to leave us with the sense that even the most complicated theories will leave something out. The problems with each account we have offered, examined from the perspective of its competitor, have illustrated precisely this point.

The pull toward Materialism comes primarily from its theoretical advantages over Dualism. If we are discontent with an appeal to nonphysical substance—the curious stuff that changes and has states, but has no size or shape and is invisible—, then the ontological simplicity of Materialism and its access to the explanatory resources of physical science make it attractive as a theory of consciousness. An explicitly third-person stance characterizes this pull. We attribute mental states to ourselves and others alike, and we generally get it right. We confidently believe that we are entitled to attribute mental states to ourselves as well as others. Thus, we believe we have evidence for one's being conscious. The details of such evidence will of course range from observational behavior to the complexities of one's brain. But we do not suppose for a moment that human persons, as perfectly good organisms of perfectly good physical constitution, must be characterized essentially by appeal to anything invisible or outside the domain of what is physical.

The first-person stance and Dualism's sensitivity to what seems impossible to capture in physical terms characterizes the pull toward the dualist's position. The problem with third-person approaches is that they must ignore what are essentially *inner* or *subjective* features of consciousness. The agonizing unpleasantness of the feeling of nausea cannot be captured in any amount of complex description of behavior or brain states viewed "from the outside." What it is like to be a conscious (nauseated, frightened, thirsty, etc.) thing requires an essentially subjective element that no objective materialist account can offer. We must then appeal to *something inherently different in its nature* than what can be gotten in purely physical terms.

And so goes the debate between Materialism and Dualism. Further empirical investigation and philosophical reflection promises continued progress on these issues.

Questions: Why does Nagel ask "What is it like to be a bat?" What does the epiphenomenalist have to say about the dualist's relationship problem? What criticism does it face?

Section 8: PERSONAL IDENTITY

A. Identity and Persons

Introduction

The traditional mind-body problem primarily concerns the nature of the mental and its relation to the physical. According to Substance Dualism, an adequate treatment of this problem must consider two quite different kinds of substance (mental and physical). An important task for the substance dualist is to explain how such different entities as mind and body can be so intimately related in a human person. According to Materialism, there is only one kind of substance, physical substance. The primary task of the materialist is to explain how mind is reducible to matter—he must explain the nature of mental states or properties in purely physical terms.

Discussions of the mind-body problem typically leave aside a separate but related topic. Consider Descartes' worry about whether "in death there is an end of me"—a worry with which we opened this chapter. Answering that question properly will depend upon our having attended to a prior question about *me*; namely, What am I, this thing about whose survival I'm inquiring? Earlier topics central to the mind-body problem are relevant here. If minds are distinct from bodies, then my mind may be able to survive the death of my body. If I am essentially a mental (thinking) thing, then, perhaps in death there is no end of me—perhaps I can exist disembodied. But if mind is a mere by-product of the body (Epiphenomenalism), or if mind just *is* body, then perhaps the destruction of my body is an end of me.

The problem of personal identity involves a number of issues, including that survival. The question of survival is a useful one, in part because attempting to answer it forces us to take stock of *what we are* (or take ourselves to be). For our purposes, the topic of personal identity primarily concerns the question, What am I?

Identity

The problem of personal identity isn't a problem about the nature of the relation 'x is identical with y.' Let's review the identity relation briefly, first getting clear on what the relation is *not*. Suppose that I worry about whether it's possible to survive my death. You might comfort me in a rather straightforward way by describing some day in the distant future, in Heaven maybe, where there exists some person just like me. You describe this person in detail, exactly similar to me in every respect, and conclude that since we can perfectly well imagine such a case, "It's possible that someone be identical with you after your death." What you have done here is to imagine someone qualitatively identical with me: the notion of identity you have in mind the one we employ in speaking of identical twins. But of course that is of no interest to me. It is of no comfort to be told that in some distant day after I die there will be this twin-like person who looks and acts and thinks just like me. When we speak of personal identity, the "identity" we need is *numerical identity*—the relation guaranteeing that the person-now and the person-a-hundred-years-from-now are the *same person*, that is, *me*.

Persons and essential properties

The main concern of discussions of personal identity is to spell out conditions under which it is correct to say that some person x is (the same person as) person y. Such conditions are sometimes called the "identity criteria" for persons. Now this way of addressing our question presumes that we're persons. We are, of course; but must we be?

Could I be a doorstep? A tree? The most general way of posing the question of personal identity, then, is to ask, for any thing (object) x, under what conditions is that thing me?

Most of us think that we not only happen to be persons, but that in some sense we must be. Whether or not that is correct, it represents an important kind of intuition. For it illustrates the fact that when asking "What am I?" we're asking about properties essentially (necessarily) belonging to me. Essential properties are properties that a thing must have in order to be the thing it is—properties without which it could not exist. If I think that I'm essentially a person, then I probably think that under no conditions could I be a doorstep or a tree.

Consider some individual x, say a small child weighing 23 pounds, with light blond hair. And consider an individual y, say a medium-sized adult weighing 134 pounds, with brown hair. By Leibniz's Law it seems we should say that since x and y don't have the same properties, x is not identical with y. But what if x is you as a child, and y is you now? Hardly anything is clearer to us than the fact that we change over time, that we lose and gain various properties with the passage of time. If we do persist, if indeed there is an enduring self, then such changes cannot be the losing and gaining of essential properties. One way of posing the question of what properties are essential to me, then, is to consider what sorts of changes I can undergo and still be me. Questions about survival are just such questions. So the question "What am I?" may be profitably discussed in the form, Given this range of possible changes I can undergo, what remains essentially the same? On what basis do we judge this individual *now* (y) to be the same individual as that one, *then* (x)? Questions about identity over time concern what we call *diachronic* ("dia-" means "through," and "chronos" means "time.") *identity*.

B. How to Think about Diachronic Identity

The Ship of Theseus

We can get clearer on how to think about personal identity by first considering a puzzle case involving changes over time in a fairly normal physical object. Consider the following story.

Theseus, a mariner, came by a neglected but seaworthy ship (call Theseus' ship "S"). He took long voyages on S with his small crew and family, sometimes staying at sea for

weeks at a time. Soon after purchasing S, Theseus imple-
mented a maintenance scheme whereby, upon each return to
port, modest renovations on the old vessel were undertaken.
A retired shipwright, now a deck hand on Theseus' ship,
would replace the oldest and most worrisome planks with
fine new ones. Slowly, plank by plank, over the course of
slightly under four years, each plank in Theseus' ship had
been replaced by a new one. Theseus was proud of his ship,
now completely renovated and looking almost new.

But the old shipwright was a clever fellow. He hadn't
thrown the old planks away, but rather had silently taken
them home to his garage, where patiently he reassembled a
ship. Slightly under four years after signing on with
Theseus, the old deck hand announced that *he* was now the
owner of Theseus' original ship S. It was a neglected but
seaworthy ship, still boasting its name in faded, chipped
paint there on the stern . . . .

The question is, Which ship is Theseus' original ship S? We'll have
differing opinions on this. Some will think that the new-plank ship is
Theseus' original ship S, others will say that it's the old-plank ship.
Those are both plausible opinions. But not just any opinion is a
plausible candidate for answering the question. What we're after here
are *principled* answers—answers based on some plausible criterion of
identity through time. Consider, for example, the idea that both
ships—the new-plank one and the old-plank one—are Theseus' original ship S. That is not a plausible candidate, clearly, because it is logically impossible. S is one ship, and since no one thing can be identical
with two things, it cannot be the case that both ship are Theseus' ship
S. Another implausible answer is that neither ship is S. That isn't
logically impossible, but it isn't very attractive either. What became of
Theseus' ship? Are we to believe that we're speaking of three ships in
this story, one of which somehow disappeared and two new ones? The
main thing we're after, then, is a plausible answer to the question: If S
does really persist, what are the criteria by which we judge its identity
over time?

Two criteria of diachronic identity

Let's think about the two reasonable answers. The first candidate is
that the old-plank ship is Theseus' original ship. This is a principled

answer, plausibly defended as follows. Everyone is willing to agree
that we can move a ship. One way we could move a ship is the way we
might move a piece of carnival apparatus, or a very large rocket: dis-
assemble it, move the parts, and reassemble it. And that's exactly what
happened with Theseus' ship S. Of course it wasn't moved all at once,
but slowly over the course of four years. What is of primary importance, then, is not how it got moved but what we have on our hands at
the end of the move. And what we have on our hands are simply *these
ship-planks*, now re-assembled into the ship. If before the move we
have these planks thusly-arranged making up Theseus' ship S, then
after the move we have exactly the same—these very planks making
up S. The criterion by which we judge identity over time is simply in
terms of the stuff making it up. In the case of a ship, it's the planks; in
the case of persons, it will just be whatever stuff makes up a person.
Call this sort of criterion a *substance criterion*.

   The second candidate is that the new-plank ship is Theseus' original ship S. A different principle employed in its defense might run as
follows. Clearly, we've got Theseus' ship at the very beginning. And
over the course of time, we find that something was simply *done to it*.
Replacing one old plank in S doesn't make S suddenly disappear or
go out of existence, and what some shipmate is doing in his garage is
irrelevant to the identity of S. Thus, all we need to do is *keep track of
Theseus' ship* the whole time, sitting there in the water, existing contin-
uously from the time we start doing things to it to the time we've fin-
ished doing things to it. The criterion by which we judge identity over
time is simply a *continuity criterion*.

   The two answers we've been discussing are common-sense answers. They cannot both be true, of course (they might both be false),
but there is nothing wildly implausible about them. Yet they are not
mere opinions, because as we have seen, they can be given a principled
support: there are good reasons for believing them. So, doing philosophy by starting with common-sense intuitions, or opinions, is all
right. That is probably the best way to start. But we mustn't stop at
that. In the present case, we attempt to give reasoned opinions by first
presenting a candidate. Then, we consider difficulties or possible
counterexamples to it as a way of isolating principles or criteria for
judging diachronic identity. In a couple of the earliest, implausible
cases, this leads to throwing certain opinions out altogether. In the
other cases, it helps us to formulate two kinds of criteria one might
employ to defend otherwise common-sense intuitions about the iden-

tity of objects over time. We'll use these sorts of criteria, now, in a discussion of personal identity.

C. Theories of Personal Identity

Dualism and minds or souls

The substance dualist encourages us to see that surely we are fundamentally more than just a body. As a conscious thinking thing, what I most fundamentally am is a mind or a soul. So I am not really this body of mine—though clearly my soul is related to it in some important way—but rather I am a nonphysical substance. This dualist thesis invokes a substance view of the identity of persons: judgments to the extent that some person x is identical with person y are judgments about immaterial minds or souls.

Before looking a bit more closely at this dualist thesis, we should remind ourselves of an important distinction. The issue of personal identity concerns a metaphysical topic. When we specify the conditions under which some person x is identical with some person y, we are making claims about the nature of some existing thing, and that is the job of a metaphysical thesis. A related but quite distinct project is to specify *how we would go about finding out* that some person x is identical with some person y. That is an epistemological matter (an issue concerning knowledge or coming to know). Now the question of how metaphysical and epistemological concerns are related is a difficult one. In the case of personal identity, for example, we might suppose that how one goes about finding out if x is identical with y will depend on one's knowing the conditions under which x is identical with y. But we might suppose, too, that uncovering the correct identity criteria will result in part from considering how one would go about determining if some person x is identical with some person y. If someone postulated criteria of identity that could never be verified or put to any test, we might wonder how these criteria were discovered and to what use they could ever be put in practical judgements of personal identity.

This last concern is relevant to the dualist substance criterion outlined a moment ago. On this view, judgments of the form "same person" are judgments of "same mind or soul." There are difficulties with establishing or verifying such claims of personal identity. Suppose that you knew me as a child, and meet me again today. On what basis do you judge me to be the same person you met as a child? Change the case slightly: you met me last night at the show, and you now take yourself to be chatting with me over coffee. According to the dualist's substance criterion, you can *see* that I'm the person you met at the show last night only if sameness of body is a reliable guide to sameness of soul. But that is at least worrisome, for since immaterial souls are unobservable, there seems to be no possible way of establishing this principle that sameness of body is a reliable guide to sameness of immaterial soul.

An important reply here, on behalf of the dualist, echoes the distinction above between metaphysical concerns and epistemological ones. *How we tell* in particular cases whether x is identical with y is irrelevant to those facts of the matter in virtue of which x and y *are* identical. The dualist is offering us a metaphysical thesis about personal identity; he is making no epistemological claims whatsoever.

Now this reply is not altogether satisfactory. As a matter of fact we *do* make judgments of personal identity (we make many of them every day), and we suppose that we get them perfectly correct. Surely we have some basis or other for making such judgments. If the dualist's thesis is correct, our judgments about personal identity seem groundless, because we have no grounds for verifying that sameness of body is a reliable guide to sameness of soul. But our judgments about personal identity *aren't* groundless; hence, the thesis that sameness of persons reduces to sameness of soul is false.

The dualist may offer a second reply here. On his account, judgments about sameness of persons aren't groundless. Surely I know that *my* soul and body are consistently found together, and from this first-person case, I can generalize to other cases. That is an inductive argument, and it is clearly a weak one for it is based on only a single case (one's self). But let that pass. The more interesting and important question is, How do I know even in my own case that a single soul has been consistently connected with my body? Nobody seriously doubts that a single person has been consistently associated with my body—indeed, that person is *me*. But what is at issue is precisely the question of whether from sameness of person we can infer sameness of soul. We can't appeal to sameness of body here, nor by fiat just assert the sameness thesis. In short, immaterial souls seem to offer no basis for identity judgments. But since we do make such judgments as "person x is identical with person y," we have nothing in mind about souls when making them. From reflections such as these, then, we may be disinclined to endorse the dualist's substance criterion of personal identity. Immaterial stuff forms no basis for the truth of claims that I am the same person you met as a child, or that I can survive my death.

Consciousness and memory

The dualist may choose to employ a continuity criterion. Let's be clear about the nature of continuity approaches. Recall that in the case of Theseus' ship S, we might judge the new-plank ship to be S because there is a continuous path traceable between them. At no time does the ship disappear, at no time does there fail to be this floating ship on which Theseus' family make their home. The basic requirement here, then, is that some relation of continuity hold between x and y in order for x to be identical with y. By "continuity" we mean that there are no moments at which clearly the object does not exist—that at each instant along the temporal path from x (x's existing) to y (y's existing) there is an entity for which we have no reasons to judge as not identical with the entity present a moment before. Typically, such criteria are not concerned with the kind of substance involved, but rather with what continuous relation obtains from moment to moment by virtue of which we judge to have the same entity.

One attempt at specifying a continuity relation by virtue of which we judge "same person" is by way of consciousness. John Locke, a seventeenth-century British philosopher, suggests that we can do this by ignoring the question of "same substance." A *man*, he says, is a living organism made of physical stuff. But, he continues:

> This being premised, to find wherein personal identity con-
> sists, we must consider what *person* stands for; — which, I
> think, is a thinking intelligent being, that has reason and re-
> flection, and can consider itself as itself, the same thinking
> thing, in different times and places; which it does only by that
> consciousness which is inseparable from thinking . . . and by
> this every one is to himself that which he calls self: —it not
> being considered, in this case, whether the same self be con-
> tinued in the same or diverse substances.[25]

"Same person" is established via continuity of consciousness, with no explicit appeal to a criterion of same substance. Locke illustrates this with his famous example of the prince and the cobbler; he says that should "the consciousness of the prince's past life enter and in-form the body of a cobbler, . . . everyone sees he would be the same

person with the prince . . . ." But clearly he is not the same man—not
the same substance. Or anyway, he is not the same physical substance.
Locke does speak of the soul as the repository of consciousness, but
that isn't central to this part of his theory. What is central is that personal identity be understood in terms of continuity of consciousness.

How should we cash out continuity of consciousness? Locke says
that it consists in the ability to "extend backward" our consciousness in
time to past actions and thoughts, that is, it consists in links of *memory*.

> For as far as any intelligent being can repeat the idea of any
> past action with the same consciousness it had of it at first, and
> with the same consciousness it has of any present action; so far
> it is the same personal self . . . .

Is memory a good criterion for personal identity? Clearly I can
remember only *my* past experiences and thoughts, and you only
yours. Thus memory does seem to be the sort of relation that appropriately hooks up me-now with me-then, not with you or anyone else.
And, if someday there exists a person that has my memories—that
remembers this very moment, say—then that person will be me.

Consider two persons—call them Bad and Good. Bad is a bad
fellow, a scoundrel, and in his recent past has committed a terrible
crime. Good is a good fellow—he once lifted up his sister's dress, but
that's it. Bad and Good die, and their disembodied spirits go to purgatory, somewhere between Heaven and Hell. In purgatory, Good and
Bad undergo an exchange of memories. Bad recalls once peeking
under his sister's dress, along with memories from boy scouts, high-
school football, and his days in the Rotary Club. Good remembers
certain evil deeds, along with memories of his youth gang, dropping
out of high-school, and his days in the Insult-Someone's-Mother
Club. What should we say here, in light of the memory criterion for
personal identity? What should God do with Good and Bad, were He a
memory-theorist of personal identity?

One might initially think that, on the basis of the memory criterion, God should allow the spirit we initially called Bad—the spirit that
animated the body that did bad things, but who cannot now remember
them—into Heaven; and He should send the spirit we initially called
Good—the one indwelling the body that did good things, but who
now recalls committing crimes—to hell. But our intuitions may be
pulled in quite the other direction, for we sympathize with the spirit

having lost the good memories, and think it unfair that the spirit loosing the bad ones should go to Heaven.

Perhaps this story is not coherent. Perhaps the mistake is to suppose that exchanges of memory could take place. Bad, we might say, merely *seems* to remember doing good things, and Good unfortunately now has false memories of doing bad things. This is an important point. You may now seem to remember certain experiences of childhood, and some day in the distant future someone may seem to remember this very moment of your present experience. But our faculty of recollection is not perfect: what you now seem to remember may not be a genuine memory at all. If memory is to serve as the grounds of personal identity, it will be important to single out *actual* memory—not mere seeming memory—as the relation guaranteeing that some future person is identical with me.

The difficulty, however, is that it's not easy to say how actual memory and mere seeming memory differ without begging the question. Suppose that I do seem to remember a childhood episode—say, hearing a performance of the Mormon Tabernacle Choir. How are we to decide if this is a case of genuine memory? (How are we to decide if there obtains a continuity of consciousness backward in time from this present memory-moment to some actual childhood-experience-moment?) The important point to see is that it won't do to say that my present seeming to remember is really remembering *so long as I actually did hear* the Morman Tabernacle Choir perform. We are trying to decide if I am identical with a person who actually heard this performance on the basis of real memory, but the present proposal attempts to guarantee real memory on the grounds that it was *me* who heard the performance. The point is simply that real memory seems to presuppose identity. (Under what conditions is person x identical with person y? Under the condition that person y has the memories of person x. Under what conditions is this real memory? Under the condition that the person seeming to remember the experience is identical with the person having the experience.) Hence, using memory as a criterion for personal identity seems to beg the question.

Perhaps this objection can be gotten around in the following way. The worry about a memory criterion is that we must rely on identity to guarantee real memory, and, hence, we cannot use memory to guarantee personal identity. But instead of saying that identity guarantees real memory, we might say that a person has real memory of the choir's performance just so long as there is the right causal connection between an actual performance and the apparent memory. If I

merely *seem* to remember the performance, there will be no appropriate causal chain between a past performance and my now seeming
to remember; but if I *really* remember, then the memory trace I now
possess of the performance will stand in an appropriate causal connection with that actual past performance. The weird so-called "switch
of memories" between Good and Bad seems better-described in the
following way. Good comes to have only apparent memories of bad
actions, and Bad comes to have only apparent memories of good actions. That is because Good's memory impressions are not hooked up
causally with any actual bad actions in Good's past, and Bad's memory
impressions are not hooked up causally with any actual good actions
in Bad's past. So Good and Bad only seem to remember these actions,
and God will not send them to the wrong places on the basis of false
memories.

Thus far we've been conducting our discussion in terms of a dualist theory of consciousness. But a story about causal chains between
actions and memory traces is difficult to envision for immaterial substances. Since the continuity approach we're considering is supposed
to be neutral between dualist and materialist accounts of consciousness, let's shift our attention to what the materialist might say about
memory criteria for personal identity.

The causal means of distinguishing real from apparent memory,
clearly, can be made intelligible in terms of memory traces in the
brain. As before, then, continuity of consciousness is cashed out in
terms of memory, and real memory is cashed out in terms of memory
traces properly causally connected to actual past episodes. It will be
helpful now to consider again the idea of survival. The possibility of
surviving death even on a materialist account may be coherent. Since
no explicit appeal is made to "same brain" but only to continuous real
memory links with past episodes, it may be possible that some future
person (in Heaven, say) have real memory links with my past
episodes. God preserves my existence by means of some appropriate
process whereby my actual memories are preserved, with all their
genuine causal connections with past episodes. He could preserve such
memories on a new brain, perhaps, or in whatever way He chooses. It
is important to realize that their means of preservation is not important
here. What makes them real memories isn't the *form* in which my
seeming memories are connected with actual past experiences, but
rather the fact that they *are* genuinely connected with them in an
appropriate information-preserving way. If God were to engage such
a memory-preserving procedure immediately upon my brain's death,

then the future being in heaven would be me because that being *has my genuine memories*. That conscious being is memory-linked with my past experiences, and hence, that person would be me.

If this is a coherent—though slightly far-fetched—story, then perhaps a materialist version of the memory criterion for personal identity can accommodate the possibility of survival after bodily death. The materialist version is not without serious difficulties, however. Consider that if God could create a memory-preserving being in the way described, then God could create two such memory-preserving beings. And then, which one am I? If the memory-criterion is correct, I am both of them. But of course, that is impossible.

Materialism and personal identity

Let's stick with materialism, and return to a substance criterion candidate for personal identity. An intuitive, important, and very simple materialist account might run as follows. What I am is this thing that is 5 feet 9 inches tall and weighs 134 pounds: I am this human body. So, sameness of person is sameness of body. This probably needs some refining—a live human body, say, with capacities such as rationality and the like. But it is intuitively plausible. You know that the person you're talking to now over coffee is me, because there's the same human organism sitting across from you now as went with you to the movies last night.

This intuitive account turns out to encounter more difficulty than one might have thought. The first worry is that I can judge my own identity—I know who I am, that I existed yesterday and had certain experiences, and so on—without having to make any judgments about my body. Recall the earlier point that we make reliable judgments of personal identity without any necessary appeal to souls, and that hence "same immaterial soul" isn't what any of our judgments of personal identity come to. Similarly, now, personal identity doesn't come down to bodily identity because when I wake up, I needn't make any judgments about my body when I consider who I am and what I did yesterday. So, this "same body" version of the materialist's substance criterion isn't much good.

What is meant by "same body"? Well, the substance criterion—of the sort motivating our intuition that the ship with all the same planks as the original ship is Theseus' original ship—seems to imply that we mean "same stuff." Here is a second worry about the materialists bodily identity criterion for personal identity. Take my body at a time t_1

and replace a particular molecule of it with a distinct molecule of the same sort. Do this again with a different molecule at t_2. Repeat this process over a period sufficiently long to have replaced all the molecules making me up with completely different ones. (And if you want to and have enough time, reassemble a duplicate body in your garage with the original molecules.) Is this the "same body?" (This replacement procedure takes place quite naturally anyway. The material stuff making up our bodies is completely "replaced" every seven years or so. But consider now the slightly less natural procedure undertaken on Star Trek when Kirk says "Beam me up, Scotty." Do all the molecules composing him get transported aboard the ship and reassembled into him? But then, it shouldn't matter: if we have the relevant blue-print for the assembly of stuff making Kirk up, why not just collect the necessary carbon and nitrogen and oxygen (etc.) sitting on board, and assemble *those* into Kirk?)

There is a third worry. It seems possible that I awaken some morning and find that I have suddenly taken on the body of a giant cockroach. That body isn't the same body I had last night. If this is at least logically possible, personal identity cannot come down to bodily identity.

We don't really care much about the body anyway, as a fourth worry seems to show. As materialists discussing personal identity, we should rather be concerned with brains. Consider a "brain transplant." Suppose identical twin brothers are involved in an automobile accident. The body of Peter is practically destroyed but his brain is fine; the brain of Ted is practically destroyed but we keep his perfectly-good body alive. Doctors take Peter's brain and put it in Ted's body (and throw the other stuff away). The survivor of this operation seems to be Peter: he is mentally like Peter in every way. Whether or not mental states are identical with brain states, mental states do seem to be dependent on brain states, and the survivor of this operation has a brain in virtue of which he has all of Peter's memories, beliefs, desires, and so on. When he awakens from the operation, he'll know perfectly well who he is. He will not insist that he is Ted, though he may be disappointed with having Ted's body. Indeed, that is a reasonable way to think of this operation: Peter had a body-transplant. When Ted's brain was destroyed, Ted ceased to exist.

This sort of reasoning is most plausibly taken to show that personal identity comes down to brain identity. But notice, too, that much of the work here is done by considerations having to do with a *continuity of psychological profile*—a renewed effort, it seems, on behalf of the consciousness/memory account discussed earlier. Perhaps then we require "same brain" to guarantee same person only insofar as we're concerned with preserving the same mental characteristics of the person. Those properties of persons that mark our individuality, that are of most value to us and to friends and family, are one's personality, one's character, one's attitudes and beliefs and so on. These properties are of importance generally in considerations of persons, and they're of ultimate importance to oneself. But nothing about the mere preservation of "same material hunk of stuff" explains the importance of these. Nor does "same material hunk of stuff" explain why I'm concerned about the preservation of these exact features of consciousness in a future person. Remember also that I seem to be able in my own case to judge "same person" without considering the body or the brain. So we need same brain only insofar as we wish to preserve same mental characteristics.

One difficulty with this renewed attempt at a continuity view is similar to one encountered earlier. Suppose that a technique is developed whereby a person's brain can be duplicated in the sense that all such psychological characteristics are preserved in the smallest detail. Should I be willing to have my own brain replaced with a duplicate? Would the survivor of that replacement-operation be me? A reason for staying with the same-brain thesis as a criterion for personal identity is, as before, that if the duplicate-brain survivor of the operation is identical with the original person, what should we say if two duplicates are made? Suppose then that we have two bodies, and make a duplicate of my brain. Put my brain into body 1—call the survivor Me-1— and put the duplicate brain into body 2—call the survivor Me-2. The same-brain theorist will say that Me-1 is me. But now, how is Me-1 to know, after the operation, who he is? Not only will looking at his body not help, but consider too, how is he to know who he is by merely introspecting? Introspection cannot tell him whether he has the original brain and is who he seems to be, or whether he has a duplicate brain, isn't who he seems to be, and just now came into existence. Finally, both Me-1 and Me-2 have perfectly good claims on the important psychological characteristics, because they're psychologically indistinguishable. One is no more like me than the other, and hence, there is no place to get started in explaining that I should be more concerned with one than the other as a candidate for my future self. In short, neither the "same brain" nor the "continuity of consciousness" views fare well. These latest reflections, on behalf of materialism, may suggest that understanding personal identity in terms of bodily identity is the best option after all.

Selves

So far we've taken it for granted that there is this single thing we call our *self*, existing at each moment, undergoing changes over time, and that the problem of personal identity is to answer the question "What am I?" in a way that specifies a criterion for diachronic identity.

There is one view of personal identity according to which that's a red herring. This view was that of David Hume, a British empiricist philosopher. We can anticipate his view by considering the following sort of argument. Identity is a relation between a thing and itself, and so never holds between a thing and some other thing. Now, a fairly innocuous principle is that a thing has the properties it has. That is just Leibniz's law, really, that says that if x is identical with y then x and y have the same properties. Clearly x and y have the same properties if x just *is* y. But then, from this innocuous truth about the logic of identity it follows that the whole idea of persistence over time makes no sense. No small thing weighing 23 pounds, with short blond hair can *be* a large thing weighing 134 pounds, with long brown hair. Generally, then, there is no persistence through change, and nothing existing at one moment can be identical with a thing existing at some other moment. As this applies to persons, the consequence is that strictly speaking there is no such thing as a persisting self, and that common treatments personal identity, of the sort we have been discussing, are based on a confusion. Here is Hume, claiming that there is no "self" of which we are ever aware at any one time, or at various times:

> There are some philosophers who imagine we are every mo-
> ment intimately conscious of what we call our Self; that we
> feel its existence and its continuance in existence; . . . unluck-
> ily all these positive assertions are contrary to that very experi-
> ence, which is pleaded for them, nor have we any idea of self,
> after the manner it is here explained. . . Self or person is not
> any one impression, but that to which our several impressions
> and idea are supposed to have reference. . . . For my own part,
> when I enter most intimately into what I call *myself*, I always
> stumble on some particular perception or other. . . I never can
> catch myself at any time without a perception.[26]

For Hume a person or self is at best a collection of conscious perceptions, each perceptual episode clearly not identical with the episode of consciousness previous to it, all of these united into a whole we call "myself." But at no one moment do we have this self.

Perhaps some illustrations will help. Suppose we go to the theater to watch a play. During the first act you must leave (you've forgotten to lock the car), and upon returning some 15 minutes later ask, "Is this the same play that I was watching a moment ago?" That might seem like a silly question. But consider that it isn't silly of you to ask if this is the same *act* that you were watching a moment ago. Here is the point: what you *are* seeing now is not identical with what you *were* seeing then. What you were seeing then was the scene in the first act where what's-his-name is courting what's-her-name; what you are seeing now is a scene in the second act where what's-her-name is killing herself. So judgments from one moment to the next about "same play" are in fact judgments about different pieces of play-acting appropriately related to one another—that is, about *parts of a play*. At no one moment am I aware of the play: the play is a temporally extended whole that at no one time is present.

Here is another example. Suppose we went to the river—down to Mohler's sand bar, say—for a picnic this afternoon. Tonight we go to the river again—to Sturgeon's Bend, far down river, for night fishing. Those are visits to the same river, we say. But we don't take that to mean that we really visited the *same thing*—the same batches of water, along the same edges of river—both times. What we saw this afternoon was a certain batch of warm afternoon water, where the river was slow and shallow and wide; what we saw tonight was a different batch of water—cold dark water, where the river runs deep and swift around the bend. So strictly speaking, I did not see the same thing tonight as I saw this afternoon. Indeed, I never saw the whole river at all, but rather different parts of it at different times. Those batches of water, and lots of other batches, appropriately related, make up one river, the whole of which I am never aware of at one time.

Hume gives the same account of personal identity. There are stretches of consciousness, that we're aware of now, and now, and now. Those are different perceptions and feelings and thoughts, from moment to moment to moment. A person is a conscious whole, composed of such parts: at no moment does the whole person exist. So personal identity does not come down to any sort of relation between some person years ago (me, as a child) and some person now (me, as an adult), or between me now and some future heavenly person. Rather, a person is something composed out of temporal parts appropriately causally related to compose a whole. Here is Hume again, describing his version of a continuity criterion for personhood.

> . . . The mind is a kind of theater, where several perceptions successively make their appearance; pass, re-pass, glide away, . . . There is properly no simplicity in it at one time, nor identity in different [times]. . . They are successive perceptions only which constitute the mind. . . Thus we feign the continued existence of the perceptions of our senses, to remove the interruption; and run into the notion of a soul, and self, an substance. . . [Consider that] in daily experience and observation, . . . the objects, which are supposed to continue the same, are such only as consist of a succession of parts, connected together by resemblance, contiguity, or causation. . . A ship, of which a considerable part has been changed by frequent reparations, is still considered as the same; nor does the difference of the materials hinder us from ascribing an identity to it.
>   . . . From thence it evidently follows, that identity is nothing really belonging to these different perceptions, and uniting them together. . . .[27]

What does unite these parts of our consciousness into a unified conscious whole? According to Hume it is a causal relation. Persons consist of person-stages or stretches of consciousness, causally hooked together into a temporal whole. Hume has his own special theory about causation, which we can ignore here. The important point to note now is that the causal element in Hume's story clearly allows for a sort of memory criterion again: where memory is cashed out in terms of causal connections between present and past conscious episodes, it is appropriate to say that the relation between two stretches of consciousness that makes them parts of the *same* conscious being is just that of memory.

> . . . as memory alone acquaints us with the continuance and extent of this succession of perceptions, 'tis to be considered, upon that account chiefly, as the source of personal identity. Had we no memory, we never should have any notion of causation, nor consequently of that chain of causes and effects, which constitute our self or person.[28]

Various objections can be raised against this Humean answer to the central question of personal identity, What am I? Consider, for example, that according to this answer, it is not strictly speaking true that Tommy-yesterday is identical with Tommy-today (since, strictly speaking, those are *different* parts of a temporally extended whole): does it still seem proper to punish Tommy-today for the bad behavior of Tommy-yesterday, if Tommy-today didn't perform the bad behavior yesterday? We will not undertake here a critical discussion of the Humean account of selves and its relation to other accounts. The temporal-parts view of selves and personal identity, however, does serve to remind us of the philosophically rich and difficult territory that discussions of personal identity attempt to clarify. The richness of the territory is due partly to the fact that personal identity concerns something that is clearly of great importance to each of us (as considerations of survival help to illustrate), and that a large range of intuitions accompany reflections about what we are. But as we have seen, even the best efforts to give some philosophical substance to such reflections—in terms of criteria for identity, say—rarely issue in clear and indisputable treatments of the difficult cases. Consider, for example, that even within the materialist camp, diverging treatments (same body, same consciousness, same brain) each attempt to capture certain intuitions but seem nevertheless to run aground of others yet worth preserving. And their worth is not merely academic, in a sense removed from personal concerns: our intuitions have to do with *what we are*, and get their purchase in concerns that are, so to speak, really "close to home." It is no wonder, then, that the Problem of Personal Identity is an old and longstanding one in philosophical circles, and that it will continue to receive serious attention for a long time to come.

Questions: What question does the Problem of Personal Identity raise? What makes a property essential? What are the substance criterion and the continuity criterion and how do they differ? What might a dualist say about the identity of persons? What might a materialist say? What problem arises from the notion of a self?

NOTES

[1]We sometimes say that a pain is in a part of the body, as when I say I have a pain in my foot. But the dualist will contend that, because pains are mental

and therefore nonspatial, they cannot literally be located in your body. First, the parts of your foot might include bones, tendons, muscles, and fat and skin cells. But you would not expect to find some additional object in your foot that is your pain. While you might be able to find some physical object, like a splinter, that is the *cause* of the pain and remove it with a tweezers, you could not remove some object called the pain itself with a tweezers. Second, just because a pain seems to be in a place doesn't mean it is really there. Some amputee victims claim they can feel a pain in a place where their amputated foot was. But since the foot is no longer there, they cannot really be feeling a pain *in* their foot.

[2]Rene Descartes, "Meditation VI," *The Philosophical Writings of Descartes, Vol. II*, Trans. Cottingham, John, Robert Stoothoff and Dugald Murdoch. Copyright © 1984, Cambridge University Press. Reprinted with permission of the publisher.

[3]Recall our discussion of epistemic possibility in Chapter 2, Section 3 ("A Modal Version of the Ontological Argument") and in Chapter 3, Section 4B ("Modality and Possible Worlds"). We call a proposition "epistemically possible" if it is possible for all we know. But a proposition can be epistemically possible and not be logically possible.

[4]Rene Descartes, "Meditation VI."

[5]Rene Descartes, "Meditation VI."

[6]Paul Churchland, *Matter and Consciousness* (Cambridge, Mass., 1984), p. 29.

[7]Thomas Hobbes, *Leviathan*, Ed. Michael Oakshott (Oxford: Basil Blackwell, 1859), Pt. 1, Ch. 1.

[8]Gottfried Leibniz, "The Monadology", section 17, Ed. L. Loemker, *Gottfried Wilhelm Leibniz: Philosophical Papers and Letters, Second edition* (Dordrecht: D. Reidel Publishing Company, 1969), 644.

[9]Gottfried Leibniz, "A New System of the Nature and Communication of Substances, as Well as the Union Between the Soul and the Body," Ed. L. Loemker, *Gottfried Wilhelm Leibniz: Philosophical Papers and Letters, Second edition* (Dordrecht: D. Reidel Publishing Company, 1969), 459-60.

[10]Gottfried Leibniz, "Considerations on Vital Principles and Plastic Natures, by the Author of the System of Pre-established Harmony," Ed. L. Loemker, *Gottfried Wilhelm Leibniz: Philosophical Papers and Letters, Second edition* (Dordrecht: D. Reidel Publishing Company, 1969), 587.

[11]Gilbert Ryle, *The Concept of Mind* (Chicago: University of Chicago Press, 1949), 18.

[12]Ryle, *The Concept of Mind*, 19.

[13]Our discussion in what follows owes much to Jerry Fodor's presentation in "The Mind-Body Problem," *Scientific American* 244 (1981).

[14]B. F. Skinner, *Science and Human Behavior* (New York: MacMillan Publishing Company, 1953), 33.

[15]D. M. Armstrong, "The Nature of Mind,"*The Mind/Brain Identity Theory*, Ed. C. V. Borst (New York: St. Martin's Press, 1970) 72.

[16]Jerry Fodor, "The Mind-Body Problem," *Scientific American* 244 (1981), 117. Reprinted with permission of the publisher.

[17]See Ned Block, "Troubles with Functionalism," *Readings in the Philosophy of Psychology, Vols. I and II*, Ed. Ned Block (Cambridge, MA: Harvard University Press, 1981), 270ff.

[18]Block, "Troubles with Functionalism," 276ff.

[19]See John Searle, "Minds, Brains and Programs," *The Behavioral and Brain Sciences* 3 (1980).

[20]Block, "Troubles with Functionalism," 304.

[21]Fodor, "The Mind-Body Problem," 122.

[22]Fodor, "The Mind-Body Problem," 122.

[23]Thomas Nagel, "What is it like to be a Bat?" *The Philosophical Review* 83 (1974), 438.

[24]Nagel, "What is it like to be a Bat?" 439.

[25]John Locke, *An Essay Concerning Human Understanding*, Ed. Peter Nidditch (Oxford: Oxford University Press, 1975) Book II, Chapter xxvii.

[26]David Hume, *A Treatise of Human Nature*, Second edition. Ed. L. A. Selby-Bigge (Oxford: Oxford University Press, 1978) Book I, Section vi.

[27]David Hume, *A Treatise of Human Nature*, Book I, Section vi.

[28]David Hume, *A Treatise of Human Nature*, Book I, Section vi.

RELATED READINGS

Armstrong, D. M. "The Nature of Mind." *The Mind/Brain Identity Theory*. Ed. C. V. Borst. New York: St. Martin's Press, 1970.

Ayer, A. J. "One's Knowledge of Other Minds." *Theoria* 19 (1953).

Block, Ned. "Troubles with Functionalism" *Readings in the Philosophy of Psychology, Vols. I and II*. Ed. Ned Block. Cambridge, MA: Harvard University Press, 1981. Originally found in *Perception and Cognition: Issues in the Foundations of Psychology, Minnesota Studies in the Philosophy of Science, IX*. Minneapolis: University of Minnesota Press, 1978.

_____. "What is Functionalism?" *Readings in the Philosophy of Psychology, Vols. I and II*. Ed. Ned Block. Cambridge, MA: Harvard University Press, 1981.

Broad, C. D. *The Mind and Its Place in Nature*. London: Routledge and Kegan Paul Ltd, 1925.

Chomsky, Noam. "A Review of Skinner's Verbal Behavior." *Language* 35 (1959). Also found in *Readings in the Philosophy of Psychology, Vol. I.* Ed. Ned Block. Cambridge, MA: Harvard University Press, 1981.

Churchland, Paul. *Matter and Consciousness*. Cambridge: Cambridge University Press, 1984.

Dennett, Daniel. "Skinner Skinned." *Brainstorms*. Montgomery, VT: Bradford Books, 1978.

_____. "Where Am I?" *Brainstorms*. Montgomery, VT: Bradford Books, 1978.

Descartes, Rene. "Meditation VI." *The Philosophical Writings of Descartes, Vol. II*. Trans. Cottingham, John, Robert Stoothoff and Dugald Murdoch. Cambridge: Cambridge University Press, 1984.

Fodor, Jerry. "The Mind-Body Problem." *Scientific American* 244 (1981).

Hobbes, Thomas. *Leviathon*. Ed. Michael Oakshott. Oxford: Basil Blackwell, 1859.

Hume, David. *A Treatise of Human Nature*. Second edition. Ed. L. A. Selby-Bigge. Oxford: Oxford University Press, 1978. Book I, Section vi.

Huxley, T. S. "On the Hypothesis that Animals are Automata and its History." *Essays, Volume 1: Methods and Results*. London: MacMillan Publishing Company, 1893.

Jackson, Frank. "Epiphenomenal Qualia." *Philosophical Quarterly* 32 (1982).

Leibniz, Gottfried. "A New System of the Nature and Communication of Substances, as Well as the Union Between the Soul and the Body." "Considerations on Vital Principles and Plastic Natures, by the Author of the System of Pre-established Harmony." "The Monadology" (section 17). *Gottfried Wilhelm Leibniz: Philosophical Papers and Letters*. Ed. L. Loemker. Dordrecht: D. Reidel Publishing Company, 1969.

Locke, John. *An Essay concerning Human Understanding*. Ed. Peter Nidditch. Oxford: Oxford University Press, 1975. Book II, Chapter xxvii.

Malcolm, Norman. "Knowledge of Other Minds." *The Journal of Philosophy* 55 (1958).

Nagel, Thomas. "What is it Like to be a Bat?" *The Philosophical Review* 83 (1974).

Parfit, Derek. "Personal Identity" *The Philosophical Review* 80 (1971).

Perry, John. *A Dialogue on Personal Identity and Immortality*. Indianapolis, IN: Hackett Publishing Company, 1978.

Reid, Thomas. *Essays on the Intellectual Powers of Man*. 1785. Essay III, Chapter 4.

Ryle, Gilbert. *The Concept of Mind*. Chicago: University of Chicago Press, 1949.

Searle, John. "Minds, Brains and Programs." *The Behavioral and Brain Sciences* 3 (1980).

Shaffer, Jerome. *Philosophy of Mind*. Englewood Cliffs, NJ: Prentice-Hall, Inc., 1968.

Skinner, B. F. *Science and Human Behavior*. New York: MacMillan Publishing Company, 1953.

Smart, J. J. C. "Sensations and Brain Processes." *The Philosophical Review* 68 (1959).

CHAPTER 5

Perception and our Knowledge of the External World

Section 1: INTRODUCTION

What do we know and how do we know it?

THERE are many things we believe to be true; fewer that we are inclined to say that we know to be true. Knowledge would seem to require something more than belief, perhaps that it be true belief grounded in good evidence. Typically we don't reflect much on what we know and how we come to know it. But certainly there is nothing strange about the idea that each of us has learned quite a lot about the world since we were born. Those of us fortunate enough to have normal healthy minds seem naturally to acquire knowledge of all sorts—that objects fall when dropped, that dogs aren't cats, that buildings far away aren't as small as they look, and so on. Much of this we take for granted, but on reflection we are immediately inclined to say that, given our prior experiences, our beliefs are supported, or at least could be supported, with good evidence.

But there are also more problematic cases. In chapters 3 and 4 we discuss the difficulty in coming to know that God exists, or that there are minds other than your own. In the first case, we produce arguments in an attempt to either demonstrated or made reasonable the belief that there is an omnipotent, omniscient, and morally perfect being. It is generally conceded that these demonstrations fail to *prove* that God exists, and to some it remains controversial whether, without proof, belief in the existence of God is rational. At the very least it is clear that, if God does exist, accounting for how we could *know* this is a difficult matter. The Problem of Other Minds proves equally troublesome. The intuitive features of Dualism—that our pains and mental images and such are private, non-spatial items—seem to clash head-on with the equally intuitive idea that we know others have pains and mental images too. While you might clearly know that you possess a mind, there seems to be just too little evidence from which to infer legitimately that there are minds other than your own.

It seems that we are on much firmer ground when it comes to knowing that your neighbor is sitting on a chair than knowing that he has a mind. Why?

One reason for this may rest with the obvious difference in the *kinds* of things about which we are trying to come to know. God and minds (according to the dualist) are non-physical objects; they are not located in space, and they don't have surfaces. In addition, both God and minds are taken to be imperceptible, at least with the common five senses. We don't have sensory access to a supernatural being such as God, nor to mental objects like minds.

On the other hand, the ordinary physical objects around us—tables, chairs, ducks and daffodils—are located in space and do have surfaces that we may see or touch. What better way to come to know about something? If you want to know whether it's raining, you go *look*; if you want to know whether duck tastes like prairie hen, you *taste* them; and so on. Our paradigm cases of genuine knowledge are precisely these cases of *empirical* knowledge—perceptual knowledge acquired by the use of our senses. In fact, one influential strain of philosophy (called Empiricism) claims that all knowledge is empirical knowledge. But whether or not Empiricism is correct, it seems clear than perceptual beliefs are among the surest candidates for genuine knowledge: we can and do know about the ordinary physical objects around us.

How this chapter will approach the issues

The purpose of the present chapter is to discuss how knowledge of the world is possible. Can we know that there are physical objects and what they are like? What is it about perception that is capable of yielding knowledge? When we perceive, what is the object of perception? These questions turn out to be far more complex and difficult than they first appear. But they are also important and interesting. Increasing our knowledge about the world is central to the enterprise of science, for example, and perception ("observation" is the word philosophers of science use) plays a central role in that enterprise. We do not simply want to have opinions about the world, or beliefs that just happen (by accident, perhaps) to be true. The knowledge we desire will consist in a body of beliefs that are true, rational, and reliable—grounded in solid evidence; the job of science is to develop such a body of knowledge about the physical or natural world.

But even if we are not interested in science, we still want to know what is going on outside our skin. Survival depends upon the fact that we don't regularly walk into walls or off high cliffs, that we know where to find food and seek shelter. Our perceptual systems provide us with access to the external world; and we suppose that the beliefs arising from our sensory experiences do in fact tell us what is "out there" and how it is. Again, it is not simply opinion that interests us: mere opinion does not reliably keep us away from the edges of high cliffs. We seek beliefs that are true, rational and trustworthy.

Our primary interest in this chapter, then, will be philosophical theories of perception as a source of knowledge. We will not be much concerned with psychological or physiological accounts that tell us only how the perceptual systems work, without telling us how they might qualify as sources of justified belief. The nonphilosopher might be interested in, say, how the retina works, or in how signals are sent through the optic nerve to the brain. But we want to know whether a belief about a certain physical object, a belief formed on the basis of some sensory experience I have had, is a rational belief. Am I justified in thinking that this perceptual belief informs me about the world? Does it count as knowledge, or is it merely opinion? And if it does count as knowledge, why does it? What is it about my being *perceptually* related to the world that puts me in a position to know things? If we can go some distance toward answering these questions, we will have significantly advanced beyond those untutored reflections we sometimes have about our knowledge of tables and ducks and cliffs.

Emphasizing an important aspect of philosophical method, this chapter explores a variety of theories about perception and knowledge. We will see that what at first appears to be a plausible theory might later need to be revised in light of objections that careful reflection reveals. Raising objections and then meeting them with revisions is crucial to philosophical progress. The theories we discuss are historically significant and remain of interest to contemporary philosophers who want to understand better our knowledge about the sensible world.

Section 2: DIRECT REALISM

A. Direct Perceptual Awareness

In this section we'll learn what generally constitutes philosophical theories of perception (that is, what sorts of questions they must answer), and we'll do this by considering a particular, seemingly correct, account of perception and perceptual knowledge. As it turns out, this theory—called "Direct Realism"—is probably one most of us find immediately acceptable; but this will not keep us from placing it under philosophical scrutiny.

What is meant by "perceptual" awareness?

Let us begin by thinking about what it is to perceive something. What is there to seeing, smelling, tasting, hearing and feeling that will be of interest to the philosopher? First, you are *aware* of something when you are perceiving. Consider what it is like to have your eyes open as opposed to having your eyes closed, or what it is like to hear when your ears are in good working order as opposed to being deaf. In the one case you are visually or auditorily aware of something, but in the latter you are not. Similar differences apply to the other senses. What we will call perceptual awareness is restricted to the experiences that arise from our common five senses. We will not consider the experience of a headache as a *perceptual* experience, although in such a case one is obviously aware of something. Still, we will often find that nonperceptual experiences such as headaches, dreams and imaginings are useful examples for our study.

The following distinction will be important to our investigation. Sometimes we are *directly* aware of things and sometimes we are *indirectly* aware of things. To be indirectly aware of something is to be aware of it in virtue of being aware of something else, as when you see someone by seeing their reflection in a mirror or you hear someone by hearing their voice over the radio. You can be said to see and hear the person, but only in virtue of being aware of the reflection in the mirror or the sound made by the speaker in the radio. To be directly aware of something is to be aware of it, but not in virtue of being aware of something else. Although it is not a perceptual experience according to our definition, the awareness one has of a headache or a toothache is direct.

Second, to perceive something is to have an experience that is in many ways different from the experiences we have when we imagine something or dream about it. When we genuinely perceive some object our experience is involuntary. Unlike the experience you might have when you imagine a tree, the character of your perceptual experience of a tree is not something you are responsible for—the experience of the tree is given to you. You cannot by force of your will make what you see change size or shape or color, although you could imagine whatever sort of tree you want to. Moreover, perceptual experiences generally are clearer and more coherent than the experience of dreams.

What kind of objects are we aware of?

Since we said that when we perceive we are aware of something, it is important to characterize the something that we are aware of. The description that seems most plausible to us immediately is that we are aware of objects that exist outside of us. After all, we have already said that we will not consider the awareness of a headache (an internal object) as a case of perception. And if we restrict our notion of perceptual experience to that which arises from the use of the five senses, then what else but an external object would be the object of our perceptual awareness?

Realism

We will need to say a bit more about these external objects. Unlike the headache, these objects are *mind-independent*. This is just to say that, unlike the headache, they could exist even in the absence of any mind, even if they were not being perceived. We will say that mental states like headaches (and beliefs, thoughts, hopes and the like) are *mind-dependent*. The view according to which there are external objects that exist and are a certain way independent of their being perceived is called *Realism*. We can discover by perceiving them that these mind-independent objects exist and are a certain way. But our perceiving them does not somehow make it the case that they exist or that they are the way they are.

Most of us are realists of some sort or other. Realism is only a very general theory about objects and our relation to them; we get particular versions of Realism depending on the details we add to fill it out. In particular, if we want a full-fledged philosophical account of perception, we'll need to specify the exact nature of our perceptual access to physical objects. And, if we want a full-fledged account of perceptual knowledge, we must say more about how perception can yield knowledge. These tasks, it turns out, are closely connected with each other and with the realist thesis.

Direct Realism

Direct Realism is a theory of perceptual knowledge that puts together two of the very commonsensical ideas that we discussed above. First, the direct realist is a realist: she believes that there are mind-independent objects in the world. Furthermore, to add the second idea, the direct realist would say that typically when we perceive these objects we are directly aware of them. That is to say that we can be aware of them without necessarily being aware of something else.

One may wonder what *else* one could possibly be aware of in such a case. There is, of course, a much more complicated story to be told about your retina, the optic nerve and certain parts of your brain. But though you might see the cup that sits on the table in front of you in virtue of these things figuring in this physiological account, none of them is *the thing of which you're aware*. According to the direct realist, when you open your eyes, what you perceive is simply the object in front of you.

By way of contrast, consider what it is to imagine a cup. In such a case, what you're aware of is in many ways like a cup, but just as certainly it isn't *the cup*. The thing you're aware of when imagining a cup is somehow "internal" to you; you in some sense create it as red or blue, as shaped in this way or that. When you perceive a cup, on the other hand, the object of your awareness is *given* to you: you open your eyes and what you see is an "external" physical object of some determinate size and shape.

But how does the direct realist explain the apparent fact that perceiving objects such as the cup on the table suffices to give us knowledge of the cup. Surely you find yourself believing that there is a cup on the table in front of you. But how can it be said that you know there is a cup there? The direct realist's answer is based on her claim that we can be *directly* aware of these external objects.

Consider an analogous case in which you are aware that you have a headache. Though you do not perceive it by means of your five senses, you are certainly aware of this pain. And clearly you are directly aware of it. You don't come to believe you have a headache because you are aware of something else that informs you of the ache. There is no other evidence for the existence of your pain than the pain itself. You make no inferences from other experiences you have. In such a case you couldn't be wrong—you're said to be infallible— about the headache's existence and nature.

Notice that the perceptual case seems to be similar. Your belief that there is a cup before you doesn't seem to be based on any inference or process of reasoning. You don't conclude that the cup is before you on the table after reviewing some other evidence. You simply see the cup on the table (or touch it) and the cup itself seems to be all the evidence you have or need. Were we only indirectly aware of the cup, say by having only seen its image on a television monitor or by listening to someone's story about the cup, we might imagine some room for error. The evidence might be misleading or the reasoning might go awry. The direct realist will say then that when you are directly aware of external objects you can't be wrong about their existence and characteristics. As a consequence our being directly aware of external physical objects puts in a position to know that these objects are as appear to be.

B. Theories of Perceptual Knowledge

Classifying theories of perceptual knowledge

Since we want to discuss several philosophical accounts of perception and our knowledge of the physical world, it will be useful to have a uniform way of spelling out the contents of any such account. Theories of perceptual knowledge, of which Direct Realism is an example, can be generally characterized by how they answer the following questions.

Q1: How should we characterize the objects that we typically say we perceive, that is, the everyday world of tables and chairs?

Q2: What sort of access do we have to these objects?

Q3: In virtue of what can we justifiably say we know about these objects? How does perception yield knowledge?

Let's quickly review the direct realist's answers to these basic questions. How do we characterize the world of tables and chairs? According to Direct Realism, tables and chairs are *mind-independent external physical objects*. What sort of access to we have to the world of physical objects? The direct realist claims that our access to tables and chairs is a *direct perceptual access*. To say that our access is direct is to say that the thing we're aware of in cases of perception is the physical object itself. In virtue of what are our perceptual beliefs about tables and chairs on solid enough footing to count as knowledge? Any good theory of perception will answer this question by underscoring the reliable nature of the perceiver's relation to physical objects. According to Direct Realism, we are justified in our perceptual beliefs simply because those beliefs are acquired directly. There is no inference performed. We appeal to no evidence beyond the object itself. Our perceptual relation to the physical object is direct, and no other means of acquiring beliefs could connect us more securely to the world of physical objects than this.

Problems for the Direct Realist

One of the appealing things about Direct Realism is that it seems immediately to capture our commonsense thoughts about perception and knowledge. One has difficulty imagining just what could go wrong with the idea that when we open our eyes and perceive the world, it is the external world that we are directly aware of. But as is often the case in philosophy, theories that at first blush seem relatively harmless and unproblematic emerge upon reflection to be quite otherwise. This is the case with Direct Realism.

According to Direct Realism we can know that objects exist and that they are certain ways simply because, when we perceive them, we are directly aware of them and the ways in which they are. We can isolate the problems with Direct Realism by considering the following questions. Are there cases in which perception fails to yield knowledge of the existence of physical objects, or of the ways they are? Are there cases of perception in which we are not directly aware of the way in which an object really is? And are there cases of perception in which we are not directly aware of any external object at all? If there are such cases, then we must take them seriously since they may indicate that we have not siezed on the appropriate sort of perceptual relation between us and the external physical world. It has been said that *direct* access to physical objects is a reliable means of acquiring perceptual beliefs. If beliefs that we arrive at by perception are sometimes unreliably acquired, then perhaps our perceptual access to physical objects is, at least sometimes, not direct. And if our awareness of external objects is sometimes not direct, is there any reason to think that it is ever direct?

Illusions

Perhaps the most straightforward problem case for Direct Realism is the phenomenon of *illusions*. Consider, for example, the notorious "bent stick" in water, familiar from our days of grammar school science. When we place a straight stick in a glass of water, the stick appears bent. We say "appears bent" because the bend is illusory—the stick is really straight. Another familiar illusion is the apparent convergence of parallel railroad tracks. And that is precisely what illusions are. They are cases in which the object appears to us to be different from the way it really is.

Now one line of reasoning might go as follows. If the thing of which we are directly aware is different from the physical object, then the thing of which we are directly aware cannot *be* (the same thing as) the physical object. The "real" stick (the external object) we assume is straight, yet we are directly aware of something bent. The stick can't be both bent and straight. So it must be that we are not directly aware of the external object.

That is a quite general consequence for any form of perception, visual or otherwise. If a faithful description of that of which we are aware ("bent," "converging," etc.) includes properties that the physical object doesn't possess at all, then that of which we're aware cannot be identical with the physical object.

Perceptual relativity

Other problem cases for Direct Realism revolve around the notion of *perceptual relativity*. Suppose you have a piece of sweet candy in your mouth, and remove it to eat something very salty. When you taste the same piece of candy a moment later, what you're aware of is not something sweet at all, but something bitter. Or consider that a distant wooded mountainside looks bluish purple from where you stand, but dark green when you are much closer to it. We are familiar with many such cases. The general point is that, relative to the same perceiver in different relations to the object, what we perceive differs.

But of course, the physical object just is the way it is. If that of which we're aware is now one way and now another ("now bitter, now sweet," or "now bluish-purple, now deep blue") and the physical object *isn't* now one way and now another, then when we describe that of which we're directly aware, we cannot be describing the physical object.

The Theory of Appearing

In both cases of illusion and cases involving perceptual relativity we find that what we are directly aware of seems to differ in some way from the external object as it really is. We are led then to conclude that Direct Realism is wrong if it contends that in perception we are directly aware of the ways external objects are.

While Direct Realism as we have spelled it out might suffer from these observations, another version might more reasonably account for illusions and perceptual relativity. Suppose we say, as does a version of Direct Realism called the *Theory of Appearing*, that while we are directly aware of external objects when we perceive them, these objects might appear to us in a variety of ways, including ways that differ from how the objects really are. The stick placed in a glass of water might appear bent to us even though it is really straight. And railroad tracks only appear to converge in the distance even though they remain parallel.

So while the initial version of Direct Realism presupposed that objects of which we are directly aware must appear as they really are, this new version acknowledges what seems reasonable, that an object can appear to be a way in which it really isn't.

If the Theory of Appearing seems to improve upon the original account of Direct Realism, it is not without difficulties of its own. At least two should be mentioned here. First, if an object can appear to be ways in which it isn't, even though we are directly aware of that object, then we must find some way to account for our knowledge of the nature of these external objects. A stick can appear bent or straight; when can we be sure that the stick is appearing as it really is?

The response to this difficulty would require a more sophisticated theory of knowledge than that which we've been contemplating so far. A defender of the Theory of Appearing might say that when the stick is perceived out of water it appears as it really is; when it is perceived in a glass of water we need only infer that it is straight since we understand the effect the medium of water will have on the visual appearance of objects to us. According to this account, knowledge of the stick's shape requires an inference based on the appearance of the object and our beliefs about the circumstances in which the object is perceived. This approach to the problem has much in common with Representative Realism, which is a theory we'll discuss in great length shortly.

Hallucinations and the time-gap argument

Now even if the defender of the Theory of Appearing can account for our knowledge of external objects despite the fact that they sometimes appear to be other than they are, another problem lurks in the background. This problem arises when we consider cases in which we have perceptual experiences in the absence of any external object that is perceived.

Consider the problem case of *hallucinations*. In an hallucination one has an experience indistinguishable from one in which one is perceiving an external object even though there is no external object being perceived. Under the influence of alcohol or hallucinogenic drugs it might appear to one as though there were blue rats running up the wall when in fact there are no such things as blue rats. How should the direct realist handle such a case? According to her view perceptual experience involves one's direct awareness of some external object. But in this case there is no external object involved. And the Theory of Appearing cannot help since in the absence of a perceived external object we cannot even talk about something appearing some way to the perceiver. If the intoxicated subject is sitting in a dark room hallucinating a group of blue rats running up the wall, what is there that could be said to be appearing to the person as a blue rat?

Another kind of case has similar consequences for Direct Realism. It is a simple fact of physics that light (or even sound waves) must travel at a certain speed. Light traveling from point A to point B does not arrive at B instantaneously. Depending on how far A and B are apart, the light might take only fractions of a second or years to cross the expanse. We know, for example, that it takes roughly eight minutes for the light to reach the earth from the sun. Thus, at the moment that the light from the sun affects your eyes, giving rise to your visual experience, the sun is eight minutes older than when that light left its surface. To take another example, consider that the lightening you see and the thunder you hear seconds later are different perceptions (at different times) of the same event. Due to the causal nature of perception there is always a time-gap between your experience of the event and the event you are said to experience.

Suppose now you are looking at a distant star from which it takes years for the light to reach the earth. Suppose further that in the time it takes for the light to travel the distance the star has been destroyed and no longer exists. At a particular time you look up in the nighttime sky and have the experience of "seeing" a star yet at that very instant that star no longer exists. What shall we say you are aware of? Can you be directly aware of a star that no longer exists? That is what the direct realist seems to be committed to. But here, as in the case of hallucinations, we seem to have a case in which we have a perceptual experience without our being directly aware of any external object.

Notice that in less extreme cases the time-gap argument is very similar to the problems of illusions. The sun still exists when I see it now though it might be slightly different (perhaps it is now closer to the horizon than it appears to be). Once again the Theory of Appearing might be able to handle this case by saying that I am directly aware of the sun even though it appears to me in a way that differs from how it really is now. But the Theory of Appearing has greater difficulty handling the possibility that I might now be having a perceptual experience when the alleged object (or event) of my experience no longer exists. In such a situation what am I directly aware of? And why should this sort of situation be any different from ordinary cases of perceptual experience?

What the problem cases call to our attention is, on reflection, quite familiar to us. Very often that of which I'm immediately aware doesn't conform to the physical world at all. They call our attention to the time-honored distinction between appearance and reality: reality sometimes *isn't* as it appears. Let us agree, then, that even with the revisions that the Theory of Appearing offers the direct realist is wrong about the perceptual access we have to physical objects through perception. The object of perception—the thing of which we're directly aware—is not the external physical object.

Questions: What is it to be directly aware of something? What is Realism? What does the direct realist say about our perceptual access to the external world? How do we gain knowledge about the world? What problems do illusions, hallucinations, perceptual relativity and the time-gap argument present to the direct realist?

Section 3: REPRESENTATIVE REALISM

A. Our Perception of Physical Objects

How do should we deal with the problem cases?

We have seen that Direct Realism fails to handle adequately the problems of illusion, perceptual relativity, hallucination and the time-gap. Given this failure, the theory simply will not suffice as a philosophical account of perception. What we must do then is attempt to construct a new theory that does not incur any of the difficulties already mentioned.

The main trouble with Direct Realism is that in at least some situations—when the world is not as it appears to be—it seems we are not directly aware of an external physical object even though we are having genuine perceptual experiences. The principle that we are directly aware of physical objects in perceptual experience must be false. But if we are not always directly aware of physical objects, of what are we aware?

We can begin to formulate an answer by thinking about the experiences we have in dreams. When we dream, although we are not directly aware of physical objects, we are clearly aware of *something*. The most reasonable suggestion in this sort of case is that we are aware of some mental image possibly accompanied by other mental phenomena such as sounds, smells, tastes and feelings. We will say that in dreams the objects of your awareness are mental.

This also seems to be a reasonable answer in the cases of illusions, hallucinations and perceptual relativity. Hallucinations are, of course, very much like dreams except that we are awake. The blue "rats" we experience aren't physical or external but (we might say) figments of our uncontrolled imagination. ("It's all in the head" we say, implying that these are mental, not physical, "rats.")

In the case of the straight stick appearing bent when placed in water, what we are conscious of, i.e., that of which we are directly aware, can only be described as *bent*; but since the physical stick is *straight*, we might conclude that we are not directly aware of the straight physical stick. Our experience, therefore, is of something mental. By this we must mean not only that what looks to be a bent stick is a mental object, but that the *whole* experience—of the stick, the water and the glass—is an awareness of something mental. It cannot be that only part of what we see is mental and the rest physical; the experience is qualitatively uniform. There doesn't seem to be any difference in seeing the glass and seeing the stick (as we might expect if the one were a physical object and the other a mental object). Or consider the situation in which from a distance a round tower looks square. As you walk closer the tower begins to look as it really is—round. But as you walk closer there is no noticeable difference in the quality of your perceptions, which you might expect if you were earlier aware of something mental and are now, when you are closer to the tower, aware of something physical. The suggestion usually offered is that you were directly aware of something mental all along.

Finally, when I perceive the food as sweet and you perceive it as bitter, what is it that we perceive? Clearly we are experiencing different taste sensations. In your own case you can experience a piece of candy as sweet one moment but less sweet, perhaps even bitter, the next. Here too the taste sensations are different. But the external object doesn't change. So we must be aware of something other than the food; the taste sensation we directly experience is mental, as is the sensation of taste you might have when dreaming about the food in its absence.

Based on these observations we might formulate the case against Direct Realism as follows.

(1) If Direct Realism were correct, then our perceiving external objects is our being directly aware of them.

(2) If we are directly aware of an object we cannot be wrong about it.

(3) But sometimes were are wrong about the external objects we perceive.

(4) So, we must not be directly aware of external objects, and

(5) So, Direct Realism must be wrong.

Several comments are in order. First, there are versions of Direct Realism according to which premise (2) is incorrect. The Theory of Appearing is one example. But such a theory introduces complications that we cannot attend to here. So we'll accept premise (2) without further debate. Second, the problems cases indicate only that sometimes our perceptions are wrong or misleading, not that they always are. If we are to claim that in these problem cases we are directly aware of something mental, can we conclude that perception is always a direct awareness of something mental? We have already suggested that in problem cases not only is the problematic object perceived in virtue of being directly aware of something mental, but also the other objects in the perceptual field must be perceived in like fashion. If the bent stick is a mental object, then so is the jar in which it's placed and the table on which the jar sits. But what about situations in which no problems arise, as when we perceive a straight stick as a straight stick? Once again we appeal to the idea that there is no difference n the experience between perceiving a bent stick in water and perceiving a straight stick out of water. The experience is just as "realistic" in the one case as in the other. We can expect the same account of perception will work for each. Let's now discuss this new account in more detail.

What are we typically aware of in perception?

So far we have been dealing with the problem cases. It seems that we are directly aware of something mental when we have perceptual or sensory experiences that inaccurately reflect how we assume the world really is. But this conclusion should apply to nonproblematic cases as well. Suppose you are now looking at a cup on a table in front of you. Think carefully about the very experience you are having; think about what it is like to experience this cup visually. Couldn't you be having this very same *kind* of experience in a dream? Couldn't a dream seem just as real, such that the cup still looked "out there" even though it wasn't? Wouldn't a hallucination of a cup be indistinguishable from the experience you are having now? And, perhaps more fancifully, might not a mad scientist directly stimulate your brain so that you had exactly the same kind of experience even though there was no cup in the room at all?

In all these cases your experience of the cup is *exactly the same* as the one you have when you see the cup as you are now. And here as well you are not aware of any physical object. The reasonable suggestion, then, is that we are not directly aware of a physical objects in *any* perceptual experience. Consider, for example, the normal experience you have of a glass of water, and then consider the experience you have of the glass of water containing a bent-looking stick. If our experience of the stick in the second case is of something mental, then so is our experience of the glass. And that is precisely what you are aware of in the first case: a mental or visual image of a glass. In each instance you are directly aware of something other than an external physical object. The thing of which you are aware in sensory experience is something mental.

The conclusion that we are directly aware of something mental—what we will throughout call "sensory ideas"—when we have sensory experience will figure crucially in our attempt to improve upon Direct Realism. We must not take it lightly or set it aside. It is precisely because the Direct Realist claimed to be directly aware of physical objects that he found himself in difficulty. Any theory that makes such a claim must deal with these problems. The important and plausible difference found in the theory we are about to develop is that what we are directly aware of in sensory experience is mental—we are directly aware only of the images, sounds, tastes, smells and sensations. And this seems to be a quite reasonable starting point for constructing a better account of perception and knowledge.

Can we perceive external objects?

If in perceptual experience we are always and only aware of sensory ideas, what can we say about our perception of external physical objects? Must we give up our belief in an external world? A certain tension can be seen to emerge between the claim about our being directly aware only of sensory ideas and our natural inclination to think we are perceiving external physical objects. Our theory can relax this tension by recalling the distinction between being *directly aware* and being *indirectly aware*. Several analogies may help to illuminate this general distinction.

Imagine looking in a shop window and seeing the reflection of someone standing behind you. If you are inclined to say you see this person, it is only because you see their reflection in the window. In this case you are indirectly aware of the person standing behind you, i.e., aware of him in virtue of being aware of his reflection in the window.

Consider the air traffic controller who is watching the blinking spot of light on a radar screen. He is not directly perceiving a plane although we can say he is indirectly aware of it, i.e., aware of it in virtue of being aware of the blinking light that represents an incoming plane.

Finally, to give a more fanciful analogy, suppose that at the moment of your birth a video screen was strapped across the front of your eyes so that you could not see anything else. Suppose also that a camera was attached to the top of your head so as to send images to the video screen before your eyes. As you look about you might "see" the cup on the table in front of you, but you are only indirectly aware of this cup since you perceive it only in virtue of perceiving the images on the video screen.

In all these examples one is indirectly aware of something—aware of something *in virtue of being aware of something else.* Contrast this with the idea of direct awareness: to be directly aware of something is to be aware of it but not in virtue of being aware of anything else. The distinction rests on whether an awareness of some second, inter-mediate, object is required. (Notice that the direct realist could claim that we are directly aware of physical objects and still admit that perception required use of the retina, the optic nerve, or brain. This is because although we are aware of physical objects by *using* our brain, it is not by being *aware* of our brain. His claim, which we now know to be mistaken, is that we are directly aware of physical objects, and this is just to say that we can be aware of a physical object without being aware of any other, intermediate, object.)

Our new theory is intended to improve upon the direct realist's theory by plausibly noting that in perceptual experience we are di-rectly aware only of our sensory ideas. Rather than give up the common sense notion that we perceive external physical objects we can now say that we perceive them but only indirectly: we are aware of them in virtue of being aware of sensory ideas.

To make this clearer, consider what you experience when you touch the surface of a desk. What you feel, i.e., what you are directly aware of, is a feeling or sensation of pressure. And it is because of this that you say you perceive or feel the desk. What you are directly aware of when you "hear a bell" is the ringing—the sound—and only by being aware of that do you say you hear the bell. Or consider the smell of a rose: isn't it the smell or the fragrance you directly experi-ence and not the rose itself? You perceive the rose by perceiving its fragrance.

How our sensory ideas are related to the external world

We are interested in developing a philosophical theory of perceptual knowledge. We want our theory to explain not only how perception works but how it yields the knowledge we suppose it does. The prob-lematic cases noted above have not made developing such a theory easy. So far we have merely concluded that when we perceive we are directly aware only of our sensory ideas and indirectly aware of external physical objects. But how are we to know that, say, the stick is really straight when all we are directly aware of is a visual (mental) image of a bent stick? How are we to know that the cup is really solid and full of coffee if we are only directly aware of sensory ideas? How are we to know anything at all about physical objects—that they even exist!—if we are only indirectly aware of them? Our theory of perception has much to explain.

Let us think of the sensory ideas that we are directly aware of as evidence for believing that there is an external world and that it is roughly the way it appears to be. This relationship is not unfamiliar to us, for we find it also in the case of where the reflection in the mirror serves to indicate the existence and nature of the object reflected. What we are directly aware of (the reflection) is evidence for what we are indirectly aware of (the object reflected).

Another analogy we have already mentioned will help make the relationship clearer. Suppose again that a video screen is fastened in front of your eyes so that you see only images projected there by a camera mounted atop your head. In this case you are still aware of the outside world, if only indirectly. The image on the monitor provides evidence about the existence and nature of the external objects. Can't you know that, say, there is a chair in front of you even if you only "see" it on the screen? Can't you still walk around it, or know what shape and size it is, even if you only have this indirect access to it?

The analogy used here is restricted only to the visual sense, and it should be clear by now that according to the present theory you could not be directly aware of the screen since that too is an external object—so we must be careful not to make too much of the example. But several points will add some insight to our new theory. First, we can know about the chair in front of us only if the camera is working properly. There must be the right sort of causal connection between the chair and the camera (light must reflect off the chair and enter the lens of the camera) and between the camera and the video screen (there must be the appropriate circuitry and signal transmission to provide an image on the screen). If the causal chain is broken or disturbed, then there is no guarantee that a faithful image of the chair will appear on the screen. Second, even if the causal connection is adequate, the image on the screen must represent the chair in just the right sort of way. It is reasonable to think the image on the screen resembles or looks like the chair. If the image incorrectly represented the chair as much smaller than it is, or slightly off to the left, or as looking more like a table than a chair, your knowledge would be deficient.

These two points regarding causation and resemblance can be seen at work in the other examples as well. You could recognize the person behind you as your friend only if the reflection you see in the window is caused in the appropriate way and adequately resembles your friend. The blinking spot of light on the radar screen provides a slightly different example. It does not look like a plane, but it must be caused in the right sort of way if it is to represent one. The air traffic controller could not tell a plane was coming unless blinking spots of just that sort were caused only by planes. The light's position and movement on the screen must approximately resemble the position and movement of the airplane in space.

Let us now look more closely at these two points as they pertain to our theory of perception.

The causation and resemblance theses

If our sensory ideas are to give us knowledge of the external world, then they must be caused in us in the appropriate way. Explaining just what this way is is the job of the scientist, in particular whoever studies the physiology of perception. Roughly we can say this much. In cases of vision light reflects .off the object and strikes the eye; an image is projected onto the retina and receptor cells are stimulated sending electrochemical impulses through the optic nerve to the brain. Of course there remains that part of the story in which the brain "produces" the visual image; but we shall ignore that for now (that won't necessarily be part of the physical scientific story).

So the account our theory provides will partly depend on the claim that when we have accurate perceptual experiences our sensory ideas are caused by the external physical objects we indirectly perceive. If the causal chain is inadequate or disturbed, then it is to be expected that our sensory ideas may not tell us much or anything about the external world. The *causation thesis* is that accurate perception requires an appropriate causal connection between the sensory ideas and the objects indirectly perceived (the objects of those ideas).

Not only must our sensory ideas be caused in the right sort of way, but they must resemble or represent the object as well. Just as the image on the video screen resembled the chair, just as the reflection in the window resembled our friend standing behind us, so our sensory ideas must resemble the objects of which we are indirectly aware. The solidity of the desk should be represented by the feeling of hardness or pressure we experience when we touch it. The sensory ideas of the chair should represent the size and shape of the chair. And this should happen if the causal connection is undisturbed. A second thesis then is the *resemblance thesis*. The resemblance thesis states that if our sensory ideas are caused in the appropriate way, then they will represent or resemble the objects we indirectly perceive.

Representative Realism

The theory of perception we are developing requires both the causation and resemblance theses. We will call our theory *Representative Realism*. It is a form of Realism since it does not deny the existence of mind-independent physical objects, and we describe it as representative since representation (the representation of physical objects by our sensory ideas) plays such an important role. Unlike Direct Realism, Representative Realism claims that we are not directly aware of external physical objects. Instead we are only indirectly aware of them in virtue of being directly aware of our sensory ideas.

In sum: *Representative Realism* is a kind of Realism according to which my being perceptually aware of an external physical object is my being indirectly aware of it in virtue of being directly aware of sensory ideas; in cases of veridical perception these sensory ideas are caused by, and will resemble to some extent, mind-independent physical objects. This theory of perception is very much like the one developed by the philosopher John Locke in the eighteenth century and so we will use Locke as its spokesman.

The theory is not yet complete, although we have already presented most of the materials we will need. Next we will show how Locke's Representative Realism handles the problems faced by the direct realist. Then we will need to say a bit more about how our perceptual beliefs (beliefs about the external world based on perception) are justified and yield knowledge. As you may already see, the causation and resemblance theses will prove to be crucial.

B. Hallucinations, Illusions, Perceptual
Relativity and the Time-Gap Phenomenon

Before looking specifically at how representative realists treat the problematic cases of illusions, hallucinations, perceptual relativity and the time-gap phenomenon, it is important to underscore the advantage Representative Realism has over Direct Realism on these matters. Consider again the nature of these cases: in each we say that the thing of which we are aware is one way while the physical object is another. The direct realist is *unable* to say this, however, because according to his theory that of which we are aware *is* the physical object. He speaks of one thing, not two, and hence there is simply no room to distinguish what we immediately perceive from the physical object, as we must do in the problem cases. The general point about Representative Realism is that, since this theory does provide this distinction, there is now room for saying that the physical object is one way while the object our awareness of it is quite another. *Two* things (sensory ideas and physical objects) now figure in the story, and the manner in which they are related can figure in the representative realist's account of illusions, hallucinations, and perceptual relativity.

How does the representative realist handle hallucinations, illusions and the time-gap problem?

In cases of illusion objects do not look as they really are. The straight stick, when placed in a glass of water, will look as though it bends at the surface of the water. We have said that this suggests that—contrary to Direct Realism—we are directly aware of something mental and not of the physical stick. How does the representative realist handle this case? Why do our sensory ideas fail to resemble the external physical object accurately?

Recall the causation and resemblance theses. If the causal connection is disturbed or inappropriate, then the sensory ideas may not resemble the object indirectly perceived. And this is what happens in the case of the bent stick. The light that is refracted from the bottom part of the stick is bent when passing from one medium (water) to another (air). This is unlike the normal causal connection between straight sticks and our sensory ideas of them in which air is the only medium. In these normal cases the stick looks straight, i.e., our visual images represent the stick as straight. Representative Realism can explain how illusions sometimes yield experiences in which objects appear to be different from the way they really are.

A similar story can be told for hallucinations. Because a chemical imbalance in the brain (or some other physiological disturbance resulting from consuming an excess of alcohol) results in sensory ideas that do not represent anything in the perceiver's vicinity, the drunk "sees" pink rats though there are no physical pink rats in the area. The causal chain that results in the perceiver's experience of pink rat images is inappropriate for resemblance—the pink rat images don't represent or resemble anything actually present.

Perceptual relativity

The direct realist also had trouble with cases of perceptual relativity. Can the representative realist do any better? One thing is clear. The resemblance and causation theses alone will not handle the job. It is not simply because our taste sensations are *improperly caused* that the candy tastes bitter to me and sweet to you. Can we say that in this situation I am wrong and you are correct about the *true* taste of the candy? Could not the same piece of candy cause a sweet sensation in one person and a bitter sensation in another? Why should your tastes accurately represent the candy and not mine? Accurate representation does not seem to be at issue here; we want to be able to say that you are not wrong in calling the candy sweet (since that *is* the way it tastes to you) and I am not wrong in calling it bitter (because that *is* the way it tastes to me).

Or consider an example that Locke uses. Suppose there are three bowls of water—one hot, one warm and one cold. If your left hand is in the hot water and your right hand is in the cold water, when you suddenly put both hands in the warm water, the same bowl of water will feel *both* hot and cold, i.e., the water will feel cold with your left hand and warm with your right hand. But how could the same water produce different sensations both of which accurately represent the water? Is there any reason at all to think that one sensation accurately represents the way the water really is and the other sensation does not?

Locke dealt with this sort of case by distinguishing sensory ideas that depend upon and resemble the intrinsic properties of the physical object from sensory ideas that do not. We must look more closely at this distinction.

Primary qualities

The current scientific story about physical objects tells us that an object is composed of molecules, or atoms. Let us simply call this structure the *microstructure* of the object. Locke thought there was some truth to this scientific story (although the current highly sophisticated story was not available in his day), and he correctly thought that some of the qualities of the object depend upon this structure. The size, shape, texture, mass, motion and arrangement of the object's molecules determine the size, shape, texture, mass and motion of the object. Locke called these qualities *primary qualities*. They are

> utterly inseparable from the body, in what estate soever it be; ... v.g., Take a grain of wheat, divide it into two parts, each part still has *solidity, extension, figure*, and *mobility*; divide it again, and it retains still the same qualities; and so divide it on, till the parts become insensible, they must retain still each of them all those qualities. For division ... can never take away either solidity, extension, figure, or mobility from any body, but only makes two, or more distinct separate masses of matter, of that which was but one before, all which distinct masses, reckon'd as so many distinct bodies, after division make a certain number. These I call original or *primary* qualities of body, which I think we may observe to produce simple ideas in us, viz. solidity, extension, figure, motion, or rest, and number.[1]

The causation thesis tells us that when we perceive physical objects our sensory ideas are caused by the objects. In particular, our ideas of the object's size, shape, texture, mass and motion will be caused by our perceptual interaction with the object's primary qualities and, according to the resemblance thesis, they will, if properly caused, represent or resemble those qualities. So as not to confuse the ideas with the qualities, let us call the sensory ideas that are caused by the qualities of the object the *primary quality ideas*.

Secondary qualities

Now qualities like size, shape or mass were not the ones that seemed to give us trouble in cases of perceptual relativity. These primary qualities exist independently of the perceivers. If you say the shape is rectangular and I say it is circular then both of us cannot be correct. The object's nature, its microstructure, determines what the actual shape is. But in cases of perceptual relativity there was no harm is saying we were both right even though we attributed conflicting properties to the object. Those properties that were relative to the perceiver were properties like sweet or bitter, warm or cold, dark green or bluish purple, etc. Locke sees qualities of this sort as distinctly different from primary qualities. These other qualities do not seem to be "in" the object at all but are to some extent dependent upon the perceiver. Locke says of them:

> Such qualities, which in truth are nothing in the objects themselves, but powers to produce various sensations in us by their primary qualities, i.e., by the bulk, figure, texture, and motion of their insensible parts, as colours, sounds, tasts, etc. These I call *secondary qualities*. (*Essay*, II, viii, 10)

> [A secondary quality may be thought of as] the power that is in a body, by reason of its insensible primary qualities, to operate after a peculiar manner on any of our senses, and thereby produce in us the different ideas of several colours, sounds, smells, tasts, etc. (*Essay*, II, viii, 23)

So secondary qualities such as being red, sweet or warm are not properties in the object as are the primary qualities. If there is anything in the object to which we are referring when we say it is red or sweet, it is at best only the power or the potential it has (because of its insensible parts) to produce in normal perceivers and under normal conditions, the ideas of red and of sweet. The object is not really (in itself) red or sweet, but in normal circumstances it will cause normal perceivers to have those experiences. We can perhaps more cautiously make the distinction by saying that while ideas of primary qualities may resemble properties of the object, ideas of secondary qualities will not. So when you say the candy is sweet in contrast to my claim that it is bitter, you are simply reporting your sensation; and that sensory idea is caused by the very same object (with the very same microstructure) that causes my sensation of bitterness.

In a very important sense the secondary qualities of an object depend on its primary qualities. Whether you taste the candy as sweet or bitter depends in part on how the molecules of the object are arranged and what primary qualities are present. But it is also important to see that which secondary quality sensation you perceive depends in part on how you are constituted. For the same primary qualities that cause you to experience red, sweet, loud, or warm may cause me to experience orange, bitter, soft, or cold. Secondary qualities, we say, are mind-dependent.

Let us summarize this discussion by noting two ways in which primary qualities differ from secondary qualities. First, primary qualities are *mind-independent* but secondary qualities are *mind-dependent.* It is because of this that at least one of us is wrong when you say the object is rectangular and I say it is circular, but both of us could be correct if you say it's warm and I say it's cold. Physical objects are not, independent of some perceiver or other, colored, sweet, warm, smooth, or loud; but they might be square, ten feet high, solid, 45 degrees Celsius and at rest depending only on the arrangement and motion of the molecules of which they are composed.

Second, our primary quality ideas, if caused in the appropriate way, will represent or resemble the primary qualities that produce them. But sensations of secondary qualities (perhaps we should call them "secondary quality ideas") do not resemble anything in the object. As Locke notes:

> ... the ideas of primary qualities of bodies, are resemblances of them, and their patterns do really exist in bodies themselves; but the ideas, produced in us by these secondary qualities, have no resemblance of them at all. There is nothing like our [secondary quality] ideas, existing in bodies themselves. (*Essay*, II, viii, 15)

So this is how the Lockean representative realist handles the problem of perceptual relativity. The properties that are relative to perceivers are secondary qualities—they are mind-dependent and not in the object at all. So there is no worry that an object must be both warm and cold, dark green and bluish purple, or sweet and bitter. We may each be aware of different sensations even though they were produced by the same object. Here is Locke explaining the hot and cold water example mentioned above.

> [Primary and secondary] ideas being thus distinguished and understood, we may be able to give an account, how the same water, at the same time, may produce the idea of cold by one hand, and of heat by the other: whereas it is impossible, that

the same water, if those ideas were really in it, should at the same time be both hot and cold. For if we imagine warmth, as it is in our hands, to be nothing but a certain sort and degree of motion in the minute particles of our nerves, or animal spirits, we may understand, how it is possible, that the same water may at the same time produce the sensation of heat in one hand, and cold in the other; .... (*Essay*, II, viii, 21)

An inference to the best explanation

Our proposed theory of perception has been able to explain the problem cases that proved difficult for Direct Realism. The causation and resemblance theses were used to explain how, in illusion and hallucination, one could be aware of sensory ideas that failed to resemble or represent external physical objects accurately. And by distinguishing primary from secondary qualities we could account for cases of perceptual relativity.

We also want our theory of perception to explain how perception can be a source of knowledge. When we are directly aware of something, we come to possess beliefs about the object in a way that requires no inference. Since there is no room for error we can say we know that the thing is as it appears to be. So, for example, you are directly aware of your mental states and because of this you cannot be wrong about them—you could not erroneously feel pain or be mistaken in thinking that the stick *looks* bent.

But we are faced with an apparent difficulty when we turn to Representative Realism. According to this theory we are only indirectly aware of external physical objects. I may know or be justified in thinking that the book *looks* rectangular, but can I know or be justified in thinking that it *is* rectangular? How can we know about objects or facts of which we are only indirectly aware?

This is the special problem facing the representative realist. Since we are directly aware only of our sensory ideas, it is as if the objects of the external world lie inaccessible to us behind a veil—a veil of perception. The representative realist's belief that there are external physical objects (and that they are certain ways) cannot be directly acquired, but rather must be a conclusion inferred from that to which he does have direct access. This inference will not take the form of a deduction since there is no guarantee (certainly no logical guarantee) that the objects in the world are as they appear to be. After all, many cases of illusion and hallucination convince people the world is one way when it is actually another ("But I saw the magician cut the woman in two;" "What do you mean there are no such things as pink rats? I saw them with my own eyes."). So, a representative realist reasons inductively. He will take his sensory ideas as evidence for his beliefs about external physical objects. This inference from, say, my perceiving a collection of cup-ideas to the existence of a cup that resembles them is a reasonable one. The existence of the cup best explains why I am experiencing these sensory ideas. We will call inferences of this sort *inferences to the best explanation.*

The representative realist's explanation for our perceptual experiences

Let us put the matter more generally. We begin with certain known facts—the data, if you will. In the case at hand, we have certain facts (to which we have direct access) about the nature of our perceptual experiences: our experiences are not the products of our own imagination (we merely receive them, they are given) and are typically very clear, vivid, orderly, uniform, and coherent. Moreover, our experiences of sensible objects is involuntary: unlike the ideas of our imagination, our sensory experiences are not under our control. These are the data that need to be explained. For example, the cup I am now perceiving is not expected to get up and walk away or turn into a lizard; the desk looks the same today as it did yesterday; the chair looks solid and, as I expect, feels solid as well.

What about the hypothesis that we are producing these ideas in ourselves, or that we are merely dreaming and there is no external world? If our sensory ideas were simply the products of our rambling minds, we could not expect this clarity, uniformity and coherence to obtain. If we were merely imagining what we take to be sensory experience, we could change the experience at will. But we cannot. Furthermore, we suppose our dreams to be the products of our minds only, and they are typically neither clear, uniform nor coherent. Such explanations of the data will not do. Consider Locke's reasoning.

> [S]ometimes I find, that I cannot avoid the having those ideas produced in my mind. For though when my eyes are shut, or windows fast, I can at pleasure recall to my mind the ideas of light, or the sun, which the former sensations had lodged in my memory; ... But if I turn my eyes at noon towards the sun, I cannot avoid the ideas,, which the light, or sun, then produces in me. So that there is a manifest difference, between the ideas

laid up in my memory ... and those which force themselves
upon me, and I cannot avoid having. (*Essay*, IV, xi, 5)

Our senses, in many cases, bear witness to the truth of each
other's report concerning the existence of sensible things
without us. he that sees a fire may, if he doubts whether it be
anything more than a bare fancy, feel it too, and be convinced
by putting his hand in it; which certainly could never be put
into such exquisite pain by a bare idea or phantom, ... (*Essay*,
IV, xi, 7)

The representative realist wants to suggest that the best explanation
we have for these general features of our sensory experiences is that
they reflect the stability and coherence of external, mind-independent,
physical objects that produce them. In the particular case, the hypothesis that there is an external, mind-independent cup causing me to
have the experience I am currently having, and that this cup is to some
extent represented by my ideas, best explains the existence and nature
of my sensory experience. So, the explanation will include both the
causation and the resemblance theses.

More on inferences to the best explanation

Of course this is only an inductive inference and so there is no guarantee that the explanation is correct. But since the external world hypothesis is better than any alternative hypothesis (say, that I'm dreaming it all up), and since it does explain why our experiences are so
forceful, clear, uniform and coherent, it is reasonable to treat it as correct. Consequently, we are generally justified in our perceptual beliefs.
In the particular case, if you are having sensory ideas of a cup and the
conditions under which you have these ideas are normal, then you
have every reason to believe there is a cup before you even though
you are only indirectly aware of it.

You are not guaranteed that your sensory ideas represent objects
accurately or even that they represent anything at all. If everything
works properly, however, then, according to the causation and resemblance theses, it is reasonable to think the chair is as you "see" it to be.
The inference from your sensory experience to facts about the world
appears to be reliable enough to yield knowledge.

Inferences to the best explanation are often used in science to justify certain hypotheses that posit the existence of entities we cannot di-

rectly observe. We cannot perceive electrons, but we are justified in believing that they exist (we say we know they exist) because by positing their existence we are best able to explain certain experimental results we can perceive—e.g., only a thing of this sort could cause the traces one observes in the cloud chamber. It is this very same sort of inference the representative realist is using. We are directly aware that the data we have include the general stability and orderliness of our perceptual experiences. We are reasonable in thinking there are external physical objects (even though we cannot directly observe them) because by positing their existence we are best able to explain these general features of our experiences. (For more on inferences to the best explanation see Chapter 2, Section 1C.)

Representative Realism and our model for perceptual knowledge

We saw earlier that Direct Realism could be characterized by the answers it provided to a certain series of questions. We can characterize Representative Realism in the same way, noting how these two theories differ in their responses to the questions.

Q1: How should we characterize the objects we typically say we perceive?

Here the direct realist and the representative realist agree: tables and chairs are mind-independent physical objects. It is this common answer that makes them both realists.

Q2: What sort of access do we have to these objects?

The direct realist will of course say that we can be directly aware of such things as tables and chairs. But as we have seen, there are problems confronting this view (in the form of illusions, hallucinations and perceptual relativity) and we have chosen to accept with the representative realist the thesis that we are only indirectly aware of external physical objects. We have only indirect access to the external world: we perceive physical objects only in virtue of being directly aware of our sensory ideas.

Q3: In virtue of what can we justifiably say we know about
these objects? How is perception a source of knowledge?

Since the direct realist claims we can be directly aware of physical
objects, he has no problem in explaining how you could be justified
in believing there was a cup in front of you when you saw one (there
is really no room for error). Of course that is precisely why the direct
realist has trouble explaining the existence of illusions, hallucinations
and perceptual relativity. If we are directly aware of the objects, then
how could we ever get things wrong? The insightful contribution of
the representative realist is to suppose that we are directly aware only
of our sensory ideas. But this leaves the external world only indirectly
accessible and makes our knowing about this world a more complicated and delicate affair.

In answering Q3, a good theory of perception must be able to
specify the reliable nature of the perceiver's relation to the external
physical object. The representative realist's answer to Q3 depends on
an inference to the best explanation. The hypothesis that our sensory
ideas are caused by, and to some extent represent, certain qualities of
external mind-independent objects best explains why we have the experiences we do and why they are so forceful, clear, orderly and coherent. Because of this we are justified in thinking that there are
physical objects and that they generally are the ways they appear to
be. The causation and resemblance theses, then, capture the reliable
nature of the perceiver's relation to external objects, and it is their
truth that justifies us in taking perception to be a source of knowledge.

It is therefore the actual receiving of ideas from without that
gives us notice of the existence of other things, and makes us
know that other things doth exist at that time without us which
causes the idea in us, though we perhaps neither know nor
consider how it does it. ... (*Essay*, IV, xi, 2)

The notice we have by our senses of the existing things without us, though it be not altogether certain as our intuitive
knowledge, or the deductions of our reason employed about

the clear abstract ideas of our own minds; yet it is an assurance that deserves the name knowledge. (*Essay*, IV, xi, 3)

Questions: According to the representative realist, what are we directly aware of when we perceive? What sort of access do we have to the external world? What part do causation and representation play in Representative Realism? How does the representative realist handle the situations that were problems for the direct realist? What are primary and secondary qualities? How are they used to explain perceptual relativity? How does the representative realist use an inference to the best explanation to justify our perceptual beliefs about the external world?

Section 4: OBJECTIONS TO REPRESENTATIVE REALISM

Berkeley objects to Representative Realism

We have used Locke as our spokesman for Representative Realism. Not long after his theory of knowledge was published, he was confronted with the criticisms of George Berkeley. Berkeley was an Irish philosopher who, while agreeing with Locke's initial assumption that we perceive only our ideas, argued that Locke drew the wrong conclusions from this assumption by failing to appreciate the force of one of his own tenets. In offering criticism of Locke's Representative Realism we will use Berkeley as our spokesman. Subsequently we will explore Berkeley's own theory of perceptual knowledge.

Berkeley issues a number of objections against Locke's brand of Representative Realism. The first two we'll look at are aimed at challenging Locke's distinction between primary and secondary qualities. The second two objections we'll discuss have to do with Locke's causation and resemblance theses. We'll see that these seem to fail to take account of the role of the inference to the best explanation on which Locke places so much weight. Finally, two more serious challenges are raised against the explanation Locke offers for our sensory experiences.

Locke distinguished primary qualities from secondary qualities in order to handle the problematic perceptual relativity cases. There is no conflict in your tasting the candy as sweet when I taste it as bitter since these are secondary qualities that are not "in" the candy as such. Our different sensations of these qualities are caused by the candy's microscopic primary properties. In short, primary qualities are in the object and determined by its microstructure; they are mind-independent qualities. Our sensory ideas of these qualities are caused by and can represent them. On the other hand, the sensations or ideas of secondary qualities that we experience are caused by the object's microstructure but do not represent anything in the object. Thus, we say that secondary qualities are mind-dependent.

Berkeley's Variability Argument

Berkeley's first objection to the distinction between primary and secondary qualities is that the so-called primary qualities, e.g., shape and size, vary as much from perceiver to perceiver as do the mind-dependent secondary qualities. Consequently we should think of these properties as mind-dependent too. He writes:

> Now, why may we not as well argue that figure and extension are not patterns or resemblances of qualities existing in Matter; because to the same eye at different stations, or eyes of a different texture at the same station, they appear various, and cannot therefore be the images of anything settled and determinate without the mind?[2]

The shape and size of a penny, for example, will vary depending on where the perceiver is situated. From straight on the penny looks circular but from an angle its shape appears elliptical. And if I hold the penny close to my eye it will perhaps look bigger than the chair that I can also see in the distance.

Now you might be inclined to say that we know on *independent* grounds that the penny is really circular and smaller than the chair, but this is an inference to which we are not at this point entitled. For we are examining only that of which we are directly aware, and on this ground the perceived shape and size of the penny does indeed vary from person to person or place to place, just as its color might vary among perceivers.

The argument here (we will call it *"The Variability Argument"*) is simply that sensible qualities such as shape and size vary according to the perceiver and his perspective and are thus relative to the perceiver. Locke's premise, recall, is that any property that varies in this way and is relative to the perceiver cannot be in the object and so must be a mind-dependent quality. Thus Berkeley draws the conclusion that since *all* qualities vary in this way, all sensible qualities are mind-dependent. There is no distinction to be drawn between primary, mind-independent qualities and secondary, mind-dependent ones.

The Variability Argument, presented formally, would go something like this:

(1) All sensible qualities vary according to the perceiver and the perceiver's circumstances.

(2) Any quality that varies according to the perceiver and the perceiver's circumstances is a mind-dependent quality.

(3) So, all sensible qualities are mind-dependent qualities.

Berkeley's Inseparability Argument

In addition to the Variability Argument, Berkeley offered another argument for the conclusion that there is no distinction between primary and secondary. In his words:

Now, if it be certain that those original qualities are inseparably united with the other sensible qualities, and not, even in thought, capable of being abstracted from them, it plainly follows that they exist only in the mind. But I desire any one to reflect, and try whether he can, by abstraction of thought, conceive the extension and motion of a body without all the other sensible qualities. For my own part, I see evidently that it is not within my power to frame an idea of a body extended and moving, but I must withal give it some color or other sensible quality, which is acknowledged to exist only in the mind. In short, extension, figure, and motion, abstracted from all other qualities, are inconceivable. Where therefore the other sensible qualities are, there so must these be also, to wit, in the mind and nowhere else. (*Principles*, Section 10)

In this argument (call it *"The Inseparability Argument"*) Berkeley contends that "even in thought" primary qualities cannot be separated from accompanying secondary qualities. One cannot imagine "a body extended and moving" without also imagining it to have some color. Or consider that you cannot now imagine the shape of a kite without also imagining some color (either some color shaped like a kite against a background, or else a kite-shaped border in some color contrasting with a background color). Now the perceptual relativity cases gave us sufficient reason to think that secondary qualities (like color) cannot be "in" the object but are mind-dependent. The candy simply is the way it is, and it does not go from being sweet to being bitter (nor is it really both sweet and bitter now) as we each taste it. Sweetness and bitterness are not really in the candy at all. Now if primary qualities are "inseparably united" with secondary qualities (as Berkeley attempts to demonstrate), then primary qualities are not in the object either. Clearly, primary qualities too must be mind-dependent.

We can also put the Inseparability Argument more formally.

(1) Alleged secondary qualities must be mind-dependent.
(2) Alleged primary qualities cannot be thought of as separate from alleged secondary qualities.
(3) So, so-called primary qualities must be mind-dependent as well.

The conclusion to these arguments is two-fold. First, all sensible qualities are mind-dependent—the shape, size, weight, motion, color, taste, smell, and sound of an object are all sensory ideas that one is perceiving. Second, if Berkeley is correct, then there is no distinction between primary and secondary qualities as Locke claimed there was.

Can we meaningfully speak about mind-independent objects?

This last point brings us to what may be called an *empiricist theory of meaning*. When I talk about the white cup full of hot brown coffee, the words 'white', 'hot' and 'brown' (adjectives or quality-terms) refer only to the sensory ideas I have (or have had). And the words 'cup' and 'coffee' (nouns or object/substance-terms) refer only to collections of sensory ideas I have (or have had). In short, the meanings of terms are only the ideas associated with them. When I say "The white cup is full of hot brown coffee" I am talking about that which I am perceiving, my perceptual experience. Thus for Berkeley, and other empiricists, if we claim to be talking, as Locke does, about things and qualities that are mind-independent, we are really doing no more than uttering meaningless words. At best our language allows us to refer only to the sensory ideas of which we are directly aware.

If we take seriously Locke's assumption that we are only directly aware of our ideas, then as Berkeley has urged, we cannot speak meaningfully about external physical objects of which we have no direct awareness. Hence, we cannot criticize only the representative realist's distinction between primary and secondary qualities. We must also object to the realist thesis itself (that there are external physical objects), along with the causation and resemblance theses. As a result of Berkeley's criticisms we shall be able to draw the conclusion that Locke's theory of knowledge is inadequate; there is no reason to think there are any external physical objects or that we could know anything of them if they did exist. Our knowledge extends no further than our ideas.

We can move now to Berkeley's criticisms of the causation and resemblance theses. In both cases we will approach the thesis from two angles. An epistemological objection will address the question, Could we ever know the thesis is correct? and a metaphysical objection will address the question, Can the thesis even be meaningfully stated? We then discuss the value of the inference to the best explanation. If there is no reason to think the causation and resemblance theses are correct, then there is no reason to think the realism thesis is correct. Consequently, Locke's theory of our knowledge of the external world can never get off the ground. Or so Berkeley will contend.

We will first consider two objections against Locke's Representative Realism that will, in the end, prove to miss Locke's point. These objections are what we might call "epistemological" objections in that they ask (rhetorically at least) how we could *know* whether what Locke says is correct. One objection is raised against the causation thesis and the other against the resemblance thesis.

How could we know that mind-independent objects cause our perceptions?

Locke's thesis is that physical objects cause sensory ideas (or, as we would nowadays say more precisely, events involving physical objects cause events involving sensory ideas—as when the light's reflecting off this object and impinging on my retina causes my being aware in such-and-such sensory ways). The epistemological question most relevant to this claim is, How can we know that certain kinds of events are causally connected? We know about causal connections only by observing them. To know that two events are causally connected (that is, related as cause and effect) one must observe them regularly conjoined. So, for example, we know that thrown rocks hitting windows cause the windows to break by having observed events of the former type (rock-like objects thrown at and hitting windows) followed unexceptionally by events of the latter type (panes of glass shattering). If we could only be aware of breaking windows and never their being hit by rocks, we would never be in a position to say reasonably that window-breakings are caused by rock-strikings. We would have access only to the effects, not the causes.

Locke's problem is that his thesis that we can be directly aware only of our ideas prohibits our knowing that his causation thesis is correct. If I can observe *only* ideas, then I cannot observe *both* the cause and the effect of any causal connection between physical objects and sensory ideas. The representative realist cannot claim that to know that events involving physical objects cause events involving sensory ideas because he has never directly observed the former. By his own admission we can never directly perceive external physical objects.

How could we know that our perceptions resemble external objects?

We can criticize Locke's resemblance thesis on two separate grounds as well. Berkeley voices his objection to the thesis in the following passage.

But, say you, though the ideas themselves do not exist without the mind, yet there may be things like them, whereof they are copies or resemblances; which things exist without the mind, in an unthinking substance. I answer, an idea can be like nothing but an idea; a color or figure can be like nothing but another color or figure. If we look but never so little into our thoughts, we shall find it impossible for us to conceive a likeness except only between our ideas. Again, I ask whether those supposed originals, or external things, of which our ideas are the pictures or representations, be themselves perceivable or no? If they are, then they are ideas, and we have gained our point: but if you say they are not, I appeal to anyone whether it be sense to assert a color is like something which is invisible; hard or soft, like something which is intangible; and so of the rest. (*Principles*, Section 8)

One way to read this passage is to understand Berkeley as simply saying that since we can only be directly aware of our ideas, we could never know whether our ideas are "copies or resemblances" of external objects. He puts his objection in the form of a dilemma, knowing full well which position a representative realist would choose. The dilemma is this: either (1) the primary or "original" qualities of the object are (directly) observed or (2) they are not. To agree that primary qualities are directly observed is tantamount to agreeing with Berkeley, since his claim is that primary qualities are not in external objects at all but are mind-dependent like the secondary qualities. This is precisely the position Berkeley attempted to establish when objecting to Locke's primary-secondary quality distinction.

Locke would surely deny that all qualities of objects are in our minds: thus he must agree (2) that we are not directly aware of the properties of the external object. But, as Berkeley objects, Locke could not then say that our sensory ideas resemble these unobservable physical objects, for we are by Locke's own admission unable to observe external physical objects and compare them with our sensory ideas. One cannot know that X resembles Y unless one can observe and compare both X and Y. If you cannot know what X is like, you cannot know whether it resembles Y.

A representative realist response

A Lockean representative realist might not be too troubled by these criticisms. First, she might say that the objections assume that one must be directly aware of mind-independent objects to know about them. This, the representative realist can contend, is not true. In fact, it is part of the representative realist's view as presented here that we can know about mind-independent objects because our hypothesis that they exist and are certain ways best explains why we have the perceptual experiences we do. We claim to know about external objects not because we are directly aware of them, but because our beliefs about them form the most reasonable theory that can be used to explain our experiences. We can have knowledge about the world because we have reasonable beliefs about the world. And this can be so even though our inability be directly aware of our sensory ideas being caused by, or resembling, these objects leaves us fallible with respect to our beliefs about them.

While the representative realist might not find these objections worrisome, other objections are more forceful. We can now turn to them.

How could an external object produce an idea?

Berkeley thought that Locke's appeal to a causal connection between the the external world and our ideas was entirely misguided and, perhaps, meaningless. As Berkeley notes:

> For, though we give the materialists their external bodies, they by their own confession are never the nearer knowing how our ideas are produced; since they own themselves unable to comprehend in what manner body can act upon spirit, or how it is possible it should imprint any idea in the mind. (*Principles,* Section 19)

Since physical objects are so radically different from mental objects, it is difficult to see how there could be a causal connection between them or in what such a connection could consist. (Berkeley would put it by asking rhetorically how an unthinking substance like matter can produce thoughts or ideas.) Locke's causation thesis cannot serve to explain the nature and source of our perceptual experiences if *it* stands in need of explanation itself.

What could we mean by "causation?" Given the empiricist theory of meaning discussed above, one can only meaningfully talk about that of which one has (or could) experience—the meaning of a term is the idea(s) associated with it. Consider for a moment what experience you have had of causal connections or of causal power. The clearest cases are those in which you, by your own will, have produced ideas by imagining or thinking of something—it is in your power to imagine or not imagine a two-headed beast. Berkeley emphasizes the active, causally efficacious nature of the mind when he says:

> This making and unmaking of ideas doth very properly denominate the mind active. This much is certain and grounded on experience: but when we talk of unthinking agents, or of exciting ideas exclusive of volition, we only amuse ourselves with words. (*Principles,* Section 28)

His conclusion is that "we only amuse ourselves with words" when we talk, as does Locke, about the causal powers of inert objects that have no wills and are by their very nature unthinking. This is just to say that it is meaningless to claim that physical objects can produce ideas, although it is perfectly coherent to hold that minds can do so. Thinking substances (minds) by their very nature think, and thinking is just the producing and perceiving of ideas; unthinking substances, simply because they are not minds, do not have that ability.

It seems that Locke's causation thesis is simply meaningless. Because of this it will not serve to support his claim that external physical objects are the source of our sensory ideas.

How could a sensory idea be like an external object?

When considering the resemblance thesis we can also see Berkeley claiming that it is simply meaningless to speak of sensory ideas resembling external objects. The former is mental and directly observable but the latter is physical and not so observable. This is the import of Berkeley's contention that "it is *impossible for us to conceive* a likeness except between our ideas" ("An idea can be like nothing but an idea"). And in the same vein he asks us to consider "whether *it be sense to assert* a color is like something that is invisible."

It is curious how one could ever think that an invisible object could resemble (look like?) a visible object. Does this make any sense? When we consider whether one thing resembles another what else do we have in mind but comparing the idea of one with the idea of the other? One could not go about comparing an idea of one thing with something that is not an idea, i.e., something that strictly speaking has nothing perceptible in common with an idea.

The conclusion Berkeley wishes to draw is not that resemblance in general makes no sense, but that it is meaningless to speak of sensory ideas resembling anything but other sensory ideas. Consequently, Locke's resemblance thesis, like the causation thesis discussed above, cannot serve to support his realism about external physical objects. If we accept his view that we are only directly aware of our ideas, then the rest of Locke's theory cannot get off the ground. There is no reason to think that physical objects cause our sensory ideas or that our ideas resemble qualities in the external world to any extent. If Berkeley is right, then these claims do not even make sense.

What has gone wrong with Locke's explanation

According to Locke's Representative Realism we are justified in believing that there are external physical objects because the hypothesis that they cause our sensory ideas best explains why our perceptual experiences are forced upon us and why our ideas are so clear, uniform and coherent. According to the representative realist, we can know that there is a cup in front of us because, under the right conditions, our perceptual interactions with it will result in sensory ideas that to some extent resemble the cup.

Berkeley has objected to this theory. He accepts with Locke the premise that we are directly aware only of our ideas, but he argues that this very premise is what prevents Locke from establishing his causation and resemblance theses. Without them Locke cannot argue that the existence of external physical objects best explains our experience; and so he cannot support his Realism thesis.

This forces us to re-evaluate our theory of perception and knowledge. The tension that is now evident is this: On the one hand, our discussion of Direct Realism shows that we are not directly aware of mind-independent physical objects. A close look at the problem cases (illusions, hallucinations, and perceptual relativity) suggests that we are really directly aware only of our sensory ideas. On the other hand, once we give up the position that we are directly aware of physical objects, it becomes more difficult to justify our initial commitment to the Realism thesis (that there is an external world of physical objects). This much has emerged from our study of Representative Realism and the criticisms of it Berkeley presents.

In what follows we will explore Berkeley's attempts to relieve this tension.

Questions: What two arguments does Berkeley have against Locke's primary and secondary quality distinction? What problems does he raise with Locke's causation and resemblance theses? How do the metaphysical objections differ from the epistemological objections?

Section 5: IDEALISM

The idealist's main contention

Idealism gets its name from the word 'idea'. Berkeley is called an idealist because in an important sense he takes ideas more seriously than do the other theorists of perception we've discussed. Indeed, Berkeley takes them seriously enough to propose that a correct theory of perception doesn't need anything else—nothing other than ideas and the minds that "have" them. This theory isn't simply hatched out of the blue, though, and it is important to see how the tension remaining from critiques of Direct Realism and Representative Realism leads quite naturally to Berkeley's Idealism.

We know from criticisms of Direct Realism that one cannot be directly aware of mind-independent physical objects. But the criticisms of Representative Realism just presented show that neither are we justified in believing that we are indirectly aware of these external objects. At first blush it seems that these conclusions cannot both be true.

What Berkeley shows us is that if we go where the arguments lead, a theory emerges according to which these conclusions *are* both true. We are neither directly nor indirectly aware of mind-independent physical objects, according to Idealism. But from this it does not follow that we are not aware of physical objects. It only follows that we are not aware of *mind-independent* physical objects. According to Berkeley, we can both satisfy our commonsense intuition that we are directly aware of physical objects (such as tables and chairs) *and* adhere to the empiricist doctrine that we are directly aware only of our ideas if we take physical objects to be collections of ideas. In short, if physical objects are things of which we're perceptually aware, and if all we're aware of when we perceive are sensory ideas, then physical objects just *are* (collections of) sensory ideas.

That is the remarkable conclusion of idealist theories. But however remarkable it is, by now we shouldn't be surprised that Berkeley endorses it. Both his Variability and Inseparability arguments are designed to show that all sensory qualities are mind-dependent. If he is correct, nothing about objects of a mind-independent sort seems to be left.

Idealism and perceptual knowledge

The general outlines of Idealism, then, are already present in Berkeley's negative remarks. Before going on to spell out the details of his positive account, let's characterize Idealism by its response to our standard questions.

Q1: How should we characterize the objects that typically say we perceive, that is, the everyday world of tables and chairs?

Realism is the doctrine that things like tables and chairs are mind-independent external physical objects. Idealism answers this first question by claiming that the world of tables and chairs is made up of mind-dependent objects.

Q2: What sort of access do we have to these objects?

Berkeley thinks it is obvious that if you perceive a chair, then that of which you're aware is the chair. This common sense view that we directly perceive physical objects is shared by Idealism and Direct Realism. Notice that there is no mediating object of which we must be aware as in Representative Realism.

Q3: In virtue of what can we justifiably say we know about these objects? How does perception yield knowledge?

The Berkeleian idealist shares part of his answer to this question with Direct Realism, since they agree on the answer to Q2. We are justified in our perceptual beliefs because they are directly acquired, and no means of securing beliefs about physical objects could be more reliable than one based upon being directly related to them. There is no need for us to bridge some gap between that of which we are aware and the world of physical objects; and we do not require a special inference. Berkeley's own account has a bit more to add here, but we'll set this aside for later.

In sum: *Idealism* states that my being perceptually aware of a physical object is my being directly aware of it, and that physical objects are mind-dependent (collections of ideas).

A. Berkeleian Idealism and What There is

Claims about what there is

Berkeley, as an idealist, says there are no mind-independent objects. There are only minds and ideas. What does Berkeley mean when he denies the existence of one sort of object and acknowledges the existence of another?

Of the great topics (metaphysics, epistemology, ethics, logic) making up traditional discussions in philosophy, metaphysics is probably the most difficult to characterize. But it turns out that much of what we do in metaphysics is relatively easy to describe: we develop theories about *what there is*. The specific study of what there is is called *ontology*. Sometimes we speak of "the ontology" to which a particular philosophical theory is committed, or perhaps even a particular person's ontology: the items in your ontology are the things that you believe exist. Dogs and daffodils are probably in your ontology, along with more philosophically interesting things like persons. Notice that we use *general terms* here, to pick out kinds of things. We could of course speak about Rover being in your ontology, along with this particular daffodil and these particular persons. But typically the most interesting philosophical questions in ontology are general ones about *kinds* of objects.

The question of what kinds of objects are in some ontology or other (yours, the idealist's, etc.) is a bit more tricky than it sounds. In unreflective moments you are inclined to talk about shadows and cold fronts, for example: but perhaps you don't *really* think there are such things. Perhaps you believe that now a certain region is cold where a nearby region is warm, and a bit later the nearby region is cold too— all this without having to speak of some other thing, a cold front moving across the country.

A slightly different wrinkle to specifying the kind of things making up one's ontology is this: often we do think that, strictly speaking, there are objects of a certain kind, but that such objects are made up of things more basic. You may think that there are clouds, for example, and at the same time believe that clouds are just collections of water droplets. If you were asked to construct the (manageably short) list of things you think there are in the air, you would be happy enough to simply talk about moisture or water droplets or whatever, without intending someone to conclude from this that you don't think there are clouds: clouds just *are* (collections of) water droplets.

The Idealist has a very sparse ontology. We have already seen that Berkeley denies the existence of Lockean external physical objects. Here is what Berkeley thinks there is:

It is evident to anyone who takes a survey of the *objects of human knowledge* that they are either *ideas* actually imprinted on the senses; or else such as are perceived by attending to the passions and operations of the mind; or lastly ideas formed by the help of memory and imagination ....

But, besides all that endless variety of ideas or objects of knowledge, there is like-wise Something which knows or perceives them; and exercises divers operations, as willing, imagining, remembering, about them. This perceiving, active being is what I call *mind, spirit, soul,* or *myself.* (*Principles,* Sections 1 and 2)

So, according to Idealism, there are only ideas (of various sorts) and minds. It doesn't follow from this that, since "persons" aren't explicitly on the list, the idealist believes there are no persons. Persons just are minds or souls—as Berkeley's adding "or myself" makes clear. Notice that Berkeley is explicit about the nature of ideas and minds. Ideas are simply the things minds have; they're what you have now as you see these words, smell or taste your coffee, decide to read two more pages and quit, daydream of better weather, and so on. Unlike minds, ideas don't do anything. Minds are "active" things, capable of perceiving, deciding (willing), imagining (daydreaming, say), and much more.

Ordinary physical objects

On the face of it, this pale ontology of minds and ideas leaves so much out that it looks rather worth ignoring. In particular, it seems to make no room for a world of objects like tables and chairs. But Idealism is not committed to the apparently silly view that there are no physical objects. When we say that ducks are shaped differently than daffodils or that the table is this way while the chair is another way, we are saying perfectly meaningful things that are either objectively true or false.

What is it to say something meaningful, according to Idealism? Recall the empiricist theory of meaning, discussed briefly in connection with Berkeley's criticisms of the distinction between primary and secondary qualities. This criterion for meaningfulness says that the meaning of linguistic expressions depends on the experiences we have (or could have).

Suppose that you are now aware of a blue triangle, and suppose you say that it is blue. What you are talking about when you use the word "blue" is the sensory idea you have now of the color blue. Similarly for the words "hot" or "sweet" or "round" or whatever. In these cases, what we intend our words to be about are the sensory ideas we have of temperature or taste or shape. If I say something like "Well, I am perfectly aware of my sensory states, but there is still the question of what the external realm of things beyond my sensory experience is like," I am beginning to talk nonsense. For an expression to be meaningful, it must be such that the difference between its being true and its being false is nothing more that a possible difference in the sensory ideas of a perceiver. This is because language is about *that of which we are aware.*

The empiricist theory of meaning

With this in mind, let's consider again what the idealist will say regarding sentences about physical objects, given his limited ontology of only ideas and minds. Berkeley puts the matter as follows:

> By sight I have the ideas of light and colours, with their several degrees and variations. By touch I perceive hard and soft, heat and cold, motion and resistance; .... Smelling furnishes me with odours; the palate with tastes; and hearing conveys sounds to the mind in all their variety and tone.
>
> ... [A]s several of these are observed to accompany each other, they come to be marked by one name, and so to be reputed as one *thing.* Thus, for example, a certain colour, taste, smell, figure and consistence having been observed to go together, are accounted one distinct thing, signified by the name apple; other collections of ideas constitute a stone, a tree, a book, and the like sensible things; .... (*Principles*, Section 1)

Here, then, is a linguistic motivation for holding one of the important theses of Berkeleian Idealism, that physical objects are collections of ideas.

More about physical objects

There are other reasons for Berkeley's conclusion found in other parts of empiricist thought. Actually, we have encountered them already. One simply begins by asking what more there is to an object than its qualities. Sensory qualities are the things we're aware of when perceiving a physical object, and from Berkeley's critique of Representative Realism we know that qualities are just sensory ideas. So, if physical objects just *are* collections of qualities, then, as before, physical objects are collections of sensory ideas.

Another line of reasoning is implicit in the linguistic argument above and perhaps most straight-forwardly captures the idealist sentiment. If we have gone so far as to see that we are only directly aware of sensory ideas, there is never any ground on which the representative realist can justify his belief that objects exist *beyond* his sensory experience. The veil of perception between sensory ideas and the supposed external object cannot be gotten rid of, as long as we agree to the thesis that the only things of which we are aware in cases of perception are sensory ideas. The idealist reminds us that, in light of this, anyone happy to accept Representative Realism and the veil of perception doctrine must be a skeptic about physical objects, since we simply are never justified in positing external physical objects. But here Idealism becomes intuitively appealing: who with any modicum of common sense can deny that we are aware of physical objects? *They* are precisely the things we perceive by sense.

Berkeley's line of thought, then, is straightforward. Of garden-variety tables and chairs and "houses, mountains, rivers, and in a word all sensible objects," he asks,

> what are the forementioned objects but the things we perceive by sense? and what do we perceive besides our own ideas or sensations? (*Principles*, Section 4)

The answer in each case is "nothing." Physical objects are things we perceive by sense; the only things we perceive by sense are sensory ideas; therefore, physical objects are (collections of) sensory ideas.

How could physical objects be ideas?

But one might protest this remarkable conclusion. "How could anyone be so silly as to suppose that physical objects are ideas? Consider a table. Am I supposed to believe that I can pile my books on a collection of ideas?" This protest is far enough off the mark to pause a moment to clear it up. First, it won't do to attack a philosophical thesis by simply asserting that it is unbelievable. You may of course find it quite fantastic, but this psychological tid-bit is quite beside the point. If you are offered reasons for a claim you cannot accept, then the only intellectually respectable way to protest is to address the argument.

If we cannot accept a claim, there ought to be reasons why we believe the claim to be false. Are there reasons offered in the protest above for why it should be false that tables are collections of ideas? Perhaps there is something lurking in the worry that one could not rest books on a collection of ideas. The worry seems to add up to this: a collection of ideas couldn't support a heavy object; if a table is a collection of ideas and my books are heavy objects, then the table cannot support my books; so, a table can't be a collection of ideas. What this line of protest seems to have in mind is that books are very dense and heavy external physical objects of Locke's sort, and that ideas are ephemeral nonmaterial breezy sorts of things that couldn't support anything. But of course books are no more external physical objects on Berkeley's account than tables: no such protest can arise unless we beg the question and *assume* precisely what Berkeley's line of reasoning is meant to render false—namely that there are external physical objects with properties that make them unsupportable by objects of an altogether different sort.

Perhaps the most important element in the idealist line of thinking offered above is the notion that we only perceive our ideas. Berkeley, remember, presumes to have satisfied us that the representative realist is on safe ground only in saying that we are aware of sensory ideas; the further claim that there are physical objects of which we are aware in some indirect way, by virtue of some inference, is unjustified. So what Berkeley variously calls "sensible things" or "things we perceive by sense" are simply ideas. Berkeley doesn't deny that we sometimes make inferences to the existence of things that we don't immediately perceive, but these, clearly, aren't *sensible* things like physical objects are. Thus:

In reading a book, what I immediately perceive are the letters, but mediately, or by means of these, are suggested to my mind the notions of God, virtue, truth, and so on. Now that the letters are truly sensible things, or perceived by sense, there is no doubt .... It seems, then, that by sensible things [we] mean those only which can be perceived immediately by sense.

[t]he senses perceive nothing which they do not perceive immediately: for they make no inferences.[3]

Unperceived objects are impossible

The Berkeleian idealist believes that physical objects are collections of sensory ideas. There are several consequences that follow from this, given other premises about the nature of ideas. Perhaps the most striking consequence is that it is (logically) impossible for physical objects to exist unperceived.

The route to this conclusion is actually very straightforward, and as before, it is important not to allow the strangeness of the view that there can be no unperceived objects to distract us.

What are ideas? They're the things you're aware of now as you look at these words and taste or smell your coffee; they're what you have when you decide to read two more pages or when you daydream of better weather. Now consider: could you be aware of these words you're reading now without being aware of them? Clearly not. It is logically impossible, and it would be a contradiction to say that you *are* sensorily aware now (of whatever), and also now *not* aware (of whatever). The case is the same for smelling your coffee or imagining better weather.

Here is Berkeley's way of putting the matter:

... the existence of an idea consists in being perceived. (*Principles*, Section 2)

That neither our thoughts, nor passions, nor ideas formed by the imagination, exist without the mind is what everybody will allow. And to me it seems no less evident that the various sensations or ideas imprinted on the Sense, however blended or combined together (that is, whatever objects they compose), cannot exist otherwise than in a mind perceiving them. ...

There was an odour, that is, it was smelt; there was a sound, that is, it was heard .... (*Principles*, Section 3)

... to have an idea is all one as to perceive. (*Principles*, Section 7)

A short aside here will help us summarize. Look again at the second of these quotations, and then consider an old question: If a tree falls in the forest and there is no one there to listen, does it make a sound? Clearly not. "There was a sound, that is, it was heard ... ." The *existence* of a sound consists in its *being heard*. And that is what Berkeley says about all sensory ideas: their *being*—their existing—just *is* their being perceived. To be is to be perceived. So, it is logically impossible that a sensory idea should exist without being perceived. To say that an idea exists unperceived is to say that a perceived thing exists unperceived, and that is a contradiction.

From here it is only a short distance to the conclusion that physical objects cannot exist unperceived.

(1) Physical objects are (collections of) sensory ideas.
(2) It is logically impossible for sensory ideas to exist unperceived.
(3) So, it is logically impossible for physical objects to exist unperceived.

Here is Berkeley's version, from a passage we've already seen in part:

It is indeed an opinion strangely prevailing amongst men, that houses, mountains, rivers, and in a word all sensible objects, have an existence, natural or real, distinct from their being perceived .... [W]hoever shall find in his heart to call it in question may, if I mistake not, perceive it to involve a manifest contradiction. For, what are the forementioned objects but the things we perceive by sense? and what do we perceive besides our own ideas or sensations? and is it not plainly repugnant that any one of these, or any combination of them, should exist unperceived? (*Principles*, Section 4)

"Repugnant" here means "incoherent" or the like: it does the same work as "contradictory." So, according to the idealist, it is impossible for physical objects to exist unperceived. (Notice something relevant to the earlier aside. If a tree falls in the forest and there is no-one there to listen, then there is no noise; but of course, if there is no perceiver, then there is no tree to fall.)

But can't one imagine an unperceived object?

One might protest here. (We know the respectable way of protesting, by now: address the argument and say explicitly where we think it goes wrong.) "But surely it's easy to imagine physical objects existing unperceived." an objector might say, "This bit about there being no tree if no one perceives a tree seems obviously false: we can easily imagine trees on the quad or in the park existing when there is nobody around." This objection can be reconstructed as an argument against Berkeley. The idea is that since we can imagine a tree existing unperceived, it is possible for a tree to exist unperceived. The premise left implicit is that if we can imagine some state of affairs, then that state of affairs is logically possible.

Here is what Berkeley says about imagining unperceived objects:

But, say you, surely there is nothing easier than for me to imagine trees, for instance, in a park, or books existing in a closet, and nobody by to perceive them. I answer, you may so, there is no difficulty in it. But what is this, I beseech you, more than framing in your mind certain ideas which you call books and trees, and at the same time omitting to frame the idea of any one that may perceive them? ... This therefore is nothing to the purpose: it only shews you have the power of imagining, or forming ideas in your mind: but it does not shew that you can conceive it possible the objects of your thought may exist outside the mind. (*Principles*, Section 23)

There are several ways we might understand this passage. A first, rather straightforward interpretation runs as follows. When we attempt to imagine a tree existing unperceived, what we do is call up in our imagination tree-ideas. Fine. But what are these ideas except *things of which we are aware*?

Now some people understand Berkeley to be saying that, once we form such tree-ideas, we aren't imagining a tree unperceived because trees just *are* ideas. So, since we're aware of tree-ideas, we are aware of a tree after all, and nothing emerges about a tree of which no one is aware. If this is what Berkeley intends, then of course it is a mistake. Recall, however, that Berkeley distinguishes ideas of sense from ideas of imagination. Real trees are collections of ideas all right, but not collections of just any ideas: they are collections of *sensory* ideas. On this second interpretation, then, Berkeley simply fails to distinguish ideas of imagination from ideas of sense. It is wrong to suppose that when we attempt to imagine a tree existing unperceived, we perceive a tree.

One thing is certain, however. When we imagine, we are aware, and when we imagine something that is essentially a perceived thing, we imagine that thing *perceived*. Now a better way of understanding the passage above—one that does not attribute to Berkeley the mistake of forgetting a distinction he made a few pages earlier—incorporates these latest reminders about imagination. Let's see how it might go.

Imagine that you are in a park, and that you see a crowd of people surrounding a large tree. These people are admiring the tree for some reason or other (it doesn't much matter why). They are, of course, perceiving the tree. Now suppose that some of these people walk away. What remains is a smaller group of people perceiving a tree. Imagine that, slowly, people begin to leave one by one. Soon there are four people perceiving the tree, then three, and then two. Finally, there is one person, perceiving the tree. And now, he leaves: there is no one left perceiving the tree. We are now imagining a tree unperceived. But wait: look again at the beginning of this story. "Imagine that *you* are in a park, and that *you* see a crowd of people surrounding a large tree." You are left there, in this imaginative story, watching the whole time, and still watching after the last person leaves—or rather, after the next-to-the-last person leaves. You were there, in the imaginative story, all the while. So what you have imagined is this: you imagined perceiving a tree along with lots of other people (though perhaps from a distance) at first, and finally alone; you imagined it as it would look from your own point of view, with your own eyes. And if you imagine perceiving a tree, you don't imagine an unperceived tree at all: you imagine a perceived tree.

Indeed that's what imagination is. When you imagine a giant orange rhinoceros, you say to yourself, "Now what would *that* look like?" and then you go on to imagine what it would be to see such a thing. Imagining a thing, then, just is imagining perceiving a thing: it is imagining that thing as it would be were it *perceived*. So no matter how hard you try, you can't imagine an unperceived tree.

The first and third ways of understanding the idealist reply seem to show this much: we cannot imagine an unperceived thing. Berkeley's conclusion, then, is that it is impossible for there to be such things. Notice that, here again, the implicit premise is that if something cannot be imagined, then it is not possible.

Phenomenalism and unperceived objects

While the "no unperceived objects" thesis is still fresh in our minds, it is worth pausing to briefly consider an alternative to Berkeleian Idealism. Phenomenalism is a theory very much like Idealism but differing from it in ways that are relevant to the thesis that physical objects cannot exist unperceived.

Recall first what motivated Idealism. Problems with Direct Realism lead us to conclude that we are not directly aware of external physical objects, but rather of mental entities called sensory ideas. But this seems to mean that physical objects are unperceived, and that by moderate empiricist standards we cannot justify claims that there are external physical objects causing and resembling our sensory ideas. Both Idealism and Phenomenalism agree with the direct awareness tenet (that we are aware only of ideas); consequently, both theories attempt to reduce physical objects, in some way or other, to sensory ideas. It should come as no surprise, then, that the idealist and the phenomenalist alike endorse the empiricist theory of meaning. Specifically, both endorse the view that any statement about the realm of physical objects can be understood in terms of statements about sensory ideas.

So Phenomenalism turns out to be very much like Idealism, insofar as both theories accept the direct awareness tenet and the empiricist theory of meaning. But these elements of common ground leave quite a lot open. In particular, the direct awareness tenet leaves open the question of exactly how to spell out the nature of physical objects (Idealism, we know, does this in terms of collections of sensory ideas). The empiricist theory of meaning also leaves open the question of exactly how to represent the meaning of physical object statements. These questions are of course related. The point to emphasize now, however, is that the phenomenalist can deny the claim that there are no unperceived objects without giving up either the thesis that we are directly aware only of ideas or the empiricist theory of meaning.

Let's begin with the linguistic story, consistent with an empiricist theory of meaning, but peculiar to Phenomenalism. The primary task engaged by Phenomenalism is to explain the concept of a physical object. It does so by translating statements about material objects into equivalent statements expressed only in terms of sensory ideas. (It is to this translation feature that we refer below when we say that physical objects, according to the phenomenalist, are *logical constructions* of sensory ideas.) These equivalent sentences, however, take particular forms. If I see a table, the sentence 'I see a table' goes over to 'I have sensory ideas _____', where the blank gets appropriately filled in by descriptions of sensory ideas like '... of a brown, rectangular, flat expanse, below which ....' etc. And where there is a table in the adjoining room that I do not see, the sentence 'There is a table in the next room' gets translated into the equivalent 'If one were to be in the next room, then one would have sensory ideas _____', where the blank is appropriately filled as before.

The important thing to notice about this way of cashing out the meaning of physical object statements is that claims asserting the existence of unperceived objects are perfectly meaningful.

Now this particular way of understanding the meaning of sentences about physical objects does not entail the Berkeleian idealist view that physical objects are *collections* of sensory ideas. Saying that sensory ideas *compose*, or are *constituents of*, physical objects differs from saying that physical objects are logical constructions out of sensory ideas. Instead of talking about a collection of ideas I *am* currently having (or have had) I can talk of ideas I *would* have if I *were* in the appropriate circumstances. The claim that P's are collections of I's entails that, if there are P's then there are I's. Where a cloud is composed of water droplets, the claim that there are clouds entails the claim that there are water droplets. This entailment does not hold if P's are logical constructions of I's, however. Look again at the logical form of the translation for 'There is a table in the next room'—it is a hypothetical, a conditional, and it does not entail that there actually are sensory ideas (of a brown, rectangular, flat expanse, under which ... etc.). It only claims that, *if* a perceiver were in such-and-such a situation (in the next room, with good lighting, say), *then* there would be such-and-such sensory ideas in that perceiver. So the Phenomenalist can perfectly well assert the existence of a physical object without committing himself to there actually being sensory ideas of the object, i.e., without committing himself to the physical object's being perceived. We might say that while the idealist identifies physical objects only with actual ideas (ideas actually had), the phenomenalist identifies *statements* about physical objects with statements about actual *and possible* sensory ideas.

It turns out that Berkeley toyed with Phenomenalism, but he never endorsed or developed it. Here are a couple of passages from Berkeley with a distinctly phenomenalist flavor.

> The table I write on I say exists; that is, I see and feel it; and if I were out of my study I should say it existed; meaning thereby that if I was in my study I might perceive it, or that some other spirit actually does perceive it. (*Principles*, Section 3)

> ... [T]he question whether the earth moves or no amounts in reality to no more than this, to wit, whether we have reason to conclude, from what has been observed by astronomers, that if we were placed in such and such circumstances, and such or such a position and distance both from the earth and sun, we should perceive the former to move among the choir of the planets .... (*Principles*, Section 58)

B. Berkeleian Idealism and Knowledge of What There Is

What causes our sensory ideas

The idealist's account of what there is must be seen as only a part of a larger account of perceptual knowledge. We know at least this much about the rest of that account: since physical objects are collections of sensory ideas, our access to the world of tables and chairs is (by the direct awareness thesis) direct. But an important question now arises: from where do these ideas come? The idealist believes that his theory accounts for the experiences we do have, and an unnegotiable fact about our experience is that we perceive a continual succession of sensory ideas of tables and chairs and the like. And yet the idealist believes that physical objects are not "out there" at all, but rather are mental objects. How is it that we ever come to have these sensory ideas?

Recall from our discussion of Locke and Representative Realism that Locke is concerned to explain the fact that our ideas of sense are typically clear, uniform and coherent. Moreover, there is the fact that, unlike ideas of imagination, our sensory ideas are given or forced on us, so to speak. We are simply the passive recipients of ideas when perceiving chairs, tables and the like. How are we to explain the difference between those ideas that we conjure up by will and those ideas presented to us by sense?

Berkeley believed, as did Locke, that our ideas of sense must be caused by something other than our wills. He notes,

> We perceive a continual succession of ideas; some are anew excited, others are changed or totally disappear. There is therefore, *some* cause of these ideas, whereon they depend, and which produces and changes them. (*Principles*, Section 26)

Could external objects cause our sensory ideas?

The intuitive response to the question, From where do my ideas of tables and chairs come? is that they are caused by those particular physical objects. But according to Berkeley, this intuitive answer is not available to us if we mean by "those physical objects" the tables and chairs existing external to us. The idealist cannot accept Locke's account of the causes of our uniform, coherent string of sensory ideas. We have already shown that Berkeley goes to great lengths to destroy Locke's theory that mind-independent physical objects cause our sensory ideas. Since the only idea we have of one thing producing or causing another is of our own mind producing ideas, this is all we can mean by 'causation'. (Remember the empiricist theory of meaning: the meaning of a term consists in the idea(s) associated with it.) Consequently, it is simply meaningless to speak of external physical objects causing anything.

The safest and most systematic way to answer the question of what causes sensory ideas is to recall again the candidates: the only things in Berkeley's ontology are ideas and minds. So either ideas or minds are the causes of our sensory ideas. Let's consider these in order.

Could other ideas cause our sensory ideas?

Are other ideas the causes of our sensory ideas? The suggestion is at first glance a plausible one. We do think that the fire causes us to feel pain if we get too close. Couldn't we say then that since fire is nothing but a collection of ideas and since *it* causes us to feel pain, ideas of fire are causing ideas of pain? Moreover, we are all familiar with "trains of thought" where one idea leads to another, and there appears to be no reason why one idea's *leading to* another can't be understood as an idea's *causing* another. Indeed, it may be that the uniformity and coherence of our perceptual experience is due to the many causal connections between ideas—one idea or group of ideas might naturally lead to (produce, cause) another, and so on.

But Berkeley resists the proposal that an idea can cause or produce another idea. Recall a distinction Berkeley draws between the nature of ideas and the nature of minds: the former are inert while the latter are active. Thus he says,

> All our ideas, sensations, or the things which we perceive, by whatever names they may be distinguished, are visibly inactive: there is nothing of power or agency included in them. So that one idea or object of thought cannot produce or make any alteration in another. ... For, since [our ideas] and every part of them exist only in the mind, it follows that there is nothing in them but what is perceived: but whoever shall attend to his ideas ... will not perceive in them any power or activity; there is, therefore, no such thing contained in them. A little attention will discover to us that the very being of an idea implies passiveness and inertness in it .... (*Principles*, Section 25)

Suppose you are entertaining an idea of red—a simple red patch, say, against a white background. Now it may be that as you are imagining this, you are imagining the patch as square and the red as bright red, but Berkeley's claim is that this idea (or group of ideas) can be nothing more than what it appears to be. All there is to an idea is what is before the mind; there can be no inside or backside to an idea; there is nothing hidden from you and no part that you are not seeing. By attending carefully to this idea it becomes evident that you are not perceiving anything active. The idea of red (or of a bright red square) is simply the passive object of your perception; it's not doing anything, it's just there to be observed. Since ideas are simply what we perceive them to be, it follows that ideas are passive in this way; it is the nature of an idea that it be passive or inert. But then we cannot say that ideas are causes, and the uniformity and coherence of our sensory ideas cannot be the result of some causal connection between them.

But why then do we say that fire causes heat? Is this not a case in which ideas cause ideas? Berkeley says no. Strictly speaking, the collection of ideas we call "fire" does not cause anything. He admits, however, that our perceptions of fire may be constantly conjoined with sensations of pain, and we are *inclined* to call this a causal connection.

> When we perceive certain ideas of sense constantly followed by other ideas, and we know this is not of our own doing, we forthwith attribute power and agency to the ideas themselves, and make one the cause of another .... (*Principles*, Section 32)

But Berkeley adds that "nothing can be more absurd and unintelligible." The constant conjunction we witness only marks a uniformity in nature, not a causal connection. There are then certain laws of nature that guarantee that we feel nourished upon experiencing the intake of food, that we feel refreshed after sleeping well, and that we feel pain when experiencing fire. But this is not to say that eating *causes* nourishment, that sleep *causes* revitalization, or that fire *causes* pain.

Could minds cause our sensory ideas?

Neither external physical objects nor ideas can be causes of our sensory ideas. By a simple logic of elimination, then, there is only one remaining candidate: minds. This does seem like the right sort of thing. As an active substance, it is the mind's job (so to speak) to perceive and produce ideas. You can call up ideas, for example, when you decide to daydream of a deep blue sky with scattered clouds and a light breeze; you can remember what your favorite friend looks like; you can calculate the sum of 29 and 137, if you choose: minds are that way. Thus, Berkeley says:

> I find I can excite ideas in my mind at pleasure, and vary and shift the scene as oft as I think fit. It is no more than *willing*, and straightway this or that idea arises in my fancy; and by the same power it is obliterated and makes way for another. (*Principles*, Section 28)

But we must be careful here. We noted earlier how our ideas of sense were, so to speak, forced upon us. The kinds of ideas involved in daydreaming and remembering and doing sums are not ideas of sense: they are not the kinds of ideas for which we are presently seeking causes. Berkeley draws this important distinction in the immediately following section:

> ... But whatever power I may have over my own thoughts, I find the ideas actually perceived by Sense have not a like dependence of *my* will. When in broad daylight I open my eyes, it is not in my power to choose whether I shall see or no, or to determine what particular objects shall present themselves to my view; and so likewise to the hearing and other senses; the ideas imprinted on them are not creatures of *my* will. There is therefore some other Will or Spirit what produces them. (*Principles*, Section 29)

It is clear that our sensory ideas are not produced by our wills or imaginations. You cannot simply haul off and see a very large rhinoceros now, or hear the Mormon Tabernacle Choir if you choose. But since the cause of our sensory ideas must be found in active substance, we must locate the cause of our sensory ideas in some mind other than our own. The only remaining candidate for filling this role, according to Berkeley, is God. Let's take a close look at why he proposes this.

God and our sensory ideas

Berkeley's reasons for thinking that (the mind of) God is responsible for our sensory ideas are relatively straightforward. The first include, as already noted, reasons for thinking that no *human* mind could be the source of our sensory experience. As a matter of fact the sensory ideas each of us have are not a product of our own wills. But neither could they be a product of any human mind, according to Berkeley. This is because a human mind is incapable of directly affecting other minds, and in addition is incapable of producing sensory ideas so orderly and coherent as those we experience. Ideas that are the products of human will are not steady and clear, and are "excited at random." Likewise, Berkeley says at one point that "it is evident that, in affecting other persons, the will of man hath no other object than barely the motion of the limbs of his body ... ."

The remaining reasons for positing the divine mind of God are best laid out in terms of the specific roles that God plays in Berkeleian

Idealism. There is, first, the general fact just noted: the existence of the infinite mind of God serves to account for the cause of our sensory ideas, and provides as well an explanation for their orderliness and coherence. Since sensory ideas must be caused by some mind, and since our minds are incapable, they are the products of another mind (though not just any mind, clearly, but one far more powerful than ours). Consider too that we could have never dreampt up or simply imagined this physical world as we perceive it, in all its detail and vividness and regularity. Even when we do our best at imagining, we are able to call up ideas that are only a fraction as clear and steady as those we get when seeing a real animal, or hearing a real choir, or actually tasting real strawberries.

The second role played by the divine mind in Berkeleian Idealism is an extension of the first, and helps put to rest a common objection against the idealist. The objection is simply that it seems implausible that the world should be annihilated when we quit looking at it—that the tree in the quad should disappear after hours, or that Mount McKinley should go away when altogether masked in dense clouds. Berkeley agrees. And Berkeley reminds us too that none of this follows from the doctrine that physical objects cannot exist unperceived. He considers the objection that

> ... the objects of sense exist only when they are perceived; the trees therefore are in the garden, or the chairs in the parlour, no longer than while there is somebody by to perceive them. Upon shutting my eyes all the furniture in the room is reduced to nothing, and barely upon opening them it is again created. (*Principles*, Section 45)

To this he responds, suggestively:

> ... though we hold indeed the objects of sense to be nothing else but ideas which cannot exist unperceived, yet we may not hence conclude they have no existence except only while they are perceived by *us*; since there may be some other spirit that perceives them though we do not. Wherever bodies are said to have nonexistence without the mind, I would not be understood to mean this or that particular mind, but all minds whatsoever. It does not therefore follow that bodies are annihilated and created every moment, or exist not at all during intervals between *our* perception of them. (*Principles*, Section 48)

Indeed, if we add to this Berkeley's common-sense claim that objects *do* exist when we do not perceive them, it would follow that some other mind holds them in existence by perceiving them all the while. And such an untiring mind—the "creator and sustainer" of all things, "by whom all things consist" (Berkeley reminds us)—can be no less than God. When asked whether physical objects would still exist were he annihilated, Berkeley replies:

> When I deny sensible things any existence out of the mind, I do not mean my mind in particular, but all minds. Now, it is plain they have an existence exterior to my mind; since I find them by experience to be independent of it. There is therefore some other Mind wherein they exist, during the intervals between the times of my perceiving them: as likewise they did before my birth, and would do after my supposed annihilation. And, as the same is true with regard to all other finite created spirits, it necessarily follows there is an *omnipresent eternal Mind*, which knows and comprehends all things, and exhibits them to our view in such a manner, and according to such rules, as He Himself hath ordained, and are by us termed the *laws of nature*. (*Three Dialogues*, Third Dialogue, 193)

Since there is very little poetry about philosophical theories, it's nice to recognize it when appropriate. Here are a couple of stanzas, the first by a fellow named Ronald Knox, and the second by, —well, your guess is as good as anyone's.

There was a young man who said, "God
Must think it exceedingly odd
    If he finds that this tree
    Continues to be
When there's no-one about in the Quad."

Reply

Dear Sir:
Your astonishment's odd:
I am always about in the Quad.
  And that's why this tree
  Will continue to be,
Since observed by
    Yours faithfully,
      GOD.

Berkeley and the problem cases

Berkeley and the direct realist disagree about the nature of ordinary physical objects. The realist, of course, takes them to be external mind-independent chunks of matter. Berkeley argues that they are collections of sensory ideas, existing only when perceived by some mind or other. But it should also be evident that Berkeley and the direct realist have much in common. Both hold that we are directly aware of physical objects: one may be perceptually aware of the coffee cup on the table without being aware of some intermediate object. And both agree that we can know things about these objects (that is, be justified in our perceptual beliefs about these objects) without inference, but simply in virtue of our being directly aware of them.

Recall, however, that it was the direct realist's claim that we are directly aware of physical objects that gave rise to his troubles with illusion and hallucination. In all these cases what we are directly aware of does not jibe with what we think the world is really like: the stick looks bent but we think it is really straight, there appear to be pink rats all around me but they don't really exist. If we are directly aware of the object, then there is no room to go wrong. Now if Berkeley also contends that we are directly aware of physical objects, should we not expect that he too will be troubled by these cases?

Berkeley's Idealism also gives rise to a rather special problem. If in *any* experience we are only directly aware of ideas, then we must have some way of distinguishing experiences of "real things" from dream experiences. Perhaps there is no distinction to be made; are sensory objects perhaps nothing more than (as Berkeley would say) "so many chimeras and illusions on the fancy?" Why should my perceiving that I am sitting on the beach enjoying a cold drink be in some cases only a dream and in other cases "real?"

We have already said that Berkeley distinguishes ideas of imagination from sensory ideas. The former are produced by our own will and are consequently not forced upon us. The latter are the result of some other mind's (God's) efforts; these ideas we passively receive. Ideas of sense, as opposed to ideas of the imagination, are also "vivid and clear." Thus we should have no trouble in distinguishing one sort of idea from the other.

Berkeley has a similar story to tell with respect to dreams.

> ... there is little danger of confounding [sensory ideas] in the visions of a dream, which are dim, irregular, and confused. And, though they should happen to be never so lively and natural, yet, by their being connected, and of a piece with the preceding and subsequent transactions of our lives, they might easily be distinguished from realities. (*Three Dialogues*, Third Dialogue, 197)

So it is the regularity, vivacity and coherence of certain ideas that marks them as "real things;" if they lack these features, they are only dreams or chimeras. There is nothing profound about this approach. How else do we commonly distinguish dreams from nondreams? Typically our dreams are more loosely connected than reality. I might dream myself in Morocco one minute but in Alaska the next; I might find myself running in slow motion while everyone else moves as quickly as normal; tables can turn into tarantulas and inanimate objects speak. We do quite easily distinguish dreams from reality and we are invited to continue in the same way. This much we might expect from Berkeley who does not want to deny any of our common beliefs about the world (except perhaps the wrong-headed belief that there are external objects existing apart from what we experience).

> ... by whatever method you distinguish *things* from *chimeras* on your scheme, the same, it is evident, will hold also upon mine. For, it must be, I presume, by some perceived difference; and I am not for depriving you of any one thing that you perceive. (*Three Dialogues*, Third Dialogue, 197)

We can distinguish our experiences of "real things" from illusions and hallucinations in pretty much the same way as we distinguish reality from dreams. Perceptions of reality fit together in a way that hallucinatory or illusory experiences do not, and not only for oneself but for others as well. Berkeley remarks that "if at a table all who were present should see, and smell, and taste, and drink wine, and find the effects of it, with me there could be no doubt of its reality." This is not to deny that when having an hallucinatory experience of pink rats, I am aware of ideas of rats. Berkeley's point is that we do not count this as an experience of reality since it would probably not fit coherently with other perceptions I might have (although I "see" the rats I cannot touch them is I would expect if they were real) and would probably not be corroborated by other perceivers around me ("Where are these pink rats? Why don't we see them too?"). Consider Berkeley's discussion of an illusion in which an oar placed in water appears bent.

> He is not mistaken with regard to the ideas he actually perceives, but in the inferences he makes from his present perceptions. Thus, in the case of the oar, what he immediately perceives by sight is certainly crooked; and so far he is on the right. But if he thence concludes that upon taking the oar out of the water he shall perceive the same crookedness; or that it would affect his touch as crooked things are wont to do: in that he is mistaken. (*Three Dialogues*, Third Dialogue, 200)

To summarize, Berkeley distinguishes experiences of real things from those of nonreal things by noting certain features of the perceptions. Experiences of reality display a special vivacity and clarity, they fit in coherently with other experiences you may have had or are currently having, certain expectations will be met (when you reach out to touch it it will be there, for example), other perceivers will report similar experiences. In general, there is a continuity and coherence that is missing in illusory, hallucinatory or dream experiences. Our experiences, though they are only perceptions of ideas, are more than "so many chimeras or illusions on the fancy."

Idealism and Representative Realism

It is important to notice that not only does Berkeley see his account of dreams, illusions and hallucinations as common-sensical, but he thinks he has succeeded where the realist could not.

> Upon [the supposition that there exist mind-independent physical objects] ... the objections from the change of color in a pigeons neck, or the appearance of the broken oar in water,

must be allowed to have weight. But these and the like objections vanish, if we do not maintain the being of absolute external originals, but place the reality of things in ideas, fleeting indeed, and changeable:—however, not changed at random, but according to the fixed order of nature. For, herein consists that constancy and truth of things which secures all the concerns of life, and distinguishes that which is *real* from the irregular visions of fancy. (*Three Dialogues*, Third Dialogue, 221)

Does Berkeley do better than, say, the representative realist in accounting for illusions and hallucinations? Certainly if we consider the *practical* grounds by which we ordinarily tell when we are hallucinating or experiencing an illusion, Berkeley has an edge. Locke's theory holds that hallucinations and illusions occur when our experiences are inappropriately produced by physical objects. But, practically speaking, how can we ever tell what sort of causal chain is responsible for our experiences? We only perceive the effects, never the causes, of perceptual experience. But on Berkeley's theory, we have only to note certain features of the perceptions themselves—are they coherent, orderly, clear, forceful?

If we consider *theoretical* grounds, however, the story is different. Although he apparently makes it easy to tell when you are hallucinating, Berkeley does not offer much to explain why experiences of that sort are not real but other experiences are. Nor does he explain why there should be any distinction between reality and nonreality at all if there is nothing to the world but our minds and ideas, that is, if there is nothing to which our ideas must conform. Why isn't all experience experience of something real? Locke, on the other hand, does assume the existence of external physical objects and so does have some reason to say that some ideas are real (those caused by, and conforming to, the physical world) and some ideas are not (those not caused in the appropriate way). He does, then, succeed on theoretical grounds whereas Berkeley does not.

Questions: How does Berkeley's Idealism differ from Representative Realism? How does Berkeley understand ordinary physical objects? What does Berkeley say there cannot be unperceived objects? According to Berkeley, what causes our sensory ideas and how does he arrive at his conclusion? How would the idealist handle the situations that gave the direct realist trouble?

Section 6: ASSESSING BERKELEIAN IDEALISM

If one were to judge the plausibility of a theory simply by how well its main tenets accord with our intuitions, Idealism would receive low marks. Still, it is remarkable how well the idealist story hangs together. We have paused on several occasions to indicate that protests of an off-the-cuff sort rarely fare well against Idealism. But setting quick protests aside isn't enough. What we must do now is engage a more sustained assessment of Idealism. In doing so, the ambition is to notice the most general sorts of difficulties empiricist theories are likely to encounter.

Problems for the idealist's thesis about physical objects

Recall that one of the weightiest considerations in favor of the view that physical objects are collections of sensory ideas was the empiricist theory of meaning. Roughly put, what this account of meaning does is to connect items of language with our ideas. Let's think about that a moment. Even if our ordinary concept of meaning is unclear, one pretty solid intuition each of us has about language is that it connects with the world—it hooks up with *what there is.* On a straightforward reading of the empiricist theory of meaning, then, it is easy to suppose that what there is—that the world we're describing and speaking about with language—just *is* the world of ideas. Now that may or may not describe the genesis of empiricist ontologies: that is not the point. The point is now to notice how unhappily it accords with our intuition that, when we talk about what there is, we speak about things that (i) we can be variously aware of and unaware of from one moment to another, and that (ii) you and I can each be aware of at the same time or at different times. If we are quite literally speaking of our ideas, then (i) and (ii) seem to be in jeopardy. It is fairly easy to see why.

Suppose that you are in pain now (you have a tooth ache, let's suppose). One thing is clear about those ideas of pain that you're now experiencing: *I* don't have them. It isn't that I don't have them because I don't have a tooth ache now. Even if I had a toothache now, *I* wouldn't have *your* pain ideas. (It is clear that this goes for all ideas of all sorts. If you hear the same choir I hear or see the same rhinoceros that I see, your sensory ideas aren't mine. If we each calculate the same sum in our heads at the same time, we don't thereby have the same ideas in our head. We have the same *type* or *kind* of ideas, but not the very same ideas.)

Now suppose again that you take a painkiller for your tooth ache. An hour from now you are not in pain, but several hours later you again have pain: you have more pain ideas. Not the *same* pain ideas as you had four hours ago. *Those* ideas you had then, *these* ideas you have now. They are the same type or kind of ideas, but they are not those very ideas. (This goes for all ideas of all sorts, as before. If you hear the flute play middle C now, and then again a moment from now, you don't have the very same sensory idea now that you did a moment ago.)

That's how we slice up the world of ideas—pretty finely. And the consequence of these facts seems to be all the worse for (i) and (ii). The ideas of which I am aware *now* are not the very same ideas that existed earlier of which I was aware then. If physical objects are collections of ideas and I cannot be aware of the same batch of ideas now as I was then, it follows that I cannot perceive the exact same object on different occasions. Similarly, if I cannot perceive the very same sensory ideas you perceive, and physical objects are collections of sensory ideas, then it would seem to follow that you and I cannot perceive the same physical object.

The Berkeleian idealist might, however, have a response to this objection. The idealist might say, for example, that we understand our talk about "same object" (as when you perceive the same object now as you did then, or when I perceive the same object as you do) to be literally speaking false. To admit this is not to deny that we still find it *useful* to speak as though we do all perceive the same object. Or, to take a completely different line, a Berkeleian could say that we do see the same object, though we each see different parts of the object— physical objects are collections of ideas that we all have. Since we can only experience our own ideas, we only ever see parts of objects: one part then, another part now; your part and my part. Berkeley himself would likely want to include the ideas of God as the ideas that "make up" ordinary physical objects. (But there are problems with this sort of response: Could God have *sensory* ideas? Surely He has no sense organs of the sort we do. Nor can the collection of ideas He holds in existence *be* the ideas we are aware of when we see the rhinoceros.)

The range of detailed replies here, in any case, is of less concern than the general point: once we accept the the idealist theory, our common ways of speaking about physical objects are difficult to preserve.

Conflating imagination and conception

Let's turn to another problem Berkeley faces. If we consider the distinction carefully, we can see that imagining something is different from conceiving something. To imagine a triangle is to form a mental picture of a particular triangle. The image in your mind must have a particular size and shape; it must be a particular sort of triangle (an equilateral or an isosceles or some other sort of triangle). But you can conceive of a triangle without entertaining any particular triangle in a mental picture. To conceive of something is to entertain the ideas corresponding to the concept of the thing. These ideas can be abstracted from any particular triangle you might see or imagine.

The difference between conceiving and imagining is perhaps most clearly brought out in the fact that while you cannot form a precise mental picture of a geometric figure with four-hundred thirty-nine sides, you can conceive of such a figure. You can think about a multi-sided figure like this without necessarily having a particular mental image of one in mind. In fact, it may well be that it is psychologically impossible to form such a precise mental image.

Imaginability and conceivability, then, are distinct faculties of thought, and many things that aren't imaginable are still conceivable.

The idealist is frequently set up to either miss or intentionally avoid this distinction (Berkeley flatly denies it). There are a few ways of understanding why this is so, but perhaps the following will serve. Recall again the empiricist theory of meaning: our linguistic terms have a meaning insofar as they are associated with sensory ideas. But abstract ideas—such as the idea of *triangle* we have that corresponds to no actual triangle of any specific sort—are not associated with anything that can possibly get cashed out in sensory experience. Our abstract concept of a triangle has built into it neither the notion of equilaterality nor non-equilaterality, and yet any particular triangle we might see must be one way or the other.

Before getting too far along, let's see how these latest points are relevant to the Berkeleian Idealism. The representative realist, as we presented him, believed that one way to account for certain cases of perceptual relativity was by appeal to distinguish primary qualities from secondary qualities. Berkeley, recall, denies any such distinction between kinds of qualities. In experience we never observe shapes without colors; we are never witness to primary qualities separate from secondary qualities. What is more, Berkeley continues, we cannot separate primary from secondary qualities *even in thought.* Take a second look at what Berkeley says:

> Now, if it be certain that those [primary] qualities are inseparably united with the other sensible qualities, and not, even in thought, capable of being abstracted from them, it plainly follows than they exist only in the mind. But I desire any one to reflect, and try whether he can, by abstraction of thought, conceive the extension and motion of a body without all the other sensible qualities. For my own part, I see evidently that it is not within my power to frame an idea of a body extended and moving, but I must withal give is some color or other sensible quality .... In short, extension, figure, and motion, abstracted from all other qualities, are inconceivable. (*Principles*, Section 10)

What Berkeley has dubbed "conceiving" here is simply the faculty of imagining. He is correct, of course. We cannot imagine the shape or motion of a body without supplying some secondary quality. Any mental image I form of a square must be shaded in and distinct from its background; otherwise I could not mentally "see" it. But from this it does not follow—as Berkeley contends—that primary qualities cannot be distinguished from secondary qualities even in thought. We can conceive of *motion*—the abstract concept of a moving thing—easily enough, without having at the same time to build into that concept any notion of color or temperature or taste or smell or the like. That we cannot imagine qualities of a certain kind separate from qualities of another kind does nothing to show that we cannot distinguish these qualities in thought as genuinely different kinds.

Is the unimaginable also impossible?

There is a second mistake the idealist makes here. The argument seems to be that since we cannot imagine these qualities except as inseparably united, they cannot possibly be otherwise. The hidden premise here is simply that what is unimaginable is impossible. But this, surely, is false. What we can imagine is limited by certain contingent facts about human psychology; but the limits of human psychology do not specify the limits of logical possibility. Why should they? Indeed, we already have an example of *an unimaginable logical possibility*: a four-hundred thirty-nine sided figure. You cannot imagine such a figure, but such a figure is logically possible. You can conceive of one, and you could go about making one.

There is a second occasion on which the Berkeleian idealist fails in the same way. Recall again the protest that "nothing is easier than for me to imagine a tree, unperceived in a park." Berkeley first argues that we cannot imagine a tree existing unperceived. Perhaps he is right. This is not to say, however, that we cannot conceive of a tree existing unperceived. The argument, however, is as follows: we cannot imagine a physical object existing unperceived; what is not imaginable is not possible; therefore, an unperceived physical object is impossible. Here is a valid argument, but an unsound one, for we know that the second premise is false.

Berkeley and indirect knowledge

The idealist offered a second argument for the impossibility of unperceived objects. It proceeded from the argument concluding that physical objects are (collections of) sensory ideas. If physical objects just are sensory ideas and it is logically impossible for sensory ideas to go unperceived, then it is logically impossible for physical objects to go unperceived. If we are willing to grant the earlier conclusion about physical objects, this is a good argument.

It is interesting to ask why we *should* accept the earlier argument that physical objects are collections of sensory ideas. That argument seems innocuous enough:

(1)   Physical objects are things we perceive by sense.
(2)   All we perceive by sense are sensory ideas.
(3)   So, physical objects are sensory ideas.

Suppose now that you are a representative realist. You will be happy to accept the premises, if understood in the right way.

(1*)   Physical objects are things we *indirectly* perceive by sense.
(2*)   All we *directly* perceive by sense are sensory ideas.

But nothing validly follows from *these* premises, so understood. By the lights of a representative realist, the argument commits the fallacy of equivocation by employing the word 'perceive' in two different senses.

A more important and interesting question is whether the idealist can offer any independent line of defense for premise (2), where we understand it to say that the *only* things we perceive by sense are what we directly perceive, namely sensory ideas. What argument could be advanced for this view? What needs to be offered is some reason for thinking that there are no objects of knowledge to which we have only indirect perceptual access.

Berkeley does have support for premise (2). It is big-picture support and we have seen it already. An *inference* is required to posit the existence of anything to which we have only indirect access. No such inference to unobserved entities can ever be justified, according to the idealist. If we side with the representative realist and claim that physical objects are mind-independent objects of which we are only indirectly aware, then Berkeley will insist that we should be skeptical about their existence. On the other hand, if we side with the idealist and claim that we can be directly aware of physical objects, we can reject skepticism and endorse the common sense: when we perceive physical objects it is those very objects that we are directly aware of.

This short rehearsal lets us see a couple of things. First, an empiricist theory of knowledge makes it difficult to posit the existence of things with which we're not directly connected via sensory experience. As we saw earlier in this section, the empiricist claim about what objects there are depends on his story about what he can know. What counts as reliable epistemic access to an object is restricted by sensory experience. So, what gets into our ontology is restricted in the same way.

The second point is that the Berkeleian idealist seems to have cheated on this part of his own game. Doesn't Berkeley posit the existence of unperceived entities of which he is not directly aware? *God* is certainly the best example here. If he is not directly aware of God in perception, how could Berkeley be sure that God exists?

Our knowledge of God

Let's set this criticism out a bit more neatly. Exactly what role does God play in the idealist program? A bit of reflection shows that God plays very much the same role played by external physical objects in the representative realist's story. Both are external. Neither are objects to which we have direct perceptual access. Most importantly, the inference by which each theorist finds himself needing to posit these external objects is the same: an *inference to the best explanation*. The representative realist and idealist alike need to account for the source of our sensory ideas. Each theory needs to account for the fact that these orderly, coherent ideas come to us seemingly from without and in a manner quite beyond our control.

To press matters a bit, if Berkeley is willing to allow inferences to the best explanation to support a belief in the existence of God, then it is reasonable to think that he should allow on the same ground similar inferences supporting belief in the existence of external physical objects.

Let us come at problems associated with the idealist's claim to know of certain unperceived objects by reviewing carefully Berkeley's own writing on the matter. Recall again the very first words of Berkeley in the *Principles*:

> It is evident to anyone who takes a survey of the *objects of human knowledge*, that they are either *ideas* actually imprinted on the senses; or else such as are perceived by attending to the passions and operations of the mind; or lastly, *ideas* formed by the help of memory and imagination .... (*Principles*, Section 1)

This passage clearly restricts the objects of human knowledge to ideas. There is no mention of minds here at all. And yet the Berkeleian idealist is happy enough to speak about the existence of minds. Do we have ideas of minds or spirits? Berkeley argues that

> a Spirit is one simple, undivided active being .... Hence there can be no *idea* formed of a soul or spirit; for all ideas whatever, being passive and inert ... cannot represent unto us, by way of image or likeness, that which acts. (*Principles*, Section 27)

If the objects of human knowledge are ideas, and we have no ideas of mind, then we have no knowledge of mind at all. Again, without an inference to something *beyond* that of which we are directly aware, the idealist is in no position to entertain seriously beliefs about minds of any sort—God's or his own. But inferences beyond that of which we are directly aware (ideas) are simply *inferences to objects that correspond to nothing in experience*, and by empiricist standards that would be illegitimate.

Our knowledge of minds

Are there any grounds on which the Berkeleian idealist can base indirect knowledge? It depends in part on how far the idealist is prepared to allow an empiricist epistemology to stretch beyond its straightforward "we know only our ideas" version. Berkeley suggests it is no count against his theory of knowledge that, strictly speaking, we have no idea of mind. Let's explore his writing further.

> But surely it ought not to be looked on as a defect in human understanding that it does not perceive the idea of Spirit, if it is manifestly impossible there should be any such idea. (*Principles*, Section 135)

We do, however, have *some* understanding of minds. Berkeley asks on one occasion "How often must I repeat, that I know or am conscious of my own being?" by which he intends to claim that, since we are spirits, we can know perfectly well what 'spirit' means.

> But it will be objected that, if there is no idea signified by the terms *soul, spirit*, ... they are wholly insignificant, or have no meaning in them. I answer those words do mean or signify a real thing .... What I am *myself*, that which I denote by the term *I*, is the same with what is meant by *soul* .... (*Principles*, Section 139)

In connection with the understanding we have of mind or spirit, Berkeley often introduces the word 'notion', saying that while we have no *idea* of mind, still we have (given ourselves as the paradigm case) a *notion* of it. Given the obscurity of a 'notion', Berkeley seems to be stretching his empiricist epistemology quite a bit.

> In a large sense indeed, we may be said to have an idea [or rather a notion] of *spirit*. That is, we understand the meaning of the word, otherwise we could not affirm or deny anything of it. (*Principles*, Section 140)

> We may not, I think, strictly be said to have an *idea* of an active being, or an action; although we may be said to have a *notion* of them. I have some knowledge or notion of *my mind*, and its acts about ideas; inasmuch as I know or understand

what is meant by these words. What I know, that I have some
notion of. (*Principles*, Section 142)

So not all human knowledge is based on ideas. It is interesting to see
Berkeley's thought here reconstructed along very common sense lines:
"A mind is whatever has ideas, and I have ideas; hence, I am a mind;
hence, we can understand at least *that much* about something of which
we have no idea."

But *that much* isn't enough. At most it legitimates claims to know
about *our* minds that, by our awareness of notions and not ideas, are
nevertheless direct or immediate ("My own mind and my own ideas I
have an immediate knowledge of ... ."). We still need some account of
things of which we are not directly aware, for it is this that Berkeley
denies the representative realist and allows for himself. Granting the
idealist knowledge of his own mind, on what grounds does he claim it
for *other minds*, and do not these same grounds justify the representative realist's claim to knowledge of external physical objects?

These are difficult questions. Berkeley has answers, as one might
expect. Let's complete this section by looking briefly at a couple of
them. Consider the following passage:

I know what I mean by the terms *I* and *myself*; and I know this
immediately or intuitively, though I do not perceive it .... I do
not therefore say my soul is an idea or like an idea. However,
taking the word *idea* in a large sense, my soul may be said to
furnish me with an idea, that is, an image or likeness of God—
though indeed extremely inadequate. For, all the notion I have
of God is ordained by reflecting on my own soul, heightening
its powers, and removing its imperfections. ... And, though I
perceive Him not by sense, yet I have a notion of Him, or
know Him by reflexion and reasoning. My own mind and my
own ideas I have an immediate knowledge of; and, by the help
of these, do mediately apprehend the possibility of the
existence of other spirits and ideas. Farther, from my own
being, and from the dependency I find in myself and my
ideas, I do, by an act of reason, necessarily infer the existence
of a God .... (*Three Dialogues*, Third Dialogue, 194)

This passage, that gestures at the grounds on which Berkeley claims to
have indirect knowledge of other minds, is immediately followed by a
passage directed to the representative realist.

For you neither perceive Matter objectively, as you do an inactive being or idea; nor know it, as you do yourself, by a [reflective] act; neither do you mediately apprehend it by similitude of the one or the other; nor yet collect it by reasoning from that which you know immediately. All this makes the case of *Matter* widely different from that of the *Deity*. (*Three Dialogues*, Third Dialogue, 194)

The four points in this last passage may be summarized in the following way: None of the grounds on which the idealist justifies his beliefs about God are grounds on which the representative realist bases claims about the existence of external physical objects. The representative realist does not have immediate knowledge of material objects, either by being directly aware of them as one is aware of ideas, or by being aware of them as one is aware of oneself. Nor does the representative realist indirectly know of material objects in either of the two ways in which Berkeley claims to know of other minds. The first of these— "apprehending by similitude"—is of the most interest to us. Berkeley spells it out in some detail elsewhere.

From what hath been said, it is plain that we cannot know the existence of other spirits otherwise than by their operations, or the ideas by them, excited in us I perceive several motions, changes, and combinations of ideas, that inform me there are certain particular agents, like myself, which accompany them, and concur in their production. Hence, the knowledge I have of other spirits is not immediate, as is the knowledge of ideas; but depending on the intervention of ideas, by me referred to agents or spirits distinct from myself, as effects or concomitant signs. (*Principles*, Section 145)

Here is an inductive *inference to the best explanation* that takes the form of an *argument from analogy* (that's what 'similitude' refers to). The conclusion that other spirits exist is offered as the explanatory hypothesis that best accounts for the fact that I see your body moving like mine moves when I hear a loud noise or notice a charging rhinoceros or experience pain. Since I am an agent and respond those ways when in those mental situations, probably you are an agent (responding to equivalent mental situations) too.

Hasn't the representative realist offered his inference to unperceived physical objects as an inference to the best explanation? He has, and Berkeley does something similar with his inference to unperceived minds. But Berkeley calls attention to the following difference. The idealist starts with something with which he is immediately aware (his own mind and ideas) and makes an inference to there being *more of those*. The representative realist can do nothing like this. Locke must start with something with which he is immediately aware (ideas) and infer to *something else* altogether different. Indeed, Berkeley thinks that Locke's inference provides no real argument at all.

> It is granted we have neither an immediate evidence nor a demonstrative knowledge of the existence of other finite spirits; but it will not thence follow that such spirits are on a foot with material substances ... if the one can be inferred by no argument, and there is a probability for the other .... (*Three Dialogues*, Third Dialogue, 195)

Conclusions

It should be clear by now that developing a theory of perception and knowledge is no easy matter. Perhaps the difficulty (or at least one difficulty) has become evident. Direct perceptual access to the external world leaves us with a clean account of how perceptual beliefs could be justified or rational, and so yield knowledge. But we face seemingly intractable problem cases (e.g., illusion, hallucination, and perceptual relativity) in which that of which we are aware cannot be the external physical object. This is the lesson we learned from our study of the direct realist's view. On the other hand, the claim that we are only indirectly aware of the external world, while freeing us from the burden of the problem cases, seems incapable of accounting for perceptual knowledge. How can perception yield knowledge if one never really perceives (directly) the world that is supposed to be known? How does one get beyond the veil of perception? This is the lesson our discussion of Locke taught us.

Berkeley attempted to salvage what was best in Direct Realism—the thesis that we are directly aware of physical objects—without incurring the trouble raised by illusion, hallucination and perceptual relativity. He did this by denying that physical objects were external. Ordinary tables and chairs are nothing more than coherent, vivid and forceful collections of ideas; illusory or hallucinatory tables and chairs are simply less-than-coherent, vivid, and forceful collections of ideas. In all cases, problematic and otherwise, we are aware of nothing more than sensory ideas and so we need not posit another item to account for the difference between appearance and reality. Notice that this difference is really, on Berkeley's account, one of degree. It is those collections of ideas that are coherent to the right degree that are called "real physical objects." And if a collection of ideas does not meet the standard it is what we call "appearance." Now this seems to go some way toward dealing with the problem cases and offering an account of how we know about physical objects (we know about them because we are directly aware of them), provided we are willing to swallow the consequence that these are not external, material physical objects.

But we must also note the additional price Berkeley has paid. He must do exactly what he criticized Locke for doing. Since we cannot be directly aware of minds, whether of man or God, we must postulate their existence as the best explanation for those ideas that we do directly experience. How else can we account for the coherence and forcefulness of our ideas? But of course if Berkeley is entitled to this sort of inference, then we must allow Locke the same. And so Berkeley's theory proves to be little better than Representative Realism.

It is here that we leave the matter. We have succeeded in clarifying the issues to some degree, we have set out the parameters that will guide any plausible theory of perception, and we have discovered some of the potholes that must be avoided. In this way we have advanced; but more remains for philosophers to do.

Questions: What problems face Berkeley's theory about physical objects? How does Berkeley think we know about God and other minds? Is this a problem for his view? In what ways is Berkeley's Idealism similar to Direct Realism? How do they differ?

NOTES

[1]John Locke, *An Essay concerning Human Understanding*, Ed. Peter Nidditch (Oxford: Oxford University Press, 1975), Book II, Chapter viii, Section 9. Hereafter all references to Locke's *Essay* will be made in the text in "Book, Chapter, Section" form.

[2]George Berkeley, *Principles of Human Knowledge*, in *Berkeley's Philosophical Writings*, Ed. David M. Armstrong (New York: MacMillan

Publishing Company, 1965), Section 14, page 66. Hereafter all references to Berkeley's *Principles* will be made in the text with section number.
³George Berkeley, *Three Dialogues between Hylas and Philonous*, in *Berkeley's Philosophical Writings*, Ed. David M. Armstrong (New York: MacMillan Publishing Company, 1965), First Dialogue, 138. Hereafter all references to Berkeley's *Dialogues* will be made in the text with page number.

RELATED READINGS

Austin, J. L. *Sense and Sensibilia*. Oxford: Oxford University Press, 1979.

Ayer, A. J. "The Argument from Illusion." *The Foundations of Empirical Knowledge*. London: MacMillan and Company, LTD, 1951.

Ayer, A. J. "Phenomenalism." *Proceedings of the Aristotelian Society* 47 (1946-7).

Berkeley: Critical and Interpretive Essays. Ed. Colin Turbayne. Minneapolis: University of Minnesota Press, 1982.

Berkeley's Philosophical Writings. Ed. David M. Armstrong. New York: MacMillan Publishing Company, 1965

Bennett, Jonathan. *Locke, Berkeley, Hume: Central Themes*. Oxford: University of Oxford Press, 1971.

Chisholm, R. M. "The Theory of Appearing." *Perceiving, Sensing and Knowing*. Ed. Robert J. Swartz. Berkeley: University of California Press, 1965.

Hirst, R. J. *The Problems of Perception*. London: George Allen & Unwin LTD, 1959.

Jackson, Frank. *Perception*. Cambridge: Cambridge University Press, 1977.

Locke, John. *An Essay concerning Human Understanding*. Ed. Peter Nidditch. Oxford: Oxford University Press, 1975.

Price, H. H. *Perception*. Westport, CN: Greenwood Press, 1981.

Russell, Bertrand. "Appearance and Reality." *The Problems of Philosophy*. New York: Oxford University Press, 1952.

CHAPTER 6 | Free Will and Determinism

Section 1: INTRODUCTION

The tension

MOST of the important and difficult problems that philosophers discuss nowadays are not new. Like the traditional mind-body problem or questions concerning the existence of God, the problem of free will and Determinism has attracted serious attention since the ancient Greek atomists. The free will controversy also arises in the way many other stubborn philosophical problems arise, from an apparent tension between two views that we might otherwise like to hold—between the existence of a benevolent God and the presence of evil, between regarding ourselves as conscious thinking, feeling things and regarding ourselves as physical objects, between free will and Determinism.

In the present chapter we will look closely at this apparent tension between free will and Determinism. What is this tension, and what importance does it have for us?

Most of us would agree that a person who could not do otherwise than perform a certain action is not morally responsible for performing it, and so should not be praised or blamed for it. If it was not up to Jones whether to embezzle the money from the bank where he worked, either because he was hypnotized to do so, or because he was forced to take the money at gunpoint, then we would not be inclined to blame him. And we would not be inclined to praise him if his assisting an elderly woman across the street was accomplished under similar conditions. The very idea that persons are morally responsible agents requires that persons are capable of acting voluntarily, of their own free will.

The idea that we might live in a universe in which no persons are morally responsible for their actions is difficult to take seriously. We quite naturally believe that it is up to us to perform many of the actions we in fact perform. You can continue reading these lines a moment from now, and you can also do otherwise than continue reading them: it is open to you now to go jogging, or to go see a movie. Of course you aren't able to do just *anything* a moment from now: you cannot become a 1957 Buick, or jump to the moon in a single bound. But for a large range of possible courses of action, many of them seem to be genuinely up to you.

If you have free will, then some of your behavior is such that you could have done otherwise—it is up to you. Call the claim that we have free will the *free will thesis*. (Sometimes we will use simply "free will" to name this thesis, as a shorthand.)

Alongside this plausible thesis of free will can be set another, equally plausible view, called *Determinism*. According to determinism, everything that occurs is uniquely determined to happen as it does by past occurrences. All of the facts about the universe at any moment, down to the finest detail, are fixed by the particular facts that obtained at earlier moments. Similarly, just as the past uniquely determines the present, so the present state of the universe uniquely fixes the state of things a moment from now. Determinism is thus a prominent assumption in the sciences. The scientist, be he a physical or life scientist, seeks to uncover laws of nature governing the transition from the past to the future. The astronomer, for example, examines the patterns of planetary motion in sufficient detail to discover laws governing their orbits. These general laws of motion, in conjunction with particular facts about the individual planets, uniquely fix the behavior of each planet at each moment of its orbit.

The tension between our belief that we have free will and our commitment to Determinism should be readily apparent. If we have free will, then we are often confronted with alternative courses of action each of which we are able to perform, and whichever we now perform, we could have done otherwise. But if Determinism is true, then given the way things actually were in the past, we could not have done otherwise after all.

In this chapter we shall find ourselves in a bind not unfamiliar to philosophers: two theses are are individually *plausible* but apparently jointly *incompatible*. Here both the thesis that we sometimes act of our own free will and the thesis that every future state of the universe is fixed by the past and the laws of nature are found to be reasonable when considered independently, and yet, when considered together, appear to be mutually incompatible. When philosophers find themselves in such a problematic situation they are forced to reject at least one of the theses. But matters are more complicated since we will also present an argument that purports to show that the free will thesis is incompatible even with the denial of Determinism. In the face of this dilemma, the only reasonable response seems to be to reject the free will thesis. But are we willing to reject the thesis that we sometimes act of our own free will? This response is particularly unwelcome when we consider that our being morally responsible for our actions demands that we be able to act of our own free will; and surely it seems that we are sometimes morally blameworthy or praiseworthy. When cherished beliefs are threatened by arguments, the philosopher's response must be to either reject the cherished beliefs or re-evaluate the arguments that pose the threat. The latter option is explored in what follows.

In Sections 2 and 3, the notions of free will and Determinism are elucidated. An argument that free will is incompatible with Determinism is presented in Section 4; and in Section 5 it is argued that our having free will is also incompatible with Indeterminism. The dilemma posed by these two consequences seems to show that free will is impossible. The dilemma is treated in Section 6. Two responses to the premises of this dilemma—one to the incompatibilist argument of Section 4, and one to the indeterminist argument of Section 5—are discussed in Sections 7 and 8 (respectively). Neither of these responses is conclusive. In Section 9 we briefly explore one philosopher's contention that being morally responsible does not require that we have free will. If defensible, this contention could remove our main motive for not rejecting the free will thesis.[1]

Section 2: FREE WILL

Our first task is to say more clearly what we have in mind when ascribing free will to ourselves and to others. Despite the quite natural belief that much of our behavior is done freely, and despite the familiarity of the expression "free will", a good deal of confusion will enter our discussion unless we say at the outset exactly what it means. Perhaps the best way to begin is with some examples.

A. Characterizing Free Will

Freedom and the will

Imagine that you are seated in the classroom, listening to a lecture. Suddenly you find your arm shooting up into the air, knocking your neighbor's notebooks to the floor as it rises. You did not intend to raise your arm. You are embarrassed that it is there and that you have appeared reckless to your colleagues, but despite all your efforts, you cannot lower it. To make matters worse, as you consider how best to apologize, you feel your mouth move and hear a voice coming from your own vocal cords, asking a philosophical question that you have never considered. The instructor responds that this is an excellent question and praises you for being an enthusiastic and insightful student. Reflecting a moment, however, you realize that you cannot take credit for the question, or for asking it, since the question had not occurred to you and and asking it was not under your control; moreover, you realize that despite what others might think, you are not blameworthy for scattering the notebooks onto the floor. You are not responsible for the question or the seemingly reckless act.

An odd situation such as this is clearly different from the more familiar case in which you do formulate a question, deliberate about whether to ask it in class, decide to do so, and then willingly and properly raise your arm to catch the instructor's attention. Under these conditions we say that raising your arm and asking the question was completely up to you, that it was a voluntary action. You don't merely find yourself doing it, "out of the blue" as we might say, as you might find yourself sneezing without the power to refrain. Here, asking the question is not against your will but in accordance with your will.

Most thinkers would not regard the first situation as one in which you acted of your own free will, reserving that description for the case in which your behavior issued from, and so was in accordance with, your decision to raise your hand and ask a question. Two questions need to be asked. First, what is it to have free will? And second, do we have free will?

What is it to have free will?

Let us begin by exploring the first question. According to philosophical and psychological tradition, the will is a faculty of the mind producing the voluntary behavior of an individual. The explanation for why Jones gave up smoking would supposedly make reference to his will, but the explanation for why Jones flinched when the attacker threw his fist at Jones's nose would not. Even though most philosophers and psychologists have abandoned the notion of the will as a faculty of the mind, the word still proves to be popular and useful in ordinary and philosophical discourse. We say that she quit smoking of her own *free will*, thereby suggesting that she has great *willpower*; that he *willfully* or *willingly* donated his time to certain charities; that she *unwillingly* took part in the embezzlement scheme; that she is *willing* to go on the mission, or that he went on the mission against his *will*; and so on.

Thus, while rejecting the idea that there is a special faculty of the mind called the will, we may still inquire into the meaning of the expression "He did action A of his own free will" or "He freely performed A."

The examples above suggest that in order to perform freely the action of raising your arm, you must have control over the rising of your arm, that it must be up to you whether you raise or don't raise your arm. Moreover, *your* having control over the motion of your arm (rather than some other power unknown to you) implies that you didn't *have to* raise your arm. To say that you raise your arm freely, then, is to say that you didn't have to raise your arm, or that, although in fact you did raise your arm, you *could have done otherwise.*

In coming to grips with what it means to deny that you *have to* do some action, we are thereby coming to grips with the closely connected issue of what it means to say you *could have* done otherwise (or to say you *can* do otherwise). If you have to do action A, then you cannot do otherwise than A. When seated in a room you might think that your staying or leaving is a matter that is up to you. If you stay, then you do so freely only if you *could have left*; and to say that you could have left is to say that (1) leaving is a course of action open to you (the door is not locked or guarded by someone who would not let you pass, for example) to the extent that (2) you have the ability to leave given the door is unlocked and unguarded (you are conscious and able to recognize doors and mobile enough to get through the door).

These two aspects of free action are important. The first stresses the requirement of *alternative courses of action.* You act freely, on some occasion, only if your action is not the only one that you could have performed on that occasion. Thus you have free will if it is sometimes true that, when confronted with incompatible courses of action (remaining seated or standing, extending our arm or leaving it at our side), you can perform any of the actions.

Notice here that if you are free, *each* of these alternative courses of action are such that you can perform it. We fail to capture the notion of free will if we say that you can perform one *or* the other course of action; for when you are tied securely to the chair, it remains true that *you can stay seated or stand.* Rather, we take ourselves to be free on this occasion when we believe that we can remain seated *and* we also can stand. (This is not meant to suggest that there is some single action you can perform that is logically impossible, such as *your sitting and standing*—i.e., your doing both at the same time. The point instead is that if you have free will, then you are able to remain seated, and you are equally able to stand.)

The second aspect of free behavior emphasizes the notion of *power* or *ability*. This feature is typically captured in terms of "what we can do" or "what we could have done". If you are now sitting in a chair, and are tied securely to the chair, then remaining seated is not a free action of yours because standing is not something that you can do. Similarly, if the person next to you forcibly raises your arm, then you are not free to keep your hand comfortably in your lap if overcoming that force is not something you can do. In each of these cases, doing otherwise is not something that you can do; in each case, it would be false to say that you could have done otherwise than you did.

While 'can' and 'could' are not easily defined, competent speakers of English readily understand them. Still, the concept associated with 'can' and 'could' in the above paragraphs—the concept of human ability or power—is very similar to other concepts that are not to be confused with the one at work in discussions of free will. Let's consider three senses of 'can' that philosophers do *not* have in mind when saying that a person can or cannot freely perform some action.

The 'can' of ability

(a) Sometimes we say that a certain event can happen, or that it could have happened, when all we mean is that *for all we know* that's the way things in fact were or will be. Suppose I say that George Washington couldn't have sailed to Greenland in 1775. In this case, I am probably claiming that given all I know about the relevant circumstances, Washington didn't make the voyage. Perhaps I know that during that year Washington was busy on the American continent leading the colonial troops against the British, allowing me to rule out the possibility of his having taken any long sea voyages. But in a case such as this, I am not suggesting that Washington lacked some ability or power to sail to Greenland. Rather, in saying that Washington couldn't have sailed to Greenland in 1775, I am indirectly saying something about what I know: I am saying that what I know about Washington rules out his actually sailing there in 1775.

Similarly, when I say that Immanuel Kant could have invented the hamburger, I am likely suggesting that, given my ignorance about who really invented the hamburger, for all I know Kant invented it. Again, I am not attributing some power or ability to Kant. Rather, I am confessing ignorance of any fact that would rule out such an accomplishment for the philosopher. Free will is not to be understood, then, as a thesis about what is or isn't possible given our state of knowledge.

(b) Nor is free will is to be understood as a thesis about what is legally permissible, or what is morally proper. Suppose that a friend confesses to you that she intends to rob the local bank. In response to this you exclaim "You can't do that!" The "can't" here is used to suggest that committing such an act would be illegal and immoral, not that your friend lacks an ability to perform it. An act that oughtn't be performed might still be performed of one's own free will. The reverse is true as well. An act that can be performed in the sense that it is legally and morally permissible may nevertheless be one that the person can't perform in the sense that they lack the ability to carry it off.

We do sometimes use "free" to describe certain kinds of political liberty. Freedom to act, in this sense, concerns primarily the absence of political constraints and restraints. While this is a perfectly good use of the word 'free', it is not the subject of philosophical debates about free will.

(c) Free will is not to be understood as a thesis about a particular human skill. Suppose that a certain philosopher is an exceptionally skilled public debater. If he is bound and gagged, he is no less a skilled debater; and yet he is not free to engage in public debate. The free will thesis does not entail that we possess certain skills or general aptitudes, but rather that we have the power to exercise whatever skills and aptitudes we happen to possess.

So, when we speak of someone freely performing an action, let us mean that that *they do perform the action* and that *they could have done otherwise than perform the action*. Attributing to them the power or ability to do otherwise, and recognizing that an opportunity to do otherwise exists, we hope to capture what is meant when saying that your free actions are up to you, that performing them is under your control.

B. Why Believe That We Are Free?

Is there any good reason to think that we have free will?

Most of us do believe that we have free will. Those who don't, or who say they don't, are probably motivated by some other philosophical theory or argument which implies the contrary (that we have no free will). But prior to examining the relevant sophisticated arguments of philosophers, assuming that we generally act of our own free will is quite natural. Is this common belief reasonable? Is there any good reason to think that we have free will?

Some philosophers have suggested that there are propositions which, if we think about them carefully and thoroughly enough, we can simply "see" that they are true (or false, if that be the case). For example, you needn't look elsewhere for evidence of the fact that every incarnadine philosopher is a philosopher. You can straightforwardly see that this is true, even if you don't know what 'incarnadine' means, because you understand how the structure of the sentence ensures the truth of the statement it expresses. Other claims that are not "logical truths" of this sort also have the feature of being transparently true. Consider the fact that you know that you're thinking now; or consider what it is like to know that you are in pain, when you are in pain. All such cases are ones in which you are eminently reasonable in believing something (we're inclined to say that you *know* it), even though you have nothing more to go on than how things clearly and undeniably *seem* to you to be. Is our belief that we have free will appropriately similar to any of these cases?

Knowing that one is free can not, of course, be placed on a par with our knowledge of logical truths. But one item that most of us would offer, if asked why we believe that we have free will, is simply the fact that we do seem to be free. When apparently confronted with two mutually incompatible courses of action, it undeniably seems to us that they are genuine alternatives for us, that we can choose to engage in either course of action equally well. That it seems to be up to us whether we shall continue reading a moment from now is uncontroversially true. By merely attending to what this and other circumstances are like, one might argue, we can tell by introspection that we have power over our future behavior. No one is in a position to inform us that it *doesn't* seem that way to us—no more than someone can inform us that we don't feel like we're in pain now or that we're not really thinking now.

Deliberation and moral responsibility

Feeling like things are up to us does count as a reason for believing that we're free, just as feeling as if we have pulled a muscle while engaging in vigorous exercise counts as evidence that we have pulled a muscle. But, this justification for our belief that we are free seems very weak. There is an important disanalogy between the cases just mentioned—between feeling like we are in pain and feeling like we are free. One cannot feel like they are in pain and fail to be in pain, for feeling that way just *is* what being in pain amounts to. Yet feeling like one is free surely is not what being free amounts to. This fact becomes clearer when we remember that in some cases feelings can mislead us. It may of course feel like we have pulled a muscle when in fact we haven't. Thus, whatever introspective evidence we might have for the belief that we have the power to follow out alternative courses of action, it is not particularly strong evidence.

But something important is lurking nearby in this introspective territory, something bolstering the claim that other common beliefs we have, if true, make it reasonable to think that we have free will. Let's briefly consider how the belief that we are free is related to other beliefs we all seem to have.

Acting of our own free will is often thought to follow some process of deliberation. One deliberates whenever one tries to decide what to do, whenever one considers the choice of pursuing this or that alternative course of action. It is what you do when (say) you enter a movie theater and pause to weigh the advantages and disadvantages of sitting in various places available to you: too near the front might give you a stiff neck, but here in the back you can't see as well. This activity of weighing options and anticipating their consequences, for purposes of making a decision, is an obvious feature of human experience.

If deliberation is a familiar, undeniable kind of human behavior, what does it teach us about free will and the reasonableness of believing that we have it?

If we are to deliberate, we cannot deny that the future, unlike the past, is "open" in the sense that we now have the power to influence, to a greater or lesser degree, what happens in the future. You can no longer deliberate about your reading philosophy a minute ago, though you may now deliberate about whether to continue reading. This point may be equally put in terms of the simple fact that we believe that often more than one course of action to be open to us. You could not try to decide what to do next if you do not believe that your future actions are not under your own control. Given that we do deliberate, then, we betray our belief that the future is open, i.e., we manifest a belief that our actions are not the consequence of something outside of our control. Thus, if we should like to judge the reasonableness of believing some view by considering how well it fits with other things we take ourselves to be justified in believing, or find self-evident and seem unable to give up, then it is reasonable to believe that we have free will.

Another common belief about the nature of human agents bearing importantly on our belief that we are free is our belief that human beings are morally responsible agents, subject to praise or blame for some of our actions. If you rob a bank, then you should be blamed, and perhaps punished, for this action; and if you save a drowning child, you should be praised, and perhaps rewarded, for such behavior. But, of course, we cannot legitimately offer praise or blame unless you really were responsible for those actions, unless you could have done otherwise than what you did. If you couldn't fail to rob the bank, say because you were hypnotized to do so, then we should not blame you for this behavior. In a similar way, we shouldn't praise you for rescuing the drowning child if this action was not under your control. Suppose, as before, that you were hypnotized to save the child, or that your body was under the control of Martians. In such a case, we should offer you no more praise than we would offer a robot.

In order to deliberate (genuinely) about future actions and to be morally responsible, we must have free will. And we do seem to deliberate often about what we regard as alternative courses of action, and it seems obvious that we are morally responsible agents, subject to legitimate praise and blame. If what seems to be the case here is indeed the case, then we do have free will.

But notice we have simply moved the initial question, of whether seeming to be free is sufficient to inform us that we are free, back a step. We must now ask whether our seeming to deliberate or to be morally responsible is sufficient to inform us that we do deliberate and are morally responsible.

The answer to this question will not be easily found. This much we can say, however. If we are to give up our belief that we have free will, then by the above reasoning, we are forced to give up our beliefs that we sometimes deliberate about what to do and that we are morally responsible for at least some of our actions. In light of this result, then, our commitment to free will is probably not best defended by looking to positive reasons for believing that we are free; rather, it is best defended by emphasizing that any reason against free will must be a very powerful one, if only because that same reason would rule against many other beliefs we hold closely.

Questions: What is it to have free will? What two important aspects of having free will are discussed? Why do we think we are free? What does freedom have to do with deliberation and moral responsibility?

Section 3: DETERMINISM

Despite the undeniable fact that we naturally regard much of our behavior as being up to us, many thinkers have encouraged us to see that we may nevertheless be wrong in this belief. Spinoza suggested that our belief that we are free is simply the consequence of ignorance:

> . . . men believe that they are free, precisely because they are conscious of their volitions and desires; yet concerning the causes that have determined them to desire and will they have not the faintest idea, because they are ignorant of them.[2]

Nearly all philosophers believe that Determinism is possibly true, and many—though by no means all—have believed that human freedom is impossible if Determinism is true. Before turning to discuss the relation between free will and Determinism, we must say more clearly what Determinism amounts to.

A. Characterizing Determinism

The thesis of Determinism is often associated with a scientifically-informed view of the universe. This view recognizes the success of science in discovering lawful explanations for events in the natural world. The universe is, at any instant of time, a certain way, and it has come to be exactly that way because it was a certain way a moment earlier. The success of science has come in uncovering the laws according to which such changes must take place.

An intuitive characterization

But we needn't consult science in order to understand and appreciate the thesis of Determinism. When you put water in an ice cube tray and place the tray into the freezer, you can expect that the water will freeze.[3] Indeed, you have probably never put water into the freezer for the purpose of making ice cubes and *failed* to get ice cubes. If on some occasion you did fail to get ice, then you were surprised, and your surprise is testimony to the fact that we believe water must freeze if placed at temperatures below 32 degrees Fahrenheit sufficiently long. Perhaps your freezer was on the blink, or perhaps you didn't wait long enough, or perhaps you didn't fill the tray pure water (certain kinds of impure water—say, water mixed with equal parts of Anti-Freeze—will have considerably lower freezing points). But given normal water and properly low temperatures, the water must freeze.

The water "must" freeze? Well, we don't suppose that it just *happens* to freeze in such temperatures, by some accident. We do not believe that the water in your ice try could be any way whatsoever after a sufficient time in the freezer, precisely because we believe that changes in the universe are constrained by laws like those governing the behavior of water at temperatures like 32 degrees. Laws governing the behavior of molecules at low temperatures make it impossible that pure water remain a liquid at sufficiently low temperatures.

Indeed, it is natural to think of laws as expressing necessary connections between events or properties of various kinds, such that if those laws (rather than some others) are true, then if certain events occur, certain others must occur. For example, given the past states of the water and the freezer before now, there must now be ice in the tray.

The past and the laws of nature

So there are two important factors that contribute to determining or fixing the way things are at a moment: the way things were earlier— the past—and the laws of nature.

When offering these intuitive characterizations of Determinism, it may be helpful to try to avoid using the words "fix" and "determine". To some ears, they may sound too much like the very notion we are trying to clarify. Let's see how to avoid them.

We've just said that according to Determinism, the present is fixed—that it is impossible for things now to be otherwise. What sense of impossibility do we have in mind, here? Presumably there are many possible futures, in the following sense. While the tree in my backyard is now actually 10 feet tall, there is nothing inconsistent or inconceivable about a story according to which that tree in my back-yard is now 35 feet tall, or doesn't exist at all. And just as there is a possible present in which it is 35 feet tall, there is a possible future in which it is 35 feet next week. All we are saying here is that there is a comprehensive and logically consistent story to be told about my tree's being 35 feet tall some time in the near future.

But there is a clear sense in which these alternatives *aren't* possible. It is *physically impossible* that my tree be 35 feet tall next week, given that it is actually 10 feet tall now. To say that it is physically impossible that my tree be considerably taller than 10 feet so soon is to say that, *given* the sort of tree it is and the way things actually have been until now, and *given* the relevant laws of nature, there is no possible world at which my 10-foot tree is 35 feet tall next week. Such a story would be plainly inconsistent—given the actual laws of nature and the actual circumstances my tree just couldn't grow that fast in one week.

There are, as we noted, *logically* possible worlds where my tree is 35 feet tall now or in the near future, but these would be worlds at which either (1) my tree's history was different from its actual history (suppose it received more rain than it actually did, or was better cared for, or was planted in better soil) or (2), while the facts about my tree's history are the same, the laws of nature are sufficiently different from our actual laws to make trees grow much differently, given those facts.

A physically possible future, then, is a future way things could be given the actual past (P) and the laws of nature (L). We can now define *Determinism*, without using the words "determine" or "fix" or the like. Determinism is the thesis that there is, at any moment, exactly one physically possible future. There are no possible worlds having exactly the same history as the actual world, and having exactly the same laws of nature as the actual world, and yet having a future different from that of the actual world.

B. Why Believe That Determinism is True?

Some people are inclined to deny Determinism on the grounds that it runs contrary to obvious facts. "Anyone can see," it may be suggested, "that Determinism is false. For if it were true, human persons would be powerless to affect the future in ways of their own choosing— powerless, that is, to avoid the inevitable future already determined to take place. But Fatalism of this kind is obviously untrue, since nothing could be more obvious than the fact that certain events wouldn't have happened if we had behaved otherwise earlier."

This way of attacking Determinism rests on a mistake. Determinism, as we are understanding it, is not the Fatalism just described. Let's get clear on the difference between them.

Determinism is not Fatalism

Confusing Determinism with Fatalism is easy, since both seem to suggest that "whatever will be, will be", or that there is only one direction future events can take. But Fatalism, or at least the common version of it sketched above, suggests only that certain future events are inevitable, that they will occur *no matter what happens in the past or present.* Given this last feature, Fatalism clearly isn't equivalent to Determinism.

Suppose, for example, that the fatalist believes you are fated to fall to your death within the year. (There probably are very few thinking people who believe that they *know in advance* what awaits us in our futures, like the fatalist just described. There are, nevertheless, many people who believe that our futures are now fixed and unavoidable.) In believing that you shall certainly meet your death in this way, he believes that no matter how events proceed, no matter what effort you make in attempting to avoid this fate, you will inevitably die in a fall. The fatalist would not be particularly surprised to learn the following about you a year from now: Your skeptical attitude toward the fatalist's prediction is tempered with mild superstition, and so you decide to move far from your Colorado mountain home to the flat Midwest, avoiding at the same time all excursions onto ladders or into tall buildings. While strolling leisurely in the afternoon sun, exploring your new flatland surroundings, you take a fatal fall into an abandoned well. "There was no escaping it," the fatalist might lament, "No efforts at avoiding such a death could have succeeded, and there was no point in trying to do anything about it."

Determinism is not Fatalism, and the plausibility of Determinism is not tied essentially to the failure or success of Fatalism as a view about the role of persons in the universe. Unlike Fatalism, determinism explicitly maintains that present actions play a role in determining what future events occur: if the present were different, then the future would be different as a result. Determinism doesn't recommend any fatalist attitude about inescapable futures of persons. This fatalist view of human actions frequently (though not always) rests on a supernatural or mystical stance that is being avoided in our discussions here. Instead, we shall be focusing on the more plausible scientific hypothesis offered us in Determinism.

Determinism and science

We have seen that one needn't consult science in order to understand and appreciate the thesis of Determinism. Still, the *plausibility* of the view that the present state of the universe is a necessary consequence of previous states is closely associated with the methods and objectives of modern science. Let's see if we can't understand a bit more clearly why many philosophers regard Determinism as a plausible scientifically-informed view.

Consider again what seems intuitively correct about our universe, namely that at every point in space and time it is a certain way, down to the very smallest detail. There are a certain number of hairs on your head now, each of them are a particular length; every grain of sand on the beach is a determinate size and shape, and stands in a precise spatial relation to every other grain of sand; and so on. To say that there is only an approximate number of hairs on your head, or that their length is indeterminate, or that the individual grains of sand have no particular shape at all strikes us as clearly wrong. What does seem correct is that we don't *know* the exact number of hairs on your head, but can at best approximate the number, and that in general we don't know the particular ways things are down to the smallest level of detail. This confession of ignorance isn't particularly troubling: we expect that if a lot were riding on knowledge of this sort, we could develop the proper scientific methods for coming by it. We expect this in part because we believe that there is something determinate there to be discovered and known.

Now the determinist has recommended that we acknowledge pretty much the same account of how *changes* occur in the universe. All of those particular facts about the universe at any moment, down to the finest detail, are fixed by the particular facts that obtained at earlier moments. Again we may not know all of these details nor the physical laws connecting them, but we nevertheless suppose there are such details and laws to be known, to be discovered and explained. Thus an omniscient being who knew all such details and laws of nature could explain why the universe is precisely *this* way, rather than some other, by citing precisely how the universe was earlier. Similarly, just as the past uniquely determines the present, so the present state of the universe uniquely fixes the state of things a moment from now. If the universe had been different earlier, it would be different now; but given the actual past and the laws of nature, things could not be otherwise than they are.

This picture of how one could in principle deduce the future states of the universe from the past and laws of nature is a picture many philosophers have recognized in the methods of science. Science, we know, does more than simply describe the goings-on in the physical universe: it attempts to explain and predict those goings-on, and in doing this modern science has been enormously successful. Leave aside prediction for a moment, and consider scientific explanation. Explaining past and present phenomenon requires that one adduce the laws that natural processes obey and the relevant antecedent conditions that obtained before the events to be explained took place. Given these, a scientist has done all there is to do in explaining why something occurs: the natural universe is subject to laws telling us that, when things are *this* way at some time, they will be a certain way a later time; things *were* that way earlier, and that is why they are this certain way now.

This little sketch of explanation captures the important elements in one of the most famous and longstanding models for scientific explanation. The *deductive-nomological* account of explanation recommends that propositions expressing the occurrence of certain events can be deduced from propositions expressing the laws of nature and prior conditions. Let P be a statement describing those prior conditions, and let L be a statement of laws of nature connecting events of one kind with events of another kind (these will likely be "if-then" or conditional statements of the form: if P, then E). How the universe is now (E) will follow from these two statements.

P (expressing the state of the universe a moment ago)
L (expressing laws that govern states of the universe)
So,   E (expressing how the universe is now)

Recall the strong connection between premises and conclusion in a valid deductive argument (see Chapter 2, Section 1B). The deductive validity of correct explanations, on this model, shows that the occurrence of the phenomenon to be explained (i.e., how the universe is now) necessarily follows from relevant facts about the laws of nature and the way things were earlier. And that is precisely the picture Determinism offers us when claiming that one could in principle deduce the future states of the universe from the past and laws of nature.

The elements of scientific explanation just presented also figure in scientific prediction. Consider the motion of a rocket. At any particular moment the rocket is in a certain place, going in a certain direction, having a certain speed and rotation and so on. Given perfect knowledge of the whole truth about the rocket at that moment, together with the laws of nature, an omniscient being could deduce the place and speed and rotation (etc.) of the rocket a moment later.

As before, it is clear that we do not know the particular facts about our universe or its laws in sufficient detail to actually perform such predictions. We are able to predict the trajectory of a rocket within only a certain range of precision, not because there is something indeterminate or sloppy about how the universe goes, but because there are some details—about hidden weaknesses in a piece of metal, factors regarding distant thermal inversions, or whatever—either unknown to us, or known to us but subject to laws we have yet to make precise. According to Determinism, it is only such restrictions on human knowledge that introduce an element of chance into our predictions: there are no elements of chance out there in the world of the objects themselves.

Recognizing this last fact, about the source of chance in our descriptions of the universe, helps to dispel one apparent difficulty with Determinism. It is sometimes thought that the random and unpredictable behavior of dice or the roulette wheel shows that determinism must be false. The proper account of this phenomenon, the determinist will recommend, must be given in terms of our ignorance. As humans we are ignorant of too much about the die's history and its present state to deduce its future state after rolling off of our hand. Given the relatively small number of possible outcomes for the die and the overwhelmingly large amount of information needed to predict successfully the actual outcome, we can use dice for "games of chance." Nevertheless, there is nothing chancy or objectively random about the behavior of the plastic cube. The cube, like everything else in the natural world, is subject to laws of nature, and its present state there on the table (showing a '6') is determined by its past circumstances and the laws of nature.

Remember that the determinist intends this sort of story, about the medium-sized and familiar objects of our universe, to apply to the universe as a whole. Given the actual past and the laws of our physical universe, there is exactly one possible future.

Questions: *How is Determinism defined? What does Determinism have to say about future events? How does Determinism differ from Fatalism? Is there any reason to think Determinism is true?*

Section 4: INCOMPATIBILISM

Earlier in this chapter we encountered the view, common among many philosophers, that free will is impossible if Determinism is true. Is this view true? If so, those finding both free will and determinism intuitively correct are faced with the uncomfortable threat of holding incompatible beliefs. Having now discussed the theses of free will and Determinism separately in some detail, let's return to take a closer look at the relation between them.

Can we be free if Determinism is true?

In focusing on the relation between free will and Determinism, we are not addressing the questions of whether we do in fact have free will, or whether Determinism is true: rather, our concern is to discover whether a person can consistently believe both theses. That is, we are concerned to discover whether free will is compatible with Determinism.

Perhaps the simplest, most direct way of expressing the intuition that free will and Determinism are *incompatible* is to emphasize the following important difference between them. According to the free will thesis, we are at least sometimes faced with alternative courses of action, each of which we can perform. Such alternative courses of action represent possible ways things could later be, that is, genuinely alternative possible futures given the actual past. According to the thesis of Determinism, however, there is at every moment exactly one possible future given the actual past. This important difference captures what seems (by the lights of many philosophers, anyway) to be a fundamental incompatibility between free will and Determinism.

Can we unpack that simple sketch of Incompatibilism? For purposes of discussion, it will be helpful to have an argument showing a bit more clearly why, if Determinism is true, we are not free with respect to any of our actions. Let us suppose for the sake of argument that Determinism is true, and then inquire whether, in such a universe, agents can act freely.

The incompatibilist argument

If Determinism were true, then every event would be determined to occur, exactly as it does, by the past and the laws of nature. Now, since any action an agent performs is an event, it would follow that any action by an agent would be determined to occur exactly as it does by the past and the laws of nature. This would be true for the event of your sneezing, and it would be true for the events of your raising your arm, sitting in the theater balcony, and so on.

Now according to our understanding of free will, an agent performs an action freely only if he could do otherwise than perform that action. And clearly, given our assumption that Determinism is true, he could do otherwise than perform that action only if he has control over the factors determining that action or event—only if at least some of the determining factors are up to him. According to Determinism, those factors are simply the past and the laws of nature. But no one has control over the laws of nature, which are true independent of what men might think or do. And clearly no one could now have control over events that have already happened, nor could it ever be up to someone what happened before they were born.

Since no agent has control over the factors determining what he does, he couldn't do otherwise than what he does. But this is just to say that he isn't free, that he has no free will. We must conclude, then, that if Determinism is true, we have no free will. Free will and Determinism are incompatible.

The argument just sketched can be put more succinctly as follows (where "S" stands for any agent whatsoever, and "x" stands for any action the agent performs).

(1) Determinism is true. (Assume for the sake of the argument)
(2) So, every event is determined by the past (P) and the laws of nature (L).
(3) So, S's doing x is determined by P and L.
(4) S could do otherwise than x only if S has control over P or L.
(5) S doesn't have control over either P or L.
(6) So, S could not do otherwise than x.
(7) So, S isn't free with respect to x.

Since this argument applies to any agent S and any action x, we can conclude that

(8) If Determinism were true, no one would have free will.

(We might have run a somewhat different argument here, beginning with the assumption that we do have free will and going on to show that Determinism would then be false.)

If this argument is acceptable, then we must conclude that the thesis of Determinism and the free will thesis cannot both be true. If Determinism is true, then the free will thesis is false; if the free will thesis is true, then Determinism is false. (Of course, it could be that both theses are false.) It is this consequence to which we shall refer with the shorthand "Incompatibilism".

Questions: What does the incompatibilist say about free will and Determinism? What argument is offered for Incompatibilism?

Section 5: INDETERMINISM

The tension between free will and Determinism is serious. Determinism is a plausible thesis about the lawful nature of change in the universe, and seems to figure as an important part of our scientific world view. And yet free will is equally plausible: it certainly seems to us that we perform many of our actions freely, and without free will we cannot be held morally responsible for any of our behavior. Faced with Incompatibilism, what should we do?

Many of us will be inclined to suggest that giving up free will is giving up too much. The notion that most of our behavior is genuinely up to us—that alternatives to our actual behavior are within our power to perform—is central to our concept of persons as moral agents. Too much *else* must also be given up, in denying free will, to make that choice a reasonable one. We must chose to reject determinism instead.

What is Indeterminism?

The evidence of contemporary theorizing in quantum mechanics seems to weigh in favor of rejecting Determinism instead of free will. As many scientists and philosophers understand it, this physical theory entails that some occurrences are indeterministic, in the sense that the physical laws and the past do not determine some events in the submicroscopic domain. An omniscient being, knowing all there is to know about the laws of nature and the prior conditions up through a certain moment, could not deduce what will happen after that moment. The actual evidence for there being such events is not our concern here; what we can say, however, is that if there are such indeterminacies in nature, then Determinism is false.

Indeterminism is the thesis that Determinism is false. This thesis does not entail that every event is undetermined by the past and laws of nature; rather, it is the view that not every event is so determined. If there is one event in the history of the universe that is not determined by its antecedent conditions and the laws of nature, then Determinism is false and Indeterminism is true.

Perhaps an example will help to clarify the relevant points of difference. Consider an electric light with a switch to turn it off and on. Normally we would say that if everything is properly wired and if there is sufficient current supplied to the circuit—in short, given suitable prior conditions—then the light must go on when we turn on the switch. Laws of nature govern what electrons will do under the conditions of a properly wired light circuit. When the switch is turned on, only one thing can happen: the light must go on. But now imagine that we have set up a certain device (sometimes called a Geiger device) rendering it a random, undetermined matter whether the light goes on when the switch is flipped on. In such a case, the laws of nature and the relevant facts about the electrons and wires and such will not suffice to determine whether the light will go on. Sometimes when we flip the switch the light goes on, and sometimes when we flip the switch the light does not go on.

Notice that if Indeterminism is true, then given the laws of nature and the past history of the universe, there is more than one possible future. Immediately prior to the occurrence of some undetermined event, there are no facts determining that the event will occur. We have, then, at least two possible futures, at least one in which the event happens and at least one in which the event does not. Each future is a physical possibility since the laws of nature, together with the past facts, do not rule out such a future's actually obtaining. In the example described above, whenever we flip the switch we face two possible futures—one in which the light goes on, and one in which it does not. Whichever event in fact occurs after a particular flipping of the switch, we can nevertheless truly say that the other event could have happened, too.

Indeterminism and freedom

Let's return again to the issue of freedom. The person who accepts the free will thesis must conclude that any human behavior determined by the past and the laws of nature can not be genuinely free behavior. Such actions are not really up to the agent to perform, because the agent could not have done otherwise than act in exactly that way. If we are to find cases in which people exercise free will, then, we must look for events that are not completely determined by the past and the laws of nature. And it is precisely this class of events which Indeterminism seems to offer us. Indeterminism entails that some events are such that, in exactly the same circumstances, they might not have occurred after all. At the moment of flipping the Geiger-switch, both the light's coming on and its failing to come on are physically possible ways the universe can go. Intuitively, this sort of case is what the free will thesis requires: according to it, we are at least sometimes faced with alternative courses of action, each of which we can perform—each of which is a genuinely alternative possible future given the actual past.

Suppose that your arm's rising during lecture a moment ago was not determined by the past (the antecedent states of your arm and your brain, etc.) and laws of nature. It is then true that you *could* either raise your arm or not raise your arm, much as it is true that the light could go on and also remain off. So, if Indeterminism is true, it looks as though there might be cases in which we perform certain actions, and it will be correctly said that we could have done otherwise than what we did. It appears that if Indeterminism is true, then having free will is at least possible.

But there is a problem with this analysis. The sense of "could have done otherwise" that arises when we consider Indeterminism is not the sense we use when we speak of having free will. If an action of ours is undetermined, then we could have done otherwise only in the sense that we *might* have done otherwise: for all we know the action might not have taken place. But this is not the sense of "could have done otherwise" that free will demands, where it is meant that we have an ability or a power to do otherwise, or that not doing otherwise was up to us. Indeterminism merely allows for other possible futures, it does not entail that agents have any control over what future will be the actual one.

If an action of yours is undetermined, then there are no determining factors, and it is not under the complete control of anything or anyone. It is said to be spontaneous or random. Consider the case in which you find your arm going up in the air, and suppose this is an undetermined event. Then you are not responsible for this happening; in fact, you will likely find it incredible and puzzling that your arm is in the air.

Indeterminism leaves us with no free will. Whether an event is determined or undetermined, we have no control over that event. It is not in our power to do either A or not-A since if A is determined to happen by the past and laws of nature, then it must happen, and we cannot force the future to go otherwise. If A is undetermined, then it is spontaneous or random, and so still is not under our control.

Questions: What is Indeterminism? Why would free will be impossible if Indeterminism is true?

Section 6: THE DILEMMA

If simple Indeterminism fails to permit free will, the original tension between Determinism and freedom might seem all the more pressing. But perhaps we should recognize instead that the tension is, in a way, resolved. On the picture that seems to have developed thus far, free will is simply impossible, leaving nothing for Determinism to threaten. Let's see how one might attempt to show that there can be no free will.

A dilemma is a form of argument in which the arguer defends his conclusion by first presenting two alternatives, together exhausting all logical possibilities, and then claiming that each alternative entails the conclusion. Since the alternatives are exhaustive, the conclusion must follow.

An argument of this sort may now be constructed to show that free will is impossible. The incompatibilist argument has shown us that if Determinism is true, then we have no free will; and we have also seen that if Determinism is false (and Indeterminism is true), then the existence of free will is again not possible. Since determinism must be either true or false, and on either account we have no free will, we must conclude that we have no free will, indeed, that we couldn't have free will. The dilemma looks like this.

(1)   Either Determinism is true or it is false.
(2)   If Determinism is true, then we have no free will.
(3)   If Determinism is false (and so Indeterminism is true), then we have no free will.
(4)   So, we have no free will.

Although the dilemma seems to show us that its conclusion is inescapable, many will find the conclusion unacceptable. Many of us do firmly believe that we are responsible for our actions, that we can be praised or blamed for behaving in certain ways, and that this necessarily entails that we are free. But if we have an acceptable argument supporting the conclusion that we are not free, what is the reasonable person supposed to do? We have, after all, defended each of the premises with other arguments, and in each case the argument seemed sound. We are faced, then, with an argument that appears to be sound for a conclusion that appears to be false.

The reasonable person, if he cannot accept the conclusion of a valid argument, must assume that one of the premises is false and that the argument used to defend that premise is unsound. Which premise do we attack? And how should we proceed to attack it? In the following sections we will look at a couple of attempts to show that one of premises (2) or (3) is false.

One way to get started is to consider whether our understanding of the views in question—free will, Determinism, Indeterminism—might have been misguided or incomplete. Determinism and Indeterminism seem to be relatively straightforward theories; since the notion of a free will, on the other hand, proves to be much more difficult to analyze, we might begin by rethinking what it is to have free will. After all, our understanding of free actions has been left rather intuitive, on the level of calling them "up to us" or of requiring that we "could have done otherwise." These expressions might be explored more carefully. In this way, we may hope to locate some misguided assumptions about the nature of free will, at work in arguments for premises (2) and (3).

Questions: What is a dilemma? What dilemma is offered for the conclusion that we do not have free will?

Section 7: COMPATIBILISM

Compatibilism is the view that the thesis of Determinism and the thesis that we have free will are compatible. Denying the second premise of our dilemma, the compatibilist will contend that an action can be both determined and free. We'll turn first to the history of philosophy and examine John Locke's account of freedom. As we'll see, Locke seems to think we can admit that persons do have freedom without denying that actions and events have causes. Next we'll look carefully at how a compatibilist might respond explicitly to the incompatibilist's argument, which was constructed to show that freedom and Determinism are incompatible.

Locke on freedom and the will

Before setting out Locke's compatibilist view we need to consider his ideas about the will and freedom (or liberty). The will, Locke tells us, is

> a Power to begin or forbear, continue or end several actions of our minds, and motions of our bodies, barely by a thought or preference of the mind ordering, or as it were the commanding the doing or not doing such or such a particular action.[4]

Willing to do something, then, seems to be no more than the mind's perferring to do something or to refrain from doing something. This preference is what orders or commands the mind or body to act or not act in certain ways. If you stand up because you willed it, then you stood up because of a certain preference the mind had for standing;

and if you did not stand because that is what you willed, then you continued sitting because that is what you preferred.

What about freedom or, as Locke often says, liberty? He suggests that

> the idea of liberty is the idea of a power in any agent to do or forbear any particular action, according to the determination or thought of the mind, whereby either of them is preferred to the other. (*Essay*, II, xxi, 8)

Notice here that as Locke defines the idea of liberty it is an idea of a power also. In this case, however, to act freely (out of liberty) the agent must have the power to do or not do something in accordance with whatever is preferred or willed.

Several comments are in order. First, the power that Locke calls "liberty" or "freedom" differs from the power Locke refers to as the will. We'll see why in a moment. Second, Locke does not talk about having free will, or about the will being free. Why not? Because "the will is nothing but one power or ability, and freedom another power or ability: so to ask, whether the will has freedom, is to ask whether one power has another power."[5] We can properly say that an agent is free (or has the power of freedom) but it is misleading at best to suggest that the will (a power itself) has the power of freedom.

Voluntary and free action

To understand more fully Locke's definition of freedom consider the following case. You find yourself in a room with someone whose company you enjoy very much. Unbeknownst to you, the only door has been locked so you could not leave if you tried to. But you don't try to leave because you prefer staying and conversing with your friend. You are imprisoned (in a sense) but you choose to stay where you are with no preference for leaving. Are you staying freely?

Something seems wrong with the idea that staying is a free act on your part. But surely the act is voluntary: you are there because you want to be. Locke explains the situation by distinguishing free acts from voluntary acts. (*Essay*, II, xxi, 10) In a voluntary act, you do what you do because you want to. In an involuntary act, you do what you do regardless of what you want. Breathing is an involuntary act (merely reflex) since you don't do it because you want to (although you may very well be happy that you are breathing and want to continue breathing). But raising your hand, or sitting in the room, might be voluntary acts: you perform them because you want to.

Now, even though you raise your hand or sit in the room because you want to, it might not be true that you could refrain from doing so if that were what you wanted. Such is the case we mentioned above. Even though the door is locked behind you, you stay because that is what you will. Your staying is said to be voluntary. But liberty or freedom requires that you be able to refrain from doing what you are doing, if that is what you should want. In the scenario we presented above, while you remain in the room voluntarily, you are not there freely because you don't have the power to do otherwise, should that be what you want.

Remember that Locke understands liberty as a power to do or refrain from doing an action, according to what one wills to do. So it is not just that you do something because that is what you willed (a voluntary action), but it must also be true that you have the power to do otherwise if that is what you will. In the locked room case, you can't do otherwise than what you do. You aren't free to stay because you lack the power to leave.

An important question remains. What determines the will? Locke, as we have seen, argues that the will is not said to be free. We cannot say that a person can will as he pleases (that he is at liberty to will) since that is to suggest that one wills to will, that one has a certain power over a power. We might then ask whether one is at liberty to will to will what he did, which leads to an infinite regress of willing to will to will, etc. But this infinite regress of willing is absurd. Instead Locke tells us that the will is determined by the mind. And what moves the mind? The mind determines the will to change because of a certain uneasiness or dissatisfaction, as when someone in pain desires to relieve it, or when someone is hungry and thereby desires to eat. The mind's motive for staying the same is its satisfaction with its present state. The general point here is that the person may have a preference for performing (or not performing) a particular action and this preference may be determined by the current circumstances.

> He that has his chains knocked off, and the Prison-doors set open to him, is perfectly at liberty, because he may either go or stay, as he best likes; though his preference be determined to stay by the darkness of the night, or illness of the weather, or want of other lodging. (*Essay*, II, xxi, 33 (first edition))

With this we can see how Locke's notion of freedom is compatible with Determinism. To hold Locke's theory of freedom, one need not deny that every event, including the event of willing something to happen or not, is determined by the past and the laws of nature. What determines the will is irrelevant to whether a person acts freely, that is, whether he acts in accordance with his will and could have acted otherwise if he so willed.

A problem for Locke's view

Although we will confront the incompatibilist's response to Compatibilism later, we should, at this point, raise at least one criticism of Locke's ideas. We need to ask, first, Can we be free if we have no power over the will? and second, Can we be free if the will is in fact determined by events and laws of nature over which we have no control? Return to the locked door example above. Suppose that instead of locking the door I make it impossible that you *will* to leave (I make you want to stay). You could leave if you wanted to, but, because I have implanted a device in your brain that controls your will, you can't want to. Locke's definition of freedom is satisfied but it is clear that you are not staying of your own free will.

Although this example is rather fanciful, a less strange example will fit the determinist's scheme. According to Determinism, every event is determined, including the event of your willing to stay in the room. Even if I do not implant a device in your brain to determine your wanting to stay, Determinism implies that past events and the laws of nature determine your wanting to stay. Could you, under those conditions, be said to be free, even if you satisfy Locke's idea of freedom?

The compatibilist's strategy

Turning from Locke's account of Compatibilism, let's look at a more specific response to the argument for the incompatibility of free will and Determinism. The argument for Incompatibilism increases the tension between our plausible belief that we sometimes act of our own free will, and our equally plausible belief that the future is determined by the past and the laws of nature (Determinism). The incompatibilist's argument, recall, concludes that if Determinism is true, then we have no free will. If we want to relieve this tension, defending the *compatibility* of Determinism and free will, we shall have to find some error in the argument for Incompatibilism.

Compatibilists, who believe that free will is compatible with Determinism, will indeed claim that there is a false premise in the argument for Incompatibilism. Their response might begin something like this. To do philosophy well, they will remind us, one must have a clear and precise understanding of the concepts one is employing. If one makes unwarranted assumptions about a concept, or if one misapplies a concept, then mistakes are bound to arise. So, let us think a bit harder about the concept of free will. We have said that to do action A freely, it must be that you could do otherwise than A. But exactly what does it mean to say that you could do otherwise? It may be that a second, deeper inquiry into the meaning of this expression will yield a much clearer understanding of free will. And perhaps having done this adequately we will see whether our reasoning for the incompatibility of free will and Determinism is flawed.

Think again about situations in which you clearly would not be acting freely, as in the situation opening this chapter: you find your arm rising without intending to raise it, asking your instructor a philosophical question you had never entertained. These are not acts of free will because because you do not will them at all, and however much you want to lower your arm and be silent, you can not. Whatever is determining your arm to rise, your action is clearly *not in accord with your wants and desires*. Your arm rises for some reason other than your decision to raise it.

A similar case arises if you desired to raise your arm but could not, perhaps because your arm was tied to your side. Here again we would say you are not free to raise your arm, precisely because your action is not issuing from your desires but from something else. Even if you desire to do otherwise than leave your arm down, you cannot do otherwise.

Now consider cases in which we would be inclined, at least in our nonphilosophical moments, to say that you act freely. Aren't these simply cases in which you do what you desire to do? You deliberate for a moment about whether to raise your arm; after deciding in favor of doing so, you raise it. You raise your arm in this situation *because* you want to, *because* you choose to. Your arm is not restrained or constrained in any way: unlike cases where you are not free, here *your action is in accord with your wants and desires*. You would have done otherwise than raise your hand, should you have desired to do otherwise.

If these reflections on the nature of free action are correct, then one way to cash out the meaning of "S could have done otherwise than A" is in terms of the conditional statement, "S would have done otherwise than A if S had wanted (or chosen) to." To say that someone *could* have done other than they did (that they have the ability to take another course of action) is to say what they *would* do were circumstances different. We shall call this the *conditional analysis* of the expression "S could have done otherwise than A."

The conditional analysis

To present an analysis of a statement or expression is to present another statement or expression that can be substituted for it without loss of meaning. Because the analysis employs more basic concepts, it makes clearer what the original meant. Thus, we might analyze the expression "being a bachelor" in terms of "being a unmarried adult male." This latter expression employs several concepts that are well-understood, and is more easily understood by someone needing an explanation of what bachelors are. If an analysis is adequate, then we can replace the one expression with the other. To say that my Uncle Joe is a *bachelor* is just to say that my Uncle Joe is an *unmarried adult male*: if the former is true, the latter must be, too.

The compatibilist's conditional analysis attempts a similar result. The expression

Agent S could have done otherwise than action A

can be replaced with the following expression, which serves as its analysis:

Agent S would have done otherwise than action A, if S had wanted to.

The conditional analysis makes explicit what we think is really crucial to freedom, namely, that one's free actions are determined by one's wants and desires. The compatibilist denies that free actions could be anything like undetermined events. Rather, to be free in the relevant sense, an agent's actions must be *determined*, but in the appropriate way: they must be determined by the agent's wanting (choosing, desiring) to perform the action. You raise your arm freely when it rises *because* you wanted it up. Your arm is thus determined to rise, but the significant determining factor is your wanting to raise it (or your deciding to raise it). This explains why we would be surprised if, having decided to raise our arm, it remained motionless: we suppose that, when we are free, our decisions to act will necessarily issue in our acting.

In Section 4 above the incompatibilist argued that if Determinism were true, then your raising your hand could not have been otherwise than it was and so was not free. You could be no more responsible for your actions than you are for catching a cold. But the compatibilist can respond that in one sense of "couldn't do otherwise" your raising your hand and your catching a cold are similar cases and the incompatibilist is correct. Given the past and the laws of nature, your catching the cold and your raising your hand were events that couldn't fail to happen. The past and the laws of nature brought about your catching the cold and your raising your hand. But there is another important sense of "couldn't do otherwise" in which the two cases are different and the incompatibilist is wrong. This is the sense in which "could do otherwise" means "would have done otherwise, if you had wanted to." It may be false to say that you could have done otherwise than catch the cold in the sense that it's false to say that *you would have refrained from catching the cold, if you had wanted to refrain from catching it.* Still, it may be true that you could have done otherwise than raise your hand in the sense that it is true that *you would have refrained from raising your hand, if you wanted to refrain from raising it.*

If your wanting to raise your arm is not a determining factor of your arm's rising, then it is false to say that you would have done otherwise than raise it if you had wanted to. In that case, you would not be free, for you would want to do otherwise—say, leave your arm down—and yet your arm would rise. Your action, we say, would not be in accordance with your desires; your action was not determined by your choice, but by something else.

A reply to the incompatibilist argument

Having offered the conditional analysis as a way of properly understanding the notion of free will, the compatibilist will recommend that we take a second look at the argument for Incompatibilism. The compatibilist will argue that acting freely is compatible with being determined to act in that manner. All that is required is that one of the determining factors in your doing A over not-A be your wanting or choosing to do A.

Recall again the incompatibilist's argument:

(1) Determinism is true. (Assume for the sake of the argument)
(2) So, every event is determined by the past (P) and the laws of nature (L).
(3) So, S's doing x is determined by P and L.
(4) S could do otherwise than x only if S has control over P or L.
(5) S doesn't have control over either P or L.
(6) So, S could not do otherwise than x.
(7) So, S isn't free with respect to x.

Premise (4) is where the expression "could do otherwise" first appears. Suppose now that we replace this expression with the appropriate conditional expression, which the compatibilist has recommended as its complete analysis. Doing so, the compatibilist will argue, will not change the argument in any way except to make clearer what it is saying. Thus, premise (4) becomes

(4*) S would do otherwise than x, if S wanted to, [but] only if S has control over the past or the laws of nature.

We might also then replace premise 6 with

(6*) So, even if S wanted to do otherwise than x, S would not do otherwise.

The idea is that, if the conditional analysis is correct, (4*) says just what (4) says, and (6*) says just what (6) says. Having this clearer version of the argument before us, the compatibilist thinks we are in a better position to ask how it fares.

The compatibilist will argue that (4*) is false. According to this premise, your doing otherwise than you do requires that you have control over the past and the laws of nature. But why believe this is correct? Even if you have no control over the past or over the laws of nature, it can still be the case that, if the past had been such that you wanted to do something other than x, you *would* have done it. You would have done other than x because freedom requires that our behavior be properly determined by our wants and desires: had you desired to do otherwise, you would have done otherwise.

Suppose, then, that you walk into the theater and decide to sit in the front row. If Determinism is true, then your sitting there was an event determined by the past and the laws of nature. So? So had the past been different, a different future would have ensued: *if* you had decided to sit near the back, you would have sat *there*. And that is all we need for freedom, surely. You sit where you decide to sit. In this commonplace example, then, we can see that acting freely is consistent with Determinism. It is consistent because acting in accordance with our desires is consistent with the past and laws of nature determining our action, so long as one of the past determining factors is a desire of ours.

And now look again at (6*). It seems clearly false, too: it simply isn't true that, if you had wanted to do otherwise than x, you would not do otherwise. Rather, when your desires are the proper determining factors of your behavior, if you wanted to do otherwise, you *would* have done otherwise.

So much the worse for the incompatibilist argument, the compatibilist will thus recommend. On a proper understanding of "could have done otherwise", we can see that the argument has at least one false premise, and indeed a false conclusion. Since the assumption of Determinism does not require us to give up the possibility that S could have done otherwise than x had he wanted to, we can avoid the dilemma of free will after all.

A problem with the conditional analysis

What can be said in response to the compatibilist's conditional analysis? Given this deeper understanding of the phrase "could have done otherwise", have we been shown that the incompatibilist's argument is unsound, and have we been thereby given good reason to believe that free will is compatible with Determinism?

In answering these questions, return to the story about your choosing to sit in the front row at the theater. Even if it is true that, had the past been different such that you wanted to sit in the balcony, you would have sat there, should we say with the compatibilist that, in the actual case, you freely sit in the front row? Remember that we are working under the assumption that Determinism is true. Thus, we are assuming that *every* event is determined to happen just as it does by the past and the laws of nature. And here is where the problem for the conditional analysis arises. Not only is your sitting where you sit determined in part by what you want to do, or by what you decide to do, but *your so desiring and deciding are determined as well*. That is, given the past and the laws of nature, you could not have desired and decided otherwise than you in fact did. Your acting as you want or choose is free only if your wanting and choosing are under your control. And clearly they wouldn't be if Determinism were true. It is of course true to say that, *if* you had chosen to sit in the balcony then you would have, but that is of no consequence here, for you couldn't have chosen to sit there.

Returning to a criticism we made of Locke's view on freedom, consider a rather extravagant case in which Martians have implanted a remote control device in your brain that completely governs your reasoning processes and fixes your wants and desires. Suppose the Martians use their device to make you deliberate in a particular way and consequently decide to make your way to the front row. You sit there because you want to, but the Martians control what you want. Again, it remains true that if you had wanted to sit in the balcony, then you would have done that. Still it is not up to you where you sit, because your wants and desires are not in your control. You would not be held responsible for your behavior by anyone who knew that the Martians controlled your desires.

Of course, we needn't appeal to such extravagant cases to make the point. Of many (otherwise healthy) comatose patients, it is true to say "If she wanted to get up and go to a movie, then she would do it;" but clearly the patient is not free to get up, because their mental states are not in their control. Even more relevant to the normal lives of you and I, we should note that if Determinism is true, there are all sorts of influences on our decisions and desires that are outside of our control. If Determinism is true, our psychological history, genetic structure, socio-economic background, among other factors, will doubtless play a significant part in wholly determining what we believe and what we want to do.

We can conclude, then, that the conditional analysis of the expression "S could have done otherwise than x" fails to capture what we have in mind when we say that a person is free. The incompatibilist argument for the conclusion that *if Determinism is true, then we have no free will* stands as a sound argument.

Questions: What is Compatibilism? How does Locke understand freedom? Why does he refuse to say that the will can be free? How are voluntary actions distinguished from free actions? What motivates the will according to Locke? What problem arises for his view? What is the conditional analysis and why would anyone think it is correct? How does the compatibilist read the incompatibilist's argument so that it appears to be unsound? What objection can be raised against the conditional analysis?

Section 8: AGENCY THEORY

Few philosophers—or even non-philosophers, for that matter—would be eager to accept the thesis that we are not free agents. The traditional problem of free will is primarily the problem of showing that we do indeed have free will. After a relatively long excursion through several views about the nature of human action and change in the natural world, we are left with the dilemma of free will, wondering now whether it is even possible to be free and to have moral responsibility.

A. Avoiding the Dilemma

The strategy

The compatibilist's attempt to show the dilemma unsound by denying premise (2)—If Determinism is true, then we have no free will—fares poorly. The conditional analysis of claims of the form *S could have done otherwise* fails to capture the sense of freedom we have in mind when describing ourselves as morally responsible free agents. If we are still concerned to rescue free will, the only remaining step seems to deny premise three in the dilemma:

(3) If Determinism is false (and hence Indeterminism is true), then we have no free will.

But denying (3) hardly looks hopeful. Our discussion of Indeterminism seems to have shown that it, too, is inconsistent with the claim that we are free agents, for if those events undetermined by the past and the laws of nature are spontaneous and random, we cannot be said to have such events within our control.

Thinking again about human freedom

Notice an important gap in our discussion of events thus far. Until now, we have supposed that events must either be determined by the past and laws of nature, or else be undetermined in the sense that they are random events over which we could have no control. That is, we've supposed that either our arm's rising *must* occur given the prior circumstances, or else our arm's rising *merely happened* to occur, and could have failed to occur, since there is nothing from which its occurrence follows. What we must now recognize is that this dichotomy may well be false: indeed, it leaves aside an important feature of our most intuitively correct descriptions of human freedom. We must see that, in cases of acting freely, if it is false that the event is determined by the past events (plus the laws of nature), and if it is also false that the event is brought about by nothing at all, then it must be true that *something other than an event brings it about*.

Consider, then, that when we typically speak of free actions, we speak naturally and plausibly of *someone's* bringing about those actions or events. If you walk to the theater balcony freely, for example, then surely it is *you* who brings it about that your legs move so as to get to the balcony. If we take this point seriously, acknowledging it as crucial to understanding the concept of human freedom, then we can understand why some philosophers object to the dilemma of free will on the grounds that it has quite ignored this option of *agent causation*. Premise (3) above, they will say, is false. While it may well be that some events are determined by other (previous) events, and also that some events are brought about by nothing whatsoever (if Indeterminism is true), an important class of events remains, namely, those brought about by agents.

What the thesis of agent causation offers, in short, is a way of driving a wedge between Determinism and the simple version of Indeterminism discussed earlier. If there can be events undetermined by the past and laws of nature but not thereby random or spontaneous, it may be possible to rescue free will after all. And there *are* such events as that, the agency theorist will tell us. On any workable view of persons as free agents, we must take seriously those natural and plausible claims to the effect that *we* do things, that things are within *our* power to perform or not perform, that it is up to *us* what we do.

Agency

Insofar as it requires persons themselves to figure centrally in the final story of human action, agency theory undeniably accords well with the intuition that humans are responsible for their actions. It does this by building into the theory explicitly the notion that human persons have powers to bring events about, and that it is ultimately them, not something else or nothing at all, which we must reckon as the causal source of free actions.

Still, this notion of human agency is far from clear. When a person raises his arm, surely he doesn't *do* anything to his arm, and still less does he do anything to his brain. One can of course do things to one's arms or brain in pretty much the same way as one does something to another's arm or brain. But if the agency theorist is not suggesting that when we walk to the balcony, we act on our arms and brains the way we act on a puppet by moving it with strings, then what exactly is meant by an agent's bringing something about?

The main point that agency theory underscores is that, when a person performs a free action, the behavior is not brought about by other events or changes within the agent; the theory denies that free action could be determined by something *other* than the agent. It is remains true that certain events will be involved in the final story of such actions: events involving certain muscular events bring about your legs moving thus-and so; certain neural events in your brain bring about those muscular contractions. But from none of this does it follow that such neural events cannot be made to happen by you, immediately prior to your moving to the balcony. Indeed, it may be precisely in this sense that your willing—your deciding or choosing—issues in your going to the balcony.

An agent, then, even if the locus of many events large and small, is not to be regarded as some mere collection of particles, nor of some series of events. Rather, an agent is an active substance—a thing with powers that by its very nature can bring about events we call free acts. When you say that you perform some act freely, you believe that the action was within *your* power, the exercise of which brings the action about, and that your exercise of power is closely associated with what we call willing or deciding or choosing. We do not say that our heartbeat or reflex actions are free acts of ours, precisely because we do not believe that they issue from our wills: we don't cause them. Since our heartbeat (etc.) is an event with which we have nothing immediately to do, and is not within our power to bring about or refrain from bringing about, it is not free behavior of ours.

If coherent, the notion that an agent can bring about an event, without some previous events determining his doing so, secures the possibility of human freedom. Genuinely free acts cannot be random, and on this account they are not: the agent brings them about. Nor can genuinely free acts be determined in the sense a determinist has in mind, and on this account they are not: to say that you acted freely in going to the balcony is to say that it is possible for the laws (L) and the prior conditions (P) to be exactly as they actually are, but you instead walk to sit down toward the front rows.

B. Remaining Questions

It could scarcely be said that agency theory is unobjectionably plain sailing. Despite the effort just expended toward clarifying the concept of an agent's bringing something about, a good deal of obscurity remains in the notion of a *thing* (substance, being), rather than an event, causing some event to occur. In closing this section, let's reflect on the difficulties associated with such a notion.

Questions about causation

Over the course of discussing a number philosophical problems, we have encountered and put to use the idea of causation often. On each occasion, we took it to be a relation between events, between happenings: the rock's striking the window, we say, caused the window's breaking. How odd it is to think of a mere *rock* (not a rock's doing something) producing an event, such as a window's breaking. Surely an inert hunk of stuff like a rock could not play the role of a cause unless it figured as part of an event giving rise to another event. Moreover, we typically think of causation in science in terms of energy being transferred from one object to another in virtue of some interaction between the two objects. But in the case of agency theory we are asked to consider not some interaction between two objects (a man and his arm), nor indeed any relation between events. We are asked, rather, to consider *the event* of his arm's rising and *the agent*. And—so far as we typically understand causation, at least—it appears that no relation between *those* two sorts of things deserves to be called causation at all.

The agency theorist says that free actions are not brought about by prior events. But if an action is not brought about by another event, isn't this just like being brought about by nothing? No, the agency theorist will say, an agent's bringing about some action is supposed here to be different from one event's being sufficient for another event, and yet it is more than an event's being brought about by nothing. But what more is there in the case where the agent produced an action? Surely the agent—his or her merely existing—is not sufficient for the occurrence of the action. How are we to understand this?

The agency theorist is likely to suggest that our notion of event causation is no less mysterious than his notion of agent causation. Even in the case of event causation, it remains difficult to say what more there is to saying "event x caused A" than there is to simply saying that x occurred and A occurred. And to whatever extent we are prepared to allow claims to the effect that x *made* A occur, oughtn't we be make a similar allowance for claims to the effect that agent S *made* A occur?

Indeed, the agency theorist may be inclined to recommend that we have a better grip on agent causation than we have on event causation. At least this much is true: we are all perfectly familiar with cases when we, as active thinking things, conjure up ideas or mental images in our imagination at will. In such cases aren't we agents producing something, namely, a mental image of some sort? (Recall here Berkeley's response to Locke's notion that inert mind-independent pieces of matter produce ideas of those ideas in us [Chapter 5].) The agency theorist might urge then that, while we really have no experience of the causal power alleged to be present when events are said to cause events, we are indeed acquainted with the power that agents exert when bringing certain happenings about, and this power, at work in cases of imagination, is no different from the power that agents exercise when willing to raise their arm.

Questions about methodology

To the extent that we judge agency theory to fall short of explaining how free will is possible, it provides us, at best, with a name for the kind of solution we would like to the dilemma against free will. Is it really possible for an agent to bring about an event, without its being some action of the agent that brings about the event? What exactly is an agent, and what is it about agents that allegedly provides for this ability? Until we have satisfactory answers to these questions, the question of how we can have free will in an indeterministic world remains problematic. We have already seen that a plausible argument can be mounted against our having free will in a deterministic world. If, when all is said and done, we really do believe that it is sometimes up to us what we do, then, as philosophers who prize rationality, we must continue to search for an adequate account of free will that avoids the dilemma presented in Section 6.

One thing this latest judgment shows is that philosophical difficulties are rarely handled in isolation: solutions to one difficulty may give raise to difficulties elsewhere. In the present case, agency theory looks promising as a way of securing the possibility of free will, but it conflicts with other commitments we have elsewhere—with certain well-entrenched views about event causation, for example.

Accepting a philosophical theory carries with it commitments. The simplest guidelines of rationality tell us that if we accept some theory, then we are also committed to accepting whatever that theory entails (its consequences). Having developed a theory to account for some phenomena or body of truths, we may discover that some of its consequences conflict with other views we have already accepted into our stock of beliefs. In our effort to be consistent, we find that we must give something up. The question facing a philosopher in such a case, as it has faced us in this chapter, is: How does one decide which of the conflicting beliefs to give up?

Contrary to what a few influential schools of philosophical thought would tell us, giving common sense the final say in decisions of this kind would be a mistake. Common sense may sometimes deserve special weight, against the threat of (say) frivolous or uncritical thought. But in the arena of philosophical inquiry, common sense must often succumb to highly developed theories, just as it often must in scientific theories: contrary to common sense, science tells us (and we tend to believe it) that strictly speaking the sun does not move, and that our chairs are mostly empty space.

Nevertheless, certain beliefs *do* seem to have a special place in our belief system, depending upon their relation to other beliefs we happen to have. One way to make a decision about which of two competing beliefs to give up—not necessarily a decision one must keep forever—is to consider carefully which of one's beliefs seem to be most fundamental, or deepest, in one's overall belief system. Not all of our beliefs are equally fundamental and momentous; rather, they stand in some order of rational preference, reflecting our present conceptual repertoire and our better and worse understanding of items in it. The most basic beliefs will be so central to our way of regarding the world that we can scarcely conceive of giving them up at all. Or, given their relation to other beliefs, perhaps giving them up would require giving up many more beliefs than if we gave up their competitors. In either case, it would be unreasonable to opt for a competitor.

Basic beliefs of the sort just described will likely include certain truths of logic, of mathematics, and about the universe and ourselves as well. That we are thinking persons, for example, seems immune to the threat of denial. And many people find the claims that we are free, that we sometimes deliberate about our actions, and that we are morally responsible to be a cluster of beliefs that we cannot reasonably doubt.

When faced with the dilemma encountered in Section 6, the rational person—should she find rationally giving up her belief that we are free inconceivable—must acknowledge that one of the premises is false. If upon some reflection she finds agency theory an initially plausible way of handling the dilemma, then, continuing in her belief that we have free will, she will attempt to defend this position. Nevertheless, she will also recognize a conflict between this way of handling the dilemma and a certain common and plausible view about causation. Should our commitment to free will run more deeply in our belief system than our inclination toward a certain view of event causation, it would be eminently reasonable to deny that event causation is the only model of how things can be brought about. From a stance such as this, a philosopher can continue rational inquiry into the possibility and nature of free will.

Questions: How does an agency theorist think about human freedom? How do agent causation and event causation differ? What questions remain for the agency theory? What is the rational person to do with the dilemma against free will if she cannot give up her belief that we have free will?

Section 9: FREE WILL AND MORAL
RESPONSIBILITY

Does moral responsibility require freedom?

We spoke above about how accepting a philosophical theory carries with it certain commitments. And earlier, when introducing the idea of free will, we suggested that having moral responsibility requires having free will. So, giving up the possibility of our having freedom seems to require that we also give up the idea that we are morally responsible for our actions. Acknowledging that the dilemma we discussed earlier has considerable force, are we at all inclined to relinquish the idea that human persons are the proper subjects of moral praise and blame? Perhaps not, and if not we are rationally obligated to reconsider the dilemma and the arguments associated with it.

But perhaps, also, we have been hasty in thinking that having moral responsibility requires having free will. In recent work on this subject, the philosopher Harry Frankfurt has argued that one could be morally responsible for a particular action and yet it still not be true that one could have done otherwise than what one did.[6] Recall that all along we have suggested that one performs an act freely only if one could have done otherwise. If Frankfurt's argument is successful, then a person could be morally responsible for an action even though he could not have done otherwise, and thus not free.

Frankfurt's counterexample

To support Frankfurt's contention we will present an example similar in form to Frankfurt's own. Suppose that a mischievous and clever spy wants a certain individual murdered but doesn't want to commit the act himself. So he finds someone, call her Patsy, who already intends to murder the selected victim. But to make sure the execution occurs, the spy fixes Patsy such that were she to change her mind, the spy would be able to make her kill the victim anyway. We might suppose that the spy has fixed Patsy's brain and nervous system such that, if her intentions change, a device will take control of Patsy and make her kill the victim. The key point is this. If Patsy keeps her intention to murder, the device will not be used and she will murder as she intends. If, however, Patsy should change her mind, the device will kick in and still she will murder the victim. Suppose, finally, that Patsy commits the murder because she wants to; her intention and not the device makes her kill the victim.

What does this example show us? As Frankfurt would have us interpret stories such as these, Patsy is morally responsible for her action. She killed someone because she wanted to. We cannot blame the spy for this murder since his device was never used (although he too seems morally corrupt). But what is interesting about the case is the fact that, given the presence of the spy's device, Patsy could not do otherwise than what she did. If she would have changed her mind, she would still have killed the victim because the implanted device would have made her. Is this then a situation in which someone is morally responsible for an action they did not perform freely?

Assessing the counterexample

We will consider two responses to the example. First, we might concede that the example does show that someone can be morally responsible for an action even though they could not have done otherwise. Does this show that someone could be morally responsible without having free will? To conclude that we also need to concede the premise that someone freely performs an act only if they could have done otherwise than they did. We earlier presented this idea as uncontroversial, but perhaps we were hasty. Perhaps there is another argument, one which does not make use of the premise that free will requires the ability to do otherwise, which can be used to show that moral responsibility requires free will. Such a plan of attack is likely to be complicated, so we will not pursue this option here.[7]

Returning to our previous discussions on Determinism and Indeterminism, a second response denies that our initial intuitions about the example are correct. What would a determinist say about Patsy's situation? Presumably, since the past and the laws of nature determine every event, Patsy's killing the victim, say by pulling the trigger of a gun, was determined to occur just as it did. Whether the cause was Patsy's intention to murder or the spy's device, Patsy is not responsible for her action (morally or otherwise). What if the act of murder was not precipitated by any cause, as would be possible if Indeterminism were true? Then again, as we discussed earlier, Patsy would not be responsible for her action. In short, the very reasoning that suggests Patsy has no free will also suggests that Patsy is not really morally responsible.

Are the arguments we raised above against the possibility of free will sufficiently powerful to convince us that we also do not have moral responsibility? If not, then perhaps the idea of having free will is not so important to us after all; or perhaps we need to look at other arguments to bolster our belief that we have free will. If the arguments we discussed are convincing, then a philosopher who believes that moral responsibility requires free will and that we are morally responsible spys must seek to defend these intuitions by exposing whatever mistakes there are in the opposing view.

Questions: What is the "Frankfurt counterexample" and what does it suggest about free will and moral responsibility? Why might someone find the counterexample unconvincing?

NOTES

[1]Our overall discussion in this chapter owes much to Peter van Inwagen's work in *An Essay on Free Will* (Oxford: Oxford University Press, 1986).

[2]Benedict Spinoza, *Ethics*, Part I, Appendix.

[3]We borrow this example from *The Problems of Philosophy, Second edition*, Eds. William P. Alston and Richard B. Brandt (Boston: Allyn and Bacon, 1974).

[4]John Locke, *An Essay concerning Human Understanding*, Ed. Peter Nidditch (Oxford: Oxford University Press, 1975), Book II, Chapter xxi, Section 5. Hereafter all references to Locke's *Essay* will be made in the text in "Book, Chapter, Section" form.

[5]Locke, *Essay*, II, xxi, 16.

[6]See Henry Frankfurt, "Alternate Possibilities and Moral Responsibility," *The Journal of Philosophy* 66 (1969).

[7] See Peter van Inwagen's work in *An Essay on Free Will*.

RELATED READINGS

Broad, C. D. "Determinism, Indeterminism, and Libertarianism." *Free Will and Determinism*. Ed. Bernard Berofsky. New York: Harper and Row, 1966.

Campbell, C. A. "Has the Self 'Free Will'?" *On Selfhood and Godhood*. London: George Allen & Unwin, 1957.

Chisholm, R. M. "Freedom and Action." *Freedom and Determinism*. Ed. Keith Lehrer. New York: Random House, 1966.

d'Holbach, Baron P. H. D. *The System of Nature*. Vol. 1 Chapters 11 and 12. Boston: J. P. Mendum, 1889.

Edwards, Paul. "Hard and Soft Determinism." *Determinism and Freedom in the Age of Modern Science*. Ed. Sidney Hook. New York: New York University Press, 1958.

Frankfurt, Harry. "Alternate Possibilities and Moral Responsibility." *The Journal of Philosophy* 66 (1969).

Ginet, Carl. "In Defense of Incompatibilism." *Philosophical Studies* 44 (1983).

Goldman, Alvin. "Actions, Predictions, and Books of Life." *American Philosophical Quarterly* 5 (1968).

Hobart, R. E. "Free Will as Involving Determinism and Inconceivable Without It." *Mind* 43 (1934).

Kenny, Anthony. *Will, Freedom and Power*. Oxford: Oxford University Press, 1976.

Lehrer, Keith. "The Conditional Analysis of Freedom." *Time and Cause*. Ed. Peter van Inwagen. Dordrecht, Holland: Reidel, 1980.

Locke, John. *An Essay concerning Human Understanding*. Book II, Chapter xxi. Ed. Peter Nidditch. Oxford: Oxford University Press, 1975.

Salmon, Wesley C. "Determinism and Indeterminism in Modern Science." *Reason and Responsibility*. Fifth edition. Ed. Joel Feinberg. Belmont, CA: Wadsworth Publishing Company, 1981.

Stace, Walter T. *Religion and the Modern Mind*. New York: Harper and Row, 1952.

Taylor, Richard. *Action and Purpose*. Englewood Cliffs, NJ: Prentice-Hall, Inc., 1966.

_____. "Determinism and the Theory of Agency." *Determinism and Freedom in the Age of Modern Science*. Ed. Sidney Hook. New York: New York University Press, 1958.

van Inwagen, Peter. *An Essay on Free Will*. Oxford: Oxford University Press, 1986.